British Communism
and the Politics of Literature
1928-1939

BRITISH COMMUNISM AND THE POLITICS OF LITERATURE 1928-1939

Philip Bounds

MERLIN PRESS

First published in the UK in 2012
by The Merlin Press
6 Crane Street Chambers
Crane Street
Pontypool
NP4 6ND
Wales

www.merlinpress.co.uk

© Philip Bounds, 2012

The author asserts the right to be identified
as the author of this work

ISBN. 978-0-85036-594-8

British Library Cataloguing in Publication Data is available
from the British Library

Printed in the UK by Imprint Digital, Exeter

CONTENTS

ACKNOWLEDGEMENTS

This book is a revised version of a PhD thesis in Politics which I submitted to Swansea University in 2003. My biggest academic debt is to my two supervisors, Alan Finlayson and George Boyce, who have both been very generous with their help. Alan was my primary supervisor and deserves special thanks for the subtlety of his comments on my early drafts. The thesis was examined by Vincent Geoghegan and Richard Taylor, whose works on the history of cultural Marxism I have long admired. I thank them for their generous remarks, their probing questions and their wise suggestions about revising the manuscript for publication. I am also deeply indebted to Andy Croft, who read the book when it was under consideration by Merlin. I fear that there is much in the following pages with which he disagrees; but I thank him for his detailed and insightful comments. It goes without saying that anyone who writes about the cultural and intellectual history of the British Communist Party will owe a considerable debt to Andy's pioneering work in the field. The librarians at Swansea University and the Marx Memorial Library in London were extremely helpful. I am especially grateful to Rosa Branson for her permission to reproduce Clive Branson's painting *Still Life* (1940) on the cover.

I would not have been able to undertake research without the extraordinary generosity of my parents, Neville and Megan Bounds, whose support has always gone well beyond the call of duty. No one else I know combines intellectual acuity and tolerance of human frailty in quite the same way. My other great source of support is Daisy Hasan, whose rare blend of magnanimity and intelligence (the latter of the razor-sharp North-Indian variety) has been much appreciated. Kya soorat hai, Daze! I have also benefited greatly from the advice and encouragement of Aftab Hamid, Adrian Howe, Mala Jagmohan, William and Rhianydd Morgan, Edward Parr, Ieuan Williams and Tony Zurbrugg. I greatly regret the fact that Margaret and Peter Bounds, two exceptionally generous relatives, died before the book was completed. The responsibility for any errors in the text lies solely with me.

INTRODUCTION

Marxist ideas had a significant influence on at least three groups of literary critics and theorists in the Britain of the 1930s. The most famous was the so-called 'Auden Circle', several of whose members (Stephen Spender, C. Day Lewis and W.H. Auden himself) produced a large body of critical writing in the period between their conversion to Marxism in the middle of the decade and their shift away from it at the beginning of the Second World War.[1] Similarly well-known to an academic audience is the handful of maverick scholars, notably William Empson and L.C. Knights, who drew briefly on Marxist and *Marxisant* sources in their efforts to extend the insights of 'Cambridge English' in a radical direction.[2] Yet the most impressive engagement with Marxist ideas was undertaken by the numerous writers who were either members of, or closely associated with, the Communist Party of Great Britain (CPGB), and whose work (now largely forgotten) had its roots in the ideas about literature and culture which emerged in the Soviet Union during the Stalin period. The aim of this book is to provide an overview of the critical and theoretical contributions of the latter group, though it will occasionally be necessary to refer to the other two groups for purposes of comparison and in order to identify influences.[3] The scholarly neglect to which the work of the communist writers has been exposed is astonishing. Nearly every historian of criticism accepts that Marxism was a dominant force in the literary culture of the 1930s, but few are willing to examine its impact in any detail. The relevant volume of René Wellek's *History of Modern Criticism*, easily the most important work of reference on the subject, devotes just two of its 400 pages to the work of only one of the Party theorists.[4] The reasons for this neglect are probably bound up with the cultural politics of the Cold War. At a time in the 1950s and 1960s when one might have expected literary historians to provide a balanced assessment of the communist writers of the previous generation, the majority of British intellectuals were deeply hostile to the Soviet bloc and regarded Marxism as a barrier to genuine thought. It might also have been the case that what Ron Bellamy has called 'McCarthy, *sotto voce*'[5] deterred a number of more sympathetic writers from tracing the history of communist criticism, though this obviously fails to explain why the literary intellectuals who openly associated with the CPGB at this time were themselves neglectful of the heritage of the Thirties. At any rate, the note of scorn which has characterised most post-war writing on the Party theorists is well captured in the following passage from John Gross's *The Rise and Fall of the Man of Letters*: 'Not even sympathizers...are likely to want to resurrect the English Communist criticism of the 1930s, and at this hour in the day it would be pointless to rake up the dogmatic pronouncements of Alick West, Philip Henderson, Jack Lindsay or the firing-squad of the *Left Review*.'[6]

In the light of passages such as this, it is necessary to be absolutely clear about why the attempt to 'rake up' the work of the CPGB's literary intellectuals is in fact justified. Gross is certainly right to say that many of the Party theorists were inclined to be dogmatic, though dogmatism was often wrongly ascribed to their work because of its use of naively partisan language – no generation of English critics has ever been more subservient to the deadening linguistic conventions of democratic politics. But at their best, there were about 15 pioneering writers (including two whom Gross impugned in the quoted passage) who moved beyond what Victor Paananen has called a 'preliminary exploration of problems and possibilities'[7] to provide a sophisticated application of Marxist ideas to the fields of literature and culture. One measure of their stature is the extent of their influence. The ideas of the Party theorists were central to the radical public sphere from which the most important creative writers of the 1930s took their inspiration, and their influence can clearly be detected in the work of Auden, Spender and even George Orwell. The attempt to identify a 'radical tradition' in English culture which occurred at the time of the Popular Front against fascism (1935-1939) would later shape the much more extensive investigations of English radicalism undertaken by writers such as E.P. Thompson, Arnold Kettle and Christopher Hill.[8] Moreover, as Paananen has pointed out, there are even similarities to be noted between the main theoretical approaches of the 1930s and those adopted by the writers who led the revival of Marxist literary theory in the Seventies and Eighties. If we want a clear picture of the sources which influenced such celebrated texts as Raymond Williams's *Marxism and Literature* (1977) and Terry Eagleton's *Criticism and Ideology* (1976), we have no choice but to give the 'firing squad of *Left Review*' its due.

My aim in the rest of this Introduction is to prepare the ground for the examination of British communist criticism by (1) outlining the argument which provides the book with its guiding thread, (2) contrasting my approach to that of earlier work on the cultural history of the Communist Party, and (3) making some preliminary observations about the relationship between the Soviet and British influences on the communist critics.

1. COMMUNIST PARTY HISTORY: THE NEW REVISIONISM

Our knowledge of the CPGB has been greatly enhanced over the last twenty years by the emergence of what some writers have described as a 'revisionist' school of Party history, exemplified by such political historians as Andrew Thorpe, Matthew Worley, Kevin Morgan and Mike Squires.[9] The guiding assumption of this book is that the central principles of the revisionist school are crucial not merely to our understanding of the CPGB's *political* evolution, but also (in suitably modified form) to our understanding of its intervention in the cultural sphere. At the core of the new revisionism is a novel account of the relationship between the British Party and the world communist movement. As is well known, the CPGB was a member between 1920 and 1943 of the Communist International or 'Comintern' (CI), the organisation which had been set up in Moscow in 1919 to co-ordinate the work of the various communist parties that came into existence in the wake of the October Revolution. The role of the CI, which styled itself a 'world communist party' and insisted that affiliated organisations such as the CPGB were merely 'national sections', was to determine the broad strategies which individual parties should pursue in their respective national contexts. The sixteenth of its 21 conditions of membership famously asserted that 'All decisions of the Communist International are binding on member parties.'[10] The relationship between the CI and the CPGB has usually been portrayed as a deeply authoritarian one. Two claims have tended to reoccur: first, that the CI was dominated by Soviet politicians (especially Stalin) who subordinated the requirements of its nationals sections to the strategic interests of the USSR; and second, that strategic decisions were enforced in such a draconian fashion that national parties had no choice but to implement them, regardless of whether they made much sense in the local conditions in which communists were obliged to operate. Although there were numerous disagreements between the various pre-revisionist historians who wrote about the CPGB, the assumption that British communists were little better than 'Moscow dupes' has united the work of Cold War liberals,[11] Trotskyists,[12] non-Marxist socialists[13] and even communists themselves.[14] The great achievement of the revisionists, many of whom have had access to the substantial archives which have become available since the collapse of the Soviet Union and the dissolution of the CPGB, has been to demonstrate that in fact the relationship between the CI and the British Party was never as rigidly hierarchical as orthodoxy insists. No one disputes that the CI was the most important institution in the world communist movement, nor that it ultimately determined the strategies which the CPGB pursued. However, it has now been recognised that there were several ways in which the British communists could *exercise a reciprocal influence on the CI*, even if they never possessed the degree of autonomy which they undoubtedly needed. It is certainly true that Soviet politicians were the dominant influence in the CI, but it is equally true that British representatives in Moscow were able to make a significant contribution to the CI's deliberations when the important decisions were made. Just as important is the recognition that there was never a time at which the CPGB simply adopted the CI's decisions in an uncritical or wholesale fashion. Because the mechanisms by which the CI sought to control the British Party were never wholly reliable (a point that Andrew Thorpe has explored in some detail),[15] it was relatively common for the British leadership simply to disregard aspects of CI policy which it saw as either unimportant or unrealistic. Equally crucially, it was necessary for all CI decisions to be adapted to local conditions by the British communists who were responsible for implementing them. The policies of the CPGB between 1920 and 1943 were therefore a product of the general principles enunciated by the CI, combined with the detailed knowledge of national politics supplied by the British leadership and activists in the localities. Most surprisingly of all, the revisionist historians have also pointed out that British communists were not merely capable of rebelling against the CI's decisions (this was already known – though rarely emphasised) but that their rebellion was occasionally important in persuading the CI to reconsider its strategic line. The most famous example of this process, explored in detail by Kevin Morgan in his biography of Harry Pollitt,[16] probably occurred when the British leadership unilaterally abandoned the CI's sectarian policy on trade unions in 1931, thereby hastening the end of the disastrous 'Class Against Class' policy which had come into operation in 1928.

There is no straightforward parallel between the CPGB's political work in the inter-war period and its intervention in culture. The most obvious difference was that there was no Party committee which had the power to enforce the cultural line being handed down from Moscow – the National Cultural Committee was not established until 1947.[17] Nevertheless, a close examination of the Party's early attempts to create a British strain of cultural Marxism, specifically in the areas of literary theory and literary criticism, yields three conclusions which are broadly continuous with those of the revisionist historians, and which can be summarised as follows:

(1)   **The work of the CPGB's early literary intellectuals can only be understood with reference to the Party's relationship with the world communist movement.** Just as the decisions of the CI determined the broad strategies which the Party pursued at a political level, so developments in the world movement shaped the intellectual context in which communist criticism at first took shape. On the one hand, the *political* decisions of the CI often had important consequences for cultural work, even when

(as in the case of the Class Against Class strategy) they appeared to lack a specifically cultural dimension. On the other hand, most communist criticism in the second half of the 1930s was profoundly influenced by the ideas propounded at the famous Soviet Writers' Congress in 1934, when the Soviet government tried to impose a cultural policy on the entire world movement. The heart of this policy was the requirement that all communist artists should observe the conventions of 'Socialist Realism'. Although the influence of what I refer to as 'Soviet theory' was reinforced by certain later writings by Soviet intellectuals, the English translation of the speeches at the Writers' Congress remained the most important document for British communists in the five years between 1934 and 1939.

(2) **The main elements of Soviet theory were elaborated by British communists in distinctive ways.** It was rare for British communists simply to parrot the ideas which had first received expression at the 1934 Congress. Their objective was usually to expand on the theoretical and critical hints which the Soviet writers had thrown out, often (though not always) by augmenting them with ideas drawn from the British tradition of cultural criticism. This can perhaps be seen as the literary equivalent of the Party leadership's attempts to adapt CI decisions to local conditions. As I shall argue later in this Introduction, the conflation of British and Soviet ideas draws our attention to certain structural similarities between the two intellectual traditions.

(3) **British adaptations of Soviet theory were often highly unorthodox.** If the CPGB was sometimes inclined to resist the strategic decisions of the CI, or else to interpret them in a highly idiosyncratic fashion, its literary intellectuals were similarly capable of producing work which subtly undermined the main elements of Soviet theory. It would be wrong to overestimate the element of outright rebellion in the writings of the British communist critics, but it is equally clear that (a) they sometimes advanced arguments which were incompatible with the fundamental ideas of Marxism, thereby illustrating the gravitational pull of non-Marxist ideas in British intellectual life, and (b) they can occasionally be read as an implicit expression of dissatisfaction either with Soviet theory or with wider aspects of communist strategy. In no sense was George Orwell justified in claiming that Party intellectuals took 'their opinions from Moscow', though he was perhaps closer to the mark when he complained that they took their cookery from Paris.'[18]

No body of work as labyrinthine as the communist criticism of the 1930s should be distorted to fit a simple thesis. The above propositions should therefore only be regarded as the book's guiding thread. My broader objectives are to clearly establish what my chosen writers actually said (something which existing work in the field has not adequately achieved) as well as to expose their work to a critical analysis. This might be the point at which to preview the material I intend to cover. Communist criticism in Britain did not begin in 1928, the point at which the book opens. Several writers in the early 1920s had expressed their support for A.A. Bogdanov's Proletcult movement in the Soviet Union – the best known appear to have been William McLaine and Eden and Cedar Paul. The work of the English Bogdanovites was subsequently attacked in the journal *Plebs* by writers such as Ralph Fox, T.A. Jackson and William Paul.[19] However, it was only in the late-1920s that British communists began to produce cultural and literary criticism in significant quantities. Their work at this time was profoundly influenced by the notorious "Class Against Class" policy, also known as the 'general strategic rule of the Third Period', which the CPGB pursued at the behest of the CI between 1928 and 1933. Rooted in the assumption that world capitalism had entered a deep crisis from which recovery was unlikely to be possible, Class Against Class was a highly sectarian strategy which stipulated that the CPGB should prepare for the forthcoming revolution by ending co-operation with the forces of social democracy (especially the Labour Party) and establishing alternatives to the mainstream trade unions. Chapter One aims to highlight the links between Class Against Class and early forms of British cultural Marxism by examining (1) the writings of P.R. Stephensen, which powerfully captured the mood of extreme revolutionary febrility which settled on the Party at this time, (2) the attempt by John Strachey and Montagu Slater to reinforce the prevailing assumptions about capitalism's terminal crisis by developing the idea of cultural crisis, and (3) the debate which occurred in the early 1930s between leading representatives of communism and cultural conservatism, notably A.L. Morton and F.R. Leavis, and which reflected a mood of disillusionment in the Party with the anti-intellectualism that was endemic to Class Against Class.

As we have already seen, communist criticism was revolutionised in 1934 when the Soviet government announced the main principles of its cultural policy at the Soviet Writers' Congress held in Moscow. Chapter Two looks at the body of doctrine elaborated at the Writers' Congress in some detail, arguing that it contained a 'prescriptive' element (i.e. a description and defence of Socialist Realism), an 'aesthetic' element (i.e. a reflectionist, anti-Kantian and anti-Formalist account of art which served to justify a political conception of literature), a 'historical' element (i.e. an attempt to legitimise Socialist Realism by pointing to prestigious cultural precedents) and a 'comparative' element (i.e. an attempt to argue that the culture of the USSR was infinitely superior to that of the capitalist nations, which had long since descended into 'decadence'). In the British context, one of the most important developments at about the time of the Soviet Writers' Congress was the establishment in 1934 of the literary journal *Left Review*, ostensibly the official publication of the British Section of the Writers International. Most of the shorter pieces of British communist criticism were to appear in *Left Review* between May 1934 and October 1938, and there are references to the journal in every chapter of the book.[20] However, it is generally accepted that Marxist literary theory only really got underway in Britain with the publication in 1937 of three seminal books: Christopher Caudwell's *Illusion and Reality*, Alick West's *Crisis and Criticism* and Ralph Fox's *The Novel and the People*.[21] Chapters Three, Four and Five examine the careers of each of these writers, seeking to identify the precise nature of their debt to Soviet theory. Drawing on his great autobiography *One Man in his Time*, Chapter Three argues that Alick West managed to combine orthodoxy and dissidence in something like equal measure. *Crisis and Criticism* had many points of connection with Soviet theory, but many of the other writings contain an implicit critique of what West regarded as the cultural (and hence political) decline of the world communist movement. Chapter Four argues that Ralph Fox's writings on the socialist novel were organised around a defence of the Soviet idea of positive heroism, but also claims that many of Fox's arguments were inadvertently non-Marxist. Christopher Caudwell's writings are given less space than those of West and Fox, not least because they have been exhaustively examined by several other writers; but in Chapter Five I briefly sketch the outlines of a new interpretation of his work. The basic argument is that Caudwell took his theoretical bearings from several important elements in Soviet theory (something which has largely been overlooked by other commentators) but that he refracted the Soviet orthodoxy through the distorting mechanisms of his distinctively autodidactic mind. The result was a body of work of high unorthodoxy. Finally, Chapter Six moves away from Soviet theory to examine the wider *political* influences on British cultural Marxism, specifically the so-called 'Popular Front' policy which the CI adopted between 1934 and 1939. At the Seventh Congress of the CI in 1935, Georgi Dimitrov famously argued that fascist movements throughout the world had gained an advantage over the left by portraying themselves as the culmination of their respective national traditions, and that communists should fight back by drawing public attention to the rich traditions of popular radicalism in their own countries. Although there was nothing especially unorthodox about the CPGB's attempt to trace the history of the 'English radical tradition', much of which was concerned with identifying the elements of radicalism in the work of Britain's most famous writers, we shall see that communist intellectuals had to develop many important ideas of their own in order to put flesh on the bones of Dimitrov's instructions.

2. EARLIER WORK ON THE CULTURAL HISTORY OF THE COMMUNIST PARTY

How can the approach outlined above be distinguished from that of earlier work on the cultural history of the CPGB? Much of the existing literature can be divided into one of two categories: (1) that which overestimates the influence of the Soviet Union on the cultural work of the British Party, and (2) that which implies that the influence of the Soviet Union was of little or no importance. The claim that British communists were little better than Stalin's cultural stooges is usually made by writers who are experts in Literary Studies rather than the history of communism, sceptical towards the left and less interested in the CPGB than in the wider literary culture of the Thirties. It can be found in either explicit or implicit form in such important works as Julian Symons's *The Thirties: A Dream Revolved* (1960) and Samuel Hynes's *The Auden Generation* (1976).[22] Even Valentine Cunningham, whose celebrated book on *British Writers of the Thirties* (1988) examines the work of the Auden Group in the context of all the literary trends of the age, occasionally says things like this: 'British Marxists had put their shirts on Comrade Radek's doctrines of Socialist Realism issued at the Moscow Writers' Congress of 1934.'[23] By contrast, the second body of work, which has been accumulating slowly since the late-1960s, goes to the other extreme in its account of the relationship between the Soviet Union and the CPGB's cultural workers. Frequently written by younger academics who are or were sympathetic to the Party (and often by people who associated with its 'Eurocommunist' wing in the Seventies and Eighties), it rarely overlooks the role of the Soviet Union altogether, yet its central argument is that the CPGB's cultural work was usually 'forged from a combination of local cultural forces and Communist enthusiasm, and developed to correspond with indigenous events, disputes and traditions' (Matthew Worley)[24]. The most distinguished work in this vein can be found in four symposia which deal either directly or indirectly with the CPGB's cultural history[25] and in a number of essays and monographs which trace the Party's approach to literature (e.g. David Smith, H. Gustav Klaus and Ingrid von Rosenberg),[26] theatre (e.g. Colin Chambers and Jon Clark),[27] film (e.g. Bert Hogenkamp and Stephen Jones),[28] philosophy (e.g. Jonathan Rée and Edwin Roberts)[29] and the visual arts (e.g. Robert Radford and Lynda Morris).[30] I will return in a moment to work which might appear to belong in this category but which actually expresses a slightly different perspective.

The tendency to deny the influence of the Soviet Union is very much a part of the small body of work which examines the history of communist criticism. With the exception of a single chapter in Raymond Williams's *Culture and Society 1780-1950* (1958)[31] and brief introductory essays by David Margolies and Hanna Behrend,[32] there are only two general surveys of Marxist criticism in Britain: Anand Prakash's *Marxism and Literary Theory* (1994)[33] and Victor N. Paananen's *British Marxist Criticism* (2000).[34] Surprisingly, neither of these books seems to have come to the attention of many other researchers in the field, perhaps because the former has only been published in India and the latter only in the USA. Paananen's important book is Volume 22 of the *Wellesley Studies in Critical Theory, Literary History and Culture*. It is primarily an annotated bibliography and contains sections on four of the most important critics of the 1930s (Alick West, Christopher Caudwell, Jack Lindsay and A.L. Morton) as well as four subsequent writers (Arnold Kettle, Margot Heinemann, Raymond Williams and Terry Eagleton). Intended as a work of reference, it nevertheless advances a number of arguments which seek to rescue the Thirties critics from what E.P. Thompson famously called the 'enormous condescension of posterity.'[35] Paananen's most interesting claim is that the approach of at least three of the Thirties critics (West, Caudwell and Lindsay) is comparable to that of their more prestigious successors, specifically in the way that it seeks to deflect our attention away from literary texts towards the process by which texts are created.[36] Caudwell's work on the economic function of poetry, West's comparisons between creativity and production and Lindsay's portrayal of culture as 'productive activity' are all precursors (or so Paananen would have us believe) of such modern theoretical initiatives as Williams's description of the utilisation of shared literary conventions by the individual writer. This argument is appealing in a number of ways (I return to it in Chapter Six) but it is also open to a number of criticisms. By placing so much emphasis on the ideas which bind the different generations of Marxist critics together, Paananen arguably pays too little attention to the other areas of criticism in which British Marxists have distinguished themselves. Moreover, the importance he ascribes to the analysis of literary production is perhaps excessive. Greeted as a major theoretical advance in the 1970s, the shift from 'finished texts' to the 'relations of cultural production' has remained too undeveloped to be of much theoretical value. How do we know what writers experience when they write? Is creativity a uniform process? What are the political advantages of focusing on the nature of literary production? We are no nearer to answering these questions now than we were thirty years ago.

Prakash's book is much more difficult to summarise. Consisting of brief essays on the six writers who dominated communist criticism between the Thirties and the Fifties (Caudwell, West, Fox, Edgell Rickword, George Thomson and Arnold

Kettle), it is neither a historian's book nor one which functions adequately as an introduction. Failing to discuss communist criticism in relation either to Soviet theory or to the politics of the world communist movement, it plunges into detailed criticism of its selected writers without first establishing exactly what they said. Insofar as it has a unifying thesis (broadly speaking, Prakash argues that communist criticism became more sophisticated but less politically engaged in the post-war period)[37] it is one that lies outside the scope of this book. Nevertheless, *Marxism and Literary Theory* has two conspicuous merits. The first is the thoroughness with which it works through its critical comments, some of which are echoed in my own examination of West, Caudwell and Fox.[38] The second is its recognition of the way that the Marxist orientation of British communist criticism was often undermined by the continued influence of non-Marxist forms of thought, specifically what Prakash terms the 'liberal bourgeois tradition'.[39] Although Prakash is not really interested in issues of orthodoxy and dissidence, his book nevertheless provides considerable evidence (at least if one is prepared to read between the lines) of the way that the collision between Soviet and English thought often had notably unorthodox consequences.

By trying to avoid the related errors of overestimating the influence of the Soviet Union and overstating the autonomy of the British communists, the present book seeks to take a different approach to the cultural history of the CPGB than either of these two bodies of work. My approach is much closer to that of a handful of writers who are usually bracketed with the second group (that is, the group which underplays the role of the USSR) but who anticipated the approach of the revisionist historians by some years. Working alongside the younger communist academics in the Seventies and Eighties were a number of much older writers, notably James Klugmann[40] and Margot Heinemann,[41] whose work on the cultural history of British communism drew extensively on their own long experience in the Party. The great virtue of their work was that it recognised the enormous importance of the USSR in shaping the context in which the British communists operated, while also drawing our attention, sometimes in a highly anecdotal form, to the local factors which reinforced, modified or subverted the Soviet influence. For instance, Klugmann wrote humorously about the difficulties which the Party encountered during the period of the Popular Front, when the CI's instruction to develop new forms of 'progressive' patriotism almost foundered on the conservatism inherent in most symbols of British identity.[42] This approach was subsequently adopted by some of the younger writers, pre-eminently Andy Croft,[43] whose work combines a detailed understanding of the history of the world communist movement with tireless research into the internal culture of the CPGB. If none of these writers has pursued a critical project which is wholly congruent with that of the revisionists, it is only because (1) they have yet to provide a detailed analysis of the balance of Soviet and English elements in the cultural politics of the 1930s, and (2) they are sometimes inclined to revert to anti-Soviet orthodoxy and argue that the British communists were primarily concerned only to 'mitigate' the influence of Soviet ideas.[44] Their account of the culture of the 1930s has nevertheless been a central influence on the argument of this book.

3. SOVIET THEORY, THE BRITISH CULTURAL TRADITION AND THE ORIGINS OF MARXIST CRITICISM

There is one other general matter which needs briefly to be addressed before we move on to Chapter One. I have already indicated that one of my main claims in this book is that the British communists created a distinctive form of Marxist criticism by combining Soviet theory with ideas drawn from the English tradition of thought about literature and culture. This claim may well seem surprising to those who believe that Soviet and British thinking had absolutely nothing in common, the latter being seen as much less theoretical, partisan and dogmatic than the former. Perhaps the British communists would always have tried to prove that the two traditions were born of common soil, even if there had been no good reason for doing so, but I would argue that Soviet and British approaches to culture evinced a number of surface similarities which provided *prima facie* evidence of their compatibility, and which prompted the British communists into recognising the possibility of creative synthesis.[45] The most obvious was a shared belief in the existence of cultural crisis. Where the Soviet theorists insisted that capitalism had stripped modern culture of every last vestige of aesthetic and intellectual significance (see Chapter Two), a long list of British thinkers, some of them going back to the early sixteenth century, provided different explanations for what they also regarded as an absolute decline of cultural standards. When the British communists read Bukharin, Gorky and Zhdanov on the spiritual poverty of bourgeois society, they surely recalled such celebrated instances of cultural pessimism as Sir Philip Sidney's attack on the immorality of Elizabethan theatre,[46] Wordsworth's onslaught on industrialism[47] and Eliot's defence of 'tradition' against modernity.[48] There was also a surprising parallel between British and Soviet thinking on the issue of reforming popular culture. At the heart of Soviet theory was the assumption that the cultural health of modern societies would never be restored until the masses had overcome their addiction to commercial rubbish and embraced the work of the Socialist Realists, in the process learning how to abolish the market institutions that were the root cause of their malaise. No British thinker had ever put such faith in the power of art, but the same belief in the ability of working people to solve the problems of culture can be seen in Ruskin's plea for a return to handicraft or Chesterton's eulogies to his beloved 'people of England'.

On a more philosophical level, it is easy to see why the British communists might have experienced a shock of recognition when exposed to the rigorously *mimetic* theory of art with which the Soviet thinkers tried to defend their conception of literary realism. The debate on mimesis (that is, the assumption that art somehow 'reflects' a pre-existing reality) had taken a particularly virulent form in Britain since the late-nineteenth century, not least because an influential group of writers and critics, most of them associated with the art-for-art's sake movement, had expressed their opposition to mimetic doctrine in a deliberately scandalous and provocative form.[49] Insisting that art was not so much a reflection of reality as the attempt to create new and more compelling worlds, apologists for art-for-art's sake often implied that there was something irresistibly disreputable about their opposition to mimetic othodoxy. For instance, it was Oscar Wilde who famously pointed out that a non-mimetic perspective commits us to the proposition that creative writers are basically engaged in an extended act of 'lying'.[50] Because of this tendency for matters of aesthetic doctrine to become bound up with issues of morality, it was common for critics of the new aestheticism to express themselves with considerable sanctimony. Responding to Wilde and the other aesthetes, G.K. Chesterton went so far as to argue that their studied immorality was one of the main contemporary threats to the Christian 'orthodoxy' whose influence he wished to defend.[51] In circumstances such as these, it is easy to see how the British communists might have regarded their support for Soviet theory as an expression of moral virtue. It could also be argued that the communists were spurred on in their attempts to fuse Soviet and English thought by the sheer eclecticism of an earlier generation of socialist writers. If we examine the pioneering writers who founded socialist criticism in Britain in the period between 1880 and 1910, it becomes clear that one of their most notable characteristics was a willingness to synthesise highly divergent traditions of thought. Edward Carpenter took ideas from Marx, Whitman and the *Bhagavad Gita* and ended up with his distinctive brand of mystical socialism;[52] George Bernard Shaw drew on Marx, Ibsen and Nietzsche in his efforts to justify the elitist politics of the early Fabians,[53] while even Oscar Wilde, the most surprising socialist of them all, employed the arguments of Kropotkin and Pater to buttress his assertion that revolutionary politics are wholly compatible with the solipsism of art-for-art's sake.[54] While many of these writers were looked upon with suspicion by their communist successors in the 1930s, it is unlikely that their intellectual adventurousness had passed unnoticed.

One way of illustrating the continuities between Soviet and British thought is briefly to examine the earliest forms of Marxist criticism in Britain, since these exemplify many of the general points which I have just made. The crucial figures in this context are William Morris, Edward Aveling and Eleanor Marx Aveling, whose pioneering work of the 1880s and 1890s remained the only significant attempts to apply Marxist ideas to the study of literature and culture until the formation of the CPGB in 1920. As is well known, Morris's work was rooted in his deep unease about what he identified as a crisis in Victorian high culture. Seeking to explain the precipitate decline in the high arts since the end of the Middle Ages (architecture was a special area of concern), Morris insisted that the quality of a nation's high culture is ultimately dependent on the quality of its popular culture. If ordinary people are able to derive aesthetic pleasure from their work, then the body of serious art which rises above them is likely to be exalted, beautiful and high-minded. By the same token, it is only when all traces of aesthetic significance are removed from the labour process that the arts go into serious decline.[55] The conclusion to which Morris came, heavily under the influence of such anti-industrial 'sages' as John Ruskin and Thomas Carlyle, was that the root cause of England's cultural malaise was the rise of industrialism and the destruction of handicraft. Whereas the older forms of craft production had catered to the worker's need for beauty, rest and a sense of usefulness, industrialism had rationalised economic life to the point where the worker was merely an 'appendage to a machine'. The recovery of high culture was therefore dependent on the abolition of industrial civilisation and the restoration of handicraft to a central position in Britain's economic life. It was this conviction which led Morris and a handful of friends to establish Morris, Marshall, Faulkner & Company (also known as 'The Firm'), the furniture company that became the focus of Britain's Arts and Crafts movement in the last 40 years of the nineteenth century. At first, Morris seems to have believed that the revival of handicraft only required a transformation in arts education and a determined effort to explore Britain's rich heritage of medieval artefacts. Fine artists were urged to put their skills in draughtmanship at the disposal of the new generation of craft producers, while the entire movement was encouraged to explore the furthest recesses of the English countryside in search of the most sumptuous examples of medieval handicraft, many of them buried away (or so Morris believed) in the silent alcoves of small churches.[56] However, in the 20 years between the beginning of his artistic career and his first exposure to Marxism in the early 1880s, Morris increasingly came to believe that the revival of handicraft would not be accomplished until the entire capitalist order had been abolished. In a society which places such a premium on competition, it is simply not possible to reintroduce time-consuming techniques of production when the constant demand is for more goods at cheaper prices. And yet, instead of following Ruskin's example and calling for the re-establishment of the sort of non-market institutions which predated the rise of capitalism, Morris began to argue that the society of the future should balance Marx's emphasis on planning, common ownership and advanced industrialism with his own preference for the simplicities of craft production. In essays such as 'A Factory As It Might Be' (1884)[57] and in his utopian novel *News from Nowhere* (1890),[58] he envisaged a future in which unpleasant jobs were taken over by sophisticated machines (though none of these machines was ever described) while the workers spent most of their time embellishing commodities with techniques handed down from the Middle Ages. Marxist criticism in Britain was therefore born of an unlikely attempt to adapt the ideas of Marx to those of precisely the sort of 'feudal socialists' whom he and Engels had satirised in *The Communist Manifesto.* [59]

If Morris's work illustrates the broad similarities between Soviet and British thought, then the literary criticism of Edward Aveling and Eleanor Marx Aveling, specifically their short book *Shelley's Socialism* (1888), provides an interesting anticipation of one of the most important critical procedures of the 1930s. Originally published in a private edition of 25 copies, *Shelley's Socialism* contained the first of what were intended to be two lectures – the second has not survived. Its central thesis was that Shelley's poetry and prose had prefigured many of Marx's most important ideas, though the Avelings refused to make the point explicitly, settling instead for the less controversial observation that 'Shelley was a socialist'.[60] At a metaphysical level, Shelley enunciated an evolutionary understanding of the natural world whose central insights, despite being couched in a 'pantheistic language', bear a clear resemblance to those of dialectical materialism.[61] He had a burning hatred for capitalism and always supported the common people in their struggles against the 'tyrants' of the middle class, insisting that the relationship between employers and workers is an inherently 'parasitic' one. He also blamed capitalism for environmental despoliation and the lengthening of the working day.[62] Moreover, there are passages in his work which anticipate the theory of base and superstructure, showing how certain non-economic forms of oppression (e.g. political tyranny and religious bigotry) are ultimately rooted in 'our commercial system'.[63] Although the Avelings provided very little evidence for any of these claims (perhaps they did so in the lost second lecture), the interesting thing about their book was the explanation it proposed for the emergence of Shelley's radicalism. Perhaps anticipating the objection that Shelley would have been unlikely to embrace socialism at a time when there was no organised socialist movement in Britain, the Avelings argued that he (Shelley) originally came to socialism by *extending and subverting the principles of liberalism.* As a 'child of the French Revolution' he initially embraced the ideals of liberty, equality and fraternity in purely 'general terms', only later seeking to apply them to the same capitalist system which bourgeois liberalism tried to protect:

> To the younger Shelley *l'infâme* of Voltaire's *ecrasez l'infâme* was to a great extent, as with Voltaire wholly, the priesthood. And the empire that he antagonised was at first that of kingship and that of personal tyranny. But even in his attacks on these he simultaneously assails the superstitious belief in the capitalistic system and the empire of class. As time goes on, with increasing distinctness, he makes assault upon these, the most recent and most dangerous foes of humanity.[64]

In effect, what the Avelings were arguing was that Shelley owed his socialism to the ambiguities and instabilities of bourgeois ideology. As we shall see, this proto-Gramscian recognition that the dominant ideology is always divided against itself was to reappear time and again in the Marxist criticism of the 1930s. It was especially important at the time of the Popular Front (see Chapter Six), when communist intellectuals were instructed by the CI to identify a 'radical tradition' in the history of English literature and culture. Since there is no evidence that the latterday communists had ever heard of *Shelley's Socialism*, it is tempting (though also rather dangerous) to suggest that they were linked to the Avelings across 40 years by what Rupert Sheldrake would call a 'morphic resonance'. The likelier explanation is that the tendency to analyse ideas in terms of contradiction and change is a natural reflex of the dialectical mind.

CHAPTER ONE

THE CRITIC AS LEFT SECTARIAN: RESPONSES TO CLASS AGAINST CLASS

Marxist literary criticism was first produced in large quantities in Britain in the period between 1928 and 1933, some 40 years after the pioneering efforts of William Morris, Edward Aveling and Eleanor Marx. This efflorescence of Marxist criticism was dominated by the Communist Party. Of the writers who came to prominence at the time, several were already members of the CPGB (P.R. Stephensen, A.L. Morton and Montagu Slater), several were on the verge of becoming members (Edgell Rickword, Douglas Garman and Alec Brown) while at least one (John Strachey) was widely regarded as what would later be called a 'fellow traveller'. The argument of this chapter is that the work of these writers was heavily influenced by the notorious 'Class Against Class' policy which the CI imposed on its member parties in the five years after 1928.[1] In the British context, Class against Class represented a sharp break with the 'united front' policy which the CPGB had been following since its formation in 1920. Rooted in the assumption that world capitalism had entered a crisis from which recovery was more or less impossible, and that socialist revolution was therefore an immediate priority in all the advanced nations of the West, the essence of the new line was a deeply irrational hatred of the 'reformist' left. After almost a decade of tireless work on the industrial front, communists were instructed to withdraw their support from the mainstream trade unions and establish unions of their own in which the militant instincts of the British workers would not be stymied by a 'class collaborationist' leadership. They were also required to adopt an attitude of unyielding hostility towards the Labour Party (an organisation to which they had previously been intent on affiliating) in order that the CPGB might rapidly establish itself as the leading force in the British labour movement. Moreover, the non-communist left was seen not merely as a drag on social progress but as the conscious ally of European reaction. For much of the period between 1928 and 1933, communists habitually referred to their former comrades in the Labour Party and the trade unions as 'social fascists' – socialist in name, fascist in nature.

A handful of writers have recently tried to revise our understanding of the Class Against Class strategy, claiming that it was neither as illogical nor as politically self-defeating as it might otherwise have seemed.[2] But the broad consensus among historians is still that the years between 1928 and 1933 were probably the most disastrous of the CPGB's history. Isolated from the rest of the Labour Movement by its own revolutionary purism, the Party saw its membership decline to 2555 (November 1930)[3] and its influence dwindle almost to nothing. Perhaps the best that can be said is that Class Against Class did not inflict on Britain the sort of political calamities which occurred on the Continent, where it divided the anti-fascist movement at the very moment when Hitler was making his bid for power. However, the revisionist historians are surely right in saying that the CPGB enjoyed a major upsurge in its *cultural* fortunes during this otherwise bleak period. Although the Party only managed to establish two trade unions of its own,[4] neither of which proved very effective, it was markedly more successful in building cultural institutions which provided British workers with a 'revolutionary' alternative to both mainstream culture and the leisure organisations of the wider labour movement. Between 1928 and 1933 it either established or assumed control of the British Workers' Sports Federation (BWSF), the Workers' Theatre Movement (WTM) and a whole host of workers' film societies.[5] In this sense, the extraordinary cultural triumphs of the period 1934-1939 clearly had their roots in the sectarianism of Class Against Class, not in a sudden outburst of creativity occasioned by the politics of the Popular Front.

The purpose of the rest of this chapter is to demonstrate what historians such as Worley, Howkins and Samuel have tended to ignore, namely that Marxist literary criticism *also* became a major part of the CPGB's cultural repertoire at this time. Section One examines the essays which the Anglo-Australian critic P.R. Stephensen wrote for *The London Aphrodite* between 1928 and 1929; Section Two assesses the accounts of the 'cultural crisis of capitalism' to be found in the work of John Strachey and Montagu Slater; Section Three surveys the sustained dialogue between communists and cultural conservatives which occurred over a period of about two years in the early 1930s. As we shall see, much of this work bears out the more sophisticated understanding of the relationship between Soviet and British communism which has emerged over the last decade. For every writer who seemed to be loyally providing the Class Against Class line with some kind of cultural ratification (Strachey), there were others who echoed it only in terms of mood (Stephensen) and others who rejected it altogether (Morton). Even when British communism was at its lowest ebb, then, its adherents were never simply following the Soviet line in a slavish or uncritical fashion. As the revisionist historians have pointed out, there was usually an ideological space in which the British communists could find some room for manoeuvre.

1. P.R. STEPHENSEN: A MARXIST FALLEN AMONG NIETZSCHEANS

In the first volume of his memoirs, *Fanfrolico and After* (1962), Jack Lindsay made the startling but little noticed claim that his friend P.R. Stephensen had 'founded Marxist literary criticism' in the articles he wrote for *The London Aphrodite* between 1928 and 1929.[6] Lindsay was scarcely the most self-promoting of men, but it is easy to see that he might have had personal reasons for wishing to make this claim. If Stephensen were indeed the man who first developed a Marxist account of literature, it follows that Lindsay (who co-edited *The London Aphrodite* with Stephensen) played a major role in the creation of an entire field of Marxist studies. He must nevertheless have been well aware that the claim was false. Even if we assume that Lindsay was only referring to Marxist criticism in Britain, he certainly knew that the application of Marxist ideas to the study of literature and culture had been pioneered some 40 years before Stephensen by writers such as Eleanor Marx, Edward Aveling and William Morris. Moreover, there is no obvious sense in which the articles in *The London Aphrodite* can even be described as unambiguously Marxist. Although Stephensen had joined the CPGB after arriving in England in 1926, and although (as we shall see) his articles clearly reflected the ambience of the Party during the Class Against Class period, his main objective in the late Twenties was to assimilate Marxism to a philosophical position with which it was basically incompatible – that is, the sort of Nietzschean individualism for which Lindsay was then an apologist.[7]

In order to understand the work which Stephensen produced in the closing years of the 1920s, it is necessary to say something about his relationship with Lindsay and the background to the establishment of *The London Aphrodite*.[8] Born in Queensland, Australia in 1901, the son of a politically-active shopkeeper, Stephensen first met Lindsay in 1919 when both men were undergraduates at the University of Queensland. Whereas Stephensen had already joined the Australian Communist Party and used his position as editor of the student magazine *Galmahra* to whip up political controversy, Lindsay saw himself as the intellectual spokesman for the quasi-Nietzschean philosophy which his father, the painter Norman Lindsay, had begun to adumbrate in books such as *Creative Effort* (1919).[9] In 1925, four years after graduating with a brilliant first in Classics, Lindsay established the Fanfrolico Press with the sole aim of publishing books which advanced his father's creed. A year later he moved to London after realising that Fanfrolico's output would be better received in Europe than

Australia. Stephensen joined him in London in 1928 to serve as the co-editor of *The London Aphrodite*, the journal which Lindsay hoped would insinuate his Nietzschean outlook into the minds of the metropolitan intelligentsia. The fact that Stephensen was prepared to work with Lindsay showed how far his commitment to Marxism was beginning to weaken. Although he joined the CPGB after arriving in Oxford on a Rhodes Scholarship in 1926, and although he continued to write for the communist press, he had evidently begun to feel that Marxism lacked a spiritual element which the Lindsays' version of Nietzscheanism possessed in abundance.[10] The essential principles of this philosophy were outlined by Lindsay in a series of essays in the new journal, notably 'The Modern Consciousness: An Essay towards an Integration' in the inaugural issue (August 1928).[11] The starting point was the assumption that the main problem facing modern culture is the breakdown of religious faith. How should people live once they realise that the universe is not the creation of a divine intelligence? If Nietzsche's response to this question was seen as more compelling than anyone else's, the whole of modern philosophy was nevertheless regarded as a sort of preparation for Nietzsche. In a characteristic attempt to summarise a vast expanse of thought in the space of a few sentences, Lindsay argued that post-Renaissance philosophy moved through five stages in its progress towards Nietzschean insight: (1) The Renaissance philosophers accepted the reality of a world without God but could only propose Montaigne's 'passive disdain' as a method for coping with it, (2) Francis Bacon reinforced the shift towards atheism but shied away from assessing its significance for mankind because of 'homosexual scepticism', (3) David Hume employed the 'abstractions' of modern science to 'sever all the knots of divine law', (4) Kant, though intending to bolster religious faith, paradoxically undermined it by providing arguments for the existence of God that buckled under the weight of their own complexity, and (5) Hegel put the idea of human evolution at the heart of philosophy by emphasising the importance of the historical process.[12]

Lindsay had several reasons for seeing Nietzsche as the culmination of this tradition. He began by arguing that the bedrock of Nietzsche's philosophy was his 'Dionysian' critique of received moral wisdom. In a chaotic universe from which all evidence of divine intelligence is absent, it makes no sense (or so Nietzsche argued) to encumber ourselves with a selfless morality that puts us at a disadvantage to those who are pitched against us in the struggle for existence. The wisest option is to abandon the very distinction between right and wrong and to assess all potential courses of action by a single criterion: To what extent do they enhance my power over other people?[13] Moreover, by plunging into the chaos of existence with scant regard for moral niceties, we not only enhance our chances of personal survival but also engage the mechanisms of human evolution. The joyous embrace of a Dionysian lifestyle is the means by which a small minority of people will ultimately be transformed from men into supermen. Lindsay evidently saw this ideal of self-transcendence as the goal by which modern culture should be guided, and summarised the absence of self-division which it implied by speaking of the superman as one who experiences a 'unity of the dynamic judgement'.[14] If all this was relatively uncontroversial in terms of the prevailing interpretation of Nietzschean thought, Lindsay displayed a hint of unorthodoxy by paying particular attention to Nietzsche's analysis of the relationship between the intellect and the instincts in the evolutionary process. His argument was that a number of writers had distorted the true nature of human evolution by indulging their own bias towards either rationalism or irrationalism. Some regarded the emergence of the superman as a predominantly intellectual process in which the individual retreats from a turbulent reality into a world of contemplation, whereas others minimised the role of the intellect and identified the 'Dionysian tumult of experience' as the source of self-transcendence. According to Lindsay, Nietzsche had in fact demonstrated that the intellect and the instincts must always be made to work in harmony.[15] The energy generated by the struggle for existence is the main force propelling us towards a new way of life, but it can only function effectively if we create a 'symbol of self-knowledge' which allows us to channel it in the right direction:

> When the self finds its own core of energy, which flows out of this intellectual symbol *into* life, stimulated by some sudden harmony between itself and the stream of the instincts, it will be filled with love and therefore with the need to perpetuate its own delighted harmony: to beget an image of itself upon life…This harmony is the moment of Eternity, the conquest of Time. For it includes both the fluid mass and the abstract construction in a third thing, the dynamic form.[16]

The philosophical element in Lindsay's work was supplemented by an ambitious attempt to survey the history of the arts, the purpose of which was apparently to encourage modern artists to adopt a distinctively Nietzschean aesthetic.[17] We will concentrate here on his remarks about literature, since (as Laurence Coupe has pointed out) it was the literary culture of England that the *Aphrodite* most wished to change.[18] For Lindsay, the challenge facing contemporary artists was to recapture the 'full proud bustling force' that characterised most Western art during the Renaissance.[19] (He implied that the basis of this force was the sudden outpouring of Dionysian energy which accompanied the breakdown of religious certainties, honed by the recognition that its disciplined use could enable human beings to transcend their limitations.) The arts began to experience a general decline in the seventeenth century, largely because writers such as John Milton tried 'to distort its [i.e. the Renaissance's] rhythm with a Gothic dispersal of energy in torment'.[20] In the three centuries since Milton's death, or so Lindsay implied, certain writers have managed to recapture the *objective* foundations of artistic greatness (that is, they have successfully portrayed the dynamism and 'imagic splendour' of external reality) but none has recaptured a sense of human beings responding to this dynamism by willing their own evolution. Surprisingly, Lindsay saw a possible model for the future in the work of Sacheverell and Edith Sitwell, whose poetry attached a 'pastoral-sweet rhythm' to visions of 'gods walk[ing] in the harvest'.[21] Yet the most startling feature of his survey of contemporary literature was its attack on modernism.[22] According to Lindsay, modernism was little more than organised pessimism: 'Convinced that life is futile, it wishes to reduce all beliefs and methods to a common intellectual Nirvana of tin'.[23] The most savagely reductive of all the British modernists was probably James Joyce, whose method was to besmirch human nature by viewing it against a background of lavatorial squalor. In the absence of an interesting or inspiring message, the only outlet for Joyce's creativity was the sort of manic wordplay which had brought his work to the brink of complete inaccessibility.[24]

Stephensen contributed six pieces of prose to *The London Aphrodite*. Apart from a brief 'Editorial Manifesto' in issue one and the single-paragraph 'Notice to Americans' in issue three,[25] there were substantial essays on Bakunin[26] and J.C. Squire,[27] a dialogue on the recent work of Aldous Huxley[28] and a highly compressed attempt to supply a political/philosophical manifesto for the modern age.[29] It was clear from all these pieces that Stephensen completely endorsed the interpretation of Nietzsche's philosophy to which Lindsay had introduced him. The goal of the individual in a post-religious age is to transform himself into a Beyond man' by observing the principle that 'blood is spirit'.[30] Insofar as Stephensen tried to comment on Nietzsche's ideas (as opposed to celebrating them in the sort of sub-Lawrentian language that implicitly rendered the *Übermensch* as a 'whole-hogging exister'),[31] he joined with Lindsay in warning against the dangers of seeing Nietzsche as either an austerely cerebral figure or a reckless explorer of the dionysian impulses. It was not true that Nietzsche had identified either the intellect or the instincts as the sole motor of human evolution. His signal contribution to modern thought (or so Stephensen implied) was to show how the intellect and the instincts could operate in tandem to propel mankind onto a new plane of self-mastery.[32]

Stephensen had two reasons for identifying a commitment to Marxist politics as an important concomitant of the Nietzschean outlook. The first was his apparent belief that only a communist society can establish the material conditions in which the quest for self-transcendence might at last be allowed to flourish. Ours is an 'Age of Wheels' in which 'The wheels have caught us' and 'whirl us centrifugally away from our centre'.[33] The advanced technology that dominates the capitalist world (and here Stephensen was simply reproducing the central tenet of romantic anti-capitalism) serves only to impede the cultivation of the spirit by delivering a succession of crippling blows to mankind's sense of equilibrium. Yet the problem lies not so much with technology itself as with the circumstances in which technological change occurs. Because the distinguishing feature of the capitalist system is ferocious competition arising from a failure to co-ordinate production, it follows (or so Stephensen implied) that each new technological innovation will primarily have the effect of reinforcing the prevailing sense of deep insecurity. If human beings are to liberate themselves from these material anxieties and turn inwards in a spirit of Nietzschean introspection, they must establish a non-market order in which economic planning allows technological development to be smoothly integrated into the rhythms of everyday life: '...when the wheel runs more smoothly it may be easier to ride upon. One hopes so. Therefore let us have a Communist revolution'.[34] The extraordinary thing about this endorsement of communism was its shameless elitism. Stephensen took it for granted that the majority of working people were too traumatised by their experience of production to serve the revolutionary cause: 'Who could hope to unite these almost-automata for collective action against the wheel's whirling?'[35] In a disconcerting example of what Leon Trotsky called 'substitutionism', he appeared to conclude that it is the vanguard and not the mass which makes history. 'Practical communists' like Lenin and Stalin were only successful because they formed themselves into a tightly-organised elite which 'quickly, ruthlessly and efficiently' deposed the bourgeoisie with acts of extreme violence.[36] Even in the society of the future, Stephensen hinted, there will only be 'individual communists' for whom self-transcendence is a viable goal.[37]

Stephensen's second reason for supporting communism was the belief that revolutionary activity often creates circumstances in which the goal of self-transcendence can be furthered. At a time of extreme social polarisation, when the future course of society is settled on the barricades in an atmosphere of paranoic tension, it is invariably the case (or so Stephensen appeared to believe) that a minority of individuals will respond to the pressure by summoning new levels of physical, intellectual and emotional strength. Yet this can only occur if revolutionary activity is approached in a certain way. The individual whom Stephensen chose to invoke when illustrating his idea of the Nietzschean revolutionary was not Marx but Mikhail Bakunin, the founder of anarcho-communism, whom Marx had famously opposed in the factional battles that consumed the First International between 1864 and 1872.[38] Describing Bakunin as a 'fore-runner in deed' whereas Nietzsche had merely 'postulated the fore-runner',[39] Stephensen implied that there were two characteristics in particular which enabled him to approach the revolutions of his time not merely as engines of social progress but also as crucibles of personal development. The first was a capacity for self-dramatisation which has only been matched in the twentieth century by that of Leon Trotsky. Because he 'dramatised his every action in terms of a preconception', Bakunin was drawn irresistibly towards the sort of perilous circumstances in which new capacities are often incubated.[40] Secondly, he also had an instinctive understanding of the way that a hunger for total destruction often results in the renewal of creativity. Without ever using the term himself, Stephensen made it clear that Bakunin's approach to revolutionary activity was essentially what later cultural historians such as Norman Cohn and Greil Marcus have called a 'negationist' one.[41] According to these writers, the hallmark of the negationist sensibility is the belief that political revolution only becomes possible when people believe that they are capable of changing *everything*. In order to provoke the masses into revolutionary activity, the negationist strives to create the impression that 'natural facts' (everything from the weather to the structure of the human body) are as susceptible to change as 'human constructs' such as politics, economics and ideology. Moreover, he expresses his belief in the possibility of total change by adopting an attitude of undiluted scorn towards the whole of his experience – the negationist is ultimately the man who screams 'no! no! no!' at everything which exists. This somewhat frenzied ethos was captured in several of the quotations from Bakunin and his contemporaries which studded Stephensen's essay:

> Let us rely upon the unquenchable spirit of destruction and annihilation, which is the perpetual spring of new life. The joy of destruction is a Creative Joy.[42]

> The revolutionist is a man under a vow...He is ready to die, to endure torment, and with his own hands to KILL ALL who place obstacles in the way of that revolution...So much the worse for him if he has any ties of relationship, of friendship, or of love.[43]

> Death to the old world! Long live chaos and destruction! Long live Death! Place for the future![44]

Stephensen's position was that this sort of demoniacal energy is effectively the hinge between the concerns of Marx and the concerns of Nietzsche. By imbuing the individual with the sense that nothing on earth can resist the desire for change, it not merely paves the way for socialist revolution but also allows a spiritual elite, that cohort of post-Christian visionaries whom Nietzsche saw as his natural constituency, to propel themselves towards a higher stage of evolution. Stephensen suggested that Bakunin probably derived his taste for negationism from the work of Hegel, which he first encountered while a student at Moscow University in the 1830s. Unlike Marx, who understood that the Hegelian dialectic portrays qualitative transformation as the result of prior quantitative shifts, Bakunin seems to have interpreted Hegelianism as a straightforward expression of a sort of apocalyptic desire for a clearing of the temporal decks: 'Only a Russian could have plumbed that well of pure idealism without leaving the world of action. Only a "barbarian newly awakened to civilisation" (Wagner's phrase) could have so far absorbed Hegel's abstract dialectic into his own fibres of concrete action as to apply "Negation" and "Overcoming" to the contemporary society in terms of physical destruction and annihilation'.[45] Stephensen's approach to the broader tensions between Bakuninism and Marxism was noticeably ambiguous. On the one hand, perhaps attracted by the thought that he was offending against Party orthodoxy, Stephensen implicitly endorsed many of the criticisms which Bakunin had levelled against Marx. Although he failed to mention the clashes between the two men over the strategic objectives of the First International, he did quote Bakunin's lukewarm assessment of Marx after their first meeting in Brussels in 1848 ('...much more advanced than I was...I called him a vain man, perfidious and crafty')[46] and argued that one of the main reasons for the failure of Bakunin's revolutionary ambitions was Marx's 'powerfully logical consistency'.[47] Stephensen's animus towards this element of 'logical consistency' in Marxism can arguably be read as the expression of a typically Nietzschean disdain for totalising systems of thought. By describing the ways in which one element of a social formation is related to all the others, Marx was guilty (or so Stephensen implied) of crippling the revolutionary impulse by portraying the existing order in dauntingly homogeneous terms. If nothing else, this reminds us that the attack on the idea of totality long predates the work of Derrida, Lyotard and the other poststructuralist thinkers who oppose the 'logocentric' logic of modern thought. At the same time, however, Stephensen was also anxious to show that his admiration for Bakunin did not preclude support for the more sober traditions of communist politics. The negationist style of politics, he now implied, is essential to the business of overthrowing the bourgeois state but a liability thereafter. Once the new society is in the process of being constructed, it is necessary to exchange the 'romanticism' and 'impetuousness' of a Bakunin or a Trotsky for the dry bureaucratic intelligence of the Stalinist elite: 'To such a climax of realism even the most heroically-carried-through revolution must come. Here is no work for heroes, flaming at heads of phalanges. Exit the Bakunin-principle, exit Trotsky. Enter Stalin, up-stage, sits at desk quietly, works...'[48]

The amount of straight literary criticism in Stephensen's articles was actually quite small. His main concern was to attack those contemporary writers whose ideas were most obviously incompatible with his own. He paid particular attention to the writings of George Bernard Shaw and D.H. Lawrence, since both men had promulgated a vision of human evolution which never (in Stephensen's opinion) attained the necessary level of Nietzschean-Marxist sophistication. Stephensen was a close friend of Lawrence's and arranged for the Mandrake Press to publish a number of his most controversial works, notably *The Paintings of D.H. Lawrence* in 1929,[49] but his ultimate verdict on his friend was that he was a 'great literary genius' who nevertheless reflected the 'hydrophobia of the lower middle-class'.[50] The biggest problem with Lawrence's work was that it posited the willing surrender to a 'mindless Unconsciousness' (this presumably meant the sexual impulse)[51] as the main engine of human evolution. If this emphasis on sexuality was broadly to be welcomed as an affirmation of the 'blood's actuality',[52] it nevertheless had the disastrous effect of obscuring the crucial role of the intellect in generating and directing the evolutionary impulses: 'He is all for *feeling* versus *thinking*, this pillar of dark blood!...[yet the] attack on Consciousness must be made with the weapon of Consciousness. There is no other weapon...'[53] Lawrence compounded the problem by associating the surrender to instinct with a return to the culture of prehistoric societies, thereby concealing his evolutionary ambitions behind an absurd idealisation of the past. This backward-looking element in his philosophy also spilled over into his political programme, notably in his 'modern Luddite' demand for the 'smash-up of the wheels' and the return to pre-industrial forms of production.[54] Nor was he always reliable in his portrayal of class. While recognising that the biggest threat to human development lay in the deracinated culture of the upper classes, he spent too much time demonising the aristocracy (e.g. Lady Chatterley) and too little attacking the bourgeoisie.[55] Stephensen's comments on Lawrence were nevertheless considerably warmer than his comments on Shaw. Whereas Lawrence had made the understandable mistake of emphasising the instincts at the expense of the intellect, Shaw was guilty of the more heinous error of emphasising the intellect at the expense of the instincts. In spite of studying Nietzsche's ideas and trying to popularise them in plays such as *Back to Methuselah*, Shaw clearly regarded the superman as a 'bloodless' intellectual who aimed to burst evolutionary boundaries through a process of pure cerebration.[56] There were some interesting parallels between this argument and the main thesis of 'George Bernard Shaw: A Study of the Bourgeois Superman', the essay by Christopher Caudwell which appeared in *Studies in a Dying Culture* almost ten years after *The London Aphrodite* ceased publication.[57] Although we have no evidence that Caudwell was familiar with Stephensen's writings, it seems unlikely that so voracious a reader would not have come across it at one time or another, perhaps during his periods of intensive study in 'the London libraries which he loved so much' (Robert Sullivan).[58] It therefore seems entirely possible that *The London Aphrodite* was one of the famously voluminous sources which Caudwell drew on when developing his own brand of Marxist theory.

The other writer whose reputation Stephensen set out to demolish was the critic J.C. Squire. Although Squire (1884-1958) is now largely forgotten, he was probably the most influential middlebrow critic in England in the period between 1914 and 1939, beginning as the literary editor of the *New Statesman* and later becoming chief reviewer for the *Observer* and publisher of *The London Mercury*.[59] As the main critical apologist for the Georgian poets, to whose third anthology he contributed a poem of his own, he was renowned for his hatred of modernism and his rubbishing of the early work of T.S. Eliot. Stephensen saw him as the embodiment of a stifling suburban respectability which had nothing to do with literature and everything to do with the insecurity of a petty-bourgeois snob who longed to be perceived as 'genteel'.[60] Squire, he argued, was an 'Apotheosis of the Average' whose work was primarily concerned with 'preserving the amenities of Oxford and of Waterloo Bridge'; inflating the reputations of 'minor (respectable) poets and essayists of the past'; condemning the representation of sexuality in literature and the other arts;[61] burnishing a superficial air of gentlemanliness (with all that implies in terms of 'metropolitan self-assurance', 'sneering' and the denigration of 'vigour') and ensuring that 'polemical expressions of definite opinion are avoided, save when Everybody would approve (*e.g.* an attack upon bawdiness)'.[62] In one of his few recognisably Marxist attempts to relate a trend in literature to its social context, Stephensen interpreted Squire's influence as a symptom of the long-term decline of the British middle classes. If the leading English critics of the past were all men of genuine sensibility, or so it was implied, this was because capitalism tends in its expansive phase to produce 'merchant adventurer[s]' in the mould of Sir Francis Drake. Now that capitalism has become an obsolescent system, it is inevitable that most of the favoured critics will reflect the cultural poverty of the class from which they are drawn.[63] But this does not mean that the damage which writers like Squire are capable of inflicting on the prevailing literary culture should be underestimated. On the one hand, simply by pouring scorn on any deviation from English respectability, they are likely to discourage young writers from producing work in which the struggle for human evolution is the primary focus. There is also the danger that their virulent brand of puritanism might ultimately provoke the demand for a tougher form of censorship. Noting that Squire and other moralising journalists such as James Douglas had recently 'succeeded in getting a book suppressed'[64] (this was presumably a reference to the suppression of Radclyffe Hall's novel *The Well of Loneliness* in 1928),[65] Stephensen feared that the 'struggle for freed expression' might soon have to be 'fought all over again'.[66] Yet his own defence of free speech was itself a remarkably elitist one, showing once again how far his conversion to Nietzsche had taken him from any faith he might once have had in the working class. Recognising that the call for censorship usually arises when a book is considered too sexually explicit to be read by ordinary people, he responded with three arguments: first, ordinary people are too busy to read anything except cheap newspapers; second, their perception of sex has already been distorted by titillating material in the commercial press; and third, most literary works are anyway beyond their comprehension.[67] Quite aside from undermining his claim to be a Marxist, Stephensen's use of these arguments also cast doubt on the extent to which he had genuinely effected a transvaluation of existing values. As a writer in the English tradition (albeit one with an Australian background) he might have been expected to oppose the puritanism of the age by invoking the 'cognitive' defence of free speech outlined by John Stuart Mill in *On Liberty* (1859). (Mill famously argued that censorship can rarely be justified because we can never be sure that the works we propose to suppress do not in fact contain the truth.) By implying that sexually explicit works tell us nothing about the human condition, Stephensen conveyed an air of sexual neurosis that was not entirely different from the sort of thing he condemned in Squire.

In what ways did Stephensen's work reflect the internal culture of the CPGB during the period of Class Against Class? Although Stephensen was clearly uninterested in striking orthodox poses, I would suggest that there were two ways in which his articles in *The London Aphrodite* connected with the wider mood of the Party. In the first place, their emphasis on negationism was arguably inspired by the extraordinary mood of revolutionary febrility which descended on a number of Party activists at this time. Judging from the work of the many historians who have written about the period, it would seem that there were occasions during the Class Against Class years when communists seemed solely motivated by a desire for chaos, especially in their behaviour towards other socialist organisations. Freed from the strategy of building a "united front" with members of the Labour Party, the ILP and the established trade unions, they vented their suspicion of their former comrades by denouncing them as 'social fascists' and exposing them to exceptionally violent rhetorical attacks. The mood of the times is summed up in the following passage from a letter which Rajani Palme Dutt sent to Harry Pollitt in 1932, offering Pollitt advice about a forthcoming debate with Fenner Brockway of the ILP: 'NO POLITENESS! No mere "difference of opinion". No parliamentary debate. No handshakes. Treatment is CLASS ENEMIES throughout. You speak for holy anger of whole international working class against the foulness that is Brockway. Make that whole audience HATE him'.[68] It goes without saying that very few communists would have justified this sort of intemperateness by invoking the example of Bakunin. Nevertheless, it is easy to see how membership of a Party grown deranged with sectarian hatreds might have inclined Stephensen towards his embrace of negationism. The second element of his work that reflected the culture of the Class Against Class period was its explicit elitism. There is no evidence that ordinary Party members lost faith in the organised working class during the bleak years between 1928 and 1933; but a surprising number of intellectuals seem to have agreed with Stephensen that the socialist revolution would ultimately be made by the vanguard acting *independently of the mass*. By resorting to what certain Marxists have called 'putschism' (that is, the belief that a small group of strategists is gifted enough to change the whole direction of society without securing the help of wider forces), they were arguably motivated by the sheer frustration engendered by the central premise of Party policy, which held that the British working class was ready for revolution at a time when it was manifestly nothing of the sort. The obvious point of comparison with Stephensen's work is J.D. Bernal's notorious book *The World, The Flesh and The Devil* (1929), still regarded by many writers as the *ne plus ultra* of biotechnological utopianism. Bernal's argument was that socialism had the potential to develop scientific knowledge to the point where 'normal man' could be liberated from his biological limitations, not least by having his brain removed from his body and suspended in a synthetic cylinder. This sort of radical cyborgism would make it possible for disparate minds to be linked in local networks and bound together by intense feelings of oceanic consciousness. However, since the knowledge required to effect these changes is only comprehensible to a tiny elite (at most to the 10 per cent of people who have received a scientific education), it follows that the society of the future should be *solely* and *unaccountably* governed by a collective of scientists. To reinforce their power over the disenfranchised masses, it would probably be necessary for scientists to achieve a position of complete physical superiority by congregating in vast 'scientific corporations', as well as permanently distracting the non-scientific mind from affairs of state by developing effective techniques of brainwashing. There might even come a time when scientists would emigrate *in toto* to a different planet, exercising their control over the scientifically illiterate across vast areas of space.[69] The fact that Bernal could propagate these ultra-technocratic fantasies while remaining a member of the CPGB (an organisation which he supported for the rest of his life) goes some way towards confirming the suspicion that wholesale elitism was central to the intellectual culture of the Party in the late 1920s and early 1930s. Just as suggestive is the fact that Bernal resorted to a much more populist position when the Party abandoned Class Against Class, insisting for much of the 1930s that the close involvement of the masses was a prerequisite of the scientific superiority of the USSR. The same cannot be said of Stephensen, who drifted away from Marxism in the early 1930s and ended up as an apologist for the Australian far-right.

2. JOHN STRACHEY AND MONTAGU SLATER: THE IDEA OF CULTURAL CRISIS

The most obvious way in which the Class Against Class policy affected Marxist criticism was by drawing attention to the idea of cultural crisis. Committed to the view that capitalism had entered a slump from which it would be impossible to recover, communist intellectuals now began to argue that the breakdown of economic order had also caused a catastrophic decline of standards in all areas of cultural activity. The idea that capitalism is profoundly inimical to cultural excellence was obviously not new to the Marxist tradition. It had been sketched out by Marx himself and developed by slightly later writers such as Franz Mehring and G.V. Plekhanov.[70] As we shall see in subsequent chapters, it was also a central part of orthodox communist theory in the second half of the 1930s. However, in Britain at least, it was only during the period between 1928 and 1933 (and primarily between 1932 and 1933) that it represented the main concern of Marxist criticism. The purpose of this section is therefore to examine the work of the two most fertile theorists of cultural crisis from the Class Against Class period, namely John Strachey and Montagu Slater.[71] Although Strachey and Slater can be regarded as orthodox thinkers, in the sense that both were trying to provide cultural ratification for a political line imposed by the Communist International, it is clear that neither was simply reproducing a pre-existing set of ideas. In the absence of any available Soviet account of why bourgeois society had entered a period of cultural crisis, Strachey and Slater were obliged to develop their own account more or less *ab initio*. Just as British communists had to draw on their knowledge of local conditions in order to translate the Comintern line into a workable strategy, so Strachey and Slater deployed their considerable cultural erudition to flesh out the CI's purely rhetorical assertions about the existence of cultural crisis. This once again bears out the revisionist point that the relationship between the CI and its national sections was usually a genuinely dialectical one.

The bulk of John Strachey's ideas were contained in Part 3 of *The Coming*

Struggle for Power and *Literature and Dialectical Materialism* (both 1932), the latter consisting of the text of a lecture delivered to the John Reed Society in New York.[72] *The Coming Struggle for Power*, still respected today for its prescient critique of Keynes, Hayek and a number of other economists who exercised a dominating influence on economic policy in post-war Britain, set out to explore the impact of capitalist crisis on the separate spheres of religion, science and literature.[73] Strachey argued that the crisis in religion took the form of a drastic reduction in the number of people who felt able to believe in God, and arose from growing public awareness of the social function of religious institutions. According to Strachey, the church has usually managed to uphold support for the existing order in two ways. In the first place, anxious to reconcile human beings to the extreme unpredictability of their physical environment, it has portrayed nature as the creation of a divine intelligence that is capable of being propitiated.[74] Secondly, it has strengthened the dominant ideology by threatening divine retribution on anyone who might be tempted to flout it.[75] Strachey's point was that religion can only function in this way if people remain unaware of what it is trying to do. Once the church is widely perceived as having a temporal as well as a spiritual agenda, support for its core metaphysical propositions begins to decline.[76] The curious thing was that Strachey made no attempt to explain his belief that the Slump had brought precisely this sort of situation about, though presumably he might have argued that when the priestly class is confronted by the prospect of capitalism's imminent extinction (as it certainly was after October 1929) it becomes so obsessed with the restoration of social stability that its spiritual concerns are simply forgotten. Nor did he explain why religious faith is necessarily threatened by the realisation that the church plays a social role. When we consider that Christianity was central to the definition of Britishness (or at least Englishness) for much of the period between the seventh and nineteenth centuries, it seems unlikely that many believers ever regarded the church as a wholly spiritual institution with no interest in earthly affairs. For someone who wrote so insightfully about fascism in other contexts, Strachey also failed to recognise that the decline of Christianity had allowed fascist ideologues to sketch the outlines of a new religion based on quasi-occult notions of human evolution. By overlooking the extent to which the appeal of figures such as Hitler and Mussolini was as much *spiritual* as directly political, he greatly weakened his account of how communism might be expected to triumph over fascism in its battle to win the support of millions of people whose distaste for bourgeois democracy was now palpable. If Strachey had paid more attention to the writings of Oswald Mosley, the politician with whom he was most closely associated between 1924 and 1931,[77] he might have recognised that the history of religion between the wars was characterised less by a collapse into atheism than by the phenomenon encapsulated in the famous aphorism that is often wrongly attributed to G.K. Chesterton: 'When men cease to believe in God, they don't believe in nothing. They believe in anything'.[78] The chapter on religion in *The Coming Struggle for Power* can nevertheless be regarded as an important landmark in the history of the relationship between British Marxism and psychoanalysis. When Strachey examined the specific ways in which the 'traditional claims of religious dogma' have been undermined in the modern age, he confined himself to reproducing Freud's famous arguments in *The Future of an Illusion*. As is well known, Freud observed that people have usually resorted to one of three arguments when seeking to justify their religious beliefs: (1) religion is true because it has been handed down to us by our 'primal ancestors', (2) there are 'proofs' of religion in the sacred texts which we have inherited from our ancestors, and (3) it is blasphemous to even *question* the truth of religion And yet, Freud continued, none of these arguments can withstand the mood of scepticism that is inseparable from the ongoing process of modernisation. The 'educated man' now accepts that 'these ancestors of ours were far more ignorant than we' and that sacred texts all contain 'contradictions, revisions and interpolations'. Moreover, he is inclined to regard the idea of blasphemy as nothing but the reflex action of an ideology which knows that its main tenets rest on an 'uncertain basis'.[79] Although there was nothing specifically psychoanalytic about these observations, it was quite unprecedented for a British Marxist to quote anything Freud had written with approval. Later in the 1930s, when the border between 'Marxist science' and 'bourgeois ideology' had been rendered more permeable by the rise of the Popular Front, Strachey's attempt to fuse Marx and Freud would be taken to much more sophisticated heights by writers such as Jack Lindsay, Reuben Osborn, Alistair Browne and Christopher Caudwell.[80]

Strachey's account of the crisis in modern science was among the first products of the so-called 'social relations of science' movement which existed in Britain for much of the 1930s. The purpose of this movement, which consisted primarily of Marxist and *Marxisant* intellectuals such as J.D. Bernal, J.B.S. Haldane and C.H. Waddington, was to explore the nature of the relationship between scientific activity and the social and institutional contexts in which it occurs.[81] Its origins are usually traced to the dramatic intervention of the Soviet delegation at the Second International Congress of the History of Science and Technology in London in 1931. Arriving in Britain in a state-of-the-art aeroplane that seemed to confirm the USSR's most boastful claims about the quality of its scientific research, Soviet intellectuals such as Nikolai Bukharin and Boris Hessen electrified their British counterparts with a series of papers exploring the relevance of historical materialism to the understanding of scientific procedures.

Strachey was not in attendance at the Congress (at least as far as we know) but appears to have taken a sustained interest in the emerging SRS movement as it began to define its principles in journals such as *Nature* in the last six months of 1931. His argument in *The Coming Struggle for Power* was that science has been undermined by a radical divergence between the needs of the capitalist economy and the trajectory of scientific research. At a time of deep recession, especially the sort of recession from which there is no identifiable means of recovery, it is inconceivable that industry will be able to invest in the new forms of technology which advances in scientific research are continually making available.[82] But this does not mean that research will suddenly cease. It is in the nature of science to continue accumulating knowledge without reference to the material needs of society. Because wasted knowledge is a sort of standing rebuke to the efficiency of the capitalist system, it is therefore inevitable that apologists for the system will begin to demand a significant scaling back of scientific activity. Strachey argued that the new mood of hostility to science had already expressed itself in the spheres of politics, economics and philosophy. Quoting from a speech of February 1932 in which the French politician M Caillaux spoke of the need to 'moderate the application of scientific discoveries to industry', Strachey anticipated a time at which governments would routinely intervene to prevent scientists from pursuing certain areas of research.[83] Equally alarming was the growing demand that capitalism should reduce its dependence on science by reverting to earlier forms of technology. Strachey pointed out that there was even a body of opinion, exemplified by a *Nature* editorial on 'Unemployment and Hope', which seemed to advocate the complete dismantling of the industrial economy and the re-establishment of market handicraft: 'What is wanted is to go back to pre-industrial methods of production. Scrap your huge-scale factories: prohibit mass production by law: and return to "small-scale cottage industries, or handicrafts", with a little gardening thrown in'.[84] In the sphere of philosophy, Strachey detected a widespread attempt to undermine scientific certainties by emphasising the ultimate unknowability of the physical universe. His rather surprising example of a modern philosopher was Jan Smuts, later to achieve notoriety as the founder of apartheid, whose 'doctrine of holism' was interpreted to mean that 'everything is one indivisible whole, incapable of analysis, and therefore not susceptible of scientific investigation'.[85]

There were obvious weaknesses in Strachey's account of the crisis in scientific culture. One of them was its tendency to exaggerate the strength of most of the forces that were supposedly trying to restrain scientific activity. The demand for government control of science was usually made by purely marginal figures, none of whom enjoyed any influence in official circles. Hostility to industrialism was largely the preserve of Distributist writers such as G.K. Chesterton and Hilaire

Belloc whose period of significant influence had ended at least a decade earlier. Although the 'holism' of Jan Smuts was indeed the product of an anti-scientific outlook, its importance to inter-war philosophy was scarcely comparable to that of the emergent school of logical positivism, inspired by Wittgenstein and led by A.J. Ayer, whose aim was not to bury scientific method but to hold it up as the only reliable means of cognition. Yet Strachey's biggest error was probably his insistence on relating the crisis in science to an excessively narrow set of economic circumstances. By claiming that support for unfettered scientific research had been undermined by the onset of a deep recession (albeit one that appeared to be permanent) he ignored the issue of whether capitalism's wider laws of motion should also be regarded as a threat to science.

A more comprehensive account of the relationship between capitalism and science was provided later in the 1930s by the physicist J.D. Bernal, whose book *The Social Function of Science* (1939) is rightly seen as the SRS movement's most important achievement.[86] Bernal argued that there are two significant ways in which capitalism imposes unneccessary restrictions on the development of science: (1) it tends to privilege 'pure' research over 'applied' research, and (2) it makes it impossible to co-ordinate research. His starting point was the assumption that scientists are at their most productive when pursuing practical objectives, and that the pursuit of knowledge for its own sake tends to give rise to a reduction of intellectual vitality. The problem with the market system is that it clouds our understanding of the enormous practical contribution that scientists are capable of making in a modern society. Because there is no guarantee that the commodities which are offered for sale on the market will actually find a buyer, there is often an enormous reluctance on the part of employers to invest in the expensive forms of new technology which science continually makes available. Moreover, it is increasingly common for the market to put scientific knowledge to profoundly anti-social uses. It is therefore unsurprising that scientists should underplay the importance of applied research and retreat into compensatory fantasies about the 'disinterested' investigation of nature. The problem is compounded by the intellectual isolation which capitalist societies impose on their scientists. Research scientists who find employment in private companies are usually forbidden from collaborating with their counterparts in other organisations, since the knowledge they generate is invariably used to secure a commercial advantage over competitors. It is also rare for scientists in the public sector to co-operate with foreign colleagues who are working in similar fields, since modern governments tend to regard scientific superiority as one of the main means by which a state can achieve economic and political ascendancy over another. Bernal was convinced that scientific culture is trivialised by this lack of co-ordination. If scientists were able to work in unison and cast a collective eye over what they were doing, they would be able to distinguish between truly essential areas of research and those of purely ephemeral significance: this would '...enable intelligence to be turned away from tasks which can be better solved by machinery and routine methods to others of great intrinsic difficulty, which as yet no one has approached'.[87] But this is simply not possible when a scientist's research horizons are defined almost exclusively by the priorities of his own organisation. Bernal's writings were suffused by the belief that the crisis in science would easily be overcome in a socialist society. Not only would the advent of economic planning make it possible for advances in technology to be utilised almost immediately, thereby creating an intellectual climate in which applied research was seen once again as the most important form of scientific activity, but the abolition of 'marketplace anarchy' would engender a research culture in which scientists collaborated freely across sectoral and national boundaries. Although 'Bernalism' was later subjected to a ferocious attack by writers such as Arthur Koestler and Michael Polanyi,[88] the latter of whom saw its emphasis on applied research as a threat to intellectual freedom, its messianic sense of science's importance can still serve as a useful corrective to the work of Thomas Kuhn, Paul Feyarabend and the other relativist sceptics who have dominated the 'cultural studies of science' over the last forty years.

Strachey proved to be a far more insightful guide to literature than to either religion or science. His account of the crisis in modern literature occasionally displayed the sort of aesthetic intolerance that disfigured so much communist criticism in the 1930s; but the remarkable thing about it was the way it anticipated several of the most important themes in the work of the so-called 'Western Marxists'. At least three aspects of Strachey's writings on literature deserve particular attention: (1) his attempt to identify the characteristics which distinguish literature from the other arts; (2) his assertion that modern writers have lost the ability convincingly to evoke the transhistorical sources of human misery; and (3) his analysis of the *fascisant* elements which he perceived in the work of several leading modernists.

In a series of highly compressed remarks at the beginning of Chapter Ten of *The Coming Struggle for Power*, Strachey expressed the view that literature characteristically addresses areas of experience that tend to be ignored by the other arts. His distinction between literary and non-literary art was by no means a clear one, in part because of his liking for quasi-scientific metaphors; but it can perhaps be summarised as follows. Music, painting and sculpture are usually concerned with material of a recognisably elevated nature. Literature deals almost exclusively with ideas and experiences of a more demotic and undeveloped kind. The musician or artist is naturally drawn towards transcendent emotions, noble aspirations and dignified philosophical ideas, whereas the writer is much more at home with 'thoughts, dreams, fantasies, concepts, ascertained facts and emotions, which [do] not fit into any other of the categories of human thought'.[89] These differences are also reflected at the level of form. The non-literary arts usually seek to generalise about the human condition, providing ideas and images which illuminate (or claim to illuminate) each manifestation of the form of behaviour they happen to be addressing. Literature, per contra, resists the lure of generalisation and deals only with 'a particular man or a particular woman at a given time and place'.[90] Strachey made no attempt to elucidate the aesthetic or political significance of the opposition between literature and the other arts; but his remarks can clearly be related to some of the wider themes which began to preoccupy the Western Marxists at about this time. One of the main features of Western Marxism has been its attempt to transcend reductionist accounts of the relationship between 'social being' and 'consciousness'. Rejecting the assumption that a society's prevailing modes of consciousness simply reflect the interests of the ruling class, one strain of Western Marxism has tried to show how thoughts, feelings and intuitions that are broadly subversive of the status quo always exist alongside (even when they are assimilated to) materials of a more obviously 'hegemonic' kind. As we shall see at several points in this book, British communists made a number of attempts in the 1930s to analyse the nature of social consciousness in a similar way, though it goes without saying that none achieved the sophistication of an Antonio Gramsci or a Raymond Williams. What Strachey appeared to be doing in his remarks about literature was relating different art forms to distinctive levels of social consciousness. He seemed to imply that the non-literary arts, with their dignified materials and confident generalisations, give expression to what might be called the 'official' consciousness of society (i.e. the outlook of the ruling class), whereas literature gives shape to the inchoate and primarily localised feelings of opposition which oppressed groups tend to experience spontaneously. To use the terminology developed by Raymond Williams in his Gramscian critique of the base/superstructure metaphor, literature reflects the 'emergent' aspects of social consciousness while painting, music and sculpture reflect its 'dominant' aspects.[91] Since Strachey was presumably implying that the different levels of consciousness usually coexist within the same sensibility, it would clearly have been preferable if he had resisted the idea that they are somehow separated out at the moment of artistic expression. But the truly noteworthy thing was that he was addressing the self-divided nature of social consciousness in the first place. In addition there was perhaps one other way in which his remarks about literature paralleled the main concerns of Western Marxism. It was during the 1930s that several writers, notably Theodor Adorno and his associates in the Frankfurt School, began to investigate the relationship between Western modes of rationality and the rise of totalitarianism. Their specific argument was that 'instrumental reason' poses a threat to democratic culture by subordinating the investigation of concrete realities to the drive to identify law-governed regularities in both the natural and social worlds.[92] When Strachey wrote admiringly about literature's ability to focus our attention on particular instances rather than bloodless abstractions, he was arguably driven by the related need to find alternatives to a style of thought that was ultimately complicit with fascism. In the British context he can thus be regarded as a distant precursor of the so-called 'new aestheticism', primarily represented by Andrew Bowie and Jay Bernstein, which regards art's ability to resist the homogenising logic of instrumental reason as the source of its political power.[93]

The largest part of Strachey's account of the crisis in literature addressed the inability of modern writers to handle the theme of tragedy. Strachey argued that the greatest writers of the past were all preoccupied with those *ineluctable* aspects of human experience that cause great misery. By addressing such 'unbearable necessities' as ageing, illness and death, they often managed to palliate human suffering by 'offering to us the example and consolation of ill fortune faced consciously and stoically by undeceived men'.[94] The problem with a great deal of modern literature is that it tends to confuse the corrigible with the incorrigible. Novelists such as Proust, Lawrence and Huxley obviously regarded their work as belonging to the 'tragic tradition'; but in practice they dealt only with problems that were (1) of recent historical vintage, and (2) capable of being resolved. Proust and Lawrence were both primarily concerned with the disappointments that accompany rampant snobbery. Characters such as Charles Swann or Mellors rise from comparatively humble backgrounds to the upper echelons of society, only to find that the culture of the aristocrats with whom they now mix is spiritually redundant.[95] Huxley was more concerned with the cultural inadequacies of the lower orders, devoting much of *Brave New World* to an anguished account of the 'production of masses of low-grade workers' in a Fordist dystopia.[96] The attempt to portray these historically-specific problems as if they were genuinely tragic (i.e. unavoidable sources of human misery) has had a devastating impact on literature's emotional range. The emboldening sense of cosmic turbulence which characterised the literature of the past has now been replaced by an enfeebled 'sense of depression'. It was this which led Strachey to suggest that the work of Proust, Lawrence, Huxley and their followers could best be described as belonging to the 'world-weary school' of writing. Although Strachey made no attempt to explain why capitalism's terminal crisis should have precipitated these developments (just as he failed to explain its responsibility for the crisis in religion), he was in little doubt as to why the world-weary school was dangerous. By lending an air of tragic inevitability to problems which human beings were eminently capable of resolving, it reinforced the belief that the social order as a whole was incapable of being changed.[97] At the moment of its greatest crisis, literature was fulfilling what Roland Barthes would later describe as the main function of 'myth'. It was translating culture into nature.[98]

Strachey used his enthusiasm for the tragic strain in world literature as the basis of an attack on what he regarded as one of the more damaging misconceptions about Marxism. Quoting from the scornful analysis of 'Communistic Utopianism' in The Modern Temper by Joseph Wood Krutch, he argued that Krutch was representative of the many intellectuals who persist in seeing Marxism as a naïve form of social constructionism.[99] Their basic claim (or so the argument went) is that Marxists tend to regard economic structures as the only determining influence on human behaviour, and therefore believe that 'perfect happiness' can easily be achieved through the simple expedient of establishing a communist society. In response, Strachey insisted that the philosophy of dialectical materialism is wholly incompatible with utopian illusions about the perfectibility of man. Far from being blind to the 'fundamental maladjustments…between the human spirit and the natural universe' which are liable to cause misery in any period of history, Marxists have never done more than assert that communism will enable human beings to confront these maladjustments at a 'different' and 'higher' level.[100] These remarks, scanty though they were, made Strachey one of the pioneers of the small school of Marxist thinkers whose optimism about the possibility of social change is balanced by a materialist pessimism about humanity's 'biological destiny'. If the most important of these thinkers is probably the Italian philologist Sebastiano Timpanaro, whose book On Materialism enjoyed a brief vogue in the 1970s,[101] it is nevertheless in the aesthetic philosophy of Herbert Marcuse that we find the most obvious parallels to Strachey's writings on literature. Some of Marcuse's later works, notably The Aesthetic Dimension from 1978, could even be used to critique Strachey's rather monomaniacal emphasis on the role of tragedy in literature. Whereas Strachey sometimes gave the impression that the evocation of 'unbearable necessities' had been the only important element in the Western tradition, Marcuse made the much more subtle case that the power of art (not only literature) derives from its complex intermingling of an 'affirmative' social vision with a tortured awareness of the 'metasocial' constraints on human happiness. According to Marcuse, the first purpose of art is to employ formal means to transfigure our awareness of our social environment. The world presented to us in the great works of art is recognisably the world in which we live, but it is also unrecognisably different: its surfaces possess an unfamiliar aesthetic lustre and its characters exhibit the 'desublimated subjectivity' which Marcuse famously regarded as the ultimate goal of social revolution.[102] Struck by the terrible contrast between the mediocrity of everyday life and the 'promise of happiness' held out by art, we are possessed by the desire to create a new world that is more consonant with the artist's vision. Yet art is not to be regarded as a vehicle of mindless utopianism. Its other great purpose is to temper the political enthusiasms which it might otherwise risk unleashing. By focusing on precisely the sort of biological predicaments which Strachey had emphasised, it 'serves to warn against the "happy consciousness" of radical praxis' and reminds us that no social order can ever protect us from anguish.[103] Moreover, its preoccupation with illness, ageing and death also has the effect of sharpening its subversive edge. When the spectre of avoidable social misery is viewed against the background of unavoidable biological suffering, our willingness to compromise with a flawed social reality is undermined: 'It [death] is the final remembrance of things past – last remembrance of all possibilities forsaken, of all that which could have been said and was not, of every gesture, every tenderness not shown. But death also recalls the false tolerance, the ready compliance with the necessity of pain'.[104] If Strachey's discussion of the tragic element in literature might have benefited from some of Marcuse's sophistication, it is also worth noting that there were several occasions on which he (Strachey) flatly contradicted his vaunted realism about the limits of human happiness. One passage in *The Coming Struggle for Power*, which Strachey felt obliged to defend vigorously in *Literature and Dialectical Materialism*, went so far as to suggest that communist society might yet engender a scientific culture so advanced that death could be 'indefinitely postponed'.[105] Presumably the function of literature in such a society would not be to reconcile human beings to their biological fate; but rather (reversing Barthes's formula) to dramatise the process by which science strove to translate nature into culture.

The other aspect of the crisis in literature which Strachey addressed in detail was the existence of what he took to be a *fascisant* strain in the work of several modern writers. Borrowing the term from an essay by Michael Gold, one of the American Communist Party's most influential literary critics in the 1930s, Strachey argued that large swathes of modern literature served to express 'The Fascist Unconscious'. This work was not explicitly fascist in outlook, nor were its authors necessarily aware that they were conveying a political perspective; but it nevertheless betrayed certain attitudes and prejudices that can legitimately be regarded as 'the mental soil out of which fascism grows'.[106] Although Strachey illustrated his theme by referring to the now forgotten poem 'Frescoes for Mr Rockefeller's City' by Archibald MacLeish, much of what he said about MacLeish can arguably be applied, *mutatis mutandis*, to the work of more important conservative modernists such as Eliot, Yeats and William Faulkner. The main assumption of the argument was that MacLeish possessed a 'strong, though perhaps unconscious, belief in what are called the standards and traditions of a gentleman in the tradition of the old American stock'.[107] This presumably meant that he yearned for the pre-industrial world of the antebellum South as completely as Eliot identified with the European 'tradition' or Yeats mourned the passing of the Protestant aristocracy in Ireland. Yet his poems were full of passages in which the Southern gentleman's poise was superseded by 'caddish' attitudinising of a sort more often associated with fascist ideologues. 'Frescoes for Mr Rockefeller's City' was an intensely patriotic poem, evidently sincere and free of Kiplingesque bombast; but its patriotism was palpably on the verge of curdling into chauvinism. MacLeish's main technique for expressing his love of America was to launch a scornful attack on expatriate artists such as Henry James who valued the 'tidier stream' of European culture more highly than the rumbustiousness of the new world.[108] There was even a stanza in which he drew bizarre parallels between the American landscape and a reclinining female nude, prompting Strachey to detect an undertow of sexual febrility that was scarcely compatible with a mature appreciation of the national culture.[109] MacLeish's portrayal of the American landscape was also linked to a distinctively proto-fascist attempt to shore up existing hierarchies by stigmatising the dispossessed. Like many other works produced by cultural conservatives with a hatred of industrialism, 'Frescoes for Mr Rockefeller's City' eulogised the 'great open spaces' that had disappeared with the rise of the urban slum. But its passages of pastoral uplift were accompanied by heavy-handed satires on 'Jewish, or immigrant, revolutionaries',[110] whose perceived spiritual bankruptcy was implicitly seen as a consequence of prolonged exposure to the claustrophobic realities of the American city.[111] Strachey's insight into the way that MacLeish used spatial metaphors to dehumanise entire categories of people was not extended to the work of other writers; but the reader is inevitably reminded of one of Eliot's more infamous excursions into anti-semitism:

> My house is a decayed house,
> And the Jew squats on the window-sill, the owner,
> Spawned in some estaminet of Antwerp,
> Blistered in Brussels, patched and peeled in London.[112]

If Strachey's gloomy account of modern culture is still one of the more famous examples of Marxist criticism from the early 1930s, the same cannot be said of the largely forgotten work on modernist painting which Montagu Slater published at about the same time. Nevertheless, there is a case for saying that Slater had a clearer understanding of the essentials of modernism than most other communist writers in either the USSR or Britain. In his essay 'The Spirit of the Age in Paint', contributed to Volume Two of Edgell Rickword's symposium *Scrutinies* in 1931, Slater recognised that modernism had its roots in a rejection of the belief that painting can somehow achieve complete realism in its depiction of external reality. Convinced that it is basically impossible to create an illusion of three dimensionality in a two-dimensional medium, the leading modernists aimed to create work which drew attention to the autonomous or non-representational status of the painted image.[113] Slater's attitude towards this project was a somewhat ambivalent one. On the one hand, in line with orthodox arguments about the existence of cultural crisis, he seemed to believe that modernist assumptions had gone a long way towards ruining the visual arts. Anticipating an argument that Tom Wolfe would make famous some 40 years later in *The Painted Word* (1978), he implied that the first problem with modernism was its tendency to subordinate practice to theory. Since the visual language employed by the leading artists of the age could only be understood by those already familiar with the theoretical principles on which it was based, it was virtually impossible for a modern painting to appeal to the average viewer.[114] Moreover, since the discourse of modernism was heavily 'aesthetic' in its orientation (that is, more concerned with general philosophical principles than with specific problems of painterly practice), it tended to rob the artist of the feel for concrete 'particulars' which lies at the heart of great art.[115] There was also a sense in which the idea of aesthetic autonomy had impoverished the *content* of modern painting. Having been told that their chosen medium is entirely lacking in mimetic potential, modern artists were reluctant to address their most deeply cherished concerns for fear of failing to do them justice. Slater underscored the point by quoting a passage by Roger Fry, the pre-eminent theorist of 'significant form', which noted that 'Cézanne was violently drawn to the female form as a model' but 'simply did not dare' to portray it on canvas.[116] However, these pessimistic remarks were balanced by a more sanguine set of predictions about the future of modernism. At times, Slater seemed willing to acknowledge that when modern artists used two-dimensional forms in their work (or when they resorted to some other technique for drawing attention to the non-representational status of what they were doing), they were simply engaging in a necessary attempt to strip down the language of painting before building it up again. Furthermore, he implied that modernism had been expanding at both the practical and theoretical levels since the culmination of its destructive phase in the late-nineteenth century. In the first place, inspired by Cézanne and the cubists, many artists had been aiming to depict the 'geometrical scaffolding'[117] which they regarded as the guarantor of the natural world's coherence.[118] By contrast, there was a growing recognition among aesthetic theorists that the idea of mimesis is fully compatible with a retreat into inner space. Quoting the work of the German psychologist Hermann Bahr, Slater argued that our spatial perceptions undergo a strange transformation when space is approached through the medium of the mind's eye. There is firstly a pronounced sense of synaesthesia, with the visual and tactile faculties seeming to translate themselves into each other, while space as a whole seems to acquire what Slater called a 'mystic apprehension of solidity'.[119] One of the goals of the modernist painter should therefore be '…"the imitation of objects in space", if by that you choose to understand the objects of the inward eye in that peculiar sort of space in which memory and imagination move'.[120] Although Slater did not address himself to the political aspects of modernism, it is tempting to argue that his survey of contemporary developments contained a tacit nod to several of the Marxist and *Marxisant* elements in the avant garde. If the reference to geometrical regularities puts us in mind of the tradition of Russian abstraction which began with Malevich and culminated with the Constructivists in the 1920s,[121] then the talk of inward eyes and mystical solidity surely recalls the surrealist attempt to combine objective reality with the world of dreams. The fact that Slater could refer even obliquely to these artists illustrates the room for manoeuvre which Marxist criticism still enjoyed in the early 1930s. Within a few short years, when the USSR had imposed its cultural doctrines on the rest of the world communist movement, few writers would have dared to invoke either constructivism or surrealism except in a spirit of deep hostility.

3. LEFT-LEAVISISM?
THE ENCOUNTER WITH CULTURAL CONSERVATISM

As a number of historians have noted, the shift towards the Class Against Class policy unleashed a virulent mood of anti-intellectualism in the British Communist Party.[122] If the Party was usually inclined to venerate intellectuals beyond their station, seeing them in some ways as a symbol of the self-fulfilment that would become possible under socialism, there was nevertheless a brief period between 1928 and 1933 when they were widely dismissed as petit-bourgeois backsliders with little or no value to the revolutionary movement. The most famous expression of this anti-intellectualism occurred in an internal memorandum which Rajani Palme Dutt, himself the Party's most obsessively cerebral leader, circulated in August 1932. Responding to the Anglo-Russian critic D.S. Mirsky and the economist Maurice Dobb, both of whom had proposed the establishment of a 'society for intellectual workers' in the CPGB, Dutt warned that intellectuals are peculiarly susceptible to ideological deviations and insisted that 'the first role of intellectuals who have joined the Party is to forget they are intellectuals and act as Communists, that is enter fully into the Party fight'.[123] It is not entirely clear why Class Against Class should have engendered this hostility to 'workers by brain', though one explanation is perhaps the mood of destructive febrility which seemed to go hand in hand with the policy of opposing other left groups (see the above section on P.R. Stephensen). Finally given permission to express their frustration with erstwhile comrades in the Labour Party, the ILP and the trade unions, there was arguably a sense among communist militants that thinking was simply incompatible with the negationist frenzy required to expose the 'social fascists'. It is perhaps also true that the necessity of rationalising an irrational policy led many communists to doubt the value of reason itself. Yet the effects of all this on the intellectual culture of the Party were not entirely negative. Most obviously, the new mood of anti-intellectualism seems to have prompted certain communist thinkers to turn outwards and engage with wider trends in academic and intellectual life. For much of the period between 1920 and the late 1960s, the majority of Party intellectuals led notably hermetic careers – they published articles in the Party press, wrote books for the Party publishing house (Lawrence and Wishart) and addressed gatherings of Party members. However, in the few brief years of their internal disgrace, they were seemingly much keener to write for non-Marxist publications and construct alliances with non-Marxist thinkers. In the area of cultural criticism, the new mood of expansiveness fuelled a remarkable attempt to forge a rapprochement with some of the leading representatives of cultural conservatism, specifically F.R. Leavis and his co-thinkers on the journal *Scrutiny*. The high point of this attempt was the debate between Leavis and A.L. Morton which occurred in *Scrutiny* between 1932 and 1933, when Morton tried to convert the Leavisites to Marxism by pointing to the ideological similarities between the two camps. At about the same time, a number of writers who had been associated with cultural conservatism through their involvement with the journal *Calendar of Modern Letters* (the most important were Edgell Rickword, Douglas Garman and Alec Brown) began to move towards Marxism and recorded their disenchantment with cultural conservatism in a series of essays and reviews.[124] These are the matters which will concern us for the rest of this chapter.

Conservative ideas about culture have played an important role in the so-called 'Culture and Society' tradition in Britain since at least the Augustan period, underpinning the work of such diverse thinkers as Johnson, Burke, Coleridge, Ruskin, Carlyle and Arnold. Yet the form of cultural conservatism which most influenced the British communists was the one associated with the emergence of modernism after the First World War. Its most important critical spokesmen were probably T.E. Hulme, T.S. Eliot and Wyndham Lewis, though the latter was in many respects a somewhat marginal figure. The task of insinuating it into academic culture fell largely to F.R. Leavis and his followers in the early 1930s.[125] Although these thinkers disagreed with each other over a wide range of issues, it can still reasonably be said that their cultural doctrines were bound together by two common features: (1) the defence of what can broadly be called the 'classical' sensibility in art against what can broadly be called the 'romantic' sensibility, and (2) distrust of modernity and the ascription of cultural superiority to premodern societies. The defence of classicism was first undertaken by Hulme in a series of essays collected in the posthumous volume *Speculations* (1924).[126] Acknowledging his debt to the French novelist Charles Maurras, one of the founders of the semi-fascist movement *L' Action Française*, Hulme implied that the essence of the classical outlook is the frank recognition of the fallen nature of man. Because the classical artist is acutely conscious of the capacity for evil which lurks at the heart of human nature, and since he realises all too vividly how strong emotion can spill over into uncontrollable aggression, he naturally favours a mode of sensibility which places 'restraint' above the expression of passion.[127] This puts him at odds with the romantic artist, whose taste for *Sturm und Drang* reflects a naïve and dangerous Rousseauian belief in the natural goodness of human beings. Classicism is also divided from romanticism by its quite different understanding of the relationship between mind and environment. Whereas the romantic artist invariably tends towards an extreme form of philosophical idealism, conveying the narcissistic illusion that the mind can somehow exert a direct influence over its material surroundings, the classicist portrays a universe in which mind and matter are permanently divided by an impassable metaphysical gulf.[128] This gloomy dualism, intended to shore up a sense of mankind's limitations, influences the style of the work of art at a number of different levels. The texture of the classical work is usually 'dry and hard', eschewing the distinctive sense of glutinous emotionality which features in much romantic art and which Hulme perhaps associated with the narcissism of the pre-oedipal period. It also displays an almost neurotic insistence on describing the surfaces of the world in minute detail, thereby acting as a powerful reminder of the sheer difficulty of bending language and the reality it represents to human purposes. Hulme's definition of classicism was extended by Eliot in two crucial ways. In the first place, acknowledging that an emphasis on restraint lies at the heart of all great literature, Eliot famously implied that the classicist seeks to discipline the emotions by effecting a reconciliation of thought and feeling. Instead of allowing the emotions to float anarchically free from all other mental functions, the artist must adapt them to the process of thinking and thereby imbue thought with its own emotional and sensual satisfactions. The problem with the great bulk of modern literature is that writers have undergone a 'dissociation of sensibility', with the result that thought and feeling have now been completely prised apart. Eliot hinted at what he meant when he said of the metaphysical poets George Herbert and John Donne that they 'feel their thought as immediately as the odour of a rose'. It was Eliot's attempt to explain this state of affairs which led him to his second great contribution to the theory of classicism, namely his influential account of the 'impersonal' nature of creativity. His initial move was to associate classicism with a specific social background. If the classical ideal was at its height in the long period between the birth of the Homeric epic and the middle of the seventeenth century, this was because pre-modern societies provided an institutional, moral and cultural context in which the orderly mind could flourish. With their rigid hierarchies, religious certainties and inviolable moral prejudices, they naturally produced men and women who favoured a balance of thought and feeling over the unrestrained expression of emotion. It was therefore inevitable that the disappearance of pre-modern societies would bring the collapse of the classical ideal in its wake. Weighed down by their liberal preoccupations with equality and moral autonomy, modern societies have disordered the public mind and engendered a literary culture to match. It follows that modern literature can only achieve greatness if the writer eschews any idea of self-expression. Rather than using his own experiences as the basis of his work, the writer must set his dissociated sensibility to one side and strive to emulate the 'tradition' of classical greatness which dominated an earlier and better age:

> ...the historical sense compels a man to write not merely with his own generation in his bones, but with a feeling that the whole of the literature of Europe from Homer and within it the whole of the literature of his own country has a simultaneous existence and composes a simultaneous order. This historical sense, which is a sense of the timeless as well as of the temporal and of the timeless and of the temporal together, is what makes a writer traditional. And it is at the same time what makes a writer most acutely conscious of his place in time, of his own contemporaneity.[129]

> Poetry is not a turning loose of emotion, but an escape from emotion; it is not the expression of personality, but an escape from personality.[130]

Leavis extended the ideas of Hulme and Eliot in a number of ways when he introduced them into the academic study of literature in the early 1930s, both in a series of books of his own and in the journal *Scrutiny*. The aspect of his work most relevant to this chapter is his elaboration of Eliot's hints about the nature of popular life in the pre-modern period. When Eliot tried to explain why pre-modern societies were more likely to produce great artists than their industrial successors, he suggested that one of the reasons was their possession of a common culture which cut across class boundaries. Works of literature were enjoyed by people from right across the social spectrum, not merely by an intellectual elite.[131] What Leavis set out to do was provide some historical ballast for Eliot's theory, examining the lives of ordinary people in the 'organic communities' of the past in order to explain their elevated tastes. Drawing on George Sturt's book *The Wheelwright's Shop*, a highly nostalgic account of life in a rural English village in the early-nineteenth century, Leavis argued that the cultural excellence of the peasantry was made possible by the satisfactions of pre-industrial labour. Whereas the modern industrial worker is so dispirited by his job that he spends his leisure hours in a state of 'decreation' (that is, recuperative passivity), the peasant felt naturally impelled to extend the creative ethos of his everyday work into all other areas of his life. Reading Shakespeare and Bunyan was a natural response to cultivating the land or attending to the needs of livestock. Faced with the suggestion that his vision of rural labour was grossly idealised, Leavis resorted to many of the stock arguments of romantic anti-capitalism in order to bolster his case. Before the onset of capitalist rationalisation, he argued, the labourer performed whole tasks which appealed to both the senses and the intellect. Membership of a small community allowed him to monitor the consequences of his everyday activity. The unchanging structures of non-market production instilled a powerful sense of the continuity of generations. The rhythms of work corresponded to the cycle of the seasons, conveying a profound sense of elemental harmony. And the ubiquity of untamed nature served as a salutary reminder of human limitations. These ideas received their most impassioned expression in *Culture and Environment* (1932), the book which Leavis wrote with Denys Thompson to introduce the perspectives of the *Scrutiny* group to sixth-form students of English. It is still widely regarded as the foundation text of British Cultural Studies.[132]

It is easy to see why a number of communist intellectuals should have been attracted to cultural conservatism in the early 1930s. Leavis's vision of unalienated rural labour may have offended against a strict reading of the materialist conception of history, but in its way it still seemed congruent with the Marxist belief that aesthetic significance would be restored to manual labour once market institutions had been abolished. There were also parallels between the conservative emphasis on classicism and the atmosphere of scholarly asceticism which characterised communist culture at this time. Moreover, as Perry Anderson famously made clear in 'Components of the National Culture' (1968), it could even be argued that conservative intellectuals were united with their Marxist counterparts by a shared hostility to prevailing academic conventions. At a time when most British intellectuals eschewed the 'totalising' modes of analysis prescribed by classical sociology, both groups were at least making a rudimentary attempt to locate culture within its broader social contexts.[133]

The writer who best illustrated the links between Marxism and cultural conservatism in the early thirties was probably A.L. Morton, later the author of the seminal book *A People's History of England* (1938). Morton had been an activist in the CPGB since 1928, but was also a friend of T.S. Eliot and an occasional contributor to such broadly conservative journals as the *Criterion* (owned and edited by Eliot) and the *Calendar of Modern Letters*.[134] At any rate, it was Morton who was responsible for the one serious attempt to propose an alliance between the communists and the cultural conservatives.[135] The attempt was made during the brief debate between Morton and Leavis which occurred in the pages of *Scrutiny* in 1933.[136] Leavis launched the debate after taking exception to an article of Morton's in the *Criterion*.[137] In 'Poetry and Property in a Communist Society' (October 1932), Morton had responded to an essay by the Catholic intellectual Gallox which described capitalism as the economic system most obviously consistent with Christian principles. Much of Morton's response was taken up with a series of observations about the status of private property in a communist society;[138] but the remarks which grabbed Leavis's attention concerned the role of the artist under both capitalism and communism. The heart of Morton's argument, which he justified by invoking a theory of cultural crisis similar to that of Strachey, was that it is only spasmodically possible to create great art under capitalism, whereas artistic excellence is as integral to communism as material abundance and the absence of class rule. The evidence of history, Morton seemed to argue, shows that significant art can only be produced under two circumstances: (1) when the artist has enough leisure to hone his creative gifts, and (2) when the existing economic system is in a state of material expansion. Although capitalism still supports a 'leisure class' of artists who are allied to the bourgeoisie, its long-term decline means that most contemporary art is 'decadent'.[139] The great virtue of communism is that it develops the material preconditions of cultural excellence to an unprecedented degree. Instead of conferring a significant amount of leisure on a small elite, it creates a 'leisure society' in which each man has enough spare time to expand his natural powers of self-expression. By ensuring that the means of production are continuously improved, it also creates the sense of permanent economic expansion that alone permits the imagination to soar.[140] Furthermore, in a passage which suggested that his approach to culture was still rooted in the classic liberal opposition between private and public, Morton speculated that the artist under communism would be sufficiently indifferent to social relations to subsist in a solipsistic world of pure sensibility:

> Poets will still have their problems and difficulties, different from ours but perhaps as great. They will solve them in their own way. Paradoxically, they may easily be more individual difficulties than our own since they are less likely to concern the relationship of the poet to society, a question which, though it presents itself individually to each one, is really only an obstacle to be overcome before the difficulties proper to the poet can be approached.[141]

Leavis decided to write about Marxism after reading Morton's essay alongside Trotsky's *Literature and Revolution* (1924), Edmund Wilson's *Axel's Castle* (1931) and an essay on T.S. Eliot by the Russian critic D.S. Mirsky. The result was a short piece called ' "Under Which King, Bezonian?" ', published as an editorial in *Scrutiny* in December 1932. At this point, Leavis had not yet developed the outright hostility towards Marxism which characterised some of his later work. He was willing to admit that 'there seems to be no reason why supporters of *Scrutiny* should not favour some kind of communism as the solution of the economic problem', though he added that 'it does not seem likely...that they will be orthodox Marxists'.[142] Yet his basic assumption was that Marxism must ultimately be regarded as a threat to cultural excellence, not only because of its political objectives but also because of its main theoretical tenets. If we accept that industrial society is profoundly inimical to the creation of great art, and if we further accept that culture can only be safeguarded by a determined effort to identify with tradition, it follows that a socialist revolution would necessarily result in a deterioration of the cultural situation. Tradition is too much of a 'delicate organic growth' to withstand any attempt to tear up society from its roots.[143] Nor is it possible to believe that a mature communist society would establish conditions in which a new culture might flourish. As the study of pre-industrial societies makes clear, great art is only created when a 'real culture' is 'shared by the people at large';[144] but ordinary people only take an interest in the arts when their work provides them with sufficient stimulation. The problem with the society envisaged by Morton is that it would not so much restore meaning to labour as abolish labour altogether, thereby creating an entire populace of 'rootless' dilettantes: 'Without being critical of Mr. Morton's generalizations one may ask: What will "social functions" be in a leisure community – a community, that is, in which the "productive process" is so efficient as no longer to determine the ordering of life?...Whether such a rootless culture...can be achieved and maintained may be doubtful'.[145]

When he turned to the more theoretical aspects of Marxism, Leavis paid particular attention to the doctrine of base and superstructure and its supposedly central category of 'bourgeois culture'. His initial objection to this category was simply that it represented a form of cultural abuse. By implying that every work since the dawn of the capitalist age has somehow reflected the outlook of the ruling class, we run the risk (or so Leavis seemed to believe) of not merely misrepresenting the works themselves but also inducing widespread cynicism about the purpose of cultural activity.[146] More interestingly, he also grounded his suspicion of the idea of bourgeois culture in a wider critique of instrumental reason. At the heart of much cultural doctrine in the inter-war period was the belief that the prestige of science (or at least the model of science associated with the Enlightenment) had created circumstances in which an emphasis on abstraction took precedence over a proper concern for 'concrete particularities'. This was held to be disastrous on both aesthetic and political grounds. Some writers, of whom Leavis was one of the most distinguished examples, argued that beauty resides only in particular things and not in generalisations; whereas others (notably Continental Marxists such as Theodor Adorno) insisted that a disdain for particularity ultimately gives rise to the abolition of individual liberty. Leavis's implication in ' "Under Which King, Bezonian?" ' was that the category of bourgeois culture is itself a product of the fetishisation of science, since its effect is to divert our attention from a heterogeneous reality towards a historically dubious 'law' of cultural production:

> To be concerned, as *Scrutiny* is, for literary criticism is to be vigilant and scrupulous about the relation between words and the concrete. The inadequacies of Mr. Wilson and Prince Mirsky as literary critics are related to their shamelessly uncritical use of vague abstractions and verbal counters. What is this 'bourgeois culture' that Mr. Eliot represents in company, one presumes, with Mr. Wells, Mr. Hugh Walpole, *Punch*, *Scrutiny*, Dr. Marie Stopes and the *Outline for Boys and Girls*? What are these 'classes', the conflict between which a novelist must recognize 'before he can reach to the heart of any human situation'?[147]

Morton responded to Leavis in a highly compressed essay entitled 'Culture and Leisure', published in *Scrutiny* in March 1933. Although he claimed that 'It is impossible for me to go into the greater number of the issues raised in ' "*Under Which King, Bezonian?*" ',[148] he actually managed to respond to most of Leavis's major arguments about the political and theoretical inadequacies of Marxism. At the level of politics, he claimed that Leavis had overestimated the extent to which a socialist revolution represents a clean break with the past. Because the society of the future is necessarily one that builds on the 'achievements of earlier periods', it is quite wrong to imagine that socialist politics entail a destructive attitude towards the existing corpus of great works. Leavis was guilty of pessimism when he claimed that tradition is too fragile to withstand major political changes, even if we assume that the changes are likely to be undesirable: 'History proves that anything which is of cultural value, far from being a "tender organic growth" possesses a quite amazing tenacity'.[149] In an interesting example of the wilful distortion to which communist writers habitually resorted when considering the work of Leon Trotsky, Morton argued that 'Trotsky's misleading formulations' in *Literature and Revolution* bore much of the responsibility for the fallacy that socialists disdained the culture of the past, even though the chapter to which he appeared to be referring ('Proletarian Culture and Proletarian Art') went out of its way to assert the *importance* of bourgeois culture in the construction of a socialist society.[150] When it came to the likely structure of communist civilisation, Morton accused Leavis of misconstruing the reference to a 'leisure society' in his earlier essay in the *Criterion*. Agreeing that a society in which everyone had been freed from the necessity to work would inevitably suffer from cultural inertia, he insisted that the goal of communism was not so much the abolition of work as the creation of circumstances in which the 'distinction between work and leisure has disappeared'.[151] However, this does not mean that work under communism will somehow acquire the characteristics of leisure under capitalism. Since intellectual and aesthetic significance is likely to be restored to the labour process by the advent of planned production, it will no longer be necessary for men and women to pass their spare time in a state of passive recuperation – work and leisure will both be characterised by the active pursuit of self-fulfilment.[152]

If these remarks were a comparatively rare acknowledgement by a thirties communist that socialism has existential as well as economic objectives (and also an early indication of how much Morton had been influenced by William Morris),[153] they were less important than Morton's response to the Leavisite critique of the *theoretical* aspects of Marxism, particularly the doctrine of bourgeois culture. Morton's initial move was to insist that the Marxist theory of culture is by no means as reductive as Leavis had implied. Noting that Leavis had tried to summarise the Marxist position by saying that culture is ultimately a by-product of the '*methods* of production', he argued that a 'small verbal point' had prevented him (Leavis) from fully understanding the doctrine of base and superstructure. According to Morton, the preferable phrase would have been '*mode* of production'.[154] Whereas the word 'methods' implies that economic activity is 'rigidly determined' and therefore incapable of being influenced by culture or indeed by anything else, the word 'mode' does the precise opposite – it implies that economic behaviour is sufficiently 'fluid' to be altered by the cultural forms it has itself called into existence. Once we realise that culture is able to influence the economic base as well as merely reflecting it, Morton implied, our hostility to terms such as 'bourgeois culture' invariably begins to disappear, since we come to recognise that their function is historical and not judgemental. That is, we recognise that their main purpose is to help us understand the relationship between cultural formations and the broader social system, not to convey the view that the only purpose of culture is to legitimise an exploitative set of class relations.[155] However, for all this verbal subtlety, the decisive moment of 'Culture and Leisure' came when Morton shifted his attention to the issue of aesthetic judgement:

> When we talk of 'bourgeois culture' we refer to the sum of the ideological superstructure characteristic of the present historical period, in which the bourgeoisie is the ruling class. This includes much that the Editors of *Scrutiny* would perhaps prefer to call a lack of culture. The novels of D. H. Lawrence and the methods of salesmanship described in Mr. Denys Thompson's article *Advertising God* do not, indeed, seem to have much in common at first sight...Bourgeois culture, then, is the result of a historic process, and cannot be accepted as uniformly valuable or rejected as entirely valueless. The purpose of *Scrutiny* seems to be to combat the harmful elements of the bourgeois 'culture complex' and to preserve what is valuable. This is entirely praiseworthy; the only question we have to ask ourselves is: what are the most hopeful means towards this end? [156]

At first sight, these sentences might simply appear to assert rhetorically what Morton had failed to prove theoretically. By endorsing the cultural forms which Leavis and his followers admired and scorning the forms which they evidently despised, Morton's clear intention was to show that the category of bourgeois culture poses no threat to the cultivation of 'critical discrimination' and that Marxists are just as adept as cultural conservatives at distinguishing the 'valuable' from the 'valueless'. And yet the real interest of the passage lies elsewhere, specifically in the fact that it anticipates two of the most important features of the work produced by cultural Marxists later in the decade. In the first place, it exemplifies what certain writers have described as the failure of the British communists to challenge the canonical certainties of the wider literary culture. Whereas Marxist writers in Europe and the USA were beginning to challenge the very distinction between 'high' and 'low' culture (or at least acknowledging that popular culture is often worthy of critical respect), their counterparts in Britain were only willing (or so it is often argued) to seek a re-evaluation of writers and artists who had *already* been admitted into membership of the canon. It was considered appropriate to argue that the radicalism of a Bunyan or a Milton had yet to be fully appreciated, but not to insist that popular verse, folk songs or commercial newspapers might also be the bearers of cultural value. This lack of intellectual nerve is often ascribed to the isolation of the British Marxists from their more adventurous continental counterparts, but Morton's article suggests another explanation – the desire to please (or at least not unduly offend) the leading representatives of academic criticism. When Andy Croft argued that writers such as Morton, Garman and Rickword 'took a kind of left-Leavisism into the Party',[157] perhaps what he had in mind was not the slightly implausible claim that the substantive ideas developed by the communists were basically similar to those of the Leavisites, but rather that Leavis and his followers had so entrenched the opposition between 'minority civilisation' and 'mass culture' that the communists were too nervous to challenge it. However, it is also clear that the perceived need to endorse the distinction between high and popular culture was not entirely counterproductive. For one thing it forced the British communists towards one of their most important theoretical innovations: the claim (or at least the implication) that there is something inherently *polysemic* about many of the more complex uses of ideology. In his efforts to justify his hostility towards commercial forms, Morton argued that the primary function of the 'mass production novel or the tabloid press' is to ensure that ordinary people are 'doped into acquiescence in a system of organized exploitation'.[158] The clear implication was that more elevated forms somehow function differently, containing elements that not only legitimise the status quo but occasionally serve to undermine it. As we shall see in Chapter Six, this belief in the janus-faced nature of prestigious cultural forms was to reappear during the later attempt to identify a radical tradition in British culture, when it was often argued that Christianity, liberalism and even the ideology of classical education all contained traces of subversive thinking which had inclined the British people towards the cause of revolution.

The other crucial feature of Morton's article was what Francis Mulhern has described as its 'conciliatory' tone.[159] There were no traces in 'Culture and Leisure' of the polemical arrogance which tarnishes so much Marxist writing on opposing ideologies. Instead of dismissing the Leavisites as purblind apologists for a decaying social order, Morton courteously invited them to reconsider their attitude towards Marxism, noting that the similarities between the two camps were greater than their divergences. In a classic attempt to win an opponent's sympathy by repositioning one of his most totemic pieces of terminology, he argued that the Leavisites and the communists both ascribed considerable importance to the idea of the 'organic community', but insisted that it was wrong to associate it solely with an irrecoverable past. While the organic community had certainly existed in the past (though in the period of primitive communism and not in the Middle Ages) it would ultimately be re-established in a higher form with the victory of socialism.[160] Furthermore, Morton seemed happy to accept that the Leavisites would take a long time to shift their position. When he wrote that '...Scrutiny is far too valuable a weapon against the Philistine to be left *permanently* in the position of the two heroes who "wept like anything to see such quantities of sand" ' (emphasis mine),[161] he appeared to envisage a lengthy period in which communists and Leavisites would co-exist within the pages of the same journal, only converging after 'Mr. Leavis....thinks things over again...[and asks] whether the struggle to "maintain the tradition of human culture" can really be carried far on a basis of ignoring the struggle of the classes with which it is inseparably connected'.[162] As I have suggested earlier, this extraordinary tactfulness was surely prompted by the miserable experience of communist intellectuals during the period of Class Against Class. Treated like a pariah by his own people and thrown into self-doubt by the Party's rampant anti-intellectualism, Morton instinctively put solidarity with other intellectuals above the desire for political purity. At the same time, as Mulhern reminds us, there was also a sense in which the Leavis/Morton debate reflected the anxiety which intellectuals *in general* experienced as the crisis of the 1930s began to take shape:

What is...interesting...is that such a *démarche* should have been attempted at all. It might be said that the thematic resemblances between the two outlooks were sufficient to create an intermediate zone which, given the ideological disorientation of the intelligentsia in the climacteric of the early thirties, was large and open enough to permit important 'territorial' gains by one side or the other. At all events, some such belief was apparently held by both parties.[163]

It seems unlikely that many readers of Scrutiny were converted to Marxism by Morton's arguments. Nevertheless, a surprising number of young intellectuals *did* make the transition from cultural conservatism to communism in the first two or three years of the 1930s.[164] The most prominent were Edgell Rickword, Douglas Garman and Alec Brown,[165] each of whom went on to play a major role in the literary culture of the CPGB.[166] The three men already knew each other through their involvement with The Calendar of Modern Letters (1925-1927), the journal which Leavis took as his model when editing the early issues of Scrutiny.[167] Rickword and Garman were the editors of the journal (along with Bertram Higgins), while Brown was an occasional contributor. The Calendar seems to have been established because Rickword, Garman and Higgins believed that Eliot's Criterion was not doing as much as it should to advance the causes of modernism and classicism. Apart from opening its pages to the likes of Lawrence, Joyce, Wyndham Lewis and Forster, it was also one of the first journals to introduce the techniques of 'practical criticism' associated with I.A. Richards to a comparatively large audience (it often sold as many as 7000 copies per issue). Indeed, as John Gross has pointed out, the *Calendar* often took its emphasis on the importance of criticism to extreme lengths, with one editorial proclaiming that '...It is no longer useful to distinguish between an act of imagination and an act of criticism...it is possible to say that the criticism in Mr. Eliot's "Sacred Wood" not only is a more valuable work than Mr Lawrence's latest novel, but takes precedence of it, makes it obsolete'.[168] However, even though the desire to advance Eliot's philosophy was crucial to the magazine's foundation, the conservative thinker who came to dominate its pages was actually Wyndham Lewis. Garman and Rickword were both converted to Lewis's virulently chauvinistic brand of cultural conservatism at some time in the mid-1920s (possibly after reading *The Art of Being Ruled* in 1925),[169] thereafter peppering their work with denunciations of 'slug humanitarianism' and 'mean-spirited equalitarianism'.[170] When Rickword, Garman and Brown began to move towards communism in the early 1930s, they drew a line under their previous beliefs by providing a number of implicit and explicit critiques of cultural conservatism in a variety of essays and reviews. This body of work is important because it demonstrates that there were definite limitations to the ecumenical ethos of Thirties Marxism. While it is true (as I have tried to show throughout this book) that the English critics often tried to supplement the Soviet influences on their work with ideas drawn from wider traditions, it is also the case that this process of ideological miscegenation was usually carried out surreptitiously (in the sense that ideological debts were rarely acknowledged) and that no system of thought was ever acknowledged as being the equal of Marxism. As the work of Brown, Rickword and Garman proves, it was also common for the English communists to launch virulent attacks on non-Marxist writers by whom they had previously been deeply impressed. Apart from anything else, this helps to explain why Morton's call for a formal alliance between the communists and the Leavisites was always doomed to failure.

The most interesting critique of cultural conservatism was developed by the novelist Alec Brown, though its main principles have to be extrapolated from a lengthy essay which focused less on cultural theory than on the work of an individual poet. In 'The Lyric Impulse in the Poetry of T.S. Eliot', an essay contributed to Volume Two of Edgell Rickword's symposium *Scrutinies* in 1931, Brown tried to rescue Eliot from the rather apocalyptic image with which his early work had burdened him. His central argument was that there is a tension in Eliot's poetry between its manifest content and its dominant mood. At the level of content it persistently evokes the whole range of predominantly biological phenomena, including ageing, illness and death, which are both ineluctable and the source of profound misery at all stages of human history.[171] In order to emphasise the transhistorical nature of these phenomena, Eliot imbues characters from a variety of different periods and civilisations with much the same sense that ultimately 'we are really in the dark' (*Portrait of a Lady*). However, the air of tragedy is radically undermined (or so Brown argued) by Eliot's talent for producing verse whose defining feature is a mood of extreme lyrical affirmation.[172] This conflation of tragedy and lyricism was exemplified for Brown by the following extract from *Mr Appolinax*, whose final two lines were said to 'really sing' in spite of depicting the inexorable drift of drowned bodies towards the bottom of the ocean:

> He laughed like an irresponsible foetus.
> His laughter was submarine and profound
> Like the old man of the sea's
> Hidden under coral islands ·
> Where worried bodies of drowned men drift down in the green silence,
> Dropping from fingers of surf.[173]

Significantly enough, Brown defined the 'lyric impulse' in poetry in terms which obviously owed a great deal to the work of I.A. Richards. Whereas Richards had described poetry in general as an 'emotive' form which makes no real reference to external reality,[174] Brown insisted that (1) 'in a lyric... every element is given over to direct positive qualities', and (2) the lyric is best regarded as a 'cosmos in itself' with 'its own laws of behaviour'.[175] Moreover, in an obvious echo of Richards's quasi-behaviourist arguments about the function of poetry, Brown argued that the 'maximally positive' mood of lyric poetry only emerges when the poet has come to terms with the unpleasant realities of human existence, especially the inevitability of his own death.[176] Conscious that his gift for lyrical digression conflicted with his disenchanted vision of the human condition, Eliot devised a number of techniques to hold his lyricism in check. The most important was his habit of implying that there is ultimately no distinction between mankind's biological and social destinies. The impression created by many of his poems is that the entropic trajectory of the human body somehow sets the pattern for the history of human institutions as well.[177] In *Prufrock and Other Observations* (1917) and *Poems* (1920), making obeisance to what Brown termed 'Goddess Drab', Eliot conveyed his distaste for life in society by forging the images of urban misery which earned him his early notoriety: 'The winter evening settles down/With smell of steaks in passageways'.[178] By the time he wrote *The Wasteland*, when his approach to social issues was becoming more consciously political, he had fully absorbed the pessimistic philosophy of history implicit in Sir James Frazer's *The Golden Bough*, with its insistence that all societies are ultimately destined to fall into decline. The effect of this sort of political pessimism was reinforced by Eliot's obsessively discursive style. According to Brown, whose taste for lengthy corroborative quotations swelled his essay to more than fifty pages, there are numerous poems in which Eliot interrupts the flow of lyricism by intruding a passage of philosophical or metaphysical speculation. Although accusations of excessive cerebrality have been levelled against modernism since its inception, the twist in Brown's argument was that Eliot's intellectualism would be more accurately regarded as pseudo-intellectualism. Look beneath the surface of his writing, Brown seemed to imply, and one often encounters a surprising paucity of thought. For instance, when he (Eliot) tried to explain his reference to the bells of Saint Mary Woolnoth striking 'with a dead sound on the final stroke of nine', the best he could manage in the footnotes to *The Wasteland* was 'A phenomenon which I have often noticed'.[179] Brown's rather heretical assessment of Eliot's intellectual status can perhaps be seen as a quirky response to Richard's seminal observation that *The Wasteland* had achieved a 'complete severance between poetry and all beliefs'.[180]

Although Brown was not explicitly concerned with cultural conservatism and did not mention Eliot's theoretical writings, it is easy to see how a rudimentary critique of cultural conservatism can be extracted from his essay. Its most obvious implication was that conservatism is burdened by an insurmountable tension between its understanding of human nature and its conception of history. On the one hand, Brown seemed to be saying, conservatives justify their preference for an orderly and hierarchical society by invoking a pre-Enlightenment notion of human sinfulness – human beings are naturally wicked and will *always remain so*, regardless of the particular society in which they happen to be living. On the other hand, they also seek to promulgate a highly idealised vision of the nation's historical inheritance. Anxious to neutralise the liberal and egalitarian impulses which bourgeois democracy has installed at the heart of modern consciousness, conservatives portray the rural, monarchical and pre-rationalist past as the site of a perfectly realised form of social unity in which the national culture acquired its essential characteristics. When Brown focused on Eliot's habit of depicting examples of human venality at all stages of human history, he unwittingly exposed the flaw in this strategy – it is simply not possible to emphasise the virtues of tradition if one simultaneously bemoans the sinfulness of those who established it. Moreover, as Brown arguably implied when considering Eliot's gloomy portrayal of life in society, there is a constant tendency among conservatives to surrender to outright political cynicism. By insisting so forcefully that the fallen nature of man is the fundamental datum of all political thought, they risk creating the impression that no human institution can ever be sufficiently untainted to act as a barrier against evil – not even the church, the family or the state. It makes no sense to see authority as a bulwark against chaos if the people who exercise it are moral cretins. Brown's essay can also be read as a critique of Eliot's defence of classicism. Whereas Eliot saw classicism and romanticism as mutually exclusive forms of sensibility, Brown implied that the mind inevitably tends to translate one into the other in a process of what Jung might have called 'enantiodromia'. If it was the classicist in Eliot who crafted the lugubrious reflections on the limitations of human nature, the sudden bursts of lyricism betrayed a streak of compensatory romanticism over which he patently had little control. Brown also seemed to suggest that Eliot's dream of a non-dissociated sensibility was similarly incompatible with the laws of human psychology. By insisting that Eliot persistently deployed passages of pure cerebration as a counter to his own lyricism, he (Brown) portrayed reason and emotion as if they were implacable enemies in a battle for control of the mind. No form of reconciliation between the two can ever be countenanced, or so the argument seemed to go.

Edgell Rickword outlined his implied critique of cultural conservatism in an essay on Wyndham Lewis which appeared in the same volume as Brown's essay on Eliot. At this time, shortly before his notorious conversion to fascism, Lewis was probably the most marginal of the cultural conservatives. He was as staunch as Eliot and Hulme in his defence of classicism, yet his spirited attempts to diagnose the forces in modern culture which undermine the classical ideal must often have seemed wilfully eccentric, not least because of his love of self-dramatisation (he called himself 'The Enemy') and the somewhat scattershot quality of his prose. There were perhaps only two ideas which distinguished him from the other cultural conservatives, one of which derived from his notorious misogyny and the other from his deep hostility to the work of Henri Bergson.[181] On the one hand, obsessed with the belief that the 'softness' and 'flabbiness' of the female sensibility are destructive of the classical ideal, he argued that the female mind has enjoyed a disastrous increase in influence since the dawn of the modern age.[182] The most obvious sign of this increased influence is the emergence of democracy, which Lewis saw as inherently feminine in its indifference to intellectual excellence.[183] Secondly, he also claimed that modern societies have experienced a precipitate decline as a result of being oriented more towards time than towards space. Insisting that the modern 'time cult' is largely a consequence of Bergson's doctrine of creative evolution, he argued that there is something fundamentally classical about a concern for the relative position of objects in space, whereas a preoccupation with time leads only to a romantic obsession with the destruction of physical boundaries.[184] John Carey captured the essence of Lewis's argument when he wrote that '...time sucked one into a soft, obnoxious intimacy where things were for ever "penetrating" and "merging"... [while]...space offered a healthy outdoor scene, with things standing apart, "the wind blowing between them, and the air circulating freely"'.[185] Although Rickword satirised many of these ideas in his contribution to Volume Two of *Scrutinies*, the heart of his attack on Lewis (and hence on cultural conservatism more generally) was an incisive though implied point about the weakness of classicism. The problem with the classical outlook, Rickword seemed to suggest, is that it insists on seeing the intellect as a fundamentally *beleaguered* force, permanently under threat from wider mental phenomena such as the 'Dionysian' emotions that we associate with great art. When the classicist seeks to defend the idea of restraint against the romantic ideal, his starting point is always the assumption that our ability to think is about to be laid waste by the mind's unrulier dispositions. The problem with this 'fear of the emotional' is that it generates a sort of continuous expectation of cerebral disaster, which itself imposes enormous and unnecessary limits on the scope of thought.[186] Much of Lewis's work shows precisely what happens when a powerful mind is crippled by intellectual anxiety. For one thing, although Lewis is an acute critic of the ills of modern society, he never makes a determined effort to sketch a workable alternative. (Somewhat ironically, Rickword made this accusation in the year that Lewis first voiced his support for Hitler.).[187] Moreover, he often resorts to a sort of callow pragmatism when assessing new ideas. Faced with the theory of relativity or some other philosophical or scientific thesis, his response is not 'is this true?' but 'is this desirable?'[188] Notwithstanding his great gifts as a creative writer, many of his works place undue emphasis on the explication of abstract ideas and ignore the essential truth that 'the aesthetic faculty...must include the emotional, the Dionysian'.[189] And in certain works such as *Tarr* and the *Wild Body*, Rickword implied, even Lewis's talents as a purely destructive thinker have been undermined by his failure to recognise the *robustness* of thought. Obsessed with the belief that human beings are everywhere losing the ability to think, he has begun to create characters who are little more than behaviourist caricatures, responding automatically and without reflection to external stimuli.[190] By overestimating the extent to which the intellect is threatened by strong emotions, Lewis has effectively destroyed the thing he claims to be defending.

Rickword hinted at another reason for his growing disillusionment with cultural conservatism in a brief review of T.S. Eliot's *Selected Essays* in *Scrutiny* (March 1933). According to Rickword, Eliot's critical writings had undergone a fundamental change in the decade or so since essays like 'Tradition and the Individual Talent'. Whereas the early essays were masterpieces of close reading, scrupulously analysing the formal means by which authors evoked a specific sensibility, the more recent work was largely concerned with issues of morality, religion and politics. Rickword believed that this transition from 'literature' to 'society' was much to be regretted. In a passage which once again reminds us of the overweening influence of I.A. Richards on the period's young literary intellectuals, he insisted that (1) literature is the most powerful means of 'redeeming the time' (that is, liberating the individual from mental chaos), (2) '...as our writings are, so our thoughts are', and (3) sensitivity to literary form is crucial to unlocking the aesthetic qualities of the individual work.[191] By abandoning his peerless gift for practical criticism and turning instead to commentary on social affairs, Eliot had gravely compromised the moral power of his criticism. This attack on political criticism might have seemed surprising from a writer who had recently converted to Marxism, but it perhaps helps to explain why so many intellectuals were able to shift their allegiance from formalism to historical materialism with such apparent ease. If an appreciation of literary technique is indeed the *sine qua non* of personal redemption, then it surely makes sense to create a society in which a sense of technical accomplishment is restored to ordinary labour. In a socialist society, Rickword perhaps meant to imply, there will be no tension between the quest for redemption through art and the conditions of everyday life – both will be bound together by a shared concern for *craftsmanship*. As we shall see in Chapter Six, Rickword's preoccupation with the reconciliation of mental and manual labour was later to take an even more utopian form.

There were echoes of Rickword's argument in the work of Douglas Garman, his former editorial colleague on *The Calendar of Modern Letters*. However, whereas Rickword had condemned Lewis for failing to sketch a plausible alternative to the chaos of liberal civilisation, Garman condemned three of the leading cultural conservatives for precisely the opposite reason. Reviewing four books by Lewis in the December 1932 edition of *Scrutiny*, he regretted the fact that Lewis, Eliot and Lawrence had moved beyond a purely 'destructive' attitude to modern society and begun to outline a definite programme of political and cultural reform. Since the most savage critics of the existing order rarely have a clear idea of how society should be reorganised, their positive suggestions were necessarily unconvincing – Eliot had retreated into a 'backwater of Anglo-Catholicism'; Lewis had put his faith in an utterly inchoate notion of the 'Not-self'; while Lawrence had achieved an 'unedifying apotheosis' by sketching a social programme whose tenets were apparently too trivial even to be mentioned.[192] Interestingly, Garman seemed to blame these developments on the gulf which had opened up in modern society between intellectuals and the 'literate public'. When intellectuals feel wholly isolated from the reading public, or so he appeared to argue, they invariably try to win new readers by coining platitudinous ideas about the way in which life can be improved. If the relationship between writers and readers had been somewhat closer in the first place, the likes of Lawrence, Eliot and Lewis could simply have intensified their exhilarating attacks on modern civilisation and left the task of envisaging the future to better qualified thinkers.[193]

Garman's most interesting attack on the prescriptive aspects of cultural conservatism was contributed to the first issue of *Left Review* (October 1934). In 'What?..The Devil?', responding to the arguments in Eliot's notoriously anti-semitic *After Strange Gods*, he appeared to predict that Eliot would soon be throwing in his lot with fascism. According to Garman, the decisive change in Eliot's recent criticism was that the idea of tradition had been supplemented by an emphasis on 'orthodoxy'. Worried that a correct understanding of the European heritage was inherently difficult to sustain, Eliot now believed that the defence of tradition should be entrusted to powerful institutions that could maintain the necessary level of ideological discipline. Although initially hopeful that the Anglo-Catholic church might assume such a role, it was only a matter of time before he transferred his allegiance to the fascist state. Apart from anything else, Garman implied, this was because his new ideas 'closely parallel[ed]' those of the fascist movement, which also claimed to be defending a traditional way of life by augmenting the power of authority.[194] If Garman's essay hardly represented the last word on these matters, it arguably inaugurated a critical obsession with the *fascisant* element in Eliot's thought which continues to this day in the work of such writers as Anthony Julius, Tom Paulin and Christopher Ricks.

There is one further irony that needs to be noted. Although much of Garman's work in the early 1930s can be seen as a settling of accounts with cultural conservatism, there is evidence to suggest that his conversion to Marxism was hastened by a novel that was not merely conservative but arguably proto-fascist. This was *Voyage au Bout de la Nuit* by Louis-Ferdinand Céline, the French writer who became notorious later in the decade for his vocal support for Hitler. Reviewing the book in *Scrutiny* in September 1933, Garman described it as a misanthropic satire on modern society which achieved its effects by portraying human nature solely in terms of the 'negative impulses'. Instead of endowing his characters with a realistic combination of benevolence and selfishness, Céline wrote as if they were entirely in the grip of 'horror and disquiet and squalor'.[195] According to Garman, one of the novel's most interesting aspects was the way it explained this level of moral blindness. Its central character, Ferdinand Bardamu, is fully aware of his predicament and 'relates his misery and failures, not to an involved metaphysical scheme or historical process, but to an immediate fact: the fact that he belongs to the exploited class'.[196] By resisting the temptation to 'generalize' about Bardamu and focusing scrupulously on his particular experiences, Céline paradoxically elevated him into a 'representative figure' for 'a generation for which the economic is, increasingly, the question of primary importance'.[197] It would be unwise to ascribe too much importance to Garman's reading of *Voyage au Bout de la nuit*, but it is easy to see how such a novel might have affected his political development. Proving that an emphasis on the primacy of economics is by no means incompatible with the creation of great art, it might well have helped to persuade him that Marxism was an ideology that a literary intellectual could embrace without fear. If so, it was a curious case of fascism engendering its polar opposite.[198]

CHAPTER TWO

REVOLUTIONARY TRADITIONALISM:
SOVIET CULTURAL THEORY IN THE 1930s

Although a British strain of cultural Marxism had been developed in the early 1930s by writers such as John Strachey, A.L. Morton and Edgell Rickword, it was not until slightly later (specifically after the abandonment of the Class Against Class policy in 1933) that a significant number of the CPGB's intellectuals became engaged with cultural issues. Their work was powerfully influenced by two contemporary developments in the world communist movement. The first was the adoption by the Soviet government of an arts policy that was considered binding on all communist artists, not simply those who lived and worked in the USSR. The second was the emergence of the 'Popular Front' strategy against fascism, which obliged communists to raise public awareness of the history of popular radicalism in their own countries. I will return to the cultural consequences of the Popular Front strategy in Chapter Six. The purpose of this chapter is to identify the central principles both of Soviet arts policy and the body of cultural criticism that was used to legitimise it.

The policy adopted by the Soviet government in 1934 was the culmination of a long debate about the nature of revolutionary art which had started almost immediately after the October Revolution.[1] The participants in the debate had polarised into two fairly distinct groups at an early stage. The first group, encompassing the members of such diverse artistic movements as Futurism, Constructivism and the so-called 'montage cinema', believed that the ideals of the new society could only be properly expressed in an art which reflected the technical innovations of modernism.[2] The second and less distinguished group (its key members were drawn from the AkhRR [Association of Artists of Revolutionary Russia] and RAPP [Russian Association of Proletarian Writers]) argued that modernism was inaccessible to the Soviet masses and that revolutionary artists should therefore confine themselves to the use of traditional forms.[3] A few observers, notably Leon Trotsky in *Literature and Revolution*, spoke in favour of a pluralist culture and urged the Soviet government to adopt an attitude of relative neutrality in its treatment of the arts.[4] For much of the early period it looked as if the Bolsheviks were throwing their weight behind the modernist camp. Narkompros, the government department with responsibility for education and the arts, gave massive subsidies to the *avant-garde* and appointed leading modernists to positions of special cultural influence – for example, Chagall, Malevich and El Lissitzky all became teachers at the famous art school at Vitebsk.[5] The propaganda materials which conveyed the government message during the Civil War were dominated by Constructivist and Futurist styles. 'No state', as Robert Hughes once wrote, 'had ever set down its ideals with such radically abstract images'.[6] Yet the period of modernist supremacy was to prove exceptionally shortlived. In 1925, mid-way through the experiment with the New Economic Policy, the Central Committee of the CPSU issued an important resolution (*On The Party's Policy In the Field Of Literature*) which stipulated that Soviet artists should 'make use of all the technical achievements of the old masters to work out an appropriate form, intelligible to the masses'.[7] Seven years later, after a period in which the traditionalists had virtually hounded their modernist counterparts out of public life,[8] the government abolished all artistic groups and established a single state-run organisation for each of the arts. It was this centralising reform which made possible the final suppression of modernism and enabled the government to enforce the main tenet of its new policy: that all Soviet artists should henceforth observe the conventions of 'Socialist Realism'.

The doctrine of Socialist Realism was explored in detail for the first time at the Congress of the Union of Soviet Writers in 1934. The Congress was by no means a staid or elitist event. Stretching across a full fortnight (August 17th to September 1st) and divided into 26 sessions, it had many of the qualities of a popular festival – one whose main purpose was to show that Soviet writers had united with the Soviet masses in a common aesthetic project. At various times there were opportunities for workers, soldiers and other ordinary citizens to declaim their views about literary policy or express their solidarity with the new generation of writers. No one seems to have complained when speeches were interrupted by the arrival of noisy delegations from the various sectors of the Soviet economy, many of them intoning wildly exaggerated economic statistics against a backdrop of traditional music. It was taken for granted that Soviet authors had not merely learned from the great writers of the past but begun to improve on them. Each of the speakers had to say his piece in a hall bedecked with immense portraits of Balzac, Cervantes, Shakespeare, Pushkin and the like. In all there were about 600 literary delegates, including representatives from 52 of the multifarious Soviet nationalities.[9] The keynote addresses were given by Andrei Zhdanov (who was soon to assume the responsibility for enforcing cultural policy), Maxim Gorky, Karl Radek and Nikolai Bukharin. The English translation of the congress proceedings (*Problems of Soviet Literature*, published by Lawrence and Wishart in 1935) was the only substantive document on Soviet policy that British communists were able to consult during the 1930s.[10] It can thus be regarded as the main source for anyone wishing to understand the intellectual context in which the CPGB's cultural critics were obliged to operate. In the account that follows I argue that its approach to the arts contained four main elements: (1) a prescriptive element, (2) an aesthetic element, (3) a historical element, and (4) a comparative element.

1. THE PRESCRIPTIVE ELEMENT

The purpose of the prescriptive element in the 1934 speeches was to specify the central characteristics of Socialist Realism, ostensibly in the case of literature but also, *mutatis mutandis*, in the case of the other arts as well. The term Socialist Realism was allegedly coined by Joseph Stalin during a discussion on revolutionary culture with Maxim Gorki and others in 1932.[11] None of the contributors to the Soviet Writers' Congress attempted a precise definition of it, but Andrei Zhdanov came closest when he said that the new art 'means knowing life so as to be able to depict it truthfully in works of art, not to depict it in a dead, scholastic way, not simply as "objective reality", but to depict reality in its revolutionary development.'[12] While this definition betrayed much of the vagueness which came to characterise Soviet criticism, it can essentially be broken down into two propositions about content and one about form. At the level of content, it insisted that Soviet art should contain a comprehensive portrait of the existing stage in the development of socialism, as well as a utopian anticipation of the communist society of the future (this latter element was usually called 'revolutionary romanticism').[13] At the level of form, it stipulated that artists should aim to make their work as accessible as possible by employing only 'traditional' techniques.

When the Soviet theorists addressed the issue of how existing society could most effectively be portrayed, they instructed artists to obey the principle of *ideinost* (the view that art should interpret reality from a Marxist perspective) as well as that of *klassovost* (the view that art should illustrate the leading role of the working class in the creation of a socialist society).[14] Both these principles were rooted in a wide-ranging critique of earlier forms of Soviet culture. It was made clear during the 1934 Congress that it was no longer acceptable for artists to express broad support for the October Revolution while eschewing a Marxist outlook. Bukharin devoted a lengthy passage to the work of several fellow-travelling poets who had come to prominence after 1917, condemning

Blok and Yesenin for their mysticism and Bryussov for his 'eclecticism'.[15] A critical note was also adopted in a discussion of the avowedly Marxist writing which had been produced over the previous 17 years, with Bukharin suggesting that much of it had been vitiated either by crude sloganeering or by a narrow preoccupation with the fine detail of Soviet life.[16] It was with these considerations in mind that Bukharin and his colleagues insisted that Socialist Realism should strive to express a synoptic or totalising vision of Soviet realities, on the assumption that art could only draw the population into political action by sharpening its understanding of the dialectical relationship between the various levels of the emerging social order. Gorky underscored the point by identifying several important themes which had yet to be addressed in Soviet literature, including the transformed role of women, the effects of industrialisation on the environment and the culture of the Soviet republics.[17]

Since the ability to think synoptically was seen as a precondition of further social progress, there was an obvious link between the principles of *ideinost* and *klassovost* and the idea of revolutionary romanticism. In the speeches of 1934, especially that of Bukharin, the issue of how the anticipated glories of the communist future could be represented in art was approached in two ways. One important suggestion was that Soviet artists should adopt the lyricism associated with European Romanticism and apply it to their treatment of Soviet realities.[18] If the everyday world of industrialisation, collective farms and other forms of 'socialist construction' were seen to evoke a rhapsodic response, then the Soviet people would soon realise that their existing institutions contained the seeds of a future paradise. This sense of millennial expectation could be reinforced, secondly, by the depiction in all forms of art of what came to be known as 'positive heroes'. The positive hero (or what some critics called the 'type') was portrayed as a sort of proletarian *Übermensch*, physically powerful and intellectually dexterous, who had advanced to a new stage of evolution because of his heightened understanding of the historical process.[19] Because his central characteristic was an encyclopaedic grasp of all aspects of Soviet life, he was held by writers like Bukharin to prefigure a communist society in which the division of labour has been abolished and the individual expresses his creativity by fulfilling a diverse range of economic roles. The probable inspiration behind this idea was the famous passage from *The German Ideology* in which Marx and Engels, in one of their few comments on the likely nature of communism, spoke of the citizen of the future as one who would hunt in the morning, fish in the afternoon, rear cattle in the evening and criticise after dinner.[20]

The idea of revolutionary romanticism raises obvious questions about the extent to which Soviet art was ever intended to be truly realistic. When we approach the issue of form, therefore, it is important to be clear that the Soviet theorists never employed the concept of realism in a strictly mimetic sense. Artists were instructed that their choice of form should always be governed by the principle of *narodnost*, which holds that the main obligation of art is to be immediately comprehensible to ordinary people. They were also told that mass influence could only be achieved through the use of such traditional forms as linear perspective in painting, rhyme and rhythm in poetry and the narrative conventions of the nineteenth-century novel in fiction. Yet they were never under a formal obligation to reproduce the surface of the world with *trompe l'oeil* precision.[21] Instead, the emphasis at the 1934 Congress was on the importance of stylistic pluralism. The orthodox view was that the treatment of a theme must ultimately depend on the nature of the theme itself (we will return to this point when examining the doctrine of the unity of form and content); while Zhdanov, in a passage that belied his reputation for aesthetic intolerance, told Soviet writers that:

> You have many different types of weapons. Soviet literature has every opportunity of employing these types of weapons (genres, styles, forms and methods of literary creation) in their diversity and fullness, selecting all the best that has been created in this sphere by all previous epochs. From this point of view.....the critical assimilation of the literary heritage of all epochs, represents a task which you must fulfil without fail, if you wish to become engineers of human souls.[22]

If this passage is to be believed (and there is no reason to suppose that Zhdanov wrote it for purely tactical reasons), it follows that the theorists of Socialist Realism wished to establish an artistic culture in which a defining commitment to traditional forms was shown to be compatible with a fair amount of stylistic freedom. Although the bulk of Soviet art eventually turned out to be straightforwardly naturalistic, this probably had more to do with the influence of a small number of leading artists (Fadeyev, Gerasimov, Ostrovsky etc) than with any real measure of government intervention.[23] Arguably this was an area in which Soviet artists imposed an orthodoxy on themselves.

Apart from sketching the broad characteristics of Socialist Realism at the level of both form and content, the prescriptive element in Soviet criticism also specified a series of reforms to the relations of cultural production in the USSR. There was considerable emphasis on the need to develop new forms of collaborative work which would enable Soviet artists to overcome the 'bourgeois individualism' that afflicted their counterparts in the capitalist countries. The establishment of the Union of Soviet Writers was justified (insofar as it was justified at all) on the grounds that it would give established authors the opportunity to exert a beneficial influence on the USSR's 'hundreds' of 'local beginners'.[24] Gorky also wrote enthusiastically about the more structured modes of collaboration that had already been adopted throughout the USSR for the purpose of educating new writers. He referred in particular to the massive works of local history which were then being published at a dizzying rate, most of which had been written by beginners under the close supervision of well-known authors: '.....this work will furnish them [i.e. the beginners] with the widest scope for self-education, for raising their proficiency through collective work on raw material and through mutual self-criticism.'[25] Yet all this paled into insignificance when compared to the most important organisational principle that was enunciated at the Writers' Congress. This was the principle of *partiinost* (roughly translatable as 'party-mindedness') which stipulated that all artists had an ethical and political obligation to submit themselves to the guidance of the Communist Party. The Party would not merely have the right to prescribe the broad ideological orientation of a work (it had effectively done this for years), but also to make detailed recommendations about subject matter and style. It was obviously not possible to describe the administrative mechanisms by which the principle of *partiinost* would be implemented, since to do so would be to reveal the true nature of Soviet totalitarianism. The only passages which broached the issue were therefore characterised by a distinctive note of vague Stalinist uplift. Zhdanov insisted that the 'thoughtful and daily guidance of the Central Committee' had prompted a 'whole army of Soviet writers' into going over to socialism.[26] Gorky claimed that 'There has never been a state in the world where science and literature enjoyed such comradely help, such care for the raising of professional proficiency among the workers of art and science.'[27] This sort of language became ever more prominent in Soviet criticism as the mechanisms of state censorship were tightened.[28]

2. THE AESTHETIC ELEMENT

The purpose of the aesthetic, historical and comparative elements in Soviet criticism was to provide intellectual support for a theory of Socialist Realism that might otherwise have been dismissed as crudely propagandistic. The aesthetic element, which sought to identify the philosophical ideas about art that were most consistent with Soviet policy, was chiefly the preserve of Nikolai Bukharin. In his paper 'Poetry, Poetics and the Problems of Soviet Poetry', Bukharin set out to do two things. The first was to sketch a reflectionist theory of art in which art's power as a medium of political persuasion was related to its qualities of *condensation* and *emotional expression*. The second was to defend the doctrine of the unity of form and content against the ideas of the Russian Formalists.

Bukharin was specifically concerned with poetry when he formulated his ideas about aesthetics, though he implied that everything he said was broadly applicable to the other arts as well. In the course of a lengthy discussion, some of it devoted to a polemic against the 'pure mysticism' of earlier Russian aestheticians, he effectively defined poetry as a form which simultaneously reflects and condenses our sense experience, with the aim of expressing an emotional response.[29] There were several ways in which this seemingly unexceptional definition was influenced by the need to legitimise Socialist Realism. By describing poetry as a record of our actual experiences, Bukharin was trying to affirm what would later be called the 'worldliness of texts' (the phrase is Edward Said's)[30] in the face of several theoretical trends which tended to obscure the links between art and society. The most important of these was modernism, with its emphasis on the 'autonomy' of art; but Bukharin was probably also thinking about Saussurean linguistics (one of the key influences on the Formalist critics of the 1920s) which had famously described language as an arbitrary medium that effectively constitutes our experience rather than straightforwardly reflecting it. This elementary mimeticism was given depth by Bukharin's emphasis on the role of condensation in artistic perception. While art is indeed a reflection of reality, he appeared to argue, it seeks to record only the most important aspects of our experiences and to eliminate everything else. In doing so it imbues its images with a 'symbolic' capacity which allows them to refer to phenomena in general, not simply to the particular experiences in which they have their roots: 'This "substitute" [i.e. the selected referent] becomes a "symbol", an "image", a type, an emotionally coloured unity, behind which and in the folds of whose garments thousands of other sensory elements are concealed.'[31] Moreover, the technique of condensation means that art should be regarded not merely as a representation of sense experience but also as the expression of a definite point of view. Yet unlike science, which expresses its general truths in the form of rational propositions, art involves a form of sensual thinking whereby images serve as substitutes for explicitly-formulated ideas.[32] Art is a vehicle of doctrine, Bukharin seemed to be saying, though its understanding of the world is felt on the senses rather than registered by the intellect. His intention here was presumably to undermine the claim that the principle of *ideinost* would compromise the arts by subordinating the cultivation of sensibility to the expression of ideology.

If Bukharin saw the ability to convey doctrine at a sub-intellectual level as a crucial determinant of art's political power, his more central emphasis was on the relationship between art and emotion. The chief function of poetry, he argued, is 'to assimilate and transmit experience and to *educate character*' (emphasis added),[33] mainly by demonstrating the appropriate emotional responses both to the existing social order and to the possible societies of the future. When he tried to identify the sort of emotions to which art usually gives expression, he defined his position against the idea that the aesthetic faculty is an inherently *disinterested* one. According to the idea of disinterestedness, which had been central to philosophical aesthetics since at least the time of Karl Philipp Moritz,[34] the artist invariably seeks to depict the world in a manner that is wholly devoid of 'desire or will' (the phrase is Hegel's).[35] Instead of viewing external reality through the prism of self-interest, he surveys it in a spirit of pure contemplation. Bukharin reminded his audience that the idea of disinterestedness had been bent to a number of philosophical purposes in the previous 150 years. Kant had used it to justify his belief that aesthetic judgements can ultimately be placed on a universal, non-subjective footing. Hegel had used it to underscore the proposition that art is one of the main means by which the 'world spirit' makes itself known to humanity. And Schopenhauer, in a move that greatly influenced Nietzsche, spoke of disinterestedness as one of the reasons why the arts could provide emotional sanctuary in a world otherwise dominated by the crude workings of 'Will'.[36]

These ideas were obviously in conflict with the Soviet principle that the primary function of art is to stimulate desire for a new social system. Bukharin's tactic was therefore to challenge the idea of disinterestedness by invoking its polar opposite. Art, he implied, should properly be regarded as one of the forms of human behaviour that expresses desire at its most uncompromising: its main emotional characteristic is that of 'active militant force'.[37] The point was defended historically rather than philosophically. It was perfectly common, Bukharin appeared to argue, for the work of the earliest artists to be judged in public by the mass audience at whom it was aimed. His main example was the so-called 'poetic contests' held in ancient Greece, when 'the poets were awarded crowns by the crowd.'[38] Since the easiest way to secure the approval of the lower orders was to reflect the intensities of mass emotion, it followed that art was defined at it origins as an expression of untrammelled desire. No form that originated in such circumstances, Bukharin implied, could ever have subsequently become a vehicle for the sort of disinterested contemplation that Kant, Hegel and Schopenhauer had celebrated.

Having defined poetry in terms of the relationship between reflection, condensation and the expression of emotion, Bukharin concluded his analysis by examining the relationship between form and content in literature.[39] His broad argument, in line with a long tradition in philosophical aesthetics, was that the *unity* of form and content is a crucial precondition of aesthetic significance. He appeared to mean two things by this, one of them entirely orthodox and the other more unusual. The orthodox claim was that a successful work of art will allow the way it says things (its form) to be determined by the things it chooses to say (its content), even though the former has the ultimate responsibility for breathing aesthetic life into the latter. Ralph Fox would later summarise this doctrine, which originated with Hegel and received the endorsement of Marx, in the following way: 'Form is produced by content, is identical and one with it, and, though the primacy is on the side of content, form reacts on content and never remains passive.'[40] Bukharin's more unusual claim was primarily concerned with what we might call the *transparency* of form. A particular formal strategy is only functioning effectively, he appeared to argue, if it allows immediate access to a work's content. If it seems to exist independently of its content, becoming an object of perception in its own right, it will have failed in its primary task of communicating an aestheticised understanding of the world.[41] The motivation behind this attitude was clearly an anti-modernist one. The formal innovations which modernism had pioneered, such as discontinuous composition in literature, atonalism in music and non-linear representation in painting, were often so startling that they appeared to contemporary observers to systematically divert attention from whatever it was that an artist wished to say. No such problem existed, or so Bukharin implied, with the more traditional forms employed by the Socialist Realists.

Bukharin's attack on the technical innovations of modernism took the form of a lengthy critique of the Russian Formalists, the group of literary theoreticians who, under the leadership of such figures as Viktor Shklovsky, Roman Jakobson and Boris Tomashevsky, had exercised a massive influence on the Soviet avant-garde between 1917 and the end of the 1920s.[42] Formalist theory was rooted in the belief that the function of literature (and of art more generally) is to 'defamiliarise' our everyday habits of perception. Since our responses to external reality tend to become sullied by routine, literature's purpose is to remind us of the sensory richness that surrounds us. The originality of the Formalists' case lay in its explanation of how this occurs. Their main argument was that defamiliarisation is possible because the forms that a work of literature employs are initially perceived in isolation from its content. When we first encounter a poem, for instance, our attention is drawn not to what it says but to the 'heap of devices' (rhyme, metre, imagery etc.) that differentiates it from non-literary uses of language. The effort to "see beyond" these devices is what moves us to concentrate our minds afresh on the richness of whatever it is that the poem describes. The purpose of much Formalist writing was therefore to identify the most powerful devices that literature has at its disposal. For instance, the Formalists argued that poetry owes most of its aesthetic force to the fact that it (1) yokes together disparate sounds in an effort to 'impede' pronunciation, (2) defies the conventions of syntax in order to facilitate the use of regular (or sometimes irregular) metre, and (3) makes widespread use of what would later be called 'multiple signifiers' – that is, words which have more than one meaning.[43] In their analysis of prose fiction, they famously emphasised the distinction between 'fabula' ('the chronological series of events')[44] and 'siuzhet' ('the order and manner in which they are actually presented in the narrative').[45] It is the tension between the two, or so the argument went, that encourages the reader to focus his attention less on the story he is being told than on the techniques of the storyteller.[46]

Bukharin's critique of these ideas began with a slightly perfunctory attack on the ahistorical nature of Formalist analysis. Echoing a point that Leon Trotsky had made in *Literature and Revolution*,[47] he argued that the Formalists were unable to account for the power of literary form because they had failed to examine the relationship between literature and society. More interesting were his comments on the likely artistic consequences of the theoretical emphasis on the autonomy of form. If intellectuals persist in claiming that form is inherently separable from content, Bukharin argued, they will end up creating a situation in which writers become wholly indifferent to meaning and produce works consisting exclusively of pure sound (the point was hammered home with the only joke to be made at the Writers' Congress: 'Down with *Faust* and long live "Dyr bull shirr"!')[48] The political stimulus behind this process was said to be the desire of bourgeois writers to ignore the revolutionary ideas that were increasingly prominent in international literature.[49] Apart from threatening the whole of literary culture with terminal collapse, the emergence of abstract literature would also have the effect of reinforcing two of the most reactionary ideologies in the contemporary world. By reducing literature to the elaboration of what were effectively private languages, it would engender support for a form of 'individualism' that was practically solipsistic.[50] And by depriving the intellect of any element of meaning to which it might respond, it would give succour to precisely the sort of irrationalism that the fascist movement had sought to revive.[51]

3. THE HISTORICAL ELEMENT

Although the historical element in Soviet criticism was less fully developed at the time of the Writers' Congress than either the prescriptive, aesthetic or comparative elements, it was already clear that the Soviet theorists had two main objectives when using historical analysis to buttress the doctrine of Socialist Realism. The first was to survey the history of the arts from the perspective of historical materialism. The second was to trawl through the past in search of artistic movements and cultural practices that could plausibly be described as precursors of Socialist Realism.

There was an obvious motive behind the attempt to apply historical materialism to the study of the arts. By demonstrating that social conditions had always played a powerful role in shaping artistic expression, the Soviet theorists intended to rebut the claim that Socialist Realism was necessarily philistine in its goal of combining art and politics. Yet very little substantive work in this area seems to have been produced in the USSR until the 1950s. It is true that the contributors to the 1934 Congress had a sort of reflexive tendency to characterise individual writers in terms of their social position, but the most that this involved was usually a very broad (and also very brief) attempt to sketch the parallels between a writer's ideology and the major events of his time. For example, Dostoevsky's pessimism was described by Gorky as the direct expression of czarism in decline,[52] while Remarque's *The Road Back* was seen by Radek as one of the most powerful exemplars of pacifist despair in the wake of the Great War.[53] The consequence of this was that the materialist analysis of the arts became the one area of cultural discourse in which there was no Soviet orthodoxy for foreign communists to follow.[54] It was therefore necessary for the international movement to use a number of earlier texts in the Marxist tradition as a source of theoretical guidance, notably Marx's and Engels's scattered comments on topics such as realism, myth and the nature of literary commitment, Plekhanov's essays on 'art and social life' and Lenin's articles on Tolstoy.[55] The work of such writers as Mehring, Lafargue and Bogdanov was not much known outside its country of origin, at least in the early part of the 1930s. Trotsky's work had been excluded from the communist canon after his expulsion from the CPSU in 1928.

The attempt to find precursors for Socialist Realism was conducted on two levels. The initial concern of the Soviet theorists was to identify comparatively recent work (that is, work from the mid-nineteenth century onwards) which employed realistic or naturalistic forms to express a dissident perspective on Russian politics. The novelists who tended to get mentioned most frequently were Tolstoy, Chernyshevsky and Gorky, while the so-called 'Wanderers' group (especially Repin and Yaroshenko) were celebrated for their revolt against Academic painting in the period after 1863. Yet at the time of the Writers' Congress it was still unusual for this tradition of 'Critical Realism' to be analysed in much depth. Better developed was what might be termed the *anthropological* element in the Soviet search for a radical cultural heritage. This involved the startling claim that the expressive forms which existed in primitive societies had effectively prefigured Socialist Realism.

The most important example of anthropological analysis in the 1934 speeches was Gorky's divagation on the nature of myth.[56] Rejecting the idea that primitive man was essentially a sort of 'philosophizing idealist and mystic'[57] (that is, someone wholly preoccupied with the influence of supernatural forces), Gorky argued that the primary function of myth was to express a plebeian yearning for the domination of nature. Myths, he pointed out, were full of scenes in which human beings employed fantastical methods in order to overcome the elements: some wore 'seven-league boots' and strode across vast distances in a matter of seconds, others made magic carpets and learned how to fly.[58] The effect of these scenes was at once psychological and practical. Apart from providing temporary respite from the uncomfortable realities of primitive labour, they also stimulated real improvements to the forces of production. 'Men', wrote Gorky in one of a number of examples, 'conceived the possibility of spinning and weaving a vast amount of fabric in one night…..[as a result of this] they created the primitive hand loom.'[59] A related feature of the mythological imagination was an awareness of the importance of representations. Myths often incorporated 'exorcism[s]' and 'incantation[s]' which sought to influence nature by depicting the desired outcome of a particular form of economic activity. These were usually addressed to the gods, 'hero[es] of labour' such as Hercules or Vassilisa the Wise, who were seen by Gorky as wholly lacking in supernatural characteristics but distinct from ordinary humanity by virtue of their immense achievements in production.[60]

The parallels between Gorky's understanding of myth and the Soviet conception of Socialist Realism are clear enough. Both forms were held to stimulate change by (1) projecting a vision of economic paradise, (2) emphasising the importance of representation, and (3) employing 'heroes' whose most vivid characteristic was a genius for transforming nature. It is perhaps less clear why anyone should have wanted to draw such parallels in the first place. The answer probably lies in the assumption that human culture was somehow purer at the moment of its origin than at any time since. By emphasising the links between Socialist Realism and myth, writers such as Gorky were implying that the new workers' state had recaptured the freshness of perception that inspired humanity at the start of its historical journey. As we shall see in Chapters Three and Five, it was anthropological speculations of this sort which often roused the British communists to do some of their most challenging work.

4. THE COMPARATIVE ELEMENT

The purpose of the comparative element in the 1934 speeches was to legitimise Soviet culture by contrasting it favourably with the culture of the capitalist powers. Whereas the USSR was said to be breathing new life into culture at all levels (especially with the development of Socialist Realism), capitalism was condemned for reducing culture to a state of permanent crisis. This crucial doctrine of cultural crisis had two distinctive elements. The first was the very broad argument that the market economy had *always* exercised a poisonous influence on culture by virtue of being aesthetically impoverished, hostile to intellectual excellence and corrupting in its effects on human nature. The second was the claim that the arts in capitalist society had undergone a particularly rapid decline in the period since the mid-nineteenth century. Both these elements need to be examined if we want to understand what turned out to be the most limiting aspect of Soviet criticism.

As is well known, the idea of cultural crisis had deep roots in the Marxist tradition. Marx's critique of capitalism was arguably aesthetic before it was economic (this was an issue on which Althusser famously had a lot to say); while his pessimism about the fate of the arts in market society often found expression in the form of aphorisms, asides and scattered critical judgements. However, it needs to be remembered that many of the texts in which he explored the idea of cultural crisis (notably the *Economic and Philosophical Manuscripts* of 1844) were largely unknown to communist intellectuals in the 1930s.[61] This helps to explain the somewhat *ad hoc* feel which characterised the comparative element in Soviet criticism, many of whose arguments seemed to have more in common with the tradition of romantic anti-capitalism than with Marxism. When the Soviet theorists tried to identify the general reasons for what they regarded as the opposition between capitalism and culture, they began by arguing that cultural decline was the inevitable consequence of an economic system that had stripped the labour process of the last traces of aesthetic significance. The modern worker was portrayed as an unmotivated dullard who regarded his job as a means to an end (that of avoiding starvation) but never as a source of self-fulfilment. The problem was blamed on the mood of *asceticism* that was held to flow ineluctably from the process of capital accumulation. Since the bulk of employers have no choice but to hold down wages in order to secure an adequate stock of investment capital, it follows that bourgeois ideology will place considerable emphasis on the virtues of self-denial: 'The less you eat, drink, buy books...the more you save, the greater grows your fortune which neither moth nor rust can corrupt – your capital' (Marx).[62] Yet the ethic of self-denial is wholly antithetical to the aesthetic impulse. The worker ceases to experience 'joy in labour' because he is infected with an outlook that regards all forms of pleasure as fundamentally immoral. Moreover, because the outlook of any given society is largely determined by the nature of its economic institutions, the aesthetic poverty that characterises the labour process will soon spread outwards to corrupt all other forms of human activity.[63]

The laws of accumulation were also central to Soviet accounts of the status of the intellect in market societies. It was Gorky who noted that capitalism tends to exert a deeply contradictory influence on intellectual culture. On the one hand, driven by the need to ensure continuous improvements to the means of production, it breeds the prejudice that instrumental reason is by far the most important of all the human faculties. The main consequences are a neglect of spiritual values and blind worship of material progress. And yet, by a strange paradox, capitalism is often quite incapable of exploiting the scientific developments which its own laws have called into being. The so-called 'anarchy of the marketplace', which makes it impossible to be sure that every commodity will necessarily find a buyer, has often discouraged (or at least delayed) investment in the more expensive forms of new technology (Gorky's example was the failure of the French to utilise the steamship for many years after its invention). When scientific discoveries are neglected in this way, the result is a mood of cynicism about intellectual activity which threatens to spill over into the sort of violent irrationalism that fascism has tried to exploit.[64] The situation is worsened by the free market's subtly corrupting influence on human nature. A society based on competition, Gorky argued, is less likely to breed a race of rugged individualists than a people for whom deviousness, calculation and dishonesty are the stuff of everyday life.[65] Proof of this is afforded by the sort of characters who have dominated both popular and elite literature since the dawn of the capitalist age:

> From the figure of Till Eulenspiegel, created at the end of the fifteenth century, that of Simplicissimus in the seventeenth century, Lazarillo de Tormes, Gil Blas, the heroes of Smollett and Fielding, down to the 'Dear Friend' of Maupassant, to Arsène Lupin, to the heroes of 'detective' literature in present-day Europe, we can count thousands of books the heroes of which are rogues, thieves, assassins and agents of the criminal police. This is what constitutes genuine bourgeois literature, reflecting most vividly the real tastes, the interests and the practical 'morals' of its consumers.[66]

But what of literature more generally? The Soviet theorists strongly implied that the crisis in bourgeois literature had begun in earnest with the emergence of the art-for-art's-sake movement (and its doctrine of aestheticism) in the mid-nineteenth century.[67] Gorky, who devoted several pages to the issue, seemed to believe that aestheticism is best understood as a deliberately antinomian response to the marginalisation of art.[68] Appalled that capitalism should have consigned them to a position of relative unimportance in modern culture, the leading aesthetes (men such as Huysmans, Baudelaire and Wilde) tried to dramatise their disaffection from the wider society by conflating art with the transgression of existing morality. The pursuit of beauty was thus seen as inseparable from sexual perversion, experimentation with narcotics and the cultivation of a self-consciously demonic outlook. Because of this descent into ethical chaos, Gorky went on to imply, aestheticism swiftly became a breeding ground for a peculiarly noxious form of authoritarian politics. Although the aesthetes were ostensibly hostile to all forms of political engagement, their brand of amoral individualism had radiated outwards from the cultural sphere and exercised a disastrous influence on public life. The nearest political equivalent to the aesthete is the 'mad animal' of fascist or Czarist persuasion who demonstrates his contempt for ordinary values by treating his opponents with the utmost savagery.[69]

Gorky made a brief attempt to apply these ideas to the particular case of Russia. He seemed to believe that Russian aestheticism had been exemplified by Fyodor Dostoevsky (this is one of the more bizarre judgements in Soviet criticism), whose protagonist in *Memoirs from Underground* embodied the aesthete's 'whining despair' in its most debased form.[70] It was therefore unsurprising that Dostoevsky's politics were among the most reactionary in nineteenth-century literature. He detested the democratic forces in Russian politics (his enduring hatred was for Vissarion Belinsky), supported Russian imperialism and regretted the abolition of serfdom in 1861. Since the majority of Russian intellectuals were profoundly influenced by Dostoevsky, it therefore follows (or so Gorky argued) that their retreat from democratic ideals after the revolution of 1905 was largely a response to his own political example. Aestheticism had conspired to frustrate the march of History.[71]

The analysis of more recent trends in bourgeois literature (those from 1914 onwards) was primarily undertaken by Karl Radek, whose paper on 'World Literature' has generally been seen as the crudest and most vituperative contribution to the 1934 Congress. Surveying the most influential work from the earlier part of this period, his main complaint was that none of it responded properly to either the Great War (seen as a clash between rival imperialisms) or the October Revolution. At the outbreak of the War, so the argument went, the literary intelligentsia had effectively become recruiting officers for the bourgeois state, producing work that glorified nationalism and obscured the economic reasons for the fighting (Radek's only example was Anatole France).[72] Even when the majority of writers had turned against the War, they could only express their opposition by resorting to a form of political quietism. Some of them, such as Henri Barbusse in *Under Fire*, spoke of the War as a cosmic necessity which illustrated once again that humanity's fate was essentially tragic.[73] Others, such as Erich Maria Remarque in *The Road Back*, embraced a world-weary cynicism about human nature and turned to provincial life as a sanctuary from high politics.[74] None of them acknowledged what Radek seemed to regard as obvious: that war would only end when socialism had triumphed over capitalism. When it came to the October Revolution, therefore, bourgeois writers had either described it as a descent into barbarism (H.G. Wells), praised its spirit but dismissed its political content (Romain Rolland) or treated it as a continuation of capitalism by other means.[75] The political ignorance which had seeped into world literature with the art-for-art's-sake movement had thus reached its apogee.

Surveying the literature of the 1930s, Radek argued that the majority of bourgeois writers had now moved in one of two directions. Those who lived in Hitler's Germany, Mussolini's Italy or Pilsudski's Poland had embraced the fascist aesthetic and become apologists for their respective regimes.[76] Their counterparts in the bourgeois democracies had opted for the less barbaric but equally dangerous path of modernist experimentation. Radek saw modernism as an attempt to justify a retreat from political action at a time of accelerated social crisis. Using Joyce's *Ulysses* as his example, he argued that its fundamental strategy was to convey the impression that humanity's natural condition is one of unrelieved banality: 'there is nothing big in life'.[77] By seeking to represent the fine detail of everyday existence, wholly eschewing the selectivity that Bukharin had identified as a condition of great art, it sought to dissolve our nobler illusions about human nature in a tangle of meaningless conversations, pointless actions and lowering physical detail. When Joyce attempted to record every action that his protagonist Leopold Bloom had committed over the course of 24 hours, he was guilty (or so Radek famously argued) of creating a work which amounted to nothing more than:

A heap of dung, crawling with worms, photographed by a cinema apparatus through a microscope...[78]

Radek implied that one of Joyce's central objectives was to encourage an attitude of 'impartiality' towards the competing trends in contemporary politics, on the grounds that no amount of political action can rescue human beings from their fallen state. However, since the modern age is one in which 'the fascists are trying to stamp out the remnants of culture and rob the workers of their last rights' (a point which Radek made in response to Wieland Herzfelde, who defended Joyce at the Congress),[79] it follows that impartiality invariably functions in the modern world as an enemy of democracy.[80] It is one of those forces which acts in what communists liked to call the 'objective' interests of the ruling class. There is also a pronounced strain of irrationalism in the modernist outlook. Most modernist works are concerned less with the conscious than with the unconscious mind, which they seek to portray (in a manner wholly consistent with the fascist yearning for *Sturm und Drang*), as a more reliable guide to human nature than the detached operations of the intellect.[81]

Since one of my aims in the rest of this book is to examine the influence of

Soviet cultural theory on the work produced by British Marxists in the 1930s, it might be helpful to summarise the foregoing material in the form of related points. Working within the four broad categories that we have identified (prescriptive, aesthetic, historical and comparative), the Soviet theorists gave particular emphasis to the following arguments:

(1) Socialist Realism, shaped by the principles of *ideinost* and *klassovost*, should aim to provide a synoptic perspective on the existing stage in the development of society.

(2) Socialist Realism should incorporate material which hints at the richness of the communist society of the future, especially by (a) adapting the romantic sensibility to the portrayal of existing realities, and (b) making use of 'positive heroes'.

(3) Artists will only achieve mass influence (thereby observing the principle of *narodnost*) if they eschew modernist experimentation in favour of traditional forms. However, the commitment to realism does not imply a naturalistic approach to the depiction of external reality.

(4) Artists must stop regarding themselves as autonomous cultural workers and submit wholeheartedly to the guidance of the Communist Party. New forms of collective creativity must be developed to challenge the aesthetic individualism which is characteristic of capitalist culture.

(5) In the process of *reflecting* reality, the arts also condense our sense experiences in order to express a particular point of view. Artistic truths are registered by the senses rather than absorbed by the intellect.

(6) Art is not a 'disinterested' medium of communication. Its ultimate purpose is to stimulate desire for change.

(7) Art can only function effectively if it achieves a dialectical unity between form and content. Work which seeks to make form autonomous from content will ultimately give rise to abstraction, solipsism and irrationalism.

(8) There is a tradition of 'Critical Realism' in European culture which established some of the fundamental principles on which socialist art should be based.

(9) Myth can be regarded as a precursor of Socialist Realism. The investigation of primitive culture is an important component of Marxist criticism, since it can help to identify the essence of human culture.

(10) The capitalist mode of production is detrimental to human culture because it (a) deprives the worker of pleasure in his work, (b) undermines faith in the power of the intellect, and (c) corrupts human nature with its emphasis on competition.

(11) Bourgeois literature has undergone a precipitous decline since the middle of the nineteenth century, beginning with the emergence of the art-for-art's sake movement and culminating with the birth of modernism.

5. THE BRITISH RESPONSE

The spirit in which British Marxists responded to Soviet theory was clearly illustrated on the rare occasions when they wrote directly about the 1934 Congress. One of the British representatives at the Congress was Amabel Williams-Ellis, an early editor of *Left Review*, who described her experiences in a long article for the journal in November 1934.[82] It was clear that what most attracted her to Soviet culture was the impression that the leading authors had all secured a mass audience. At various times during the Congress, often in the middle of important speeches, proceedings would be halted so that delegates from different sectors of the Soviet economy (mining, agriculture, defence etc.) could express their thanks to the new generation of writers for the high quality of its work. On one extraordinary afternoon the Congress delegates adjourned to an outdoor stadium at the Park of Rest and Culture, where they witnessed a number of writers being cheered by 10,000 ordinary citizens. Williams-Ellis described these events without betraying the slightest suspicion that they were less spontaneous than the authorities had implied.[83] She also revealed a great deal about the kind of deference which foreign Marxists were expected to display in the presence of their Soviet hosts. During the discussion that followed Radek's contribution on world literature, she described Radek as 'very able' but criticised him for overestimating the influence of certain British writers (Shaw, Wells, Joyce) and underestimating the influence of others (Huxley in particular). It is not clear whether she received a direct response to her comments; but something seems to have happened which convinced her that she and other critics of Soviet theory were suffering from a sort of residual petit-bourgeois prissiness about literary judgement. 'The effect of the conference', she wrote in a suitably chastened state, 'will certainly be to help the creators in their age-old battle against the prigs.'[84] It was an interesting example of the way that the cultural arguments of the 1930s were often won by those who could lay claim to the greatest amount of proletarian authenticity.

At the same time, as Valentine Cunningham has pointed out,[85] there was at least one respect in which Williams-Ellis's article included material which the Soviet authorities might have regretted. Towards the end of her piece she devoted a lengthy passage to a speech by the novelist Ilya Ehrenburg, author of *Julio Jurenito*, which had adopted an unusually critical line on existing examples of Socialist Realism. Ehrenburg, it was pointed out, had condemned the obsession with technology and neglect of emotion that characterised many Soviet novels, chastised younger writers for their avoidance of political controversy ('They carefully steer round any themes which seem difficult')[86] and questioned the wisdom of continually drawing parallels between the industrial worker and the creative artist.[87] By the time that the congress proceedings were published in book form, the text of Ehrenburg's speech had been suppressed.

One of the other British writers who commented directly on the Writers' Congress was Montagu Slater, who reviewed *Problems of Soviet Literature* in *Left Review* in October 1935.[88] Slater's approach was to focus on a single similarity between Soviet and English criticism. The issue he chose was the analysis of form and its consequences for the public role of the writer. Slater implied that when Bukharin advocated the study of form (see above) he did so because he believed that it would enhance the writer's ability to communicate with a mass audience. The more a writer knows about the technical aspects of his art, Bukharin had seemed to argue, the greater the likelihood that he will eschew formal obscurities and seek to perform a genuinely bardic function. Slater's point was that the leading English proponents of formal scholarship had also perceived the links between the analysis of form and the extension of literary culture. Shortly after T.S. Eliot undertook the painstaking analysis of seventeenth-century verse forms, he became obsessed with music hall, jazz and other forms of popular entertainment. The result was his play *Murder in the Cathedral*, whose debt to popular narrative bespoke a 'longing for an audience organized on something more than an academic basis'.[89] Slater's other example of a formal scholar turned literary populist was Robert Graves, whose early exercises in practical criticism had stimulated an interest in nursery rhymes, street songs and folklore. The only real difference between the Soviet and British writers (or so Slater implied) was that the former lived in a society which encouraged their democratic aspirations, whereas the latter had been frustrated in their attempts to bring literature to the masses by the elitism of the dominant cultural institutions.[90]

Slater's argument was hardly a strong one. Neither Eliot nor Graves had ever made a serious attempt to produce work that would be accessible to a mass audience, nor (especially in Eliot's case) did they necessarily believe that it would be desirable to do so. Graves was so appalled by Slater's account of his work that he wrote a sarcastic letter to *Left Review*, published in December 1935, in which he claimed that:

> The trouble with writers like Mr. Slater is not that their political sympathies are misplaced, but that, by trying to rally literature, art and several other interests under the banner of politics, they are bound to be more ignorant of literature, art and so on than wise about politics.[91]

Yet the crucial thing about Slater's article was not the accuracy of its critical judgements so much as its attitude towards Soviet criticism. By showing – or claiming to show – that the Soviet theorists were interested in much the same things as their English counterparts, it helped to create the intellectual context in which the CPGB's cultural critics did their most important work. It is this body of work that we must now examine.

CHAPTER THREE

ALICK WEST: LOYALTY, DISSIDENCE
AND THE POLITICS OF COMMUNITY

The Soviet Writers' Congress of 1934 had a major impact on the intellectual culture of the world communist movement. By establishing the outlines of an 'official' understanding of the arts, it provided Marxist intellectuals outside the USSR with a body of ideas on which they were expected to build. The British writers who responded most successfully to the challenge were Alick West, Ralph Fox and Christopher Caudwell, each of whom published a major work of literary theory in 1937: *Crisis and Criticism* (West), *The Novel and the People* (Fox) and *Illusion and Reality* (Caudwell). The purpose of the next three chapters is to bring the work of these writers into focus. I will try to show that West, Caudwell and Fox had a more ambiguous relationship to Soviet theory than has sometimes been supposed. While each of them tried to build on the theoretical insights of Bukharin, Gorky, Radek and their colleagues (something which has not always been recognised in commentary on their work), they were never reduced to simply parroting the Soviet line. All of them made an effort to flesh out Soviet doctrine by combining it with ideas drawn from the Western tradition, often to the point where their work bordered on outright unorthodoxy. West can best be regarded as a communist of semi-dissident instincts who used his work to express an implicit critique of the CPGB's understanding of culture. Fox was ostensibly the most loyal of communist intellectuals, frequently using critical language of a naively partisan kind; but there were several occasions on which his fidelity to basic Marxist principles seemed questionable. By contrast, Caudwell developed a richly idiosyncratic brand of Marxist criticism by filtering the tenets of Soviet theory through his distinctively autodidactic habits of mind.

Of the three founding fathers of Marxist literary theory in Britain, it was only Alick West (1895-1972) who survived into old age.[1] One of the fruits of his longevity was a remarkable volume of memoirs, *One Man in his Time*, which he began writing in 1956 but only completed shortly before its publication in

1969.[2] The book was clearly intended as a sort of loyalist's critique of the politics of the world communist movement. After more than 40 years as one of the CPGB's most respected intellectuals, West revealed that he had begun to doubt the Party's strategic thinking almost as soon as he became a member in 1935, and that his doubts had persisted throughout the whole of the post-war period. His criticism of the Party and of 'official' communism more generally can be fairly easily stated. At some point since the establishment of the USSR, or so West insisted, the international communist movement has gone into decline for largely *cultural* reasons. Its members have lost sight of the fact that the majority of people are drawn to communism by the prospect of a revolution in consciousness, specifically one which challenges individualist assumptions and encourages a heightened sense of community. Instead of fighting to create a society in which human solidarity is the overarching principle, the majority of communist organisations have become preoccupied with issues of economics and politics to the exclusion of everything else. The price of this failure is a growing sense of frustration among genuine communists which often results in spectacular outbursts of revolt against the dour apparatchiks who control the world movement. An inevitable consequence is the sort of savage repression which occurred in Hungary in 1956 and Czechoslovakia in 1968. If international communism is ever to move beyond its authoritarian impasse, it has no choice but to reconnect itself to the cultural vision which accounts for much of its appeal.[3] Since West evidently regarded himself as a representative communist dissident, these arguments were largely conveyed through the medium of his own personal history. As we shall see, *One Man in his Time* is essentially a record of West's own engagement with the idea of human solidarity. It traces his enthusiasm for the communitarian ideal to the experiences of his early childhood, evokes its central role in his conversion to communism (while making it clear that other factors were also important) and charts his disappointment on seeing it betrayed by his own Party. At the same time, it would be wrong simply to regard the book as a straightforward expression of political disillusionment. In its closing pages, writing movingly about the rich insights which membership of the Party had brought to his life, West made it clear that he remained a loyal member and that 'I still believe that communism is necessary to the freedom of mankind'.[4] As such, some 20 years before the emergence of a revisionist school of Party history, he displayed precisely the blend of loyalty and dissidence which the revisionist historians have since described as the central feature of communism in Britain.

There is an obvious danger in basing an account of West's work on information drawn from his memoirs. In the absence of any biographical work on West, there is no means of knowing whether *One Man in his Time* provides an accurate account of its author's life. The problem is compounded by the remarkably elusive nature of much of the writing. *One Man in his Time* is surely unique among autobiographies in being almost wholly devoid of explicit statements about its author's character. Instead of using slabs of discursive prose to draw out the significance of the various events which he relates, West expects his readers to piece together an impression of his personality from the narrative alone. Nevertheless, I would suggest that there are two reasons why *One Man in his Time* should serve as a frame for any substantive discussion of West's critical writings. The first is that it throws an enormous amount of light on the way that West's critical and theoretical assumptions were shaped by his personal response to developments in the world communist movement. Once we have read the book, the *political* subtext of many of the critical writings suddenly becomes clear – at least if we make the effort to read between the lines. This suggests that it can largely be trusted as a record of West's ideological development, even if its wider biographical reliability remains uncertain. Secondly, it is important to remember that West intended *One Man in his Time* as a contribution to the ongoing debate about the future direction of the communist movement. When he wrote about his overwhelming need for community, his belief that the communitarian ideal is best served by Marxism and his disappointment at the degeneration of world communism, he was advancing an argument which he hoped would be instrumental in setting the movement on a new course. In other words, the book deserves a place in any account of West's critical writings because it is arguably his most important critical work. The first section of this chapter therefore provides a reading of *One Man in his Time* which tries to show how the entire narrative is structured by West's communitarian ideals. Section Two examines *Crisis and Criticism* in some detail, describing it as a largely orthodox book which nevertheless extends Soviet theory in highly innovative ways. Sections Three and Four turn to the more unorthodox elements in West's work, the former claiming that his essays and reviews of the 1930s were often an expression of his opposition to the 'Popular Front' strategy, while the latter (the only section of the book which goes beyond the 1930s) characterises his post-war writings as a disguised expression of hostility to the 'reformist' politics embodied in the CPGB's programme *The British Road to Socialism*.

1. BECOMING A COMMUNIST: A READING OF ONE MAN IN HIS TIME

As we have already seen, the biggest problem facing the reader of *One Man in his Time* is that the book is written more like a novel than an autobiography.[5] Instead of explaining why the events he described were of such enormous personal significance, West seemed largely content to let them speak for themselves. My aim in this section is therefore to provide an outline of the book which relates its main events to what I take to be its central theme – West's overarching belief in the importance of community. The narrative of West's life was effectively divided into three distinct phases: (1) his discovery of communitarian values while still a child, (2) his unhappy flirtation with individualism in the years between 1914 and 1926, and (3) his return to communitarianism in his years as an active communist. By showing how ideological insight was achieved early, disregarded for many years and then triumphantly regained, West was probably trying to portray his life in terms of a dialectical process of development.

Alick West was born in Warwickshire on 4th March 1895, the son of an affluent but chronically unsettled engineer who had served as a missionary in India in the 1880s and later become a charity worker.[6] After the death of West's mother in 1900 the family moved to Highgate in London, where West attended Highgate School. He made it clear in *One Man in his Time* that the personal preoccupations that dominated his life had all taken root while he was still very young. The first was a persistent sense of self-division arising from his conscious mind's interference with such involuntary areas of experience as emotion, aesthetic pleasure and intuition. When his father told him of his mother's death ('Mother's gone to stay with Jesus') West was puzzled to discover that he was unable to surrender himself fully to his grief, since he seemed to be in the presence of 'a little man inside me' who was monitoring his response.[7] He presumably came to recognise that these feelings of self-consciousness are universal; but he also appeared to believe that he suffered from them more acutely than the majority of other people. At any rate they formed the basis of his other life-long neurosis, which can broadly be described as paranoia about the nature of authority. Since West believed that his own 'little man' was cruel, unpredictable and incapable of being propitiated, he now projected these qualities onto anyone else who occupied a position of real or imagined power – especially God, whom he saw as a cosmic tyrant handing down punishment without regard for moral goodness or piety. As a young boy he spent long hours worrying that a minor act of folly such as lying, losing a present or cribbing in an exam would lead to either himself or a member of his family being 'taken'.[8]

It was the desire to escape the trauma of self-division which pushed West towards the one positive commitment that recurred throughout his work. This was a belief in the redemptive power of community. He seems to have believed from an early age that divisions in the self are ultimately related to divisions in society. The early pages of *One Man in his Time* showed him groping precociously towards a defining principle: If societies based on individualism are likely to cause the dissociation of basic mental functions, then communitarian societies (those in which 'we are' takes precedence over 'I am') will be more likely to harmonise them. From the start he appears to have associated communitarian values with the culture of working people. On his own street in Highgate, studiously bourgeois, he was constantly struck by the 'separating silence' that divided one family from another – curtains were always drawn, children instructed to avert their gaze from other people's windows.[9] Yet in the streets of 'slummy cottages' which he walked through on the way to school, the whole idea of privacy was apparently unknown. This was a culture of open doors and easy intimacy. West's belief in the greater sociability of working people was reinforced by the summer holidays which he and his sister took on a farm in Warwickshire, where 'Joe Smith, a vigorous redhaired man of about thirty ..., liked to rub his ginger stubble against our cheeks until we screamed'.[10] Some readers would perhaps identify an element of homoeroticism in descriptions such as these.

Fear of self-division and anxiety about authority, combined with the belief that these could be overcome by the healing power of collective experience, were the three forces which pushed West forward throughout the whole of the rest of his life. Yet his extraordinary experiences during the Great War began a phase of his development which in many senses proved aberrational. In September 1914, the month in which he was due to take up a place at Balliol College, Oxford, West was one of several thousand Britons interned by the German authorities in a prison camp at Ruhleben. (He had been in Germany on holiday and was unable to leave when war broke out in August.)[11] His four years at Ruhleben had a revelatory effect upon him. The German authorities devolved the responsibility for running the camp to its inmates, who immediately established a network of societies reflecting their wide range of intellectual, cultural and professional interests. It was West's involvement in the Dramatic Society which apparently led him to believe that he had found a cure for his earlier difficulties. While playing the role of Lavinia in Shaw's *Androcles and the Lion*, he found that acting was the one activity that could erase his feelings of self-division – the need to create a satisfying dramatic spectacle was so absorbing that the diverse areas of his mind seemed temporarily to work in harmony.[12] Moreover, while his faith in drama proved somewhat shortlived, the intellectual influences to which it exposed him exercised a much firmer grip on his imagination. Sometime in 1915, anxious to understand his experiences while acting, West read Nietzsche's *The Birth of Tragedy* and became an instant convert to its powerful vision of human self-development.[13] He now seems to have thought of himself as a sort of apprentice *Übermensch*, alone in a Godless universe, whose primary objective was to exercise the will-to-power by achieving a transvaluation of all values. The influence of Nietzsche was reinforced by readings of Ibsen and also of Max Stirner, the one-time adversary of Marx and Engels whose *The Ego and His Own* (1845) is often seen as the starting point of philosophical egoism as well as a key text in the history of anarchism. The irony of this shift in perspective can scarcely be overstated. Having arrived at Ruhleben as an instinctive communitarian, West was now a disciple of three of the most uncompromising individualists in the Western tradition. It would be more than a decade before he began to slough off his individualist convictions and embark once again on his search for community.

However, West made a point of emphasising that during this period (approximately 1915-1926) the type of individualist doctrines to which he subscribed became markedly different to those of Nietzsche, Ibsen and Stirner. West remained a passionate Nietzschean for most of his years at Ruhleben, only occasionally worrying that he had made the transition from timid believer to aggressive atheist with unseemly haste;[14] but his beliefs changed rapidly after his release in 1918. Choosing to pass up his place at Oxford, apparently because of his growing disillusionment with the British establishment,[15] he now spent three years (1919-1922) as a student of classics and modern languages at Trinity College, Dublin.[16] While living in Dublin he also acted at the Abbey Theatre and struck up an acquaintanceship with 'A.E.' (George Russell), the occult poet who had exercised so decisive an influence on the work of the early Yeats. There appear to have been two reasons for the distrust of Nietzschean philosophy which he acquired at this time. The first was his growing suspicion that Nietzsche was not so much a prophet of mental unity as an essentially pre-Freudian thinker who anticipated the distinction between the id, the ego and the superego. As such, his work contained a set of assumptions which reminded West of one of the things he feared most – the division of the mind into warring factions.[17] Secondly, West also came to feel that his timid and introspective personality was wholly inconsistent with the Nietzschean emphasis on the transvaluation of all values. One evening, irritated by the chatter of the students who surrounded him in the college refectory, he consoled himself with the thought that he could, like Zarathustra, simply defy the rules and stage an indignant walkout. Then the revelation was borne in upon him: 'I realized that I couldn't. Being what I was, I would sit there. It had no sense to say with Zarathustra, "Become what you are", for I was already myself, bound by cause and effect.'[18]

West graduated in 1922 and spent much of the next four years living a peripatetic life in continental Europe.[19] He worked occasionally as an English tutor in Switzerland and registered for a PhD in German Literature at the University of Berlin, though his thesis was never completed. His break with Nietzsche seems to have ensured that this was a period of what can best be described as intellectual mortification. Having abandoned the optimistic individualism expressed in *Thus Sprach Zarathustra*, with its exhilarating belief in the possibility of human evolution, he now began to explore a more *agonistic* brand of individualism which yoked an emphasis on the atomised sensibility with a tragic vision of the human condition. It was as if West, in a fit of anger at having succumbed to individualism in the first place, now felt obliged to atone for his intellectual lapse by immersing himself in doctrines that made him bitterly unhappy. His main influences were Freud (he had read *The Interpretation of Dreams* and *The Psychopathology of Everyday Life* while still at Ruhleben) and Oswald Spengler, whose work he now subjected to a highly unorthodox interpretation. Whereas fascist intellectuals throughout Europe had characterised Spengler as a theorist of cultural decline who regretted the passing of medieval stability and the rise of democratic chaos (Oswald Mosley was the British representative of this trend),[20] West implied that it was quite wrong to interpret his apparent nostalgia for premodern society as a sign of communitarian sympathies. When he spoke of the circularity that had characterised the trajectory of Western civilization, what he chiefly had in mind was the process by which the 'Faustian' values had emerged, achieved dominance and then passed away. *Decline of the West* was ultimately an apologia for precisely the sort of heroic individualism which West had himself abandoned only a short time previously.[21]

If the work of Freud and Spengler had provided West with his only intellectual sustenance at this time, he might well have developed into one of the rootless nihilists whom Karl Radek would later identify as the driving force behind modernism. And yet, even at the height of his flirtation with individualism, he remained open to a number of influences that helped to sustain the communitarian impulses he was otherwise trying to suppress. His interest in cultural conservatism, the most important of these influences, was stimulated by a close friend whom he had met at Ruhleben and subsequently lodged with in Berlin. Paul Farleigh had developed a cyclical theory of history which clearly owed a great deal to the writings of Ruskin, Carlyle, Eliot and the other conservative traditionalists who had dominated English cultural criticism since the nineteenth century.[22] Its starting point was the assumption that the birth of Christ had ushered in a new phase in the history of Western civilization in which 'the individual had existed only as part of the whole'.[23] The dominant culture was rigorously enforced by the Catholic Church, which illustrated its belief in the subordination of the part to the whole in its theology, rituals and sacred buildings. However, the strength of Christianity was not enough to prevent the eventual rise of individualism, which Paul appears to have attributed solely to developments in philosophy. The important figure in this regard was Descartes, whose efforts to put human knowledge on a sure foundation ('*cogito ergo sum*') succeeded only in driving a dualistic wedge between mind and body. The drawbacks of individualism became apparent almost immediately, not least because 'the individual was unable to bear alone the tragic consciousness of transience and death';[24] but Western civilisation responded to its crisis not by seeking a return to collectivism but by developing a form of 'weak' individualism, the main aim of which was to confer a sort of spurious glamour on the idea of the suffering individual. Romanticism had been the main representative of this trend.[25] It was only more recently, with the emergence of 'collective associations'[26] such as political parties and trade unions, that a yearning for genuine community had once again become prevalent throughout Western societies. The task of the intellectual (or so Farleigh seems to have implied) was to help translate this yearning into a culture that combined the ethos of the Middle Ages with the material advantages of modernity .

Although cultural conservatism, in the guise of Farleigh's theory of the 'three realities', was the most rarefied of the intellectual interests which kept West's individualism in check during the early to mid-1920s, there was also a more demotic influence at work – popular fiction. For several months towards the end of 1925 and the beginning of 1926, West was treated for tuberculosis at a sanatorium in Switzerland.[27] (He had first been diagnosed with TB while a student at Dublin.) One night, in an effort to banish his feelings of claustrophobia, he borrowed a copy of *The Three Hostages* by John Buchan and immediately became immersed in it. Whereas the literary novel tends to impose a rigid separation between its characters and its intended readers, West now found himself 'living vicariously' through the character of Richard Hannay.[28] The self-styled individualist had merged his consciousness with that of an imaginary English spy. This experience, presumably repeated on many occasions with other works of popular fiction, seemed to confirm West's belief that the communitarian ideal was better served by popular culture than by the culture of the bourgeoisie. It also stimulated a long-standing interest in commercial writing which culminated in two remarkable essays on the detective novel, published in *Left Review* in 1938 (see Section Three).

In 1926, after five years of comparative rootlessness, West was appointed to the position of Lektor in English at Basle University.[29] The most decisive phase of his development was now underway. In the period up until 1935, when he resigned his university position and returned to England, he at last found the strength to abandon his Freudo-Spenglerian prejudices and return to the communitarian values of his youth. The culmination of this process was his decision to join the Communist Party after settling in Stepney. It was personal tragedy which appears to have been the catalyst for West's retreat from individualism. After a traumatic engagement to a Swiss woman named Sonja was brought to an end by his fiancée's suicide, he seems to have concluded that the relationship was effectively destroyed by individualism. By imagining that personal redemption could somehow be achieved through a romantic relationship, he and Sonja had retreated so far into themselves that neurasthenia became all but inevitable. Badly affected by Sonja's death and tempted by the thought of suicide himself, West could only summon the strength to go on by returning with increased conviction to the cardinal insight of his pre-Ruhleben days – the human spirit can only flourish in strong communities.[30] The long years of individualist misery were thereby laid to rest, though at the cost of great personal suffering.

If West's conversion to communism was essentially a consequence of his return to communitarian values (a point we shall return to in a moment), there were nevertheless a number of other factors which helped to draw him towards the communist movement in the first place, and which arguably throw a lot of light on the popularity of revolutionary politics amongst young intellectuals in the 1920s and 1930s. West seems to have been familiar with a range of Marxist and *Marxisant* arguments for most of his adult life. In his early weeks at Ruhleben, even before he had joined the Dramatic Society and read Nietzsche, he was informed by an inmate called Thompson of what amounted to the orthodox Leninist explanation for the outbreak of the war: '...Britain wasn't fighting Germany for moral reasons. She wanted to smash a business competitor.'[31] He perhaps had cause to remember this critique of imperialism when, serving as an assistant to Leslie Hynes on an archaeological dig in Egypt in 1921-1922, he found himself discomforted by the colonial arrogance with which his English colleagues treated the contents of Egyptian graves.[32] Yet it appears that he was only persuaded to take politics seriously by the breakdown of liberal values which afflicted European society from the mid-1920s onwards.[33] The General Strike of 1926 made a particular impression on his mind. Convinced that the strike had been deliberately provoked by the British government,[34] he now seems to have come to the view (presumably without reading the developing literature on fascism) that economic dislocation was being used throughout Europe to justify the suppression of democratic liberties. Although *One Man in his Time* failed to give a clear impression of his motives at this time, he perhaps concluded that the freedom he valued as an academic could only be safeguarded by a political movement that was capable of restoring economic order. At first he put his faith in the social-credit movement, whose doctrines (specifically those of Raymond Soddy) he had heard expounded by a speaker in Hyde Park.[35] Yet in the Spring of 1929, shortly after incorporating Soddy's ideas into a series of lectures on the novels of Galsworthy, he was challenged by a communist student at Basle to describe the way in which the principles of social credit could be translated into concrete policies. Realising that it was not possible to do so, he accepted the student's invitation to attend a communist meeting on the economic policy of the USSR.[36]

Once West had been drawn into the orbit of communism, there seem to have been three things (other than its evident commitment to collective values) which sustained his interest. The first was the sheer suggestiveness of the Marxist interpretation of history. Preparing for a course on 'The English Family in Life and Literature' in 1929, he read *The Origins of the Family, Private Property and the State* by Friedrich Engels and was immediately transfixed by the panoramic ingenuity with which it explained the historical process.[37] (His translation of the book would be issued by Lawrence and Wishart in 1940.) The second was the reputation that communists had acquired for defending civil liberties. Having been drawn into politics by a fear of authoritarianism, West was struck by the way that ordinary people seemed automatically to assume that communists would be heavily involved in any form of agitation against fascism. When the Reichstag was burned down in 1933, he was part of a small crowd in Basle which gathered around a newspaper office to read about the news: 'Der Reichstag brennt!'[38] A rumour immediately began to circulate that communists were to blame. Since the respectable citizens of Basle were wholly opposed to communism, West perhaps saw their willingness to believe the rumour as a sort of negative affirmation that it was only the communists who could now be relied upon to safeguard democracy.[39] The third factor which predisposed him to communism was of a more historical nature. He seems to have ascribed great importance to the realisation that communism was not a purely modern movement (in the sense of embodying an entirely novel set of values) but one which had its roots in a venerable tradition of popular revolt. In an extraordinary passage which immediately rings bells for any reader of *Rabelais and his World* by Mikhail Bakhtin, West described the experience of attending Lent Carnival in Basle and being exposed to images of rebellion which dated back to the Middle Ages: '...huge rectangular lanterns slowly advanced upon us. Carried on long poles by animal figures, preceded and followed by masked drummers, they displayed on their painted and illuminated sides savage caricatures of the Basle Government (for the town was an independent Canton), the leaders of the political parties, rich and notorious citizens and their wives and mistresses. The people shouted and clapped and hooted.'[40] West's enthusiasm for the historical roots of communism was perhaps a reaction to the ahistorical evolutionism of his Nietzschean period, when he presumably believed that the individual could transform himself without reference to the past.

Yet in the final analysis (and to make the point for the last time) the whole of *One Man in his Time* converged on a single proposition – Alick West became a communist because he believed that his dream of human community could only be realised in a socialist society. When West returned to England in 1935, equipped with a letter of introduction from a leading Swiss communist, he settled in the Brixton district of London and immediately applied for membership of the CPGB. His early experience of life in the Party was one of extreme contrasts. On the one hand, picked out straightaway as a man of intellectual and literary gifts, he was offered a place on the editorial board of *Left Review*, encouraged to write for the Party press and given extensive lecturing responsibilities at Marx House. On the other hand, mindful of the assumption that 'the first role of intellectuals who have joined the Party is to forget they are intellectuals and act as Communists' (Rajani Palme Dutt),[41] he willingly undertook many of the more onerous duties of Party membership – chalking slogans on walls, speaking at sparsely attended Branch meetings, selling the *Daily Worker* outside factories and underground stations.[42] In a couple of extraordinary passages, the first describing the production of the *Daily Worker* and the second evoking a speech by Harry Pollitt in the Kingsway Hall, West made it clear that he was drawn to the CPGB not merely because of its attachment to communitarian values but because it had somehow *prefigured* the community of the future in its own internal culture:

We found the premises [of the *Daily Worker*] in a drab side-street, and went up a dark flight of stairs into a big loft with bare boards, crowded with small tables, and men sitting at them and moving quickly between them and standing in intent conversation amidst the rattle of typewriters. Always when I came to the head of the stairs...I felt on the brink of an absorbed urgency of people working with a pressure which this old building could hardly support....These men, each with his own responsibility, all had their energy bent on the paper for tomorrow and on the revolutionary future.[43]

I went to a meeting at the Kingsway Hall called by the committee which had been set up to demand the release of Dimitrov, whose trial was soon to begin at Leipzig. The hall was packed to the roof. I had been at theatres and concerts in the Albert Hall; now for the first time I was one of a body of people who wanted not only to see and hear but to do. The excitement and unity mounted, and there was a storm of applause when Harry Pollitt got up from his seat on the platform and stepped forward, and in dead silence began. Never had I seen such a man, nor heard such oratory. Drawn towards him, the whole hall, tier upon tier of people, became a great wave curving over to break, as his impetuous, unconquerable voice soared and struck and rang, "Fight fascism".[44]

If passages such as these revealed the extent of West's loyalty to the CPGB, it was also true that his doubts about the Party's strategic direction were already taking shape, prompted in the main by its support for the idea of a Popular Front against fascism. I would suggest that these conflicting feelings were reflected in West's work of the 1930s in two ways. Although there are traces of rebelliousness in *Crisis and Criticism*, the major work of theory which he published in 1937, the book must ultimately be regarded as an innovative but uncontroversial attempt to extend the insights of Soviet theory. However, if we look at West's shorter writings (especially the contributions to *Left Review*), we find that many of them were implicitly shaped by a deep hostility to the Popular Front. These are the issues which are up for examination in the next two sections.

2. CRISIS AND CRITICISM

Crisis and Criticism was organised around an argument which directly related to West's preoccupation with collective experience. According to West, recent literary culture had been thrown into crisis by its cautious rejection of individualist ideas about the nature of creativity.[45] Many of the leading writers and theorists who had come to prominence in the period since the Great War (notably Eliot, Herbert Read and D.H. Lawrence) had questioned the idea that the literary work is primarily an expression of the personality of an individual author, and had tried instead to describe creativity in more collaborative or collective terms. For example, Eliot had spoken of the writer's duty to assimilate his sensibility to that of the 'tradition' of European literature, whereas Read had tried to revive the Keatsian doctrine of 'negative capability'. The basis of this theoretical shift was the emergence of a definite strain of collectivism in English culture as a whole, characterised by incipient feelings of social solidarity and the 'thrill of metaphysical awe'[46] which goes with them. Yet the revolt against aesthetic individualism did not mean that the literary intelligentsia had undergone a conversion to Marxism. When writers such as Eliot, Read and Lawrence tried to modify or discard the idea of individual creativity, they did so by introducing new critical assumptions which tended to reinforce their support for bourgeois society. West blamed this problem – the failure of the literary intellectuals to realise that their taste for collectivism would only find its logical culmination in a commitment to communist politics – on what he saw as the most glaring deficiency in Marxist writings on culture: the absence of a theory of aesthetic value. In *Crisis and Criticism*, therefore, he set out to do three things: first, to examine the crisis in literary studies in greater detail; second, to suggest a Marxist theory of aesthetic value which emphasised the idea of an unconscious identification between the writer and the process of production; and third, to trace the continuities between his own critical project and that of the English Romantics in the early-nineteenth century. We shall examine each of these themes in turn. Although many of West's arguments had their roots in Soviet theory, there was nothing especially unorthodox about the highly innovative ways in which the Soviet influences were developed. As such, *Crisis and Criticism* provided further proof that orthodoxy was no necessary barrier to critical ingenuity.

2.1 *West's theory of cultural crisis*

As we saw in Chapter Two, Soviet writers such as Bukharin, Gorky and Zhdanov invoked a bewildering variety of causes when trying to explain the 'crisis' in modern culture. One of the things which distinguished their more interesting British counterparts was a preference for monocausal explanations.[47] Christopher Caudwell blamed the lack of vitality in modern culture on the so-called 'bourgeois illusion of freedom', which holds that freedom can only be achieved *outside* society and not within it.[48] Although Alick West's theory of cultural crisis was not worked out as meticulously as Caudwell's, nor applied to as many areas of activity, it shared the same inherent simplicity – literary culture has been plunged into confusion by the growing recognition that creativity is primarily collective and not individual. Another factor which distinguished West from the Soviet theorists was his less upbraiding tone. Whereas the Soviet writers associated the crisis with a catastrophic collapse of standards, West seemed to regard it as the by-product of a conceptual shift which Marxists would be broadly advised to welcome. If literary intellectuals are indeed moving beyond individualism and embracing a collectivist understanding of creativity, then it surely follows (or so the argument went) that they are ripe for conversion to communist politics. The task of the Marxist critic is not to expose bourgeois culture to a series of unflattering comparisons with the developing 'proletarian' alternative, but rather to show how the nascent anti-individualism of men like Eliot, Read and Lawrence can only find its logical culmination in a commitment to communism.[49] In the early chapters of *Crisis and Criticism*, West applied these ideas to three individual writers (Eliot, Read and I.A. Richards) and one artistic movement (surrealism). Since the relationship between Marxism and cultural conservatism is a recurring theme in this book, I shall focus here on West's insightful account of Eliot's literary criticism.

We have seen in Chapter One that Eliot's approach to literature was itself a response to the perceived existence of cultural crisis.[50] As a defender of 'classicism' against 'romanticism', he believed that the classical virtues arose naturally in the hierarchical societies of the past, only to be destroyed by the debased values of the modern era. If the modern writer wishes to produce work of any consequence, he has no choice but to suppress his own personality and identify with the 'European mind' which found expression in the literature of the past. This account of the proper relationship between 'tradition' and the 'individual talent' was seen by West as one of the most significant retreats from literary individualism ever to occur in English culture. Falling back on his stock explanation for the growth of communitarian feeling in the capitalist countries, he seemed to regard it as a manifestation of the yearning for collective experience which had entered mass consciousness as a result of the October Revolution.[51] Yet for all that, West insisted, it would be wrong to see Eliot's doctrine as a sort of staging post on the road to communism. It is actually a deeply reactionary response to the decline of liberal civilisation. Apart from the fact that Eliot was obviously invoking the certainties of the past in order to undermine the democratic values of the present (a point which West's friend Douglas Garman had already made in the pages of *Left Review*),[52] this was largely for two reasons. The first was that Eliot persistently discussed the idea of tradition in either non-political or inadequately political terms. His decisive move was to ascribe the superiority of pre-modern culture to the fact that the European mind still remained 'homogeneous', thereby imbuing the writer with a distinctively classical concern for aesthetic and intellectual coherence. But when he tried to account for this background of moral, religious and racial unity, he tended to deviate wildly between political and theological explanations. In some of his earlier critical writings, such as *The Sacred Wood* from 1920, he appeared to recognise that the classical sensibility was at least partially rooted in the static and hierarchical structures of the feudal mode of production. But in later works, notably *The Use of Poetry and the Use of Criticism* (1933), his frame of reference was almost wholly non-political. The collapse of the classical virtues was now attributed to the 'fragmentation' of the European mind, which had itself been caused by the downgrading of religion in the seventeenth century. The central point was that these interlocking processes were ascribed less to political developments than to the operation of malign spiritual forces. In the final analysis – and West recounted this point with some incredulity – the unravelling of European literature was viewed by Eliot as the work of the Devil.[53]

These remarks were supplemented by a subtle account of the way in which Eliot avoided political analysis in his essays on individual authors. West's example was the section on Wordsworth's poetry in *The Use of Poetry and the Use of Criticism*. Eliot was especially concerned with Wordsworth's famous 'principle of poetic diction', enunciated in the Preface to the second edition of *Lyrical Ballads* in 1800, which held that the duty of contemporary poets was to experiment with 'the language of the middle and lower classes of society.'[54] As West implied, this sort of statement was potentially a source of considerable danger to a depoliticising critic like Eliot, since ultimately it could only be understood by referring to the political beliefs of its author. If we want to know why Wordsworth tried to experiment with a style of language that had previously been dismissed as wholly unpoetic, we have no choice but to invoke his sympathy for the French Revolution and his dismay at the effects of industrialism on the English countryside. So how was Eliot able to deal with Wordsworth's principle while simultaneously steering clear of any substantive discussion of politics? On the one hand, West seemed to argue, by resorting to a sort of critical sleight of hand. At one moment he acknowledged that Wordsworth's poetry was indeed to be understood in political terms (his specific call was for the investigation of its 'purposes and social passions');[55] while at the next he suddenly turned his attention to purely literary matters, pointing to the conformity between Wordsworth's desire to 'imitate' the language of the lower classes and Aristotle's doctrine of mimesis. The reference to 'social passions' *appeared* to satisfy the need for a properly historical analysis, whereas Eliot's sole actual concern was to displace political considerations onto aesthetic ones.[56] Moreover, the attempt to depoliticise Wordsworth's poetic theory was reinforced by Eliot's use of what can perhaps be called the archetypes of English authority. Shortly after raising the non-issue of Wordsworth's indebtedness to Aristotle, Eliot wrote that 'It was not from any recantation of political principles, but from having had it brought to his attention that, as a general literary principle, this would never do, that he [i.e. Wordworth] altered them' [i.e. his poetic ambitions].[57] According to West, the point about this passage was that it employed the distinctive tone of the 'schoolmaster' or 'bank manager' (note the 'this would never do') and therefore bypassed its readers' critical faculties by invoking the spectre of 'traditional authority'. Eliot had advanced his case not by making an argument but by exploiting the strain of deference at the heart of English culture.[58]

The issue of critical authority was also central to the second element in West's critique of Eliot. For West, one of Eliot's most distinctive habits as a critic was that he often made magisterial judgements on other writers without referring to the textual evidence. His essays were full of *de haut en bas* evaluative passages which referred to writers but not to their work. At one point in *The Use of Poetry and the Use of Criticism*, to use West's own example, Eliot remarked that John Keats's scattered observations on poetry were clearly evidence of genius, though only because Keats had been a young man when he made them. Not only was this passage a signal instance of damning with faint praise, it also failed to identify what Eliot found acceptable in the Keatsian view of poetry and what he thought was missing from it. The anomaly in this sort of critical behaviour was that it completely reversed the desired relationship between 'tradition' and 'individual talent' which Eliot had outlined in his theoretical writings. Instead of suppressing his own personality and making himself receptive to an alien sensibility, Eliot was deliberately eliding the work of another writer in order to justify his pose of critical superiority. (There are interesting parallels here between West's remarks about Eliot and Harold Bloom's later work on 'the anxiety of influence'.)[59] The implication was that his behaviour was thus more consistent with the bourgeois individualism he claimed to loathe than with the communitarian impulses he professed to represent.[60] West's verdict on the passage about Keats was one of the most scathing of his career: 'The style subordinates Keats to Mr. Eliot. Mr. Eliot does indeed extinguish his personality in dogmatic appeals to received ideas; but it is Keats, not himself, who is sacrificed.'[61]

West's remarks about Read, Richards and Surrealism were more exiguous than his comments on Eliot. The only book of Read's which he examined was *Form in Modern Poetry* from 1932. Written before its author had become the leading figure on an anarchist left that also included the likes of George Woodcock, Alex Comfort and Marie-Louise Berneri, its main thesis was that the writer should strive to make his sensibility as malleable and discontinuous as possible, on the grounds that this is the only way of making himself receptive to the two most important creative forces – 'negative capability' (in the Keatsian sense) and the unconscious mind. For West, the problem with this argument was that its break with aesthetic individualism was more apparent than real. By emphasising the importance of mental capacities that might otherwise seem alien to the creative mind, Read's real purpose was to put the old idea of the individual personality on a broader and more interesting footing, not to locate the origins of creativity in sources *outside* the individual writer.[62] Although the theoretical writings of I.A. Richards can be seen as one of the main influences on *Crisis and Criticism* (a point to which I will return in due course), West was more interested in Chapter Six in the experiments in 'practical criticism' which Richards had famously conducted while teaching at Cambridge. As is well known, Richards's method was to distribute unsigned pieces of poetry and prose to his students and then to ask for their immediate responses. The famously anomalous results, which (to use an example that amused George Orwell)[63] saw the light verse of 'Woodbine Willie' being rated more highly than the poetry of John Donne, convinced Richards that the audience for serious literature had undergone a dreadful coarsening of taste. West's concern was that when Richards tried to explain this lack of receptivity to literary art, he focused more on secondary symptoms (such as the fear of appearing sentimental) than on their real cause – the prohibition on communal feeling that lies at the heart of capitalist culture.[64] Surrealism was subjected to an even less rigorous critique. In a series of rather perfunctory remarks, West acknowledged that the purpose of surrealism was to create the psychological preconditions of socialist revolution by promoting a synthesis between 'perception' (objective reality) and 'representation' (the imagination). The main flaw in this project was that it smacked of philosophical idealism. By insisting that political changes would follow on inevitably from the transformation of the individual sensibility, as if the mind exercised a direct and mysterious influence on the world around it, the surrealists were guilty of ignoring the cardinal Marxist belief that social being determines consciousness.[65]

How convincing is West's theory of cultural crisis? Perhaps its most serious defect is the inflexibility with which it approaches the opposition between individualism and communitarianism. Despite insisting that the ideas of Eliot and his contemporaries were inherently reactionary, West seems to have built his theory around the following assumptions: (1) capitalism is necessarily individualist, (2) socialism is necessarily communitarian, (3) it is not possible for any society to achieve an admixture of individualism and communitarianism. This enabled him to imply that any deviation from individualism on the part of the literary intellectuals could be regarded as either an actual or potential challenge to bourgeois society, regardless of its precise ideological content. The obvious weakness with this chain of reasoning is that it overlooks the extent to which bourgeois ideology (assuming the term to be meaningful) has usually sought to maintain social cohesion by balancing an emphasis on individualism with an account of the characteristics that bind human beings together. When West wrote about Eliot's attempt to harness the idea of tradition to the defence of capitalism, he gave the impression that this was somehow a unique innovation in the history of modern thought. But the whole conservative tradition to which Eliot belongs has been preoccupied with specifying the ways in which the public authorities can offset the anarchy of market institutions by inculcating a sense of what Maurice Cowling has called 'moral solidarity'.[66] Nor is there any recognition in West's work of the way that other branches of bourgeois ideology, notably the various forms of post-Enlightenment liberalism, seek to ground the idea of individual freedom in an overarching conception of universal human nature. West might have been justified in supposing that Eliot, Read and Richards were all unusually hostile to bourgeois individualism; but he was wrong to imply that any body of thought which emits a whiff of communitarianism can *necessarily* be regarded as a threat to the stability of capitalism.

This obviously raises the question of why a thinker of West's subtlety should have adopted such an undialectical approach in the first place. On a personal level, West's misunderstanding of bourgeois ideology was perhaps related to the guilt he experienced in the 1930s because of his attitude to fascism. In a remarkably self-revelatory passage in *One Man and His Time*, West admitted that he had often felt attracted to the doctrine of group identity that lay at the heart of fascist ideology. Still influenced by Paul Farleigh's theory of the Three

Realities, with its emphasis on how medieval societies were bound together by their submission to theocratic rule, he seems to have recognised that the fascist version of communitarianism embodied a sort of hierarchical and mystical grandeur that was simply absent from its communist equivalent. And yet, instead of confronting his feelings directly, he 'remained silent even to myself' in the hope of overcoming his shame.[67] It seems possible that by overstating the element of individualism in bourgeois ideology (and by denying that any system of thought could defend market institutions by appealing to collective values) West was partly motivated by the desire to overcome his unorthodox ideological yearnings by consigning fascism to the realm of theoretical impossibility. He came close to admitting as much when recalling his father's response to *Crisis and Criticism*:

> When my father read the book, he said that it had no centre. I think he was right, inasmuch as I had not penetrated to what was for me at the heart of the conflict. For I only described an imaginary bourgeois intellectual torn between socialism and an ideology prior to fascism. When I spoke of the uneasiness about 'I' and 'we', I said nothing about the fascist 'we' nor about its power to release collective emotion. This was the real intellectual and political issue, and the book was weakened because it did not face it.[68]

If we try to identify the wider influences on West's theory of cultural crisis, it becomes clear that in some respects he was simply giving a novel twist to an idea which had circulated widely among literary intellectuals in the first few decades of the twentieth century. As John Carey has pointed out in *The Intellectuals and the Masses* (1992), there was widespread concern in this period that individualism was under threat from the 'herd mentality' of the masses. Terrified that the advent of mass literacy had destroyed the foundations of a hierarchical society, writers as diverse as T.S. Eliot, H.G. Wells and Virginia Woolf all foresaw an age in which 'natural aristocrats' like themselves would be swallowed up by the dionysian excesses of mass culture. At the heart of this body of opinion was the tendency to conflate mass consciousness with the mentality of the crowd. Convinced that working men and women are *always* motivated by the sort of group instincts which co-ordinate the behaviour of large crowds, regardless of whether or not they are physically united with other people, the intelligentsia seemed incapable of thinking about modern society without surrendering to paranoid fantasies about bloodthirsty *canailles* whipped up by savage demagogues. The origins of this version of cultural crisis can therefore be traced outside Britain to several continental texts which aimed to provide a 'scientific' understanding of crowd psychology, notably Gustave Le Bon's *The Crowd* (1895), Sigmund Freud's *Group Psychology and the Analysis of the Ego* (1921) and Elias Canetti's *Masse und Macht*.[69] By agreeing that individualism was indeed under threat from the new forms of group consciousness, West was arguably seeking to convert his fellow intellectuals to Marxism by pandering to their most virulent prejudices, pausing only to enter one all-important caveat – the death of individualism is a good thing.

Staying with the issue of the wider influences on West's theory of cultural crisis, it is also worth examining Christopher Pawling's throwaway claim in his book on Caudwell that '*Crisis and Criticism* is clearly a reply to [I.A. Richards's] *Principles of Literary Criticism.*,[70] Although the links between the two writers are by no means as clear as Pawling implies, except in the obvious sense that they both ascribe great importance to the analysis of literary form, there is perhaps a sense in which their respective theories of cultural crisis are bound together by a shared concern with integration. As is well known, Richards believed that the crisis of modern culture had largely been caused by the decline of religious faith (this was obviously not an original position) and that its most terrible effects were at the level of personal psychology. Once it became impossible to think of the world as the organic creation of a divine intelligence, it was more or less inevitable (or so Richards argued) that the individual mind would begin a long descent into incoherence. To be modern is to feel that one's every 'impulse' is somehow at loggerheads with all the others. Displaying a faith in art that Frank Kermode has rightly described as 'messianic', Richards insisted that one of the main solutions to the problem of mental incoherence is to become a more sensitive reader of poetry. Because poetry has a 'coenaesthetic' function (that is, it arranges disparate impulses into cohesive wholes), it serves as a model of mental efficiency from which the individual reader can learn to transform self-division into unity.[71] Just as West believed that modern literary intellectuals were obsessed with replacing the chaos of individualism with the order of community, so Richards believed that their primary function was to encourage a similar act of integration at the level of the individual sensibility. As we shall when we examine his remarks about romanticism, West often took a curiously indirect approach to acknowledging his main influences, mentioning them in print but eliding the ideas which had affected him most deeply. This arguably makes it all the more significant that the chapter on Richards in *Crisis and Criticism* makes little reference to his theoretical principles, limiting itself to his experiments in practical criticism.

2.2 West's theory of aesthetic value

If bourgeois literary criticism had indeed moved away from individualist theories of creativity, why had its leading exponents failed to translate their taste for collectivism into a commitment to communist politics? West's answer to this question was very simple – they had been put off by the absence in Marxist literature of a theory of aesthetic value. Although Marxism had done a great deal to illuminate the relationship between art and society, it had failed to say much about (1) the ability of literary texts to convey aesthetic pleasure, and (2) the criteria by which good writers can be distinguished from bad ones. According to West, this failure of understanding was partly the result of a philosophical misconception. Many Marxists had mistakenly come to believe that speculation about aesthetic matters was the sole preserve of the Idealist school of philosophy, presumably (though West did not make this clear) because of the importance of aesthetics to the great school of German Idealism which began with Baumgarten and later embraced the likes of Kant, Hegel, Schopenhauer and Nietzsche.[72] There was also a political aspect to the problem. Since it was common for reactionary movements to conceal their true nature behind public spectacles of intense grandeur, it was understandable that many Marxists should have conflated aesthetic experience with the defence of capitalist society.[73] The latter point would have seemed especially forceful at the time of a confident and expanding fascism, which (in Walter Benjamin's famous observation) owed much of its success to the fact that it had 'aestheticised politics'.[74] West's main purpose in *Crisis and Criticism* was thus to formulate a Marxist theory of aesthetic value, specifically in the context of literature. As we shall see, his theory had four main elements:

(1) A preparatory attempt to use anthropological data to show that language and poetry both had their origins in the economic activity of primitive societies.
(2) The argument that the impulse to write is rooted in the writer's identification with the energies which fuel production.
(3) An adaptation of the Soviet emphasis on the unity of form and content which holds that the aesthetic power of literary form can only be realised if the writer appreciates the forces in society which lead to economic progress.
(4) An account of literature's social function.

Let us begin with the anthropological dimension of the argument. In our survey of the historical element in Soviet cultural theory (Chapter Two), we saw that Maxim Gorky attached great importance to identifying the characteristics that linked Socialist Realism to myth.[75] The desire to establish this link perhaps reflected the belief that human culture was somehow purer at the dawn of its existence than at any time since. Gorky's remarks were probably influenced by the much more dramatic anthropological speculations of G.V. Plekhanov, who tried in his *Unaddressed Letters* (1895) to substantiate the base/superstructure metaphor by claiming that art had grown *directly* out of the economic requirements of primitive societies. Art, Plekhanov argued, originally took the form of collective rituals in which men and women tried to sharpen their skills as hunters by imitating the movements of wild animals.[76] Although the British Marxists of the 1930s were probably unfamiliar with *Unaddressed Letters*, not least because it was only translated into English as late as 1953, some of them developed anthropological ideas which often read like an extension of Plekhanov's.[77] Most importantly, Christopher Caudwell and Alick West both argued that it was not merely art but also language itself which had its origins in the primitive economy. The strategic motivation behind these ideas seems clear enough. By proving (or seeming to prove) that the emergence of art and language was inseparable from economic factors, Caudwell and West were trying to legitimise the more urgent task of analysing contemporary literature in terms of its social function.

The anthropological sections of *Crisis and Criticism* took the form of a critical summary of recent work by a number of prominent linguists, anthropologists and cultural historians, many of whom were also cited in the equivalent chapters of Caudwell's *Illusion and Reality*.[78] Chief among them were Ludwig Noiré, Richard Paget, G.A. de Laguna, Nikolai Marr (a Soviet thinker) and Karl Bücher. As proof of the claim that language was initially developed in response to problems in the sphere of production, West referred to Noiré's work on the distinctive nature of linguistic signification in primitive societies. One of the most salient features of primitive languages, Noiré had claimed, was that their frame of reference was almost wholly economic. The majority of nouns denoted aspects of the physical environment that had already been transformed by human labour, and usually combined a reference to an object with an indication of the sort of labour which had been practised upon it: '...[primitive] language describes the things of the objective world not as being forms, but as having been formed; not as active beings that exercise an effect, but as passive beings on whom an effect is exercised.'[79] Nor was it simply the case, West went on to imply, that the main effect of the invention of language was the consolidation of existing methods of working. In a passage which anticipated Raymond Williams's argument that language should be regarded not merely as a part of the superstructure but also as one of the forces of production,[80] he claimed that the emergence of speech precipitated a major transformation of the primitive economy. It did so by allowing human beings to congregate in bigger and more complex groups than ever before. Proof of this was furnished by Marr's observation that in certain primitive languages there were no verbs which referred simply to the act of speaking, only verbs which characterised speech in terms of integration into a broader social group: 'The word for "speaking" in Grusinian [Georgian]', West wrote, 'literally means "being Scythian"...That is, speaking is social existence in a particular mode.'[81]

The general argument was supplemented by some speculative remarks about the precise circumstances in which language had emerged. According to West, drawing heavily on the work of Paget, there were two reasons for supposing that the decisive occurrence was probably the invention of tools. The first was that the use of tools made it significantly more difficult to communicate through gestures, which had previously been the established method of co-ordinating economic activity.[82] The second was that the new ways of working had 'refined the powers of distinguishing and grasping',[83] thereby giving rise to a more complex and differentiated conception of the natural world than had existed earlier. It thus became urgently necessary to evolve a means of communication that was sufficiently adaptable to convey the new sense of nature's diversity.[84] If this eventually took the form of words, West wrote, it was probably because 'pantomimic gestures of the tongue'[85] had always been an important accompaniment to human labour. When primitive man undertook some complex task, he would often roll his tongue around his head in order to increase his concentration – this established a link between economic efficiency and orality (that is, the capacity to produce sounds from the mouth) whose ultimate consequence was the birth of language.[86]

West's brief comments on the role of poetry in primitive societies formed an important bridge between his anthropological concerns and his ideas about the relationship between form and content in literature. Following the lead of Karl Bücher, whose *Arbeit und Rhythmus* was one of the few theoretical works he identified by name, West suggested that poetry (or, more precisely, the sort of metrical chants which often accompanied primitive labour) had its origins in 'the regularly repeated movements of the body in work.'[87] When employed in an economic context, its purpose was to liberate supplies of collective energy which might otherwise have gone untapped. By imposing a new regularity on individual actions and by 'co-ordinating the action of one individual with others',[88] poetry engendered a ferocious sense of group resolve which enabled primitive societies to scale heights of economic achievement which had previously been beyond them. This emphasis on poetry as a *transformational* force was an early sign of West's impatience with the 'reflectionist' element in Marxist thought, with its tendency to regard literature and the arts as little more than elegant props for the existing social order.[89] As with Caudwell, Fox and most of the other aestheticians in the world communist movement (though arguably with a much greater sense of theoretical clarity) West's interest was in the idea of literature as a force which points humanity towards a better future. This brings us on to the second element in his argument.

Having prepared the ground for a materialist theory of aesthetic value by arguing that poetry performed a directly economic function in primitive societies, West now turned his attention to the question of how literary texts can convey aesthetic experience. At the heart of his explanation was an attempt to link the expressivity of texts with the productive capacities of the wider society. Its point of departure was a startling proposition about the origins of literary inspiration. An individual is moved to write, West implied, because he is drawn towards the majesty of the economic process by powerful feelings of identification, which imbue him with the desire to transform the human sensibility in much the same way that production transforms the environment.[90] When a writer tries to restore our experience of the world to a state of rude sensual health – to 'defamiliarise' it, in Shklovsky's phrase – he does so by *unconsciously* striving to emulate the protean energies that enable human beings to shape the external world in accordance with their own wishes:

> The good writer does not take for granted. In some way, of which at present we know very little, he actively feels the productive energy of society and identifies himself with it. He realises, not necessarily consciously, but perhaps through the alternations of energy and fatigue, that neither the world nor our living in it are mere plain facts. They are the facts to make songs about.... With this sense in his body of the productive energy that alone continues the existence of us and our world, the writer's language is quickened. His whole writing expresses that participation in social energy through which he feels the life of the world.[91]

Literary form, the source of a text's aesthetic power, is as much rooted in economic procedures as the writer's original impulse to create. It can best be understood as the result of an unconscious effort to mimic the techniques of production at the level of language – or, more precisely, to mimic the states of mind which accompany economic activity. The emotional states and intellectual procedures which characterise the labour process are broadly similar under any system of production, and have their precise parallels in the formal arrangements that confer aesthetic significance on works of art.[92] This idea was initially explored in relation to the flow of energy during work. West's argument was that the individual is necessarily ambivalent about the prospect of engaging in productive activity. The desire to labour is invariably balanced by an inclination to shirk. This is partly for biological reasons (or so one assumes) but also because the majority of people have a preference for consumption over production – the result of being excluded from economic activity during their earliest years. The different stages in the flow of economic energy are associated with different attitudes towards membership of the broader social group. The individual will regard himself as an integral member of society when he is fully committed to playing an economic role; but is likely to experience feelings of either rebellion or exclusion during periods of lesser activity. The crucial point is that this set of tensions (tensions between 'energy and stasis', 'acceptance and rebellion' and 'inclusion and exclusion') provides the basis for the binary patterns which structure the presentation of emotional states in all forms of literature. The heightened sensibility that we associate with great literature is nothing, in the final analysis, except the everyday experiences of the ordinary worker evoked in primary colours.[93]

The argument was then extended to matters of a more cognitive nature. In a passage which recalled Marx's famous description of the architect who 'raises his structure in his imagination before he erects it in reality',[94] West implied that there are two related forms of intellectual activity which allow production to occur. The dispassionate investigation of external reality, oriented towards the question 'how does it all work?', is balanced by the more subjective attempt to anticipate the ways in which knowledge can be used to humanise the environment – that is, to transform it in accordance with human needs. West's belief was that this fundamental distinction is reflected by literature's central devices, some of which (e.g. non-figural imagery) make a direct reference to the external world, whereas others (e.g. comparative imagery) seek to describe the 'human and non-human in terms of one another'. The continual alternation between the two modes was what West held responsible for much of literature's power.[95]

West's argument about form was saved from reductionism by his willingness to acknowledge what can perhaps be called the relative autonomy of form. He appeared to argue that there are two characteristics which are present in literature but absent from the economic processes in which it is rooted. The first is a capacity for reconciling opposites. Whereas economic activity is always characterised by the sort of emotional 'conflicts' to which we have just referred (conflicts between energy and stasis, acceptance and rebellion and inclusion and exclusion), literature usually makes a virtue of fusing its disparate elements into a cohesive whole.[96] Secondly, it displays a feel for ambiguity which is unequalled in any other form of communication. A genuine work of literature deliberately activates the multiple denotations attached to a whole range of individual words, though not in such a way as to sabotage the reader's ability to extract a continuous meaning.[97] The effect of these characteristics is subtly to alter our understanding of social organisation. By flirting with verbal anarchy while retaining a fundamental coherence, literature 'conveys the sense of power to achieve organisation and to use its energy'.[98] And by reconciling affective states that would otherwise be in conflict, it 'gives a sensation of a more harmonised organism than the social organism actually is'[99] (this is presumably to be admired for prefiguring the social harmony that will exist under communism, as well as invigorating the outlook of the individual worker). If the formalist assumptions which dominated academic criticism in the 1930s were a clear influence on the whole of West's thinking (a point to which I will return in due course), this was nevertheless the only part of his argument which evinced a clear debt to *specific* British thinkers. It was I.A. Richards, excoriated in Chapter Six of *Crisis and Criticism*, who popularised the idea that poetry's central characteristic is that of 'coenaesthesis' (that is, the ability to reconcile conflicting impulses), while the notion of ambiguity had been increasingly influential in critical circles since the publication of William Empson's *Seven Types of Ambiguity* in 1930.[100] West presumably chose to rework these ideas, albeit without acknowledgement, in order to establish some common ground with an intended readership of 'bourgeois intellectuals'.

The third element in West's aesthetic theory provided a criterion by which literary works could be evaluated. It may be correct to characterise literary form as a sort of verbal correlative of the states of mind which prevail during production; but it is also clear that not all works of literature are as effective as others in using their formal resources to express a compelling aesthetic vision. What is it that distinguishes the successful work from the less successful one? In order to answer that question, West proposed a highly unusual variation on the doctrine of the unity of form and content. As we have seen in Chapter Two, this doctrine was held by the Soviet theorists to encompass two related beliefs: (1) that the nature of a work's form is ultimately determined by the nature of its content, and (2) that a work's form should never strive for 'autonomy' but should always function as a more-or-less 'transparent' bearer of meaning. West's innovation was to reformulate the first of these beliefs in the light of the similarities he perceived between writing and production. Since literary form has its origins in the writer's identification with productive activity, it follows that its aesthetic power will only be fully realised in those works that display an understanding of the inherently *dynamic* nature of the economic process. 'Literature', West wrote, 'gives us not only the sense of the social organism, but of the changing social organism…sensitiveness to the process of social change characterises all great literature.'[101]

The writer's understanding of society will only be suitably dynamic, West continued, if he is able to identify the forces in his own age which must ultimately lead, either in the short or long term, towards a complete transformation of the economic system. He must be able to evoke the continuous development of the productive forces (technology, scientific knowledge, labour power etc.) as well as to describe the process of 'class war' which pushes this development forward.[102] At the same time, West seemed to imply, it is not necessary for the writer to refer *directly* to any of these things. Many of the greatest works of literature, including the shortest lyric poems, have represented the dynamism of economic affairs in wholly symbolic or allegorical form. West's example was Milton's *Paradise Lost,* conceived as a lengthy meditation on the rise of capitalism, in which Heaven served as a symbol of declining feudalism and Paradise as a symbol of the emerging bourgeois order.[103] Nor is it the case that the forward movement of society can only be depicted by writers whose political opinions are consciously progressive: 'A work may talk revolution; but if it does not show revolution through society's creative movement, it is not fulfilling its function as literature...a work may talk reaction; but if it conveys the sense of the social movement it condemns, the manifestly reactionary work is more valuable than the manifestly revolutionary.'[104] By emphasising this point, West was aligning himself with an important tradition of Marxist criticism, beginning with Marx and Engels themselves and stretching forward through the likes of Lukács and Marcuse, which is suspicious of 'tendentiousness' in art and seeks instead to emphasise the potential subversiveness of aesthetic form as such.[105] It has sometimes been suggested that endorsement of this tradition was one of the main ways in which the communist aestheticians of the 1930s implicitly distanced themselves from the element of crude sloganeering in much Soviet or Soviet-inspired art.[106] If this argument seems especially plausible in the case of West, it is perhaps because of the complete absence from the theoretical – as opposed to critical – sections of *Crisis and Criticism* of any reference to a work of Socialist Realism.

West's emphasis on the dynamism of the artist's vision, linked as it was to a broader attempt to reformulate the orthodox account of the relationship between form and content, prepared the ground for the remarks about literature's social function that served as a capstone to his aesthetic theory. The ultimate purpose of literature, West now argued, has been to stimulate political action by disseminating a more compelling vision of social change than has been available elsewhere: 'Because literature, as content and form, expresses and is social change, it hastens it. Literature is therefore propaganda.'[107] The thing which distinguishes literature from other forms of discourse, making it more effective as an instrument of political persuasion, is its habit of depicting social change in a manner that is simultaneously even-handed and disinterested. In the first place, West implied, the literary imagination is set apart by its sense of *inclusivity*. It works by casting a balanced eye across both the hegemonic and emergent elements in a social formation, identifying as much with the former (God in *Paradise Lost*, for instance) as with the latter (Satan in the same poem).[108] Only then, having registered the divided loyalties which necessarily exist when an established way of life is under threat, will it begin to guide the reader towards a less equivocal identification with the forces of change.[109] It does so by freeing our perception of social evolution from narrowly personal or utilitarian considerations. When literature is working its magic upon us, we cease to ask 'what does this mean for me?' and begin to perceive the sheer grandeur of the technological and class forces which are pushing society forward. This stimulates our desire to make a contribution to their further development. The argument at this point took the form of a partial critique of Bukharin's remarks about the idea of 'disinterestedness' in art. Taking issue with Bukharin's rejection of the entire Kantian tradition in aesthetics, West resorted to a vivid analogy in order to illustrate his belief that the idea of disinterestedness should not be simply discarded but retained in a modified form:

> ...if, instead of merely waiting for the train to come, as trains always do come, we look down the tunnel, feel the wind begin to blow out of it, then see the gleam from the approaching train, the sense of excitement may make us momentarily forget whether we are waiting for a Highgate or a Golders Green train. In that sense, we are disinterested. The train is not a given object, by which we travel to Highgate, which we consume. We look at it without reference to our desire to get to a particular station. But it is untrue to say that it exists for us only in an intellectual way, without any reference whatever to desire or will. We see it with a sense of exhilaration that there should be any trains at all, with a feeling of the social energy that has created them. We do not want only to use trains, but to take part, in our field, in the activity that produces them. The element of truth in Hegel's idea is that in an aesthetic experience we do not desire as mere consumers; but we do desire as producers, and this desire, though not necessarily the only one, is dominant.[110]

Each element in West's theory of aesthetic value is open to criticism, beginning with his anthropological speculations about the origins of language and poetry. As Robert Sullivan has pointed out in his book on Caudwell, the idea that language and poetry both arose in response to economic needs has a respectable anthropological pedigree, appearing for the first time in E.B. Tylor's *Primitive*

Society in 1871.[111] As such, it would be going too far to follow the lead of René Wellek and simply dismiss it as a convenient fiction or 'phantasy', conjured into existence to buttress Marxist preconceptions.[112] It is nevertheless clear that this is an area in which certainty is simply impossible – all theories about the roots of human communication are ultimately the product of informed speculation and nothing else.[113] The perspectives which West shared with Caudwell and Plekhanov can reasonably be criticised for overstating economic considerations and ignoring or eliding other possible reasons for the emergence of language and poetry.[114] For example, there seem to be many anthropologists and linguists who insist that language had its roots either in genetics (a sort of natural propensity to operationalise the 'deep structures' of an innate grammar)[115] or in a straightforward love of mimesis (the desire to imitate the sounds of birds and wild animals).[116] The interesting thing from a historical point of view is that alternatives to the Plekhanov/Caudwell/West thesis were occasionally proposed in the 1930s by *other English Marxists*, notably by W.H. Auden in his important essay 'Writing' (1932).[117] It has often been argued that members of the so-called 'Auden group' were torn for much of the Thirties between two incompatible conceptions of art. On the one hand, traumatised by the rise of fascism and the threat of war, they tried to create a 'parabolic' form of writing that could be used to convey important political truths to the public. On the other hand, indebted to the legacy of European Romanticism, they instinctively believed that the main purpose of art is to evoke the private moods of the gifted individual.[118] The striking thing about 'Writing' was that it provided an account of the origins of language which aimed to legitimise both these perspectives. If we wish to identify the 'first language', Auden suggested, we should look no further than the purely expressive sounds that existed before the emergence of language proper – that is, sounds such as 'ow', 'coo' and 'ee-ah' that directly expressed emotion without referring to definite signifieds.[119] This primitive form of language was partly a response to the urgent need to co-ordinate economic activity,[120] but it also reflected a deep-seated desire to reinforce feelings of intimacy by laying bare the speaker's inner world: '…it was used to express the feelings of the speaker; feelings about something happening to him (the prick of the pin), or attitudes towards other things in the world (the other hungry dog; the darling baby).'[121] However, when a more authentic form of language finally superseded the older system of semi-articulate noises, the reason for the change was more existential than economic. At a certain point in their development, Auden wrote, primitive societies lost the 'telepath[ic]' sense of person-to-person intimacy which bound them together. Remembering the heightened sense of belonging that usually resulted when they communicated through sounds, primitive men subsequently came to feel that the group consciousness of the past could somehow be recaptured if only their language was elaborated into something more systematic and genuinely referential. Language thus emerged from the desire of primitive man to 'recover the sense of being as much part of life as the cells in his body are part of him.'[122] Although these arguments were much sketchier than those of either Caudwell or West, they provided interesting early evidence of the way that the Marxist Auden (the one who emphasised the economic reasons for the birth of language) would eventually be drowned out by the Romantic Auden who primarily saw language as a key player in the drama of the human soul.

What of West's belief that literature arises from feelings of identification which draw the writer towards the process of production? Although it stands at the centre of *Crisis and Criticism*, there is perhaps a sense in which it is undermined by one of its own premises. When he insisted that the feelings of identification between writer and society are 'not necessarily' conscious, West arguably did two things: (1) he reduced his argument to the status of an unverifiable hypothesis; and (2) he cast doubt on their explanatory power by failing to assign them a suitably prominent role in the writer's conscious existence. If the awe which the writer experiences in the presence of 'social energy' is really so fundamental as to spur him into writing, one might at least expect it to make some sort of impression on his conscious mind – there is, after all, no ethical or cultural reason that would obviously justify its suppression. The suspicion that West's analogy between literature and production is therefore somewhat forced, though perhaps not wholly misleading, is underscored by the relative paucity of his remarks about literary form. While *Crisis and Criticism* makes some interesting suggestions about literature's use of figurative and non-figurative language and its capacity to express emotion, it fails to indicate how a whole range of other formal devices can plausibly be related to the nature of the labour process. For example, in what sense is it possible to see rhythm, tone and texture as verbal correlatives of the states of mind that characterise human labour? On the credit side, however, it should also be noted that West's emphasis on the unconscious roots of creativity was of pioneering significance in terms of the development of Marxist theories of culture. A number of Marxists had tried to integrate psychoanalytic ideas into their work by the time that *Crisis and Criticism* was written; but West was one of the first to reject the idea that the unconscious mind is merely a repository of anti-social impulses (as in the Freudian orthodoxy) and to see it instead as a crucible of progressive intuitions. In the period after the War, especially during the great flowering of Western Marxism between 1945 and 1970, this idea became central to various forms of Marxist theory. Since we know that the work of the thirties aestheticians was familiar to many of the Western Marxists, we cannot rule out the possibility that West's theory of literature exercised a distant influence on such writers as Ernst Bloch (who saw the unconscious mind as the locus of the utopian imagination)[123] and Herbert Marcuse (who saw the 'desublimation' of the Freudian eros as one of the main objectives of political revolution).[124]

Viewed from another perspective, West's theory can perhaps be seen as a conscious attempt to update (and hence to displace) an earlier account of the nature of creativity. As George Steiner has recently pointed out in an important series of books and essays, notably *Real Presences* (1989) and *Grammars of Creation* (2002), there has been an entire movement in Western aesthetics which regards creativity as the product of the artist's tendency to identify with the mind of God. Convinced that his own powers are just as demiurgic as those of his creator, the artist conjures aesthetic worlds of his own (or so the argument goes) in order to assuage his disappointment at not being responsible for the act of divine inspiration which created the universe. Whether or not he sets out to explore religious ideas, he identifies so completely with God at the moment of creation that his work necessarily embodies a sense of the numinous. It is important to remember that traces of this theory can be detected in the work of many of West's contemporaries. Looking back towards the end of his life at his experience of writing, it was D.H. Lawrence (the subject of West's last essay) who wrote that 'I always feel as if I stood naked for the fire of Almighty God to go through me – and it's rather an awful feeling. One has to be so terribly religious to be an artist.'[125] The similarities which link West's ideas to those of the earlier tradition are surely clear enough. There is the same emphasis on the artist seeking to emulate an external source of creativity (God on the one hand, production on the other), and the same insistence that the artist has no choice but to refer to certain subject matters. The idea that Marxism often functions as a substitute religion has been greatly overplayed, but this is arguably a clear case of a Marxist writer preserving the structure of a religious doctrine while changing its substantive content.

Even if West's understanding of the nature of creativity were wholly convincing, the observations about the unity of form and content which flow from it would still be problematic. By insisting that the expressive power of literary form can only be activated when the writer evokes the forces of economic progress in his own age, West is obviously placing drastic limitations on what the writer can be expected to achieve. Implicit in West's theory is the assumption that no successful work of literature can ever evoke social stasis or decline (where does this leave Swift, Gibbon and Dickens?) or even the forces of economic progress *from an earlier age.* This makes it all the more ironic that three of the writers who have won most praise from Marxist critics, namely Shakespeare, Scott and Balzac, each created epic works about social transformations that occurred before they were born. The other main problem with West's theory relates to its account of the effects of literature on the reader's *conscious* understanding of economic processes. When form and content work in unison, West argued, three things tend to occur: (1) the forces of economic progress are perceived in comparatively 'disinterested' form, (2) productive energies which clash in everyday life are portrayed as part of a continuum, and (3) ambiguities of meaning remind us of the miraculous way in which the economy unites diverse individuals in a common effort. What is missing from this account is any explanation of why a work's content should be perceived as distinctively economic in the first place. Given that social realities are often portrayed in literature in a highly refracted form (as West implicitly acknowledged), there would seem to be no particular reason why the reader should look beyond a work's manifest content to the economic forces that inspire it. The point can be illustrated by referring to two of the theorists who influenced West. When I.A. Richards spoke of literature's capacity to reconcile opposites, he interpreted the impulses that submit to reconciliation not as forms of productive energy but as 'instincts' that might otherwise threaten mental coherence. Similarly, when William Empson drew attention to the proliferation of ambiguities in poetry, he saw them primarily as an expression of disparate impulses in the poet's personality. There was no attempt to relate them to disparate individuals coming together in a common act of economic creativity. In a culture which has tended since the nineteenth century to regard literature as the record of personal psychology, these ideas are likely to seem rather more plausible than West's.

To the majority of West's contemporaries, however, the philosophical integrity of his ideas was probably a lot less important than their wider political function. As has often been pointed out, it seems clear that the strategic ambition behind *Crisis and Criticism* was to provide Socialist Realism with some sort of philosophical justification.[126] If it is indeed the case that the most powerful literature is that which successfully evokes the forces of economic progress, West seemed to be saying, then it follows that the Socialist Realists are the most important writers of the age – Marxist content is the condition of significant form. By the same token, modernism has been condemned to aesthetic poverty by the reactionary opinions of its main exponents. West tried to illustrate this argument in the two notorious chapters which brought *Crisis and Criticism* to an end. These consisted of an extended comparison between Joyce's *Ulysses* and *The Gates of a Strange Field* by Harold Heslop, one of the few genuine proletarians to write socialist fiction in the 1930s.[127] Whereas Heslop's book was complimented on its unusual vitality, Joyce was condemned (though not without receiving a great deal of incidental praise) for his failure to translate his anti-clericalism into a wholehearted opposition to capitalism and imperialism. If *Ulysses* displayed a lack of formal coherence which prevented it from achieving genuine greatness, it was Joyce's ignorance of Marxism that was ultimately to blame.[128] Although the chapter on Joyce was often a lot more insightful than this brief summary would suggest (it was later described by the non-Marxist critic Stanley Edgar Hyman as 'absolutely first-rate'),[129] West's encomium to Heslop might reasonably be seen as the *ne plus ultra* of thirties dogmatism. Unsurprisingly, it was omitted from the new edition of *Crisis and Criticism* that was published in Britain after West's death.[130]

2.3 Romanticism as a precursor of Marxism

We have seen in Chapter Two that the Soviet theorists often tried to legitimise Socialist Realism by portraying it as the culmination of a whole series of prestigious cultural forms. These ranged from the fertility myths of ancient society to the novels of Tolstoy and the paintings of Repin and Yaroshenko. It is less often realised that the Soviet theorists also employed a similar strategy to confer historical legitimacy on their own work, usually by invoking non-Marxist writers from the nineteenth century who had explored the relationship between art and society from a radical perspective. It was common for Soviet writers to claim direct descent from Belinsky, Chernyshevsky and Dobrolyubov, each of whom had combined a taste for realism in the arts with a commitment to anti-czarism in politics.[131] Yet in Britain, even during the period of the Popular Front when interest in the history of English radicalism was at its height (see Chapter Six), it was only Alick West who showed any real interest in relating Marxist criticism to a wider tradition of aesthetic thinking. According to West, Marxist criticism should essentially be seen as a recapitulation (albeit at a much higher level of political sophistication) of the ideas developed by the main Romantic theorists in the late-eighteenth and early-nineteenth centuries.

West's starting point was the assumption that the Romantics had a similar relationship to their theoretical predecessors as his own generation of Marxists had to theirs. Whereas the Marxists were trying to build on the undeveloped strain of collectivism in writers such as Eliot, Read and Richards, the Romantics tried to extend the inchoate collectivist insights in the work of Augustan critics such as Pope, Warburton and Hurd.[132] For much of the eighteenth century, West claimed, English intellectuals had been preoccupied with the issue of the diversity of human taste. Faced with a revival of scholarly interest in medieval, Scandinavian and biblical literature, combined with a 'growing acquaintance' with the culture of non-Western countries such as China and India (the result of the growth of imperialism), the leading Augustans distanced themselves from the orthodox assumption that aesthetic standards are of transhistorical or 'timeless' significance. They did so by forging a relativist form of criticism which employed sociological assumptions to justify the fundamental tenet that each age has aesthetic standards of its own. Because literature always bears the imprint of its social environment, it follows that tastes will change with each significant transformation of the social structure – it makes no sense to judge the work of one age according to the standards of another. Although West accepted that these ideas were a significant advance on the aesthetic individualism of the sixteenth century, he also claimed that the Augustans failed to develop a properly historical understanding of human personality. When they wrote about the relationship between the individual and society, they still assumed that personality is essentially shaped *outside society* and that the social influences on the individual are therefore of purely secondary importance.[133] In other words, they failed to challenge what Christopher Caudwell had called the 'bourgeois illusion of freedom' – the assumption that the individual is ultimately free of social determinations. This was the theoretical weakness which the Romantics tried to put right.

Although West ranged widely in his account of Romanticism, referring at various times to theoretical statements by Blake, Wordsworth and Shelley, his argument was chiefly based on a highly unconventional interpretation of Coleridge's writings on literature and aesthetics. According to West, Coleridge regarded literature as a force which mediates between man and God. The ultimate goal of the poet is to transfigure his personality by achieving direct communion with the mind of God, but this state of grace can only be reached after a long process of spiritual endeavour. If the poet is to stand any chance of success, he must firstly acquire a basic sense of the numinous by looking beyond everyday experience towards the 'organic unity' which represents the main evidence for God's presence in the world. This process is itself a gradual one. To use the sort of mystical language by which West occasionally seemed attracted, spiritual wisdom does not begin with a premature quest for the divine oneness at the heart of all creation. Its real starting point is the attempt to identify the traces of organic unity in purely *local* forms of experience.[134]

It was this emphasis on organic unity, West argued, which allowed Coleridge to make a decisive break with the ideology of aesthetic individualism. For one thing it forced him to dismantle the opposition between society and the individual which had survived unscathed in the work of his Augustan predecessors. Since the idea of organic unity implied that the universe is bound together by a network of mutually determining relationships between its constituent elements, it no longer made sense to attribute a fixed nature to the individual and thereafter to describe the influence of social factors as purely contingent.[135] In Coleridge's work, the self is wholly shaped by its dialectical interactions with the social environment: 'But for my conscience, that is my affections and duties towards others, I should have no self.'[136] In West's opinion, Coleridge expressed this recognition by insisting that the primary function of literature is to evoke the forms of organic unity which operate *in society* – or, as he liked to call it, the 'body politic'.[137] Seen from this perspective, the role of the writer is to lay bare the mode of interaction that unites society's diverse elements into a cohesive whole. Yet West rejected the idea that Coleridge was trying to project a misleading unity onto a social system that remained deeply conflictual. At the heart of his work, he argued, was the recognition that social cohesion is regularly being undermined by the conflict between opposed forces. These forces were often described in highly abstract terms. Coleridge once distinguished between the 'indeterminable, but yet actual, influences of intellect, information [and] prevailing principles' (what we might now call the hegemonic ideology)[138] and 'the regular, definite and legally recognised powers' (established political institutions).[139] He also distinguished between 'latent or dormant power' (which appears to mean the will of God) and 'actual power' (the sources of temporal authority).[140] Yet in his more concrete moments he made it clear that the main responsibility for the threat to social cohesion lay primarily with the growth of capitalism.[141] The problem with the market system, he once wrote, is that it contravenes 'the sacred principle recognised by all laws, human and divine, the principle, indeed, which is the the groundwork of all law and justice, that a person can never become a thing, nor be treated as such without wrong'.[142] The responsibility of literature, in circumstances such as these, is to demonstrate that social unity can only be maintained in spite of, not because of, the commercial forces which dominate the age.

West was not suggesting that Coleridge or any other of the English Romantics had been revolutionary socialists *avant la lettre*. Because Romanticism emerged at a time when a disorganised proletariat was confronted by a powerful alliance between the aristocracy and the industrial middle classes, it was more or less inevitable that its anti-capitalist instincts would be diverted into a series of political cul de sacs.[143] But it is surely clear why West should have perceived so many similarities between Romantic theory and his own contribution to Marxist aesthetics. Where the Romantics were responding to the emergent collectivism of the late Augustan period, West was responding to the emergent collectivism of men like Eliot, Read and Lawrence. Where the Romantics (or at least Coleridge) believed that the purpose of literature is to reflect the organic unity at the heart of society, West proposed that literature's aesthetic power derives from deep feelings of identification which bind the writer to the economic process. And where the Romantics thought that capitalism poses an incalculable threat to social cohesion, West believed that the highest task of literature and literary theory is to hasten the abolition of capitalism and the establishment of a new society in which human solidarity can flourish. However, there is still one question that needs to be answered. To what extent did West convey an accurate impression of Coleridge's ideas? There is a case for saying that his chapter on Coleridge was ultimately vitiated by one serious omission. Although Coleridge's theoretical and critical writings are notoriously digressive, most commentators have agreed that the core of his aesthetic system is the doctrine of imagination outlined in Chapter Thirteen of *Biographia Literaria* (1817). According to Coleridge, the essence of imaginative activity is the attempt to recreate the initial act by which God created the world. Conceived as the driving force behind all genuine poetry, imagination is a 'repetition in the finite mind of the eternal act of creation in the infinite I AM.'[144] Far from being a form which mediates between man and God by evoking the temporal evidence of God's existence, poetry reflects the brief moments in which the poet gropes towards an understanding of the demiurgic powers that resulted in the creation of the universe. I have already suggested that ideas of this sort (that is, ideas which regard the root of creativity as the artist's desire to identify with the mind of God) might well have been the primary influence on West's own understanding of the creative process. The fact that the doctrine of imagination was elided in *Crisis and Criticism*[145] only serves to reinforce this impression – as we have seen, West was the sort of writer who often performed bizarre acts of expurgation on his most powerful influences. Yet the issue of West's fidelity to his sources is not really important. The crucial point about his work on Romanticism is that it represented the most sustained attempt in the 1930s to legitimise Marxist criticism by invoking a non-Marxist theoretical tradition. As we shall see in Section Four, West's taste for non-Marxist ideas was to be of increasing importance as his relationship with the Communist Party became more strained.

3. OPPOSING THE POPULAR FRONT?
WEST'S OTHER WRITINGS FROM THE 1930s

Crisis and Criticism was by no means the only work of Marxist criticism that West published in the 1930s. Apart from contributing the important essay 'On Abstract Criticism' to Betty Rea's symposium *5 on Revolutionary Art*, he also wrote 15 essays for *Left Review*, four essays for *Labour Monthly* and seven articles for the *Daily Worker*.[146] If *Crisis and Criticism* was a largely orthodox book, extending the insights of Soviet theory in innovative directions but rarely seeking to challenge them, much of this other writing served notice that West had already developed doubts about the CPGB's strategic orientation, especially its commitment to the so-called Popular Front strategy. As he later admitted in *One Man in his Time*, West could never quite escape the feeling that 'Popular

Frontism' undermined the very objectives which had brought him into the Party in the first place. By insisting that communists should temporarily subordinate the struggle for socialism to the broader effort to establish a united movement in defence of bourgeois democracy, the CPGB was guilty (or so West believed) of sabotaging the communitarian passions which drove its members forward.

> We reassure those who believe only in bourgeois democracy that the government of the Spanish Republic is not communist. But the movement we ask them to support is directed to a different democracy than theirs. 'We communists', the *Manifesto* said, 'scorn to conceal our aims'. We conceal ours for the sake of unity, and all we achieve is a false unity with Gollancz and the Left Book Club; and by that compromise we take away from our own aim its power to inspire real unity.[147]

When read in the light of passages such as this, several of West's occasional pieces from the 1930s suddenly take on a new significance. Especially important are the essays and reviews in which West expressed an uncompromising critique of several of the literary and artistic groups which communist intellectuals were seeking to entice into the Popular Front. We shall concentrate in what follows on his attacks on (1) progressive Christians, (2) left-wingers in the *Scrutiny* group, (3) the Auden circle, and (4) the surrealist movement. Although West was never explicitly critical of Party policy, it seems clear in retrospect that one of his objectives was to problematise the idea of a Popular Front by attacking nearly all its non-communist supporters. Anxious not to offend against the principles of democratic centralism, it was as if he could only maintain his public support for the Party by channelling his doubts into cultural criticism.

West's first attack on the Christian element in the Popular Front was prompted by two letters by Eric Gill which appeared in *Left Review* in June 1935.[148] Although Gill was a Catholic distributist whose social radicalism owed more to Ruskin, Carlyle and G.K. Chesterton than to any socialist writer, he was nevertheless the most prominent non-Marxist artist associated with the Artists' International Association (AIA).[149] His two letters were originally published in the *Catholic Herald* after the AIA was attacked by one of the paper's critics for disseminating 'Marxist propaganda'. The letters were republished in *Left Review* because they were held to represent 'currents of thought among English intellectuals which ought not to be ignored'.[150] Gill's main concern, in response to the claim that the AIA had corrupted art by linking it with politics, was to defend the idea that great art is necessarily a form of propaganda. If we examine the works of art that have dominated the English imagination, including the Gothic cathedrals of the middle ages and the 'effigies of eminent politicians in Westminster Abbey and

Parliament Square',[151] we find that they all expressed a distinctive view about how society should be organised. If artists abandon social themes and engage only with their personal concerns, they end up producing work that expresses little more than a blasphemous form of 'self-worship'.[152] In order to reinforce his insistence that there is no meaningful distinction between the aesthetic and the political, Gill condemned the prevailing definitions of art for creating the impression that artistic activity is 'performed *in vacuo*'.[153] Instead of limiting our idea of art to such forms as painting, literature and music, we should try to acknowledge that all forms of human labour (including cooking a Christmas pudding and manufacturing a gas oven) encompass the element of creative endeavour that is the hallmark of the artist's sensibility.

West's response to Gill was concerned with what he seemed to regard as the hidden agenda not merely of the two letters but of the entire Christian faction in the Popular Front.[154] Progressive Christians, West implied, devote much of their energy to identifying the assumptions which communism and Christianity have in common, and in so doing risk obscuring the more important assumptions which divide the two ideologies one from another. Gill showed that he was typical of this tendency by implying that Catholic artists and communist artists are ultimately bound together by the 'expression of collective emotion in protest against bourgeois exploitation and individualism'.[155] By emphasising the emotional similarities between the two camps, he was guilty of ignoring the crucial differences in ideology that distinguish Socialist art from devotional art. Whereas Socialist art embodies a Marxist understanding of bourgeois society and emphasises the need for proletarian revolution, Catholic artists are unable to pursue Marxist insights because 'the Holy Roman Catholic and Apostolic Church has declared Socialism incompatible with Catholic piety'.[156] West detected a similar concern to elide the differences between Catholicism and Marxism in Gill's attempts to widen the definition of art. There is much truth in the idea that 'art' and 'craft' are both areas of activity in which human beings can experience aesthetic pleasure; but it is equally true that the artist *directly reflects* social relations (that is, society is one of his manifest subject matters) whereas the craftsman does not. Gill's attempt to conflate art and craft was bound up with his belief that the crucial element in a work of art is not social vision but emotion, and therefore reinforced his dangerous assertion that the cultural politics of catholicism and Marxism are basically the same. At the same time, West pointed out, there is always a danger that an unbalanced concern with the emotional dimension of art will end up inspiring precisely the sort of solipsistic aestheticism that Gill had rightly condemned. West would later explore some similar ideas in his review of *Christianity and the Social Revolution*, the famous symposium from 1935 in which a number of Marxist intellectuals (e.g. John Lewis and W.H. Auden) joined with their Christian counterparts (e.g. John MacMurray and Karl Polanyi) to assess the relationship between their respective creeds.[157]

The small number of Marxists who wrote for *Scrutiny* in the early 1930s had abandoned the journal by the middle of the decade.[158] But *Scrutiny* retained the loyalty of certain intellectuals who aimed to reconcile a Leavisite understanding of cultural history with a commitment to socialist politics. The most important of these was probably L.C. Knights, whose study *Drama and Society in the Age of Jonson* came out in 1937.[159] West's hostile review of this book, strangely entitled 'Ben Jonson was No Sentimentalist' (*Left Review*, September 1937),[160] was another sign of his scant willingness to treat potential allies in the Popular Front with much comradely feeling. Not even mentioning the fact that Knights had a history of activism on the left, West argued that the main purpose of his book was to provide a sketch of Elizabethan and early-Jacobean culture that substantiated the reactionary Leavisite account of how the decencies of pre-modern society had been disastrously overtaken by the barbarism of emergent capitalism. It tried to achieve this (or so the argument went) by portraying Jonson as a dramatist who ruthlessly criticised the new market order by invoking the luminous standards of feudal Britain: 'His [i.e. Knights's] main conclusion is that the dramatists brought to bear on the significant economic developments of their time...a traditional morality inherited from the Middle Ages.'[161] By portraying pre-modern England as a lost paradise of civilised values, Knights was guilty of grossly idealising feudal society and creating the impression that a return to the 'small community' was modern culture's 'only hope'.[162] West's response to all this was to reject the idea that Jonson had ever been quite the hard-line traditionalist whom Knights described. Although many of Jonson's plays are critical of capitalism, they also embody a Renaissance man's optimism about the creativity, energy and grandeur which commerce brings in its wake.[163] One of the best examples of this self-divided approach to Elizabethan society is found in *Volpone*. When Volpone disguises himself as a dying man in order to wheedle presents out of credulous visitors who hope to inherit his wealth, he is undoubtedly intended to satirise the dishonesty on which the free market is based. But Jonson portrays him with such humour and affection that he simultaneously strikes us as a powerful model of personal dynamism. Referring to the scene in which Volpone bursts out laughing at the spectacle of an old man's avarice, West wrote that 'Its mood seems to me to be not the steady recognition of human limitations, based on the traditional morality of "the mean", but the laughter of a young man at the decrepitude of age; and beneath the laughter, the *memento mori*, not of Catholicism, but of the Renaissance.'[164] Other examples of the loveable capitalist rogue in Jonson's plays are the two 'swindlers' in *The*

Alchemist, who go conspicuously unpunished in spite of their 'jolly' commercial misdemeanours. Nor was it the case that characters who portrayed the feudal virtues were always portrayed in a favourable light. Although Justice Overdo is resolved to expose the 'enormities of the age' in *Bartholomew Fair*, he is thwarted by the 'discovery that his own wife has been recruited by a pimp and become "a twelvepenny lady"'.[165] If Jonson felt a keen regret at the passing of the feudal age, West implied, he also knew that capitalism was simply too progressive for the clock to be turned back.

Knights felt sufficiently traduced by West to send a brief letter of response to *Left Review*, published under the title 'Mr. Knights Replies to Alick West' in October 1937.[166] Denying that he had either romanticised the middle ages or failed to recognise the combination of modern and pre-modern elements in Jonson's work, Knights nevertheless argued that a Jonsonian attempt to assess the present by the standards of the past was potentially of great importance to left politics. It is perfectly true, he acknowledged, that the establishment of a socialist society is now 'necessary and desirable': 'I hope Mr. West didn't think me a Distributist.'[167] Yet socialists need to recognise that the danger of alienation is likely to exist in any large-scale industrial society, whether it be capitalist or socialist. There is always the possibility that the individual will be so overwhelmed by the realities of mass organisation that he loses his capacity to establish deep human relationships. It is in this context that the example of the small communities of the past can be of such value, since it serves to remind us of the sort of face-to-face relationships in which intimacy can flourish. The culture of the past can best be 'possess[ed]' through the medium of 'great literature', so long as the reader exercises enough 'sensitiveness' and 'critical ability'.[168] Although these arguments were reminiscent of A.L. Morton's earlier attempt to reconcile Leavisism with Marxism (see Chapter One), they appear to have made little impact on West. He never replied to Knights's letter.

Although the writers who belonged to the so-called 'Auden group' were among the most prestigious participants in the Popular Front, their work was not always received with enthusiasm by the CPGB's intellectuals. At various times in the 1930s it was either attacked or damned with faint praise by the likes of Edgell Rickword, Montagu Slater and Christopher Caudwell. The distinctive feature of West's critique of the Auden group, which he outlined in a brief but highly compressed review of Rex Warner's novel *The Wild Goose Chase* (*Left Review*, November 1937),[169] was that it primarily focused on the group's use of form.[170] Anxious that they should play their part in mobilising their readers against fascism and the threat of war, Auden and his associates had repeatedly employed the conventions of the parable in their efforts to imbue modern literature with an element of political didacticism. Yet the implicit point of West's piece was that the parable is basically unsuited to the effective dissemination of revolutionary ideas. *The Wild Goose Chase* is chiefly the story of George, a young man from The Convent (symbolising ' "culture" in very inverted commas'),[171] as he cycles through the countryside in search of the Wild Goose. The main action occurs when George falls in with the 'country people' and leads their revolution against the Town (seen by West as 'representing imperialism'). While accepting that Warner was 'a good story-teller with a good story',[172] West pointed to several reasons why his novel failed to work as a manual of revolution. In the first place, presumably because parables tend to eschew the accumulation of detail in favour of rapid narration, there is no account of the process by which the country people were politicised. This has the effect of limiting our identification with the revolutionary cause: 'Because the work necessary to get the country people on the march is not felt, the reader's sense of their achievement is lessened.'[173] There is similar evidence of oversimplification in Warner's portrayal of George's personality. As a product of the Convent with its pretentious traditions of 'arty talk', George is making a complete break with his past when he resolves to go over to the side of the people. But Warner presents his conversion as if it were simply a matter of abandoning one set of convictions and acquiring another, conveying none of the ambivalence that necessarily acts as a brake on revolutionary enthusiasms. At the same time there is a curious tension between George's motivations and those of the people he leads. When the people revolt against the domination of the Town, they do so in order to create a society based on communitarian feeling. Their leader, on the other hand, only becomes a revolutionary because he sees it as an opportunity to catch up with the Wild Goose, which West interprets as the symbol of an essentially *private* quest for spiritual transcendence. The implication was that Warner's main achievement was to write a novel which exemplified the intelligentsia's continuing difficulties in identifying with the cause of revolution. If residues of bourgeois ideology remain in his work, it is probably (or so West hinted) because his conscious intentions were subtly undermined by the historical associations that parable brings in its wake. Noting that the particular idea of transcendence to which Warner subscribed was one which emphasised the benefits of irrationalism and 'the delightful blood', West observed that *The Wild Goose Chase* was sometimes reminiscent of 'D.H. Lawrence at his worst'.[174] The parable, he seemed to suggest, is simply too bound up with the reactionary wing of English modernism to be appropriated for radical ends.

If West was comparatively unusual in attacking radical Christians and left-wing members of the *Scrutiny* group (though not so unusual in attacking the Auden circle), he was only one of a large number of communist writers who inveighed against surrealism. The disdain in which surrealism was held by orthodox communists, regardless of the fact that it was ostensibly part of the cultural wing of the Popular Front, can probably be explained in two ways: first, it was an unambiguously modernist form and therefore offended against one of the main tenets of Soviet theory; and second, there were occasions in the 1930s when British surrealists seemed close to displacing the communists as the leading force in radical culture, especially in the field of the visual arts.[175] The latter point is especially worth emphasising. Shortly after the Artists' International Association (AIA) adopted a Popular Front policy in 1936, its communist stalwarts probably came to seem hidebound and dogmatic in comparison to new surrealist recruits such as Herbert Read, Roland Penrose and Roger Roughton. The communist counter-attack was led by West, Anthony Blunt and A.L. Lloyd,[176] each of whom wrote fiercely critical articles at about the time of the famous surrealist exhibition at the New Burlington Galleries in July 1936. The surprising things about West's article, entitled 'Surréalisme in Literature' and published in Left Review in July 1936, were its complete disregard of surrealist doctrine and its uncharacteristic note of aesthetic puritanism. According to André Breton, surrealism's undisputed leader and chief ideologue, the main purpose of a surrealist work is to synthesise external reality with the 'superior reality' of dreams.[177] Starting from a broadly Freudian perspective, he insisted that dreams are essentially an expression of the 'marvellous' desires which human beings have banished from their conscious minds but which will nevertheless form the basis of everyday life in the revolutionary societies of the future. By employing techniques such as 'automatism', defined by Breton as the '[the dictation of] thought…in the absence of any control exercised by reason, exempt from any aesthetic or moral concern',[178] the surrealist artist can begin the process of reintegrating unconscious desire into our waking lives, thereby placing a strain on the capitalist system that will ultimately result in revolution. Although West would go some way towards engaging with these ideas in his rather inadequate remarks on surrealism in Crisis and Criticism (see the previous section), he chose to ignore them altogether in his article in Left Review, claiming instead that surrealism should basically be understood as a systematic attempt to undermine the stability of language. By forcing words into highly unusual contexts (West quoted Breton's observation that '…a nose is perfectly in its place beside an armchair'),[179] surrealists aim to defamiliarise language by weakening the established relationships between its denotative and connotative levels. This subversion of language is seen as the first stage in the subversion of the wider society. Having misrepresented the surrealist project in this way, West appeared to suggest that its radical credentials were suspect for at least three reasons: (1) the surrealists had tended in practice to substitute the subversion of language for the subversion of the existing order,[180] (2) there is necessarily an element of hidden conservatism in the surrealist outlook, since it is only possible to generate verbal shocks if settled linguistic conventions remain in place,[181] and (3) the 'senselessness' which surrealists regard as a precursor of revolution is more accurately seen as a cause of political impotence: 'If a man is consciously fighting the bourgeois world with all his power and not only with the liberty of words, he either never experiences that sudden sense of disorientation, or he considers it a momentary weakness, not the highest vision.'[182] West was presumably unaware that some of these arguments could also be deployed against aspects of the Soviet orthodoxy, specifically the view that progressive art should combine an element of 'realism' with an element of 'revolutionary romanticism'. By attacking the idea that the denotative and connotative levels of language should be prised apart by using words in unusual contexts, he was effectively stipulating that art should be realistic and nothing else, since (as even a cursory inspection of Soviet art makes clear) it is impossible to portray the future in a utopian light without undermining the connotations of a whole host of everyday words. Although the theoretical sections of *Crisis and Criticism* show that West was actually quite comfortable with the visionary dimension of Socialist Realism, it is noticeable that a preference for realism over revolutionary romanticism was a pronounced feature of a great deal of English communist art in the 1930s. This is especially true of much of the work produced by the visual artists associated with the AIA, including the so-called 'Three Jameses' (James Boswell, James Fitton and James Holland),[183] many of whom favoured dour portraits of industrial decline and domestic poverty to upbeat anticipations of the socialist future. There is perhaps a sense in which the suspicion of utopian art was an unintended consequence of the orthodox attack on modernism. Because many of the leading modernists strove to draw attention to the 'non-mimetic' status of language, there were probably a lot of communists who believed that any departure from naturalism represented a grave act of compromise with the doctrines of the cultural enemy. This feeling was perhaps especially strong in England, where the anti-mimetic theories of the modernists had already been described as immoral and irreligious by writers such as G.K. Chesterton. Another important cause of the unspoken hostility to utopianism might well have been the continued influence of nonconformity, whose attack on the aesthetic indulgences of High Anglicanism was part of a wider ethic of self-denial to which many British communists remained wholly committed.

The other area in which West showed considerable independence of mind during the 1930s was the analysis of mass culture, though in this case his unorthodoxy had nothing to do with his suspicion of the Popular Front. The serious investigation of forms such as film, popular literature and advertising had scarcely got underway by the time West was writing and tended to be dominated either by members of the *Scrutiny* right (e.g. F.R. and Q.D. Leavis) or mavericks on the non-communist left (e.g. George Orwell and C.L.R. James). There was nevertheless a series of stock arguments to which communist writers tended to adhere. The basic assumption was that the popular arts are condemned to ideological and aesthetic poverty by the economic circumstances in which they are produced. Because the culture industries are owned by very rich men whose main concern is to safeguard the capitalist system, it follows (or so the argument went) that its products will primarily be concerned to brainwash their target audience into an acceptance of the existing order.[184] West implicitly challenged this view in a two-part essay on detective fiction which appeared in 1938 in the January and February editions of *Left Review*.[185] Perhaps conscious of the way that a critical attitude towards mass culture can easily spill over into a condemnation of the masses themselves (a point that would later be emphasised by Raymond Williams in the famous 'Conclusion' to *Culture and Society*),[186] he portrayed detective fiction as a complex and rewarding form that should not simply be dismissed as what Philip Henderson had called 'pabulum for the lower middle classes'.[187] Tracing the origins of the form to the late-eighteenth century, his first strategy was to characterise the detective novel as an outgrowth of the technical developments which revolutionised 'serious' fiction at about this time. More precisely, he claimed that detective fiction had been made possible by (1) the abandonment of first-person forms of narration by novelists such as Samuel Richardson, which enabled the writer to create an air of mystery about the ultimate fate of his characters,[188] (2) the 'new quality of suspense' engendered by the '...alternation between depths of boredom and heights of ecstasy' in the work of such poets as Pope and Young,[189] and (3) the appearance in Horace Walpole's novels of an emphasis on 'serendipity' (that is, the ability to make far-reaching deductions on the basis of scanty physical evidence) which allowed detectives to be portrayed as prodigies of intellectual flair.[190] Having thus linked this ostensibly 'mass' form to the sphere of high culture, West then went on to demonstrate that its political sympathies had undergone important shifts in the course of the previous 150 years, disproving the idea that it had always been a straightforward conveyor belt of bourgeois ideology. In many of the detective novels that appeared in the period between about 1790 and 1820, notably William Godwin's *Caleb Williams* (which H.N. Brailsford has described as a dramatisation of the anarchist doctrines contained in Godwin's *Political Justice*),[191] there is a persistent tendency to portray the criminal as superior to, though not usually victorious over, the detective who seeks to bring him to justice. Far from being a knee-jerk expression of the desire for law and order, these novels 'share in the confused revolutionary and reactionary feeling of the romantic movement.'[192] It was only during the 60 or so years after 1840 that detective fiction expressed a more conservative outlook, with writers such as Collins, Poe and Doyle seeking to palliate the 'bourgeois fear of revolution'[193] by writing books in which the detective was always an object of veneration. However, more recent work (such as that of Chesterton and Edgar Wallace) once again displays an element of ideological ambiguity. Although the modern detective novel is by no means as seditious as its Godwinian forebear, it does tend to create the impression that criminals are more interesting than the forces of law and order. This is partly because the criminal characters are often swathed in mystery until their guilt is established in the closing stages of the narrative, but also because the individual detective has been superseded by 'mass investigation by the police.'[194] Moreover, it is difficult to admire the police when the majority of crimes are now solved not with the aid of deductive ingenuity but through chance: '...a man repairing telephone wires happens to look into the window of a room where the criminals think themselves unobserved, and his evidence gives a vital clue.'[195] In a passage of great subtlety, West seemed to suggest that this emphasis on chance also conveys a valuable lesson about the relationship between human beings and their environment. By drawing our attention to the inability of the criminal to erase all evidence of his guilt from the areas in which he moves, it serves to remind us of the overwhelming importance of environmental influences on the human condition – in this sense, West implied, modern detective fiction is a thoroughly *materialist* form.[196] On the other hand, in order to prove the point that the modern thriller writer is not so much a thoroughgoing subversive as someone who seeks a productive tension between hegemonic and emergent forms of thinking, the essay concluded on a rather pessimistic note:

> The social function of the detective story now is not so much to relieve and reassure, as in the middle period, as to divert a confused desire for social change into safe channels. It keeps it concerned with crime, and with a police force that has nothing to do but arrest murderers, never makes a baton charge, and always wins, because the very structure of society is its ally and the enemy of the criminal. Ignoring the real function of the law and the police, and the real struggle against them, detective stories are finally dull, even though one cannot lay them down...But the significance of the shift of interest back to the criminal must also be kept in mind. Millions read the detective story, not because they are decaying with capitalism, but because they want to live and don't know how. The detective story is also a sign of revolt against decaying capitalism, while endeavouring to make that revolt harmless.[197]

As we saw in Section One, West first became interested in popular fiction after reading John Buchan's *The Three Hostages* in a Swiss sanatorium and finding that he was able to 'live vicariously' through the central character.[198] The most surprising omission from "The Detective Story" was therefore any consideration of the 'subject positions' which popular fiction offers to its readers. If West had paid closer attention to his experiences in Switzerland, he might have concluded that elite novels seek to hold the reader at a distance whereas popular narratives invite his close involvement – an insight which Pierre Bourdieu has taken up in his seminal account of the cultural relationship between 'dominator' and 'dominated' classes. A more serious defect with West's essay is its failure to attempt a theoretical explanation for the polysemic characteristics which it implicitly ascribes to the popular arts. The outlines of a theoretical account of polysemy were nevertheless sketched by the poet Charles Madge, one of the two founders of the Mass Observation movement, in a remarkable essay which possibly influenced West's account of detective fiction (it appeared a few months earlier) and which certainly proved that West was not alone among British communists in his opposition to mass-culture theory. In 'Press, Radio, and Social Consciousness', published in *Left Review* in June 1937 and later included in C. Day Lewis's symposium *The Mind in Chains*, Madge argued that modern popular culture is a sort of hybrid formation which balances the ideas of the ruling class against the sensibility of the masses. On the one hand, or so Madge argued, it is obviously the case that elite domination of the culture industry means that films, newspapers and radio programmes are all saturated in bourgeois ideology. However, the need to secure a large audience means that the same forms must also reflect what Madge called 'mass-wish'[199] – that is, the lurid complex of erotic and violent impulses which exists just below the surface of the working-class mind in most industrial societies. The presence of this 'sensational and vulgar' material tends to compromise the media's ability to win support for the existing order, and for three reasons. In the first place, Madge argued, it is impossible for the conventions of bourgeois society to seem quite so natural and ineluctable when refracted through the 'queer poetry'[200] of media sensationalism: 'The newspaper-reader is temporarily in the state described by Coleridge as a "willing suspension of disbelief"…it means that we regard it [i.e. the news] not as objective fact, but as poetic fact. It also means that when we stop reading it, the news ceases to have the same hard, inescapable force that the objective fact has; it becomes a poetic memory, affecting our feelings but not our actions.'[201] By appealing to desires which would otherwise have remained suppressed, the media also creates 'formidable psychological reserves of dissatisfaction'[202] which must one day subvert the ethic of self-denial on which capitalism depends. Moreover, in its endless search for new sources of sensationalism, it frequently dredges up material which serves only to portray the existing system in a more morbid light than ever: 'Even when ostensibly benevolent, capitalism cannot help being the bearer of evils; and even when, vice versa, it is simply out to win a big circulation, the newspaper cannot help being a good influence, and eventually an influence subversive of itself. Though it may carry political propaganda and exploiter-class advertisement on one page, on another it will print the story of a starving unemployed family, simply because it is a good human story. The class-basis of the proprietors determines the politics; the class-basis of the readers at least helps to determine the rest of the news.'[203] If the work of writers such as West and Madge scarcely represents the last word on the nature of popular culture, it is nevertheless of some historical importance because it tends to undermine one of the founding myths of Cultural Studies. Nearly everyone who has surveyed the history of Cultural Studies insists that radical writing on popular culture was almost entirely crude and reductive in the period up to the 1970s,[204] not least because it portrayed the working-class audience as 'passive dupes'[205] in the face of an all powerful culture industry. What a reading of West and Madge demonstrates is that ideas about polysemy and active consumption long predate the attempts of such writers as Stuart Hall, Dick Hebdige and John Fiske to dismantle the assumptions of mass-culture theory.[206]

4. THE CAUTIOUS DISSIDENT: WEST IN THE POST-WAR YEARS

West's suspicion of communist policy did not come to an end once the era of 'Popular Frontism' had passed. For much of the period between the defeat of fascism in 1945 and his death in 1972, West seems to have been convinced that the CPGB had shamelessly abandoned the revolutionary policy of its early years for a 'reformist' accommodation with British capitalism. Although he chose not to leave the Party and continued serving as an English teacher at the Soviet Embassy in London throughout the 1940s and 1950s,[207] he now saw himself as something of a communist dissident. If much of his work in this period was shaped by the cultural orthodoxies that had taken root in the 1930s, parts of it can also be interpreted as a coded (and sometimes not so coded) attack on the whole direction in which world communism was heading. The purpose of this final section is to illustrate this reading of West's later work by glancing at: (1) the essays from the period 1947-1951 which contrasted an instrumental approach to culture with the idea of cultural revolution, (2) the attempt in *The Mountain in the Sunlight* and elsewhere to recuperate writers whom communist orthodoxy had condemned, and (3) the rejection in the late essay on D.H. Lawrence of the entrenched belief in cultural crisis.

The political developments to which West was responding can be summarised fairly briefly. After the dissolution of the Comintern in 1943, the world communist movement adopted a "polycentric" strategy which recognised that socialist revolutions would invariably take different forms in different parts of the world. The strategy developed by the CPGB had a number of interlocking components. Rejecting the insurrectionary approach of its 1935 programme *For Soviet Britain*, the Party argued that the 'all-round strengthening of Socialism and the tendencies and developments towards it throughout the world'[208] (i.e. the Soviet colonisation of Eastern Europe) now made it possible for socialism to be established in Britain through a combination of parliamentary action and extra-parliamentary mass mobilisation. It was envisaged that the transition to a new society would be overseen by a radical Labour administration, buoyed by the support of a disciplined phalanx of communist MPs. Since it was not considered possible to abolish capitalism immediately, it was argued that the first duty of such a government would be the implementation of an intermediate programme to shift Britain in a radical direction. The policies at the core of the intermediate programme were those of extended public ownership, demand management, decolonisation, planned trade and constitutional reform. This vision of how socialism might be achieved, first outlined by Harry Pollitt in his book *Looking Ahead* (1947), formed the basis of the various editions of the CPGB's programme *The British Road to Socialism* (*BRS*) that were published between 1951 and 1977.[209]

Although the *BRS* paid lip-service to the ideal of moving beyond capitalism, there were many British communists who feared that an intermediate programme of left-Keynesian reforms now represented the height of the CPGB's ambitions. The thing that distinguished West from other critics was that he interpreted the 'surrender to reformism' in predominantly cultural terms.[210] The communist movement had compromised its revolutionary principles, he now believed, because it had lost sight of the profound cultural transformations which the establishment of a socialist society would make possible. Communists had largely forgotten that the primary goal of socialism is to eliminate individualism and restructure human consciousness along communitarian lines, and had therefore lost their main motivation for abolishing capitalism rather than merely reforming it. Matters were compounded by the fact that communists were so intent on seeing culture as an *instrumental* force (that is, as something which could be utilised in the struggle against existing social relations) that they had become virtually incapable of seeing it as an end-in-itself:

At the school [a CPGB school on culture in 1953][211] I said that culture... heightens our consciousness of the world we want to win and our energy to win it. In this sense it was true that culture is a weapon in the fight for socialism. But the truth depended on the recognition of the greater truth that socialism is a weapon in the fight for culture. For our final aim was not the establishment of a political and economic structure, but the heightening of human life. Without this recognition, the slogan became a perversion of the truth, since it degraded culture into a means to a political end. It seemed to me that the political end itself was thereby perverted, and that this was the weakness of *The British Road to Socialism*...At a meeting of the Cultural Committee, of which I was a member, I said that since the enrichment of human culture was our final aim, the Cultural Committee should have equal standing with the Political Committee in the leadership of the Party. The proposal met with no response, and I said no more.[212]

Having failed to win the support of his colleagues, West proceeded to give disguised expression to his dissatisfaction with the Party's approach to culture in a series of articles between 1947 and 1953. In 'New People', published in *Communist Review* in November 1947, he gave his fullest account of his vision of socialist culture, stressing that the communitarian outlook of the classless societies of the future would provide the basis for a 'promethean' transformation of human nature.[213] In 'Marxism and Culture', written for an edition of *The Modern Quarterly* which marked the 100th anniversary of the first publication of the *Communist Manifesto* (Spring 1948), he ostensibly celebrated the cultural achievements of the British revolutionary movement over the course of the previous century; but actually poured implicit scorn on its instrumental approach to culture by identifying only five writers whose work had contributed to the struggle against capitalism. Significantly, none of them was a Socialist Realist – not even Robert Tressell rated a mention.[214] In one article, a brief contribution to the so-called 'Caudwell Discussion' in *The Modern Quarterly*, West even came close to making an outright attack on the Party leadership. The Caudwell Discussion was the vigorous debate about the merits of Christopher Caudwell's work which erupted when Lawrence and Wishart issued a new edition of *Illusion and Reality* in 1948.[215] It was essentially a symptom of the disagreements that undermined the Party's cultural work in the period after the war. In 1947, shortly after Andrei Zhdanov had reaffirmed the main principles of Soviet cultural policy in a series of hardline speeches, the CPGB established a National Cultural Committee (NCC) with the aim of co-ordinating the work of its growing body of artists, writers and musicians. Although the NCC contained a number of the Party's most talented intellectuals, including Jack Lindsay, Margot Heinemann and West himself, it was dominated by machine politicians whose understanding of radical cultural activity was quite different from that of the creative workers they sought to instruct. Whereas the group of intellectuals around the journal *Our Time* had been trying to create a progressive cultural movement along pluralist lines, eschewing the opposition between modernism and Socialist Realism which had dominated the work of the 1930s, NCC members such as Emile Burns and Sam Aaronovitch insisted on a rigid adherence to the Zhdanovist orthodoxy.[216] When Maurice Cornforth initiated the Caudwell Discussion with a fiercely critical article in the Winter 1950-51 edition of *The Modern Quarterly*,[217] he was widely seen as opening a new front in the undeclared war between the two groups. As one of the most zealous members of the CPGB's Executive Committee, a position he held in spite of his philosophical brilliance (he had once been a research student of Wittgenstein's), Cornforth was perceived as the voice of Party authority whose demolition of Caudwell was effectively a warning to Party 'creatives' that they should toe the NCC line. This alone was enough to ensure that Caudwell's work was defended by over twenty of his admirers, including Arnold Kettle, Alan Bush and George Thomson. In his original article, probably one of the crudest he ever wrote, Cornforth made four main allegations against Caudwell's writings: (1) they misunderstand the Marxist account of social change,[218] (2) their sub-Freudian account of the clash between 'instinct' and 'environment' conveys an excessively static conception of human nature,[219] (3) they fail to specify the precise relationship between literature and society,[220] and (4) their analysis of cultural crisis is too one-sided, relying too heavily on the so-called 'bourgeois illusion of freedom' as an explanation for the spiritual poverty of the modern age.[221] However, when West responded to the article, he focused on a passage in which Cornforth berated Caudwell for referring to mankind's 'inner energy'.[222] According to West, Cornforth's dislike of the phrase implied a disabling nervousness in the face of the human capacity for aesthetic experience: 'Maurice Cornforth appears to me to fight shy of subjective activity.'[223] West's immediate intention was to show that the reference to 'inner energy' was consistent with a Marxist account of human personality; but, if one reads these passages in the light of his wider critique of world communism, it becomes clear that what he probably had in mind was the failure of senior communists such as Cornforth to remain inspired by a non-rational vision of the communitarian culture of the future. There was also a passage in which West seemed to signal an important development in his understanding of literature. By denying the reality of 'inner energy', Cornforth was failing to recognise that literature not only reflects the present but also anticipates the future: '…poetry…makes an image of the future reality which through the exercise of his labour-power and – in class society – through the class struggle he [i.e. man] will bring into existence.'[224] As we have already seen, West had argued in *Crisis and Criticism* that a writer can only harness the aesthetic potential of literary form if he evokes the progressive elements in a given social formation; but he now seemed to be claiming that one of the main functions of literature is to evoke the mental atmosphere (to use George Orwell's phrase) of the society that will come into existence when the progressive elements in the present have worked their revolutionary course. He would make it clear over the next 20 years that what he particularly valued in literature was its vision of human community.[225]

After his contribution to the Caudwell Discussion appeared in *The Modern Quarterly* in the Summer of 1951, West remained comparatively silent until the publication of his third book in 1958.[226] Consisting of five closely observed chapters on the work of Bunyan, Defoe, Walter Pater, Oscar Wilde, J.B. Priestley and Jack Lindsay, *The Mountain in the Sunlight* could easily be mistaken for a more or less orthodox attempt to identify a radical tradition in English literature. Once again, however, it is more accurately regarded as a further veiled attack on the cultural politics of international communism. In the brief theoretical remarks which opened the book, some of them stimulated by F.R. Leavis's hostile response to Jack Lindsay's study of Bunyan (see Chapter Six),[227] West made it clear that he now regarded literature as one of the most powerful transmitters of precisely the sort of communitarian consciousness which official communism had evacuated from the revolutionary process. Since all societies have their roots in close co-operation between disparate individuals, it follows (or so West implied) that a yearning for the 'unity of free and conscious association'[228] is one of the most enduring of human impulses. The sense of heightened fraternity is at its greatest at moments of social crisis and revolution, regardless of the fact that they rarely result in a sustained increase in social cohesion. Moreover, in a passage which closely resembled the discussion of aesthetic disinterestedness in *Crisis and Criticism*, West argued that the intensity with which literature evokes the feeling of fraternity stimulates our desire to 'transform the given unity of conflict into the voluntary unity of brotherhood'[229] – that is, to create a society in which human solidarity is the overarching concern. In defiance of the crudely instrumental approach of the Soviet theorists, West was therefore suggesting that literature not only precipitates the desire for change but also fixes our attention on the transformation in consciousness which a socialist society must ultimately seek to establish. What had merely been implied in the essay on Caudwell was now made explicit.

The other noticeably unorthodox element in *The Mountain in the Sunlight* was West's attempt, specifically in his comments on Walter Pater, to identify a strain of radicalism in the work of writers whom communists had usually dismissed as worthless.[230] As we have seen in Chapter Two, the emergence of the art-for-art's sake movement in the late-nineteenth century was regarded by the Soviet theorists at the moment at which bourgeois culture began its long slide towards the outright decadence of modernism. As the author of *Historical Studies in the Renaissance* (1873), famously described by Oscar Wilde as the 'golden book' of British aestheticism, Pater might have seemed an unlikely candidate for inclusion in the radical tradition, but West insisted that his work nevertheless contained 'contradiction[s]'[231] which made it 'worth study.'[232] The main argument was that Pater, in spite of his reputation for rejecting 'society' in favour of a private world of aesthetic sensation, often practised a form of historical criticism which forced the reader's attention away from aesthetic artefacts towards the social forces which help to shape them. For instance, one of Pater's main themes was the emergence in modern art of what he called a 'relative spirit' – that is, the recognition that moral and aesthetic standards are historically variable.[233] After claiming that the relative spirit first found expression in the thirteenth-century cathedral of Amiens, he argued that it arose more or less naturally from the quasi-communist outlook of the people who built it: '...those lay schools of art, with their communistic sentiment, to which in the thirteenth century the greatest episcopal builders must needs resort, would in the natural course of things tend towards naturalism.'[234] In passages such as these, West seemed to be saying, Pater not only belied his aestheticism but implicity defined communism as the modern period's most vital cultural trend.

The publication of *The Mountain in the Sunlight* was followed by another period of comparative silence, punctuated only by occasional essays on such figures as John Osborne, Swift, Adam Ferguson and Kafka.[235] The final stage of West's career effectively began with the publication of *One Man in his Time* in 1969. The distinguishing feature of this stage, which lasted until West's death in 1972, was the willingness to move beyond what Lenin might have called the 'Aesopian' language of his earlier works to outright criticism of the world communist movement. The main themes of *One Man in his Time* were those which have framed my presentation of West's work throughout this chapter. Because the world communist movement has forgotten the yearning for community which attracts people to communism in the first place, it has created a situation in which the depredations of Stalinism become inevitable. The only solution is a reassertion of the communitarian vision by the movement as a whole. The point was underscored in an important companion piece to *One Man and his Time* which West prepared in the last months of his life. In this piece, an essay on D.H. Lawrence that was eventually published in a posthumous edition of *Crisis and Criticism* issued by Lawrence and Wishart in 1975, West at last expressed his doubts about the critical orthodoxies which had shaped the communist view of art since the 1930s.[236] At one level, 'D.H. Lawrence' simply extended the arguments about the communitarian dimension of literature which West had put forward in *The Mountain in the Sunlight*. In language of a surprisingly Heideggerian nature, West argued that the 'impulse' of Lawrence's work was 'the consciousness of our participation in being'[237] – that is, the consciousness that human beings are bound both to each other and to their physical environment by indestructible ties. Convinced that our grip on 'being' has been loosened by the destruction of settled rural communities, Lawrence devoted much of his work (or so West argued) to analysing the inadequate means by which human beings have tried to sustain a sense of community in the industrial age. Sexual love, religion and the nuclear family all come in for attack in novels such as *Sons and Lovers* and *The Rainbow*.[238] What was genuinely new about West's essay was his attempt to discuss this communitarian understanding of literature in relation to the entrenched communist belief in cultural crisis. If a writer like Lawrence was able to give such powerful expression to the experience of community, West seemed to be arguing, then the idea that 'bourgeois' culture is mired in crisis is surely false. Interestingly, as if it were only possible to emphasise the sheer unorthodoxy of what he was saying by exposing the weaknesses of Britain's most respected communist critic, he illustrated his argument by pointing to a 'contradiction'[239] which threatens to undermine the theory of cultural crisis developed by Christopher Caudwell. On the one hand, West pointed out, Caudwell dismissed the literature of the modern age because of what he regarded as its excessive individualism. By investing in a 'bourgeois illusion of freedom' which holds that the individual can only achieve personal fulfilment when he is liberated from social ties, most forms of literature since the Renaissance have reflected the 'loneliness' which necessarily occurs when human beings suppress their gregarious instincts.[240] On the other hand, there is also a brief passage in Caudwell's writings which seems to explore a more nuanced view:

> He [Caudwell] says also that the individualism of bourgeois poetry does not express merely the individualism of the particular poet; 'it expresses the collective emotion of its era'. According to this interpretation, bourgeois poetry is not bourgeois in the sense that it speaks only for the bourgeoisie; it is bourgeois in the sense that it is the expression of bourgeois society.[241]

Although these insights go unexplored in Caudwell's writings, West seemed to regard them as a tacit recognition that modern literature is not really in crisis at all. Far from being aesthetically substandard, or so he implied, it is actually one of our most powerful means of dissolving individualism in a radiant vision of community. Once we have absorbed this truth, we can restore literature to the place where it belongs – at the heart of communist politics: 'In literature there is the consciousness of life, and for this reason the revolutionary movement can learn from literature. It has more to learn than it has yet done.'[242] West's essay on Lawrence seems to have received little attention at the time of its publication, nor has it seemed especially significant to subsequent writers.[243] Yet its importance to a history of Marxist criticism in Britain is surely obvious. It marks the moment at which the orthodoxies of the 1930s were finally abandoned by one of their most distinguished exponents.

CHAPTER FOUR

RALPH FOX: POSITIVE HEROISM
IN THE SOCIALIST NOVEL

It is common for Ralph Fox's *The Novel and the People* (1937) to be grouped with Alick West's *Crisis and Criticism* and Christopher Caudwell's *Illusion and Reality* as one of the three founding texts of Marxist literary theory in Britain. Yet the insistence on classifying Fox as a theorist has arguably had a distorting effect on our understanding of his work. Only a handful of writers have devoted more than an odd sentence to *The Novel and the People*, and many of them have focused primarily on Chapter Two ('Marxism and Literature') in which Fox made a rather half-hearted effort to defend the base/superstructure metaphor against charges of reductionism.[1] This obscures the fact that *The Novel and the People* was actually the most *prescriptive* work of Marxist criticism to be published in Britain in the 1930s.[2] Its central argument, implied throughout but never explicitly stated, was that the novel is the literary form which can most easily be adapted to the aesthetic of Socialist Realism. Effectively a form of 'modern epic' in which heroic individuals seek the wholesale transformation of their material circumstances, the novel provides the only setting (or so it was implied) in which the 'positive heroes' demanded by Soviet theory can be convincingly delineated. Fox underscored his case with a dramatic though implicit argument about the danger of fascism. Since the novelist 'expresses his country' more completely than any other artist, his books are often used by foreigners to gauge the spiritual health of the country in which they originate. Because the British novel has undergone a rapid decline in the period since the early nineteenth century, it has played its role in convincing the fascist powers that Britain is little more than a decadent civilisation in need of outside assistance. If the communists fail to resuscitate the novel by transforming it into a vehicle of Socialist Realism, they will therefore have made an inadvertent contribution to strengthening international fascism in its 'drive to war'.[3]

This chapter tries to show that *The Novel and the People* can only be properly understood if Fox's prescriptive intentions are continuously borne in mind. After providing a brief outline of Fox's life, it goes on to examine the following aspects of his theory of the novel: (1) his belief that the novel is best regarded as a 'modern epic', (2) his lengthy account of the development of heroic individualism in the history of the novel, and (3) his proposed solutions to the sort of practical problems which socialist writers invariably face. The final section of the chapter goes beyond *The Novel and the People* and briefly examines some of Fox's other cultural writings from the 1930s. I will make the case that although Fox was ostensibly the most orthodox of British Marxist critics, there were several arguments in his work which were inconsistent not merely with Soviet theory but with the fundamental principles of Marxism itself. This strain of unorthodoxy was undoubtedly the product of many different influences, but chief among them were a number of contemporary trends in non-Marxist cultural theory – especially the sort of liberal humanism associated with writers such as E.M. Forster. In contrast to some of West's writings, which implicitly expressed their author's *conscious* opposition to the direction in which the world communist movement was heading, *The Novel and the People* thus betrayed an element of what can perhaps be called unconscious dissidence. As such, it provided further evidence that the relationship between Soviet and British criticism was rarely one of absolute consonance.

1. GENTLENESS AND HEROISM: A BIOGRAPHICAL SKETCH

There is one theme which tends to crop up time and again in the scanty biographical literature on Ralph Fox.[4] Writers as diverse as Jeremy Hawthorn, Ann Brett-Jones, Alan Munton and Alan Young have all drawn attention to a curious split in Fox's personality. On the one hand, or so it is said, Fox was a sensitive and scholarly man who often behaved uncertainly in his relationships with other people. Writing eight years after his tragic death in the Spanish Civil War, his friend Mulk Raj Anand recalled his 'poet's pale face, his fine nose, delicate lips and gentle grey eyes'[5] – qualities which come across strongly in the photograph of Fox reproduced in his book *The People of the Steppes* (1925). On the other hand, as befits a critic whose main theme was the novel's depiction of personal heroism, Fox seems to have been preoccupied with living a life of action. Far from taking the path of the reclusive scholar or indolent man of letters (and in spite of writing more than ten books in his short life), he spent much of his time travelling to remote countries and wilfully putting himself in dangerous situations. By combining writing and adventure in equal measure, he exemplified the desire of thirties communists to strike a creative balance between 'theory and practice'.

Fox was born in Halifax on 30th March 1900, the son of a senior executive in a local firm of engineers. He received the bulk of his secondary education at Heath Grammar School in Halifax, though in 1916 he transferred to the Sixth Form at Bradford Grammar School in order to study for the Oxford Entrance Exam. He entered Magdalen College, Oxford in January 1919 and received a first-class degree in French in 1922. There is some evidence that his desire for heroism was stimulated (or at least inflamed) by an experience which he shared in common with many of the young writers of his generation – that is, the experience of guilt at being slightly too young to fight in the Great War.[6] Whether or not this is true, the first thing he did after graduating was to serve as a member of a Friends Relief Mission which toured through Central and Southern Russia in 1922. Although his main job was to distribute aid in areas which had been hit by famine during the Civil War, he clearly conceived a deep romantic attachment to the people, landscapes and cultures of Kazakhstan, Mongolia and elsewhere. He seems to have been especially attracted to the USSR's muslim population, which he evoked in darkly mysterious terms in *The People of the Steppes* (an autobiographical account of his trip to Russia) and his first novel *Storming Heaven* (1928):

> Through the blue smoke peered the high cheek-bones of the Kazaks, whose veins held the mingled blood of all the Turko-Mongol peoples, conquerors of the world, shepherds, soldiers, justice-givers to mankind, men who had made Asia in their day. They were like the dreams that an old story brings to birth, like the imaginings that rise from some old inscription found in the waste to bear sole witness to a high glory dead.[7]

Fox was not a member of the Communist Party at the time of his trip to Russia, in spite of the fact that he had begun to call himself a Marxist as early as 1919. There is no agreement in the biographical literature as to precisely when he joined the CPGB. Until recently it was widely supposed that he first became a member in 1926 (perhaps as a result of the General Strike), but his niece Ann Brett-Jones insists that he 'spent many of his evenings on Communist Party matters' as soon as he returned from Russia.[8] It seems probable that Brett-Jones is correct, not least because Fox returned to the USSR in 1925 to work for the Far East section of the Comintern.[9] He would hardly have been entrusted with a position of such importance if he had still been a mere 'fellow traveller'. At any rate, shortly after getting back to London in 1927 (along with his new wife Madge Palmer, whom he met and married in Moscow), Fox began to acquire a reputation as a Marxist literary critic. Most of his early articles on literature were published in the *Sunday Worker*, which served as the main outlet for the views of the National Left Wing Movement between 1925 and 1929. While the *Worker*'s role in the development of Marxist cultural theory was scarcely very important, there is no doubt that its arts page (which Fox oversaw with T.A. Jackson) alerted thousands of working-class readers to the political importance of literature. One of Fox's great strengths as a cultural journalist was his enormous range. Between April 1927 and September 1929 he wrote on about sixty topics for the *Sunday Worker*, ranging from early history ('When and Why Did...Men First Build Ships?') right through to the most recent novels from the Soviet Union.[10] He typified the polymathic ambitions of the Marxist intellectuals of his day.

Perhaps as a consequence of his cultural journalism, Fox spent most of the period between 1930 and 1933 as the English Librarian at the Marx-Engels Institute in Moscow. These were the years in which he began to make a genuine though minor contribution to Marxist scholarship. After helping to prepare scholarly editions of Marx's articles for the *New York Daily Tribune*, he drew on the abundant materials at the Institute to write a series of important works on the history of the socialist tradition. These included *Marx, Engels and Lenin on the Irish Revolution* (1932), *The Class Struggle in Britain in the Epoch of Imperialism* (two volumes, 1933) and *Lenin: A Biography* (1933). His standing in the CPGB seems to have been very high when he left the Institute and returned to Britain in 1933. In rapid succession he was elected onto the Party's Central Committee, became a leading contributor to *Left Review* and the *Daily Worker* (he was responsible for the 'Worker's Notebook' column for a period of about seven months) and travelled throughout Europe to gauge the strength of the anti-fascist struggle. He also became an enthusiastic contributor to the workers' education movement. One female trade-unionist remembered him as a 'sympathetic' teacher whose 'gentleness of character made young people feel at ease with him'.[11] His success in keeping his classes going was not always shared by his Marxist contemporaries.

The events which brought Fox's life to a premature end began to unfold in the Autumn of 1936, when he travelled to Spain to fight on the Republican side in the Civil War. For a brief period he served as a Political Commissar to Number One Company of the International Brigade's British Battalion in Madrigueras. His attitude to the job exemplified the mood of extreme democratic idealism which existed on the Republican side at the beginning of the War. Instead of trying to exercise conventional military authority (a task which clearly ran counter to his nature), Fox treated the volunteers in the British Battalion as equals and sought to win their loyalty by appealing to their political ideals. One of his most important themes was that each member of the International Brigades had to learn to tolerate the eccentricities of everyone else, not least because the anti-Franco army was one of the most authentically multi-national in history.[12] However, when he finally went into battle (as an Assistant Political Commissar with the XIV International Brigade), he acquitted himself with a sort of reckless courage which rapidly curdled into foolish irresponsibility. The journalist Hugh Slater contributed a highly disconcerting account of his death to a memorial volume published in 1937:

> Ralph Fox was with the brigade commander on the road halfway up the hill [the events being described occurred near Andújar in Andalusia] when it became evident that there was an unforeseen possibility of our machine-gunners establishing invaluable positions covering the enemy's right flank. Fox set off running, bending low across some open ground, to organize this manoeuvre. It was a supremely brave thing to do; the bombing and the machine-gun fire were at their most intense, and it was almost certain death for anybody to leave cover. Fox knew this, but he considered it necessary to take the risk.[13]

As Munton and Young have argued, Fox's behaviour in the last few minutes of his life was so reckless that '...it is difficult to resist the conclusion that he threw his life away.'[14] Perhaps his yearning for heroism, combined with residual feelings of guilt about his failure to fight in the Great War, had finally induced a mood of almost suicidal selflessness. He died on January 2nd 1937 at the age of 36. His publishers had begun to distribute the first copies of *The Novel and the People* about a week earlier. Its emphasis on the positive hero must have brought considerable anguish to those of his friends and admirers who were aware of the circumstances of his death.

2. FROM ODYSSEUS TO ROBINSON CRUSOE: 'THE NOVEL AS EPIC'

Although the Soviet theorists regarded a 'positive hero' as an indispensable feature of any work of Socialist Realism (see Chapter Two), they never defined their idea of positive heroism with much clarity. It is nevertheless clear that the majority of Soviet writers employed a similar formula when devising their main characters. Positioned at the centre of the narrative and offered to the reader as a possible object of identification (or at least of emulation), the positive hero was the character in the book who displayed the greatest ability to contribute to the onward march of social progress. If the steel had to be tempered (as in the famous novel by Nikolai Ostrovsky) or some other aspect of 'socialist reconstruction' had to be pushed forward, it was invariably the positive hero who precipitated the necessary changes. He was portrayed as being at once entirely representative and dauntingly exceptional. On the one hand he embodied all the most obvious characteristics of the particular social group (usually the working class) whose collective power the artist wished to affirm; yet he also prefigured the well-nigh superhuman level of personal development which the individual might be able to achieve in the communist society of the future. He was someone for whom manual labour and intellectual activity were largely continuous, not the paired terms of an irreconcilable contradiction. With his synoptic or 'totalising' grasp of the various elements in the existing historical conjuncture, he gestured towards an age in which common ownership and material abundance would enable the individual to experiment with a diverse range of economic roles. The outward signs of his distinction were usually a statuesque physique and a permanent expression of serene thoughtfulness, the latter suggesting that his formidable resources of intellect were continuously being applied to the business of creating a better future.

The central assumption of *The Novel and the People* was that the hero in the 'bourgeois' novel provides a basis on which the socialist writer can profitably build when shaping the positive heroes in his own work. Starting from the premise that the novel is merely the latest in a long line of 'epic' forms, Fox developed his case by comparing the typical protagonist in a Greek epic (specifically the *Odyssey*) with the typical protagonist in the realist novels of the seventeenth, eighteenth and nineteenth Centuries (specifically *Robinson Crusoe*).[15] In a passage which recalled Marx's famous comments on classical culture in the 'Introduction' to the *Grundrisse* (1857),[16] Fox argued that the Greek epic was the product of a society in which 'the individual does not feel himself in opposition to the collective, any more than he feels himself in conflict with nature'.[17] Odysseus was not an isolated being but the exemplar of a wider community. Denied any sense of history by the unchanging structures of the classical economy, his aim was to restore a former state of equilibrium (in Tzvetan Todorov's phrase) rather than establish new conditions of existence. Taking it for granted that the natural world was the creation of divine forces which required continual propitiation, he aspired only to a *modus vivendi* with his environment and not to a position of dominance. The protagonist in the bourgeois novel is driven by more ambitious goals. Estranged from both his environment and the rest of humanity by the reified structures of the market, Robinson Crusoe (who played the same exemplary role in *The Novel and the People* as in the work of the early economists)[18] pursued his quest for redemption without reference to the needs of other people. He did so not merely by seeking a wholesale transformation of his personal circumstances, thereby reflecting the sudden awareness of historical change which capitalism had brought in its wake, but also by bending nature to his own will:

The novel deals with the individual, it is the epic of the struggle of the individual against society, against nature, and it could only develop in a society where the balance between man and society was lost, where man was at war with his fellows or with nature...Robinson renounced the past and prepared to make his own history, he was the new man who was ready to command nature, his enemy. Robinson's world is a real world, described with a vivid and understanding feeling for the value of material things.[19]

Although the bourgeois hero's individualism is simply too uncompromising to be consistent with the socialist vision, his belief in the possibility of wholesale change through the domination of nature makes him a valuable model (or so Fox implied) for the positive hero in the revolutionary novel. The socialist writer can also learn from the great technical strides which bourgeois writers have taken in their portrayal of character. Whereas the pre-modern epic was concerned only with actions, the greatest novelists have always combined a record of action with a detailed account of their characters' inner lives. Paraphrasing E.M. Forster, whose influential distinction between 'flat' and 'round' characters had been drawn as recently as 1927, Fox argued that 'the great feature which distinguishes the novel from the other arts is that it has the power to make the secret life visible'.[20] It is especially important that the socialist writer should be able to move easily between the subjective and objective aspects of human experience, since this is the only (or at least the best) way of showing that history is pushed forward by conscious choices and not by a purely mechanical response to external stimuli.[21]

The most surprising thing about this account of positive heroism was that it tended to create the impression that the relationship between the individual and his environment is essentially a *contingent* one. By portraying the hero as someone who invariably succeeds in shaping his world according to his own desires, Fox seemed to be reinforcing the belief that human nature is ultimately free from the influence of material circumstances.[22] It goes without saying that this belief is wholly at odds with the materialist axioms of Marxism. The unorthodox cast of Fox's remarks was perhaps a symptom of the difficulties which Marxists faced in adapting 'bourgeois' forms to the aesthetic of Socialist Realism. If we accept the argument that the novel had its roots in the rise of individualism, then it follows (or so a number of literary theorists have insisted) that its characters will usually be portrayed as 'floating free' from the environments in which they live. When Fox failed to indicate how a socialist novel might illustrate the opposing belief that the relationship between human beings and their environment is actually a *mutually constitutive* one, he was therefore illustrating the virtual impossibility of making a clean break with an entire aesthetic tradition. Because E.M. Forster was one of the few theorists of the novel whom Fox invoked in the whole of his book, there is a case for saying that it was Forster's *Aspects of the Novel* (1928) that was primarily responsible for reinforcing an orthodox (or non-Marxist) idea of characterisation in Fox's mind.[23] The two chapters on character in *Aspects of the Novel* are best regarded as a disguised expression of the longing for human intimacy which permeated the Bloomsbury group, and which received its clearest formulation in Forster's famous remark that '...if I had to choose between betraying my country and betraying my friend, I hope I should have the guts to betray my country'.[24] Their main argument is that the novel serves to deepen our sensivity to other people by revealing everything about its characters' inner lives. Our relationship with real people is invariably compromised by our ignorance of what they are truly thinking and feeling; but when we read a novel we are able to achieve total communion with someone else's (admittedly fictional) soul. What is sometimes overlooked is that Forster used these ideas about character to justify the novelist's habit of driving a wedge between the individual and his environment. Quoting the 'interesting and sensitive French critic who writes under the name of Alain' (Emile Auguste Chartier), Forster insisted that a form which specialises in the depiction of inner states will invariably prefer the 'pure passions' to 'external causes' as an explanation for its characters' behaviour.[25] The famous distinction between flat and round characters also played its part in advancing this argument. Recognising that the unfettered portrayal of character is usually impossible, not least because a novel's protagonists are invariably put at the disposal of the developing narrative, Forster argued that the great virtue of round characters (i.e. many-sided characters who surprise the reader with their continuous transformations) is that they are sufficiently unpredictable to lessen the sense of disjuncture when they are placed in incongruous circumstances. The whole emphasis is on the novelist *protecting* his characters from environments that might undermine their aesthetic integrity. To understand why Fox should have taken these ideas so seriously (assuming he did), we have to remember that Forster was an enthusiastic supporter of the Popular Front who enjoyed considerable popularity among communists in the 1930s. It seems to have been common for Marxist intellectuals to approach his work less critically than that of other liberal writers, even if this resulted (as it clearly did in the case of the *Novel and the People*) in a willingness to absorb perspectives whose relationship to 'orthodox' Marxism was at best tenuous. It was one of the more curious ways in which the fringes of the liberal tradition served to domesticate British Marxism during the years of the Popular Front.[26]

3. A BRIEF HISTORY OF THE HEROIC INDIVIDUAL

Fox supplemented his theoretical observations with a brief account of the novel's historical development. Although this part of *The Novel and the People* has sometimes been dismissed as a mosaic of random observations which gives 'very little information' and 'nothing for the student to underline',[27] its primary purpose was to indicate the ways that the portrayal of the heroic individual has altered over the course of the last 400 years. Fox was especially concerned with (1) the invention of the heroic individual in the seventeenth century, (2) the politicisation of the novel in the eighteenth century, (3) the slow decline of the novel in the nineteenth century, and (4) the 'death of the hero' in the modernist novel.

The core assumption was that the pioneering work of Rabelais and Cervantes provided the novel with two archetypes of heroic individualism which later writers would aim to synthesise.[28] In *Gargantua and Pantagruel* (a book which has exercised an enduring fascination for Marxist critics)[29] Rabelais created heroes who derived an explosive energy from their immensely permissive attitude towards physical pleasure. Driven forward by the injunction 'Do what you will!', the Rabelaisian hero bludgeons his world into submission by indulging his appetite for food, drink and sex. The role of Cervantes was to provide the novel with a sort of countervailing refinement. Don Quixote's most important characteristics are a subtle line in irony (which he uses to distance himself from his world) combined with the ability to enter into deep personal relationships. When Rabelais' elemental power was synthesised with Cervantes' more rarefied form of subversion, the great age of the heroic individual was born.[30] Both writers also went a long way towards breaking down the barriers between poetry and prose, not least in the way that they endowed their characters with a sort of visionary lustre. Nor has their work ever been bettered: 'They were universal geniuses and no work equal in stature to theirs has since been written in that variegated prose fiction which we call the novel.'[31] They owed their pre-eminence not merely to the fact that they lived through the most dramatic years in the transition from feudalism to capitalism (a characteristic they shared with Shakespeare) but also to their status as 'men of action' who had first-hand experience of the individual's transformative power.[32]

Having located the origins of heroic individualism in the work of Rabelais and Cervantes, Fox shifted his attention to English fiction in the first half of the eighteenth century. He argued that the flowering of the novel at this time was made possible by the emergence of a materialist strain of English philosophy in the wake of the English Revolution, especially in the work of John Locke.[33] Since the novel is primarily concerned with the struggle between the individual and his environment, it tends to be the case that the novelist will gain much inspiration from a philosophy which emphasises the dependence of mind on matter. Fox reserved most of his praise for Henry Fielding, whom he seemed to regard as the first writer to appreciate the *political* significance of the novel. At one level, this was a matter both of content and of Fielding's involvement in practical politics.[34] At a time when primitive accumulation had reached new heights of barbarism and English imperialism was intensifying its 'horrible' and 'immoral' offensive against India, Fielding cast a disenchanted eye across the behaviour of the ruling class and made a powerful case for the rights of the individual in respect of the state. Yet Fox also seemed to believe that there was a political dimension to Fielding's experiments with form, specifically his habit of interspersing his narratives with lengthy chunks of discursive prose. Although this aspect of Fielding's work has been extensively criticised, especially by exponents of art-for-art's-sake who regard it as a violation of aesthetic autonomy, it should actually be seen as part of a laudable effort to transform the novel into an instrument of social agitation by imbuing it with an element of propagandist clarity: '…if the sermons were all removed, the social criticism would be there just the same, implicit in his story, and we should have lost some of the best essays in the English language.'[35] The implication was that Fielding had been so inspired by the dynamism of his heroes, especially Jonathan Wild, that he had effectively tried to harness it to everyday political affairs.[36] On a less positive note, Fox also recognised that the eighteenth century novel was partly responsible for triggering a long-term decline of the form, not least in the way that it frequently upset the balance between subjective and objective elements that had characterised the work of Rabelais and Cervantes. Whereas Fielding, Daniel Defoe and Tobias Smollett were largely interested in writing about events, Laurence Sterne and Samuel Richardson tended to ignore events altogether and retreat into the inner lives of their characters. In the case of Sterne, whose *Tristram Shandy* was described as the first 'relativist' novel, the preoccupation with subjective experience led not merely to an attack on linear narrative but also to a view of the world which was practically solipsistic. If the work of Fielding and other 'objective' novelists had been inspired by philosophical materialism, then the Sternean school of fiction derived much of its credibility from the idealism of Bishop Berkeley.[37]

Notwithstanding the many Marxist critics who have approached the greatest achievements of nineteenth century fiction in a spirit of reverence, Fox saw the period after 1750 as one of prolonged decline in which the novel gradually lost most of its epic qualities. The hallmark of the decline was a failure of nerve in describing the human environment. Instead of portraying an awful reality which the heroic individual proceeded to transfigure, the majority of novelists now depicted the world in a curiously *sanitised* fashion. Fox argued that the process of decline took very different forms in England and France. There were several ways in which the English novelists of the nineteenth century fell short of the realistic standards that Fielding had set them. Charles Dickens engaged with the most important contemporary realities but viewed them through a prism of sentimentality.[38] Jane Austen took a more 'critical' and 'ironical' approach but described only those portions of reality (notably the 'world of sheltered gentility') which she personally found congenial.[39] And Walter Scott, despite his unrivalled ability to evoke fundamental historical changes, 'ran away from it [i.e. contemporary Britain] altogether into the idealized and romanticized past'.[40] The immediate cause of what Fox called 'The Victorian Retreat' was the transformation of the British economy which had occurred since the 1750s. Once the Industrial Revolution had polluted the landscape, widened inequalities of wealth and transformed labour itself into a commodity, it was simply too painful for the bourgeois novelist to devise stark environments for his heroes to overcome.[41] The situation was made worse by the growth of a mass audience for the novel, epitomised by the thousands of ordinary Britons who rushed to buy the monthly instalments of Dickens's stories as they appeared in periodicals. Whereas the Augustan novelists were able to write freely about British society because they knew that their work would only be read by an educated elite, their Victorian counterparts (anxious to retain their class privileges) were crippled by the assumption that there are 'things you cannot say to the masses if you are a decent middle-class man'.[42] Although Fox was quick to repudiate the idea that the growth of a mass reading public must invariably lead to the decline of artistic standards, there were still passages ('...[the novelist] was to be tormented by his *public*, by that great mass of the semi-educated lower middle-class or self-educated working class')[43] in which he came perilously close to sounding like a sort of poor man's Ortega y Gasset, bemoaning the effects of mass literacy on the pristine culture of the bourgeoisie.

The situation in France was somewhat different. The French Revolution, combined with the revolutionary wars that succeeded it, made it virtually impossible for French novelists to either ignore or sanitise contemporary affairs for much of the period between 1789 and 1848. Reality had to be directly faced. The result was that novels of genius were still being produced in France at the time when Scott, Austen and Dickens were squandering Fielding's legacy in Britain.[44] In a passage that quoted extensively from Engels's famous argument about Realism in his 1888 letter to Margaret Harkness, Fox wrote enthusiastically about Balzac's ability to transcend his royalist sympathies and produce a rich portrait of the inevitable triumph of the bourgeois revolution: '...Balzac was politically a legitimist; his great work [i.e. the *Comédie Humaine*] is a constant elegy unto the irreparable decay of good society; his sympathy is with the class that is doomed to extinction. But for all that his satire is never more cutting, his irony more biting than when he sets in motion the very men and women with whom he sympathizes most deeply – the nobles. And the only men of whom he speaks with undisguised admiration are his bitterest political antagonists, the Republican heroes of the Cloître-Saint-Merri, the men who at that time (1830-36), were indeed the representatives of the popular masses.'[45] But the impact of the French Revolution on the development of the novel was by no means wholly positive. The events of 1789 might indeed have created the passionate interest in politics that allowed Balzac to do his greatest work; but they also released the sort of utopian expectations which can never be realised in the confines of bourgeois society. This engendered a creeping sense of disillusionment which imbued most of the French novelists who came to prominence after 1848 with a deep loathing of all forms of politics.[46] The representative figure in this regard was Gustave Flaubert, whom Georg Lukács famously condemned as the assassin of authentic realism in a series of books which provide an interesting point of comparison to *The Novel and the People*. Fox implied that Flaubert's emphasis on the 'god-like objectivity of the artist' was actually intended to prepare the way for a complete break with the representation of external reality. By conceiving of reality in essentially synchronic terms, Flaubert was able to exorcise his hatred of society by portraying it as if it were 'frozen and static'.[47] In turn this enabled him to hold out the prospect that the novel of the future would be 'a book about nothing, a book without any attachment to the external world, which would support itself by the inner strength of its style, just as the world supports itself in the air without being held up'.[48] If none of Flaubert's contemporaries managed to create a self-reflexive novel along exactly these lines, some of them (notably Edmond de Goncourt and Joris-Karl Huysmans) nevertheless succeeded in producing books whose sole concern was the artist's interior life. The vogue for the novel of sensibility was reinforced by at least three wider developments: first, the acceleration of rationalisation in industry, which encouraged the artist to regard himself as a narrow specialist in the area of consciousness;[49] second, the emergence of psychoanalysis;[50] and third, the pre-eminence throughout the nineteenth century of Idealist philosophers such as Kant and Hegel.[51]

The crisis of the novel eventually came to a head (or so Fox argued) in the early decades of the twentieth century. The most striking characteristic of modernist fiction was its complete abandonment of the hero, even the sort of etiolated hero who featured in *Madame Bovary*.[52] English modernists have contented themselves either with self-regarding displays of knowledge (Huxley), poetic evocations of passing moods (Lawrence) or demeaning efforts to capture the lavatorial underbelly of 'ordinary' life (Joyce).[53] It is hardly surprising that bourgeois novelists have failed to respond imaginatively to the heroic example of the modern proletariat, since the cultural gap between the upper and lower classes is still too vast to allow mutual comprehension. But neither has any novelist tried to base his protagonists on the scientists and 'millionaire ruler[s]' who represent the last vestiges of heroism in bourgeois culture.[54] The 'death of the hero' has not only been precipitated by the internal history of the novel, but also (and more importantly) by the state of capitalist society as it approaches its final crisis. If a modern novelist tried to depict the external world being transformed by an individual hero, he would risk drawing attention to the only change which can now rescue society from its present state of decay: the overthrow of capitalism. It follows that the epic qualities of the novel can only be revived by the growing number of writers who have made a conscious commitment to Socialist Realism.

There are a number of obvious objections to this brisk survey of the novel's history. For every hero or heroine who combines the physical exuberance of Rabelais with a Cervantean gift for irony, there are several who clearly do not. Most of Fox's attempts to locate individual novels in their historical context were marred by reductionism. His hostility to contemporary writing was rooted in an absurd conflation of modernism and moral degeneracy. But the most surprising thing about the historical section of *The Novel and the People* was the way it departed from orthodox accounts of the cultural crisis of capitalism. Although the Soviet theorists had argued that capitalism was inimical to cultural excellence from the moment of its inception, they also insisted that the degeneration of the arts only truly began in the second half of the nineteenth century.[55] They also took it for granted that the greatest bourgeois novels were written in the first 50 years of the nineteenth century, specifically by pioneering realists such as Balzac and Tolstoy. When Georg Lukács tried to develop these assumptions in his work on the realist tradition, he famously identified 1848 as the moment at which the 'totalising' ambitions of realism were superseded by naturalism's obsession with surface appearances. As we have seen, Fox also traced the onset of decadence to the period after 1848 in his account of the *French* novel, yet in his much longer account of the literature of his own country he took the unprecedented step of arguing that the novel had reached its apogee in the Augustan period and subsequently gone into a slow decline. There was nothing specifically un-Marxist about this preference for Defoe and Fielding over Scott and Dickens; but it was so much in conflict with the norm as to require some explanation. We can speculate that there were perhaps two main reasons for Fox's lack of orthodoxy. The first might well have been a desire to parallel the anachronistic tastes of many working-class readers. As Jonathan Rose has pointed out in his pathbreaking study *The Intellectual Life of the British Working Classes* (2001), it has been common for the reading habits of working people to lag several decades behind those of their middle-class counterparts, which presumably meant that there were still thousands of proletarian autodidacts in the inter-war period who revered eighteenth-century literature but knew practically nothing about the writers who came afterwards. This extreme literary conservatism had its roots in a nexus of economic, commercial and educational circumstances. Because the majority of working-class readers were simply too poor to buy new books in the period before the emergence of paperbacks, they often had to limit themselves to what they could find in second-hand bookshops and market stalls. Even in the 1920s and 1930s, when Victorian literature was no longer modish enough to escape being discarded by fashion-conscious readers, it seems likely that it was still far easier to locate second-hand copies of the Augustan and Victorian classics than anything more recent. Although many publishers issued cheap editions of the classics in an attempt to cater to the mass market, they were limited in their freedom of manoeuvre by the 1911 Act which stipulated that a book only went out of copyright after its author had been dead for 50 years. Rose illustrates the effect of this Act by pointing out that J.M. Dent was only able to issue an Everyman edition of *Middlemarch* in 1930, a full 58 years after its original date of publication. There is also evidence that teachers in working-class schools were often wedded to a self-constructed canon that rarely went 'beyond the Victorians'.[56] Since Fox was deeply involved in the working-class education movement,[57] it seems reasonable to suggest that his account of the novel's history was intended to appeal (consciously or otherwise) to the literary prejudices of his target audience. Nor is it fanciful to suggest that his perception of proletarian tastes owed a disproportionate amount to the example of one man. The great T.A. Jackson (1879-1956) was one of the few working-class intellectuals to exercise much influence in the CPGB in the 1930s, and many of his middle-class counterparts would presumably have derived their understanding of proletarian autodidacticism primarily from him.[58] Jackson was a famously erudite man whose literary tastes ranged from Homer to Sholokhov (though not to Huxley, Mauriac or Joyce); but he always insisted that 'Mentally speaking I date from the early 18th Century'.[59] His love of Augustan culture could be traced to his early experiences of reading the books in his childhood home: 'A fine set of Pope, an odd volume or two of the *Spectator*, a *Robinson Crusoe*, Pope's translation of Homer, and a copy of *Paradise Lost.*'[60] In his essays on eighteenth-century fiction he praised Defoe for supporting the rights of Dissenters; described Swift as a stalwart supporter of Irish nationalism; commended Sterne's ability to disregard class distinctions in his judgements on human character; took pleasure in Fielding's relaxed approach to personal morality (especially in the light of Richardson's puritanism) and discerned a Hogarthian facility in Smollett's evocations of 'low life'.[61] In 1937 he was one of the three men who edited the tribute volume *Ralph Fox: A Writer in Arms* after Fox was killed in Spain.[62] If his 'talent for preaching Marxism in Burkean prose' (Rose's suggestive description)[63] was not the source of Fox's conviction that the working class was more at home in the Age of Enlightenment than in the twentieth century, it surely did a great deal to reinforce it.

Another possible explanation for Fox's unorthodox approach to the history of the novel was the presumably unconscious influence of D.H. Lawrence. Although Lawrence was categorised in *The Novel and the People* as one of the modernist writers most responsible for the 'death of the hero', I would suggest that Fox gave the impression in many sections of the book that he was effectively *recasting* Lawrence's ideas in Marxist terms. There are two ways in particular in which the work of these otherwise very different writers seemed to coincide. As we have already seen, Fox believed that the hero of a novel should ideally be a person of great physical bearing who succeeds in achieving a wholesale transformation of his material circumstances. In his essay 'Why the Novel Matters' (posthumously published in 1936, the year in which *The Novel and the People* was being written), Lawrence argued a similar case while advancing his distinctive ideas about the relationship between sexuality and human evolution. Lawrence believed that there is something intrinsic to the narrative form which forces novelists to invent characters who live in a continuous state of 'flow and change'. The novel is therefore full of people who call on every last ounce of *physical* vitality in order to cope with the flux of their everyday existence: '…my body, me alive, *knows*, and knows intensely. And as for the sum of all knowledge, it can't be anything more than an accumulation of all the things I know in the body…Let us learn from the novel. In the novel, the characters can do nothing but *live*.'[64] By forging a close association in the reader's mind between bodily health and the possibility of change, the novel goes a long way to reminding us of the crucial role of sexuality in the process of human evolution. It can thus be regarded as the most 'moral' of literary forms. The other area in which there are clear parallels between Lawrence and Fox is the analysis of cultural crisis. Both men seemed to regard the decline of the arts as the consequence of an unwillingness to confront unpleasant or disconcerting physical realities. Fox argued that the onset of industrialism made it too unpleasant for novelists to depict undesirable material circumstances, thereby depriving the hero of the impetus he required to demonstrate his genius for self-transformation. Similarly, Lawrence put the blame for falling artistic standards on a certain squeamishness about the human body. In his great essay 'Introduction to his Paintings', written at the instigation of P.R. Stephensen in 1929, he effectively argued that the problem with modern culture is that artists are so neurotic about sex that they no longer portray the body in appropriate physical detail. Moreover, he agreed with

Fox that the novel degenerated sharply after the eighteenth century. Whereas Fielding, Swift and Smollett retained an earthy concern with physiological processes, the romantics ushered in an era in which 'physical consciousness gives a last song in Burns, then is dead'.[65] This preference for the eighteenth century was continued in Lawrence's comments about painting. The works of 'Watteau, Ingres, Poussin and Chardin have some real imaginative glow';[66] but the English landscape painters tried completely to banish human beings from the work of art ('...landscape is always waiting for something to occupy it')[67] while the main objective of the modern abstractionists is to sever the last ties between painting and physical reality. It is perfectly possible that the parallels between the critical ideas of Lawrence and Fox were purely coincidental; but several admiring references to Lawrence in *The Novel and the People* suggest that Fox was familiar with far more of his work than might otherwise be supposed. Ostensibly committed to the orthodox view that Lawrence was little more than a reactionary modernist, he nevertheless described *Sons and Lovers* and *The Rainbow* as a 'brilliant beginning' and applied the adjectives 'strange, beautiful and mystical' to the poems and stories.[68] He also emphasised the fact that Lawrence was one of the few successful English writers to emerge from the working class.[69] This suggests that the influence of Lawrence on Fox was probably direct.

4. PROBLEMS OF REVOLUTIONARY FICTION

The account of Socialist Realism that brought *The Novel and the People* to its conclusion was the longest piece of prescriptive writing to be produced by a British communist in the 1930s. Acknowledging that Socialist Realism was still in its infancy and that no writer (with the partial exceptions of Mikhail Sholokhov, André Malraux and Ralph Bates) had so far managed to apply its principles with complete success, Fox made a brief attempt to list the characteristics which a revolutionary novel might ideally possess.[70] Its primary goal would be to revive the sort of totalising grasp of history that Fielding had introduced into the novel, presumably by focusing on the transition from capitalism to socialism and the various stages in the development of post-capitalist society. Social change would be analysed and not merely described, with the aim of laying bare the 'essence' (i.e. the fundamental political significance) of any given character or situation. The narrative would pivot around the activities of a positive hero, usually a member of the working class, portrayed as a representative of his wider social group. And as much importance would be attached to the inner lives of the characters as to the structure of 'external' events, since this is the best way of showing how human personality is shaped by (and in turn shapes) material circumstances.[71] If these remarks were uncharacteristically vague, it was probably because Fox was less interested in defining the ideal work of Socialist Realism than in confronting the difficulties which prevent it being written. There are two main problems, he seemed to imply, which have prevented the socialist novel from achieving the epic qualities of its bourgeois predecessor. The first is the tendency of socialist writers to overcompensate for the individualist bias of earlier novelists. Aware that the ultimate goal of their work is to steer the working class towards a revolutionary perspective, they have too often treated their characters as if they were merely ciphers of Marxist ideology and not unique individuals with distinctive characteristics and ambiguous motivations.[72] This failure of characterisation has been compounded, secondly, by the dominant stereotypes of working-class life.[73] Unable wholly to abandon the prejudice that working people have been condemned to a position of social inferiority by a tendency to behave passively, it is unsurprising that socialist writers have never created the sort of vibrant proletarian characters who can function credibly as makers of history.

Much of *The Novel and the People* was devoted to a consideration of how these difficulties could be overcome. It is especially important (or so the argument went) that the revolutionary novelist should not allow 'tendentious' writing to spill over into outright propaganda. Quoting again from Engels's letter to Margaret Harkness, Fox insisted that a novel's message must 'never obtrude…it should appear quite naturally from the circumstances and the characters themselves'.[74] If the writer surrenders to the temptation to 'preach' his socialist message, he will end up creating characters who seem more like walking megaphones than authentic human beings: 'It is only too easy to substitute lay figures for men and women, sets of opinions for flesh and blood, "heroes" and "villains" in the abstract for real people tortured by doubts, old allegiances, traditions and loyalties, but to do this is not to write a novel.'[75] However, it is essential that the injunction to create complex characters should not be taken too far. While the novelist should undoubtedly portray the feelings of ambivalence which afflict the individual at times of great social upheaval, he must also leave the reader in no doubt that his revolutionary heroes are steadfast in their commitment to change. There should, in particular, be no contradiction between the hero's political vision and the quality of his sensibility. He should always be endowed with a poet's capacity to derive inspiration from his everyday life, since a sustained attachment to the 'poetry of revolution' can only be nurtured by a continuous supply of 'earthly satisfaction'.[76] The novelist should also make it clear that the hero's militant outlook is all of a piece with the traditions of his native country. Invoking the examples of Zachariah Coleman (the protagonist of Mark Rutherford's *The Revolution in Tanner's Lane*) and Tyl Ulenspiegel (Charles de Coster's hero in *The Legend of Tyl Ulenspiegel*), Fox noted that both characters are continually related back to the revolutionary traditions of England and Belgium respectively. Coleman is portrayed as the successor to the Puritans, the Wesleyan miners, the Luddites and the Chartists; whereas Ulenspiegel seems to share many of his characteristics with the subversive characters who are dotted through the folklore of Flanders.[77] The importance that Fox attached to this strategy reflected the depth of his commitment to the central strand in the cultural politics of the Popular Front, namely the attempt to prove that each country possessed radical traditions which had prepared the ground for the emergence of modern communism.[78]

If revolutionary novelists wish to have plausible models on which to base their leading characters, Fox went on to argue, they should open their eyes to the many cases of real-life heroism that the communist movement has inspired. His argument seems to have been influenced by a speech on the role of the positive hero which Georgi Dimitrov delivered to the Soviet Writers' Union in 1935.[79] Speaking two years after his famous acquittal in Nazi Germany on charges of burning down the Reichstag, Dimitrov had a more instrumental idea of positive heroism than the one explored at the Soviet Writers' Congress in 1934. Whereas Bukharin and his colleagues regarded the positive hero as a means of prefiguring the transformations of human nature that would allegedly occur in a communist society, Dimitrov saw him more as a device for sucking readers into the plot (and hence the book's ideological universe) by providing them with a potent object of identification and emulation. He also made an important point about the way that novelists should present their characters. Perhaps influenced by the growing interest in structuralist narratology among a number of Soviet intellectuals, he argued that the novelist should always aim to foreground the hero's positive qualities by counterposing them against the 'negative' traits of a less-principled character. Having made these general observations, he then asked why no revolutionary novelist had so far recognised the dramatic potential of his own story: 'I may be permitted to express a certain astonishment that this Leipzig trial, this enormous collection of material, invaluable stock-in-trade of revolutionary practice and thought, has not been studied or utilized.'[80] Fox responded to the challenge by trying to imagine a novel in which Dimitrov was the central character. He implied that the great merit of Dimitrov's story was that it exemplified the sort of dramatic reversal of fortune that often defines the contours of an epic narrative. At the beginning, taken into custody for a crime they never committed, the main suspects were reduced to a state of whimpering degradation by the brutality of their gaolers. It was only Dimitrov who saw the experience as a test of his spiritual and intellectual resources. In the months leading up to his trial he acquired a detailed knowledge of German law, improved his command of German in order to represent himself in court, surreptitiously informed foreign communists about his imprisonment and strengthened his 'mastery of life' by immersing himself in Shakespearean texts. The trial itself provided an extraordinary example of the inversion of established hierarchies (to use Bakhtin's phrase) in which Dimitrov humiliated the Nazi prosecutors and provoked Herman Goering into shouting 'Wait until I get you out of the power of this court!'[81] If Fox made a strong case for seeing the Leipzig trial as what Samuel Hynes has called the 'scenario for a strong political novel',[82] it was nevertheless surprising that he seemed to regard Dimitrov more as an isolated colossus than as a 'type' of the revolutionary workers:

> After the trial the three Bulgarian prisoners met in a common cell for the first time and Dimitrov summed up the struggle they had made. "There were four of us, Communists – four armed fighters. Torgler is a deserter, for he threw down his rifle and ran from the field of battle. You two did not throw down your rifles, you remained in position, but you did not shoot, and I had to shoot alone all the time." He shot alone, but his fire was strong enough to subdue the enemy's and finally to rout him.[83]

More surprising than Fox's strictures against preaching in the novel were his extended remarks on the appropriate use of language. 'The art of writing good prose', he insisted, 'is largely the lost one of calling things by their right names',[84] by which he appeared to mean that writers must strive at all times to employ language that is both immediately comprehensible and free of unnecessary ambiguities. If this was simply a partial restatement of the Soviet emphasis on the unity of form and content, it was nevertheless linked to a much more unorthodox claim about the inherent superiority of plebeian speech. In any society that is divided into classes, Fox appeared to argue, it is likely to be the common people who employ language most clearly and expressively. Since productive activity depends on their ability to co-ordinate the efforts of large numbers of individuals, they must go out of their way to ensure that each sentence conveys a precise and immediate impression of their intentions. By contrast, the language of the ruling class is constantly being robbed of clarity by the need to obscure the true nature of an unjust social order. In a passage that might well have influenced the thesis of George Orwell's great essay 'Politics and the English Language' (1946),[85] Fox observed that 'the evolution of our language has been towards this bloodless, blameless ideal of the BBC, an evolution conditioned by the fear of the truth of life that is the most striking feature of the intellectual existence of our class society'.[86] The purity of plebeian speech, he went on to argue, has tended to ensure that the greatest works of English literature owe a considerable stylistic debt to the language of ordinary people. Literary historians have obscured this fact by emphasising the influence of the King James Bible, but the point which needs to be grasped is that the style of the King James Bible was itself based on the 'ordinary speech' of the Elizabethan masses.[87] By insisting that socialist writers should also resort to everyday language in an effort to achieve the necessary degree of clarity, Fox was not merely engaging in proletarian one-upmanship (important though this was) but also seeking a solution to the cardinal problems of portraying the positive hero. Because working-class habits of speech are shaped by a predominantly *active* relationship to external reality, it therefore follows (this at least was the implication) that their use in the novel will galvanise the writer into creating characters who completely lack the passivity that is wrongly attributed to the proletarian way of life. Although Fox recognised that the language of the British workers had lost some of its lustre in the early decades of the twentieth century, he nevertheless emphasised that sources of linguistic renewal could be detected in some unlikely places. At a time when the left (as well as some sections of the right) were beginning to condemn American popular culture as a synthetic and demobilising imposition on the 'authentic' culture of the masses,[88] Fox endorsed the 'living style' which he encountered in the work of the 'hard-boiled' American novelists. Another model of stylistic virility was provided by Rudyard Kipling, whose reactionary politics could not conceal the fact that he was 'soaked...in the folk speech of England and America'.[89]

Fox's defence of proletarian language was perhaps derived from a controversy that had blown up among Marxist critics earlier in the decade. Shortly after the British Section of the Writers' International was established in 1934, a number of sympathetic writers, critics and academics were asked to comment on its founding statement in *Left Review*.[90] The most vigorous intervention was made by the novelist Alec Brown, formerly one of the main contributors to *The Calendar of Modern Letters*, who addressed the issue of how revolutionary literature could be made more appealing to working people. Nearly every important writer in the English tradition, with 'rare' exceptions such as Bunyan and Defoe, had alienated ordinary readers by employing the incomprehensible 'jargon' of the ruling class. If socialist writers were to stand a better chance of communicating with their target audience, they had no choice but to turn their backs on the example of the English canon and submit to 'the proletarianisation of our actual language'.[91] Brown summarised his proposal in three upper-case slogans which have since become synonymous with the worst excesses of Stalinist aesthetics:

LITERARY ENGLISH FROM CAXTON TO US IS AN ARTIFICIAL JARGON OF THE RULING CLASS; WRITTEN ENGLISH BEGINS WITH US.

WE ARE REVOLUTIONARY WORKING-CLASS WRITERS; WE HAVE GOT TO MAKE USE OF THE LIVING LANGUAGE OF OUR CLASS.

ALLUSIVE WRITING IS CLIQUE WRITING: WE ARE NOT A CLIQUE.[92]

These startling sentiments were endorsed in a much more thoughtful essay by J.M. Hay (March 1935), whose ideas about proletarian language were often identical to those that subsequently featured in *The Novel and the People*. Hay argued that the most important lesson which the writer can learn from working people is that meaning is more clearly conveyed by concrete words than by abstract ones. Concrete words predominate in everyday speech for broadly economic reasons, and evince a polysemic quality that tends to make them inherently poetic: 'The concrete word is rooted deep in the practical acts of everyday life and has, because of its practical roots, developed a wide range of secondary associations which give it colour and psychological force.'[93] But Hay also recognised that Brown was being too simplistic in assuming that proletarian language could be straightforwardly adapted for use in the novel. The problem with everyday speech, he implied, is that it lacks the grammatical resources which allow complex thoughts to be easily expressed. The true goal of the socialist writer is thus to combine a proletarian vocabulary with the complex structures that only exist in great works of literature. Brown's ideas received a much more scornful response from other contributors to the debate. Douglas Garman and Montagu Slater attacked Brown for advocating the rejection of the entire literary tradition, with Garman (Brown's former editor at *The Calendar of Modern Letters*) suggesting that the function of the revolutionary critic is to use Marxism to explain the literature of the past and thereby render it useful to a new generation.[94] Hugh MacDiarmid argued that any attempt to proletarianise language would end up reinforcing the terrible linguistic deprivation which capitalism imposes on ordinary people, and that the true aim of revolutionary art is to employ the 'entire jargon…of Marxism' to raise the workers to a new cultural level.[95] Lewis Grassic Gibbon, writing in the month before his untimely death, insisted that membership of the Writers' International should only be open to 'revolutionists' who 'have done work of definite and recognized literary value'.[96] If Fox's version of linguistic fundamentalism escaped such criticism, it was probably because the publication of *The Novel and the People* coincided almost exactly with his death in Spain. He was now a martyr to be honoured; not a promising critic whose work was up for debate.

Nevertheless, there are two aspects of the prescriptive sections of *The Novel and the People* which require further comment. The first is Fox's insistence that the socialist writer should eschew deliberately 'tendentious' writing in favour of a more balanced survey of social realities. Although Fox invoked Engels's letter to Margaret Harkness in support of this position (he could also have invoked the similar letter of 1888 to Minna Kautsky),[97] it is clear that his hostility to tendentiousness differed from that of Engels in significant ways. When Engels advised radical writers to avoid approaching the novel as if it were merely an instrument of propaganda, he did so because he believed that a less hectoring approach would have a beneficial effect on the quality of their work. In the first place, he argued, it would ensure that socialist novels were primarily concerned with exploring the deficiencies of the existing system, not to sketching speculative portraits of the socialist future. This would have the effect of drawing in readers who were open to a critique of capitalism but not yet convinced that an alternative system was feasible. Secondly, an absence of tendentiousness would prevent writers from imbuing their socialist characters with an unrealistic degree of moral or intellectual virtue. Yet the obvious point about *The Novel and the People* was that it openly advocated the very things which Engels found distasteful, especially in its insistence that the main duty of Socialist Realism is to show positive heroes ushering in the new revolutionary age. As writers such as Phil Watson have implied, it is tempting to argue that Fox's opposition to tendentiousness was more a matter of strategy than aesthetics.[98] Quietly appalled by the increasingly totalitarian nature of Soviet cultural politics, perhaps he was trying (or so the suggestion goes) to register an implicit critique of an overbearing system that imposed intolerable restrictions on freedom of speech in its efforts to ensure that the Party line was correctly transmitted. If this is true, it means that *The Novel and the People* was one of the only works of the 1930s to call the entire principle of *partiinost* into question. It should nevertheless be noted that in some of his other writings, especially his essay 'Abyssinian Methods' (*Left Review*, November 1935) and his eulogy on Maxim Gorky, Fox came close to characterising the Soviet cultural system as a sort of foolproof mechanism for the production of artistic masterpieces.[99]

The second noteworthy aspect of the prescriptive sections of *The Novel and the People* is Fox's approach to language, specifically his related claims that (1) the novel has characteristically been written in the language of working people, and (2) the socialist novel should be written in the language of the *modern* working class. If these arguments now seem too dated to be worth considering directly, it is nevertheless clear that the assumption which underpins them is still prevalent in the cultural politics of the left and needs to be examined. When members of the 'working-class writing movement' or the radical theatre call for the 'language of the class' to be given a more prominent role in radical art, or when they commend writers such as James Kelman and Irvine Welsh for their skilful use of proletarian vernacular, they seem to imagine (as Fox did before them) that it is somehow possible to create an alternative linguistic space from which all 'bourgeois' impurities would be excluded. But can this in fact be achieved? The obvious starting point for a critique of the cruder forms of linguistic populism is the 'dialogical' theory of language developed by Mikhail Bakhtin in the 1920s.[100] At the core of Bakhtin's theory is the recognition that each language is subdivided into a series of different 'speech types', and that the variety of speech types broadly correspond to fundamental social divisions. Working people use language differently from their employers, just as men use language differently from women and people of colour use language differently from whites. Since the existence of 'heteroglossia' (Bakhtin's term for the internal divisions of linguistic communities) is invariably seen as a threat to social cohesion, there are 'centrifugal' forces in every age which seek to unify language by universalising the grammatical, syntactic and semantic habits of the dominant groups. The 'official' language of the ruling class is held up as an ideal to which the rest of us must aspire. The main consequence of these centrifugal pressures is that our every 'utterance' is implicitly situated in relation to other speech types, usually in a way which benefits the exponent of the more prestigious speech types. Whenever a worker employs the language of his class, the smoother linguistic habits of people further up the social scale establish a sort of spectral presence above his own utterance which admonishes him for his linguistic inferiority. Language can thus be regarded as one of the most powerful means of reinforcing social divisions. The corollary of Bakhtin's theory is that it is simply impossible to create forms in which proletarian language stands alone.[101] Even if a radical novelist could construct his work entirely from the vernacular of the lower orders (and not even virtuoso *pasticheurs* such as Welsh and Kelman have achieved that), it would still be impossible to prevent the reader from situating the language against the other speech types from which it derives its social meanings. This is not to say that Fox was entirely wrong in encouraging socialist writers to experiment with the language of their target audience. It was Bakhtin himself who recognised that the novel is often peculiarly well-suited to challenging the linguistic hierarchies on which the status quo depends. But this challenge can only occur if the novelist takes a fairly promiscuous approach to the depiction of disparate social voices. Because it is a form in which the 'the internal stratification of any single national language' is 'artistically organized', the novel potentially enables us to distance ourselves from the dialogical relationships between the various speech types and reorder them in a consciously progressive manner.[102] The role of the socialist writer is therefore to create hybrid forms in which the vigour of working-class language is used to satirise the more formal stylings of bourgeois speech; it is not (as Fox would perhaps argue) to try and create a sense of linguistic self-containment by employing proletarian vernacular to the exclusion of everything else.

Why should Fox have believed that a non-dialogic novel written in proletarian language was possible in the first place? This is obviously an issue on which we can only speculate; but it is reasonable to suggest that there were at least four factors which weighed on Fox's mind when he addressed the question of language. The first was the debate in *Left Review* to which we have already referred. The second was the extraordinary popularity among working-class readers of 'hardboiled' detective novels by the likes of Dashiell Hammett (a member of the American Communist Party), Raymond Chandler and James M. Cain. As Ken Worpole has pointed out in his important essay on the reception of detective fiction by British readers, it was the ability of the hardboiled novelists to capture the language of the American streets that convinced many ordinary Britons that fiction was an area in which they could legitimately take an interest. William Keal, described as a 'retired trade-union and labour movement militant', told Worpole in an interview that 'I read H.G. Wells, Arnold Bennett, all those people, but they weren't my kind of people. You always had the edge of class; and what intrigued me about the American writers – of course they had a class system as well – but they were talking the way we talked...What came through with the Americans was really a brutal and realistic attitude in language.'[103] The point about this 'brutal and realistic attitude in language' was that it was so unusual, so obviously a manifestation of proletarian defiance, that it must have convinced hundreds of working-class readers that the genteel language of the bourgeoisie could simply be excluded from the novel by sheer force of expression. Given that the hardboiled novel was singled out for praise in *The Novel and the People*, this was surely something of which Fox was aware.[104] The third influence on Fox was arguably the distinctive culture of the British working class. In their sustained attempt in the 1960s to identify the 'peculiarities' of British history, Perry Anderson and Tom Nairn famously argued that working people in Britain differ from their European counterparts in possessing a 'corporate' and 'hermetic' culture which effectively constitutes an 'alternative moral universe'. Traumatised by the brutality it encountered at the moment of its formation, the working class has persistently turned inwards and asserted its difference from the bourgeoisie in order to ensure its psychic survival.[105] By arguing that the novel has always been characterised by a more-or-less exclusive reliance on proletarian language, Fox might very well have been recasting this mentality in literary terms. By contrast, the fourth influence on his thinking about language was quite possibly the tradition of cultural conservatism. As we have seen in Chapter One, there was a preoccupation with the idea of linguistic homogeneity among many of the cultural conservatives who dominated literary culture in the inter-war period. When writers such as Eliot and Leavis tried to justify their belief that premodern societies were culturally superior to the modern industrial democracies, they often argued that premodern writers had benefited from the existence of a unified literary culture based on a common language. Since English was subsequently fragmented into a number of different speech types by the coming of industrialism, one of the main duties of the poet (at least according to Eliot) was to 'purify the dialect of the tribe'.[106] Although Fox's predilection for the language of the working class was a world away from the elitism of Eliot or Leavis, it is easy to see how the work of the cultural conservatives might have reinforced his belief in the possibility of linguistic unity. If so, it was one of the more bizarre examples of the interchange between Marxism and conservatism which extended throughout the 1930s.[107]

5. OTHER WRITINGS

Fox was an extremely prolific writer but only a fraction of his work was devoted to cultural themes. Apart from *The Novel and the People* and a series of articles in the *Daily Worker*, the only other cultural writings of the 1930s were an essay on Marxist literary theory in the symposium *Aspects of Dialectical Materialism* (1934), a eulogy for Maxim Gorky published in the house magazine of Martin Lawrence (later Lawrence and Wishart) and nine essays in *Left Review*.[108] Much of this work is of purely ephemeral significance; but two aspects of it need to be noted if we require a rounded impression of Fox's critical project: (1) his implicit response to the charge that Marxism compromises the prestige of the arts, and (2) his analysis of the nature of ideology in periods of systemic crisis.

Many of the intellectuals who flirted with Marxism in the 1930s were ultimately put off by what they seem to have regarded as its tendency to devalue the arts.[109] Because of its habit of relating developments in culture to the prevailing economic circumstances, Marxism was widely charged with infiltrating a spirit of grubby utilitarianism into the temple of aesthetic experience. The interesting thing about Fox's general writings on Marxist cultural theory, especially his contribution to *Aspects of Dialectical Materialism* ('The Relation of Literature to Dialectical Materialism'), was their implicit attempt to refute this charge by showing how the most elevated ideas about art can be incorporated into a Marxist aesthetic. One of Fox's strategies was to pander to the mood of residual romanticism which prevailed among many literary intellectuals. Although the work of Hulme, Eliot and other 'classical' writers had done much to undermine the dominance of romanticism, it was still common for many literary theorists (among them John Middleton Murry, Herbert Read and G. Wilson Knight) to endorse the sub-Wordsworthian view that art represents an agonised struggle by an individual genius to express his 'unique' vision. If this emphasis on uniqueness seemed incompatible with Marxism, particularly with the view that art has its roots in the shared experiences of society, Fox nevertheless tried to retain the main elements of romantic individualism in modified form. The artist by no means resides in an aesthetic universe of his own making, since his basic subject matter is the social relations into which he is born; yet the essence of art is its maker's attempt to imbue these common materials with something wholly idiosyncratic: 'On the forge of his own inner consciousness the writer hammers out reality, beats it out madly by the violences of thought, if I may steal a phrase from Naomi Mitchison. The whole process of creation, the whole agony of the artist, is in this violent conflict with reality.'[110] Fox displayed similar ingenuity in his brief discussion of the historical status of aesthetic values. Many intellectuals in the 1930s believed that Marxist aesthetics implied a rejection of the belief that art provides *universal* insights into the nature of the human condition. If art is indeed conditioned by the social relations of its day, then it surely follows (or so the argument went) that it can only investigate forms of human behaviour which exist for specific periods. Fox responded by drawing a rigid distinction between the ideological and the affective dimensions of art. The *ideas* which art expresses are indeed historically specific, but the emotional responses that form its core remain remarkably constant throughout time and space: '…because they deal with human passions, human emotions, with the experiences of flesh and blood, works of art have a value for all time, a meaning for all time.'[111] The argument was buttressed by the audacious claim that a commitment to Marxist politics might ultimately lead to a *deepening* of art's universality. Since the dawn of the capitalist age, Fox implied, writers and artists have been haunted by the ideal of global expressivity. The creation of a world market, combined with the resulting disappearance of 'national onesidedness' (Marx's phrase), has nurtured the belief that art should reflect the experience of living in a world society. Yet every attempt to express the new forms of global consciousness have necessarily been stymied by the national rivalries which are endemic to capitalism. By seeking to absorb the various regions of the world into a highly integrated system of planned production, the communist movement will therefore establish conditions in which the artist's dream of total communication can at last be realised.[112]

Fox's most original piece of cultural criticism was probably the essay on T.E. Lawrence which he published in *Left Review* after Lawrence's death in 1935. Proving that his interest in heroism went beyond purely literary matters, Fox wanted to know why Lawrence was effectively the only person in England to be elevated to heroic status in the period since the Great War. His answer was that Lawrence embodied *in extremis* the Janus-faced characteristics of capitalist society in crisis. Ostensibly a servant of the ruling class, he nevertheless held a number of beliefs which objectively undermined the stability of the existing system. After being sent to the Near East to advance the interests of British imperialism, specifically by fomenting revolt against the Ottoman Empire, he developed a romantic attachment to the forces of pan-Arab nationalism. And although his obsession with aeroplanes might have seemed like an endorsement of capitalist technocracy, he actually believed that improvements to technology were most likely to result from the ingenuity of working people: 'To me it is the multitude of rough transport drivers filling all the roads of England every night, who make this the mechanical age. And it is the airmen, the mechanics, who are overcoming the air, not the Mollisons or Orlebars.'[113] Whether or not this interpretation of Lawrence's career was correct, the important thing about it was its implications for the theory of bourgeois ideology. By insisting that only someone as radically self-divided as Lawrence could have effectively symbolised British capitalism in its post-war decline, Fox seemed to be implying that a period of systemic crisis invariably gives rise to ideological formations which do as much to subvert the existing order as to legitimise it. His essay can thus be seen as part of the wider attempt by British communists to challenge the belief that ideology simply consists of a straightforward representation of the opinions of the ruling class. Insofar as it concerns itself with the ideology of imperialism, it also anticipates the preoccupation with self-undermining imperial representations which dominates the work of such 'post-colonial' critics as Edward Said, Homi Bhabha and Gayatri Spivak. Its subtlety suggests that Stanley Edgar Hyman was probably justified in saying that Fox's literary essays evinced an 'aesthetic sensibility capable of breaking through the fetters of his straight political criticism, had he lived'.[114]

CHAPTER FIVE

CHRISTOPHER CAUDWELL:
ORTHODOXY AND THE AUTODIDACTIC MIND

The work of Christopher Caudwell has been analysed at length in a number of books and articles, most obviously in the distinguished monographs by David Margolies, Christopher Pawling and Robert Sullivan.[1] Much of this writing has tried to relate Caudwell's ideas to the vast number of predominantly Western thinkers whose work he cited in the bibliography to *Illusion and Reality* (1937). My purpose in this comparatively brief chapter is to indicate how Caudwell's work can also be interpreted in accordance with my broader thesis about the relationship between Soviet and British criticism. I shall argue that Caudwell owed as much of a debt to Soviet ideas as either West or Fox, in the sense that the main assumptions of his work were all derived from the 1934 Writers' Congress, but that he significantly modified (or even subverted) these ideas by refracting them through the sort of intellectual assumptions which tend to characterise the autodidactic mind. When he made use of ideas from the Western tradition, as he did on innumerable occasions, it was usually in such a way as to throw his autodidacticism into relief. I shall illustrate these arguments by looking at the two most important elements of Caudwell's work: (1) his theory of poetry, and (2) his theory of cultural crisis.

1. CAUDWELL'S ROAD TO MARXISM: A BIOGRAPHICAL SKETCH

Anyone who wishes to understand the culture of the world communist movement must address the issue of autodidacticism, since communist parties throughout the world were uniquely successful in producing large numbers of worker-intellectuals who had received little or no formal education.[2] Many of these autodidacts only displayed their erudition in conversation or debate, which helps to explain why the British Communist Party was once renowned for the excellence of its orators, but a certain proportion also made careers for themselves as journalists and writers. While most of these men and women came from working-class backgrounds, Christopher Caudwell was an autodidact of an altogether different kind – a middle-class intellectual who had been denied a university education because of family poverty.[3] Born Christopher St John Sprigg in Putney on 20th October 1907, his mother was a self-employed artist and his father a prominent journalist who had once been literary editor of the *Daily Express*. After attending a Catholic preparatory school in Bognor Regis and the Benedictine Priory School in Ealing, he had no choice but to leave formal education at the age of fifteen because his father could no longer afford to pay the school fees. Caudwell's solution to his family's financial problems was to follow his father into journalism. He spent the two years between 1923 and 1925 as a reporter on the *Yorkshire Observer* (the paper was based in Bradford), later returning to London to edit an obscure trade journal called *British Malaya*. This seems to have been the period in which Caudwell's remarkably diverse intellectual interests began to take shape. Obsessed with science and literature and determined to resist the lure of specialisation, he spent much of his time acquiring a basic knowledge of all the sciences and reading his way through the history of English poetry. It was his interest in science which prompted him to collaborate with his brother Theodore in a number of publishing ventures between 1926 and 1933, each of them intended to popularise information about the burgeoning aeronautics industry. Apart from serving as the editor of *Airways* (the first monthly magazine to devote itself to aeronautics), he was also the co-founder and Joint Managing Editor of a press agency called Airways Publications Ltd. He also made a small reputation for himself by writing a series of well-received books on aeronautics, including *The Airship, Its Design, History, Operation and Future* (1931), *Fly with Me: An Elementary Textbook on the Art of Piloting* (1932), *British Airways* (1934) and *Great Flights* (1935). While most of these books sought merely to codify existing knowledge, some of Caudwell's other writings betrayed a definite strain of scientific originality. His article 'Automatic Gears: The Function of the Moving Fulcrum in Determining Design' (*Automobile Engineer*, October 1929) is said to have stimulated considerable interest among experts in the field, though ultimately its detailed proposals for a new form of automatic gear came to nothing.

It is thought that Caudwell made a great deal of money from his various publishing concerns. However, his period of affluence came to an abrupt end in 1933 when Airway Publications Ltd went bankrupt. As a result, in the three or four years before his death he made an extraordinary transition from technical journalist and amateur scientist to novelist, aesthetician and Marxist.[4] His first response to the problem of renewed poverty was to throw himself into the writing of detective novels, no fewer than seven of which appeared between 1933 and 1937. (A more serious novel entitled *This My Hand* appeared in 1936 – the first of his books to be credited to Christopher Caudwell rather than Christopher

St John Sprigg.) He also continued working as a technical journalist, tirelessly offering stories on the aeronautics industry to whichever publication agreed to accept them. Yet most of this work now seemed entirely meaningless to him. His real passion in the final years of his life was the Marxist ideology to which he converted at some point in 1933 or 1934. While at one level his conversion was undoubtedly a response to the widespread phenomenon of middle-class insecurity, it also seems to have been rooted in a sense of intellectual crisis which arose directly out of his autodidacticism. Most obviously, as he made clear in a widely quoted letter to his friends Paul and Elizabeth Beard in November 1935, Caudwell had begun to feel an urgent need to unify his exceptionally broad range of knowledge in a single theoretical system: '...I think my weakness has been the lack of an integrated Weltanschauung, I mean one that includes my emotional, scientific, and artistic needs. They have been more than usually disintegrated in me...'[5] The great attraction of Marxism was that it provided a theory of history which related each aspect of human activity to all the others, making it easy for Caudwell to identify the links between intellectual interests which had previously seemed troublingly heterogeneous. It might also have been the case that Marxism answered to Caudwell's perceived need to live a life of 'action'. As Robert Sullivan has pointed out in a fascinating analysis of the unpublished story *The Way the Wind Blows* (1934 or 1935),[6] Caudwell seems to have been haunted in the 1930s by the sense that his relationship with the world around him was a wholly ineffectual one. Convinced that his intellectual achievements were more or less worthless (a common anxiety among autodidacts), he longed to be liberated into a life of courage, activism and decisiveness. With its emphasis on the 'unity of theory and practice' and its ambitious programme of social reform, Marxism naturally appealed to Caudwell by insisting that the main test of intellectual principles was whether or not they contributed to the onward march of social progress. Just as seductively, it also hinted that the isolated and hesitant bourgeois intellectual could overcome his awkwardness by immersing himself in the culture of the working class.

If a less sedentary existence was what Caudwell wanted when he threw in his lot with the Marxists, he was not to be disappointed. After joining the Communist Party in 1935 he settled in a working-class neighbourhood in Poplar and immediately threw himself into Party life. (His behaviour in this regard can be compared to that of Alick West, who also moved to a working-class area once he joined the CPGB.) Apart from attending endless meetings of the local branch, selling the *Daily Worker* on the streets and propagandising at factory gates, Caudwell also became involved at a very early stage in the violent struggle against British fascism. In June 1936 he was attacked by supporters of Oswald Mosley at a demonstration against the British Union of Fascists (BUF) in Victoria Park, only to be arrested and beaten up by the police. Subsequently found guilty of assaulting the police after various members of the constabulary perjured themselves in court, he now became convinced that the British state was rapidly moving towards an openly fascist position. This was one of the factors which made him determined to fight in Spain once the Civil War had broken out in July 1936. He arrived in Barcelona in December of that year, spending about two months as a Party functionary while receiving basic military training. He eventually went into action as a member of the British Battalion of the International Brigade in early February 1937. As is well known, he was destined to participate in only a single battle. He was killed in the afternoon of February 12th during the famous battle near the Jarama River in Madrid, still eight months short of his thirtieth birthday.

2. CAUDWELL'S THEORY OF POETRY

Although literary historians have recently made great strides in investigating the history of autodidacticism,[7] they have done very little to identify the intellectual habits to which the self-taught are often prone. This is not the place in which to try and repair their omission, but it is worth noting that many of the CPGB's autodidacts were bound together by a lot more than their lack of formal education. If we read the work of such influential self-taught Marxists as William Paul, T.A. Jackson and Caudwell himself, it rapidly becomes clear that a handful of distinctive intellectual characteristics tend to predominate. The first is a pronounced taste for intellectual drama. Perhaps because they have never been obliged to absorb ideas in order to achieve an academic qualification, autodidacts often seem to differ from professional intellectuals in experiencing a sort of naked wonder when engaging with the history of human thought. This arguably means that they tend to assess ideas more by aesthetic than by cognitive criteria. If an idea is exciting or dramatic enough to send a shiver down the spine, it is likely to be better received by an autodidact than an idea which merely purports to identify the truth. One aspect of this search for intellectual drama is a liking for monocausal explanations. Whereas the trained thinker usually emphasises the complexity of the natural and human worlds, drawing our attention to the variety of causes which precipitate any given effect, autodidacts tend to favour theories which reduce immense clusters of events to a single cause. (This doubtless helps to explain why a resolutely 'totalising' theory such as Marxism should have been so popular among the self-taught intellectuals of the nineteenth and twentieth centuries). By a curious paradox, however, it is rare for an autodidact's theories to be entirely consistent. Because of his voracious appetite for knowledge and a distinct lack of caution in traversing disciplinary boundaries, he is likely to advance an argument by drawing in thinkers from a bewildering variety of intellectual traditions, regardless of the fact that their main ideas are often incompatible with his own. Moreover, since monocausal explanations are notoriously difficult to defend successfully, his work is often characterised by what Jung might have called 'enantiodromia' – that is, the tendency of 'everything eventually [to go] over into its opposite.'[8] At a certain point in his argument, apparently unaware of what he is doing, he will begin to expound a thesis which is diametrically opposed to the one he claims to be advancing, only to return to his original position a few paragraphs later. As such, there is a sense in which the combination of 'blindness and insight' that Paul de Man identified in all intellectual work is especially well illustrated in the writings of the self-taught.[9]

One way of approaching the work of Christopher Caudwell is to see it as an autodidact's response to Soviet theory, though it is necessary to emphasise at once that Caudwell had a range of knowledge that that was unusual even by the standards of other self-taught communists. Let us begin with his theory of poetry, expounded at length in *Illusion and Reality* and arguably the most important element of his work.[10] As we have seen in Chapter Two, one of the central aspects of Bukharin's contribution to the 1934 Congress was his opposition to the idea of 'disinterestedness' in art. Recognising that art which displays no traces of 'desire or will' (Hegel) is unlikely to mobilise people to create a better world, Bukharin rejected the entire Kantian tradition in philosophical aesthetics and declared that the essence of art is actually the expression of 'active militant force'[11] in the face of external reality. There is a case for saying that Caudwell's theory of poetry was a dramatisation of this already dramatic idea.[12] Where Bukharin emphasised the role of primitive feeling in the arts, Caudwell went one better and described poetry as a manifestation of our 'instincts' – that is, the anarchic cluster of desires with which we are born and which are 'incompatible' with our physical environment. Influenced by thinkers from the psychoanalytic tradition (Freud, Adler *and* Jung – a nice illustration of the autodidact's eclecticism) as well as modern behaviourism,[13] Caudwell argued that the world represented in poetry is not a reflection of reality but a paradisical vision of the human environment transfigured by instinct – in other words, poetry shows us what the world would be like if it were capable of meeting our innate desires.[14] At the same time, probably drawing on the ideas of I.A. Richards,[15] Caudwell also insisted that poetry is more of an expressive medium than a referential one. When we read or hear a poem, even one which we already know, our sense of its 'external referents' is altogether vaguer than our awareness of the feelings which it brings to the surface.[16] Caudwell explained the link between poetry and instinct by developing an ingenious theory about the nature of rhythmic language.[17] The point about poetry's use of rhythm is that it induces a mood of 'emotional introversion' which directs our attention to the 'natural periodicities' in our own bodies – the beating of the heart, the ebb and flow of respiration and so on. Once we have retreated into our bodies, we become aware once again of the instinctual drives which needed to be sublimated before our life in society could begin: 'In emotional introversion men return to the genotype, to the more or less common set of instincts in each man which is changed and adapted by outer reality in the course of living.'[18] Moreover, since an awareness of our instincts reminds us of the things we have in common with other human beings, poetry is a necessarily *collective* force. Even when a poet writes alone, he is inspired by a ferocious sense of group consciousness into taking an active approach to external reality – this is why poetry always transfigures our world rather than simply reflecting it. Caudwell thus believed that the function of poetry is ultimately an 'adaptive' one. By depicting a world which has been remade in the image of our most uncompromising desires, poetry convinces us that it is possible for our instincts to receive some kind of expression in our everyday lives, and therefore contributes to the whole process of sublimation which transforms unrealistic desires into realistic ones.[19]

If all this talk of instincts, genotypes and adaptation was only vaguely compatible with Soviet theory, Caudwell veered towards outright unorthodoxy with the theories of language and poetic form which buttressed his ideas about poetry. Perhaps recognising that he had tended to make poetry seem curiously remote from everyday life, not least by claiming that it prioritises expression over reference, Caudwell seems to have ascribed great importance to showing that the poet's use of language is ultimately not so dissimilar to everyone else's. As such, he developed a theory of language which held that *all* forms of speech and writing combine a reference to the external world with an element of emotional expression.[20] Whenever language is used, even in a scientific context, it always tells us something about the 'common perceptual world' (that is, the complex of events and objects which exist independently of the speaker or writer) as well as registering a response in the sphere of the 'common affective world' (that is, it evokes the attitude of the speaker or writer towards the events and objects to which he refers). This combination of reference and expression reflects the fact that language had its origins in economic activity. While there was nothing particularly unorthodox about these ideas, what was interesting was the way that Caudwell seemed to undermine his account of language's objectivity with the examples he used to illustrate his theory. Speaking of the common perceptual world, he placed less emphasis on what already exists than on private images which an individual might wish to make available to other minds:

The word is spoken and heard. Let us call the parties to this act speaker and hearer…The speaker wishes to change the hearer's perceptual world so as to include the thing the word symbolises. For example, he may say, 'Look, a rose!' He wishes the hearer to see a rose, or be aware of the possibility of seeing one. Or he may say, 'Some roses are blue'; in which case he wishes to modify the hearer's perceptual world to the extent of including blue roses…What, then, has been the result of this transaction? A blue rose, which was in the *speaker's* perceptual world, but not in their *common* perceptual world or in the *hearer's* perceptual world, has been formed in the common perceptual world and introjected into the hearer's perceptual world. Hence both the hearer's perceptual world and the common perceptual world are changed. Thus, if now the speaker says, 'A blue rose is scentless', the sentence will have a meaning it would not have had before, because blue roses now exist in the common perceptual world of speaker and hearer.[21]

The impression which Caudwell created with these examples, no doubt inadvertently, was that language is not to be regarded as a 'reflection' of reality (as Bukharin had insisted and as the theory of Socialist Realism demanded) so much as a signifying system that tells us more about the structure of the human mind than about the properties of the object world. (It is interesting that Saussure's *Cours de linguistique générale* was listed in the bibliography to *Illusion and Reality*, though it was not referred to directly in the text). This is perhaps one of the things that Maurice Cornforth had in mind when he claimed over ten years later that Caudwell's ideas were tainted by philosophical idealism.[22] Even more unorthodox were Caudwell's remarks about the nature of poetic language. In his efforts to explain the priority of expression over reference in poetry, Caudwell sketched a theory of poetic form which appeared to owe a great deal to what David Lodge has called 'modern symbolist poetics'.[23] The basic argument was that poetry is more concerned with the emotional connotations of language than with the properties of the world around us – or, to put it more precisely, it yields its effects by enhancing the 'affective associations'[24] of language (that is, the 'latent content contained in the original word')[25] rather than the things to which it refers (that is, the 'portions of external reality which the words symbolise').[26] By bringing together words which tend to resonate at the same emotional frequency, or by juxtaposing words whose emotional 'tones' are sharply opposed, the poet interposes a layer of affective material *between* the reader and the poem's content.[27] The interesting thing about this theory was its wholesale incompatibility with Soviet ideas about the unity of form and content. Whereas the Soviet writers insisted that literary form should always serve as a sort of transparent medium for the transmission of ideas and images, Caudwell's argument was that a disjuncture between form and content is absolutely crucial to the way that poetry works. This belief in the autonomy of poetic form perhaps helps to explain the note of modernist experimentation in his own creative writings, especially his poetry, which nevertheless stood in sharp contrast to the orthodox denunciation of modernism in books such as *Illusion and Reality*.[28]

2.1. The Obsession with Instinct

As we have seen, one of the biggest problems facing Marxist writers on literature is the assumption that poems, novels and plays are essentially private forms which have nothing in common with wider political realities. The problem was especially acute for the communist aestheticians of the 1930s, who not only sought to explain literature sociologically but also to encourage writers to take up the idea of Socialist Realism. The tendency to see literature as a record of private experience makes it all the more surprising that Caudwell should have ascribed such importance to the *instinctual* element in poetry. By insisting that poetry gives expression to a set of innate desires and impulses which are wholly incompatible with life in society, Caudwell tended to give the impression that the poet naturally resides in a world of pure sensibility. Even when he emphasised that the function of poetry is to adapt the instincts to the environment, his painstaking theoretical observations still paid far more attention to the artist's interior life than the highly politicised work of his contemporaries. (It is interesting to note that one commentator has dismissed the idea that *Illusion and Reality* is authentically Marxist, seeing it instead as a veiled expression of Jungian principles.)[29] Given that the doctrine of instinctual expression was always likely to create problems, it is perhaps worth asking two questions: Why should Caudwell have placed such emphasis on it in the first place? And in what ways did he seek to compensate for its depoliticising implications?

The second question is easier to answer than the first. When Caudwell wished to emphasise the irreducibly political nature of poetry, he resorted to precisely the sort of anthropological arguments which can be found in the work of Plekhanov and West. Surveying the history of primitive societies in Chapter One of *Illusion and Reality* ('The Birth of Poetry'), he argued that not only had poetry always played a social role but that it had its origins in the primitive labour process.[30] Far from reflecting the private moods of the isolated individual, it was originally a collective form which functioned as a stimulus to hunting or agriculture. The thing which distinguished Caudwell's arguments from those of other communists was his scrupulous attempt to make them consistent with the doctrine of instinctual expression. His essential point was that primitive poetry always invoked a 'common perceptual world' that was directly economic. Since human beings have no instinctive desire to work, or so the argument went, it is necessary for all societies to adapt the instincts to the demands of production. The chosen method in primitive societies is to hold tribal festivals in which (1) poetry is buttressed by 'dance, ritual and music' (an essential point), and (2) attention is focused on the economic paradise which will surely ensue when the necessary work is done:

> The real object, the tangible aim – a harvest – becomes in the festival a phantastic object...As man by the violence of the dance, the screams of the music and the hypnotic rhythms of the verse is alienated from present reality, which does not contain the unsown harvest, so he is projected into the phantastic world in which these things phantastically exist. That world becomes more real, and even when the music dies away the ungrown harvest has a greater reality for him, spurring him on to the labours necessary for its accomplishment.[31]

By conjuring a vision of 'granaries bursting with grain' at precisely the moment that it drags the instincts to the surface of the mind, poetry plays the essential role in transforming the recalcitrant tribesman into a willing worker. Moreover, since verse is always chanted collectively in tribal festivals, it also generates the sense of group consciousness which is indispensable to primitive agriculture. The only jarring note in Caudwell's argument was its contradictory emphasis on the *clarity* of the 'phantasy object'. As we have seen, one of Caudwell's most important theoretical insights was that poetry is more expressive than referential – that is, it tends to work by emphasising its affective element and allowing its objective referents to float hazily on the outskirts of consciousness. The problem with his comments on tribal festivals was that they seemed to reverse this schema, ascribing a sort of hallucinatory vividness to primitive verse which has been absent in subsequent forms of poetry. It was an object lesson in the perils of autodidactic theorising. Anxious to show that poetry can be instinctive and political at the same time, Caudwell showed that he was more than willing to substitute a minor inconsistency for a major one. One of the consequences was that his comments on primitive verse were ultimately more compatible with the Soviet doctrine of form and content than his general poetic theory.

Before we try to explain Caudwell's preoccupation with the instincts, it is worth making the point that no other Marxist thinker (with the possible exception of Wilhelm Reich) has ever ascribed such importance to them. The impression one carries away from *Illusion and Reality* is that the unmodified instincts represent a grave and continuous threat to the mind's equilibrium. There are times when

Caudwell's attitude to human nature seems even less sanguine than that of the psychoanalytic thinkers who influenced him. Instead of supposing that the instincts can be permanently sublimated at an early age (thereafter remaining trapped in the unconscious), Caudwell seemed to regard them as a daily source of instability in the minds of even the most mature adults. Indeed, in his fine essay on psychoanalysis in *Studies in a Dying Culture*, he criticised Freud for the element of dualism in his thinking, insisting that the relationship between the conscious and unconscious minds is not one of stark opposition so much as interpenetration: 'Consciousness and unconsciousness are not exclusive opposites…they are in mutual relation, like the positive and negative poles of a battery activating a circuit, and it is only by abstraction that we separate out the complex called consciousness, as we might separate out the threads forming the pattern on a tapestry.'[32] All of this suggests that Caudwell's interest in the instincts must have arisen from something very deep in his personal experience. It is surely the case that no thinker would have placed such emphasis on the mind's unrulier emotions unless he felt threatened by them himself. What I want to suggest here is that Caudwell was probably suffering from a species of emotional turbulence which is very common among autodidacts. Cursed with the sort of mind that continually tries to arrange first principles into vast edifices of logic, he seems to have worked himself into fits of intellectual tension on a more or less daily basis. (Anyone who reads his notoriously inspissated prose immediately understands what Geoff Dyer had in mind when he said that thought can sometimes be experienced as an 'almost physical act of labour.')[33] As befits a man who wrote so insightfully about Freud, his solution (or so it can be inferred) was to fantasise about retreating into a pre-oedipal world from which the horrors of logic had been permanently banished. At any rate there is evidence of this not merely in his creative writings (which often evoke the dark underbelly of human experience) but also in theoretical statements such as the following: 'It [i.e. infantile regression] is the path that perpetually appeals to man when, as to-day, his consciousness seems to fail him at the tasks with which he is faced…'[34] If Caudwell looked to poetry to adapt the instincts to civilised life, it was perhaps because the lure of the primitive was more familiar to him than to many of his contemporaries. In an irony he would surely have relished, he showed what happens when obsessive intellectualism is transformed into its dialectical opposite.

2.2. Caudwell and Day Lewis

While it is sometimes recognised that the work of the Party theorists helped to shape the ideas of the Auden Circle, it is rarely acknowledged that the influence occasionally flowed in the opposite direction. This makes it all the more significant that Caudwell's theory of poetry was clearly anticipated in the writings of C. Day Lewis. As David Margolies has pointed out, there are some marked resemblances between the anthropological arguments in *Illusion and Reality* and those of Lewis's essay 'Revolutionaries and Poetry' (*Left Review*, July 1935).[35] Like Auden's essay 'Writing' (analysed in Chapter Three), 'Revolutionaries and Poetry' is poised uneasily between activist and individualist conceptions of art. On the one hand, anxious to ensure that 'fellow travel[ling]' poets like himself were not obliged to sell their souls to the Communist Party, Lewis argued that creative writers are naturally inward-looking and should not be expected to write excessively partisan verse. Although left-leaning poets should indeed attempt to 'assimilate Marxism through theory and practical activity',[36] they must also recognise that theirs is a distinctly idiosyncratic view of the world and write accordingly. When they address themselves to public issues (and Lewis accepted that they had a duty to do so), they should evoke contemporary realities from the perspective of a well-informed but not wholly engaged individual. They should make no attempt to express the forms of collective consciousness which lie at the heart of political activity, nor should they degrade their language by dealing in 'slogans and...*direct* propaganda.'[37] They should also accept that a great deal of their work will address purely personal themes such as falling in love, the beauty of nature and despair. On the other hand, acknowledging a debt to Stephen Spender's book *The Destructive Elements* (1935), Lewis also argued that poetry could not be expected to survive unless it once again achieved a mass audience. This could only occur if poems began to speak directly to the experiences of the urban working class, especially their experience of industrial production. It was at this point that Lewis deployed an argument that might have come straight from the pages of *Illusion and Reality*. Seeking to prove that poetry had once been the most collective of forms (and that a new form of popular poetry was therefore eminently achievable), he not only argued that verse had played a directly economic role in primitive societies but that it had done so by educating the emotions:

The successful hunt, the terror of natural phenomena – earthquake, hurricane, eclipse, the hopes and fears for the harvest, the horror of barren winter and the delight in spring's fertility – all these were expressed by primitive man rhythmically, in dancing and poetry. They were a release of emotion, of directed emotion; and that release meant, like the bursting of a thunder-cloud, refreshment in the end...Poetry was one of the chief instruments through which primitive man, by expressing his emotions, gained strength to fight against the economic conditions which gave rise to those emotions. It is bound up therefore with our emotional life, and there seems no reason to suppose that it is less necessary to us than it was to our early ancestors.[38]

Lewis's implied point was that the new urban poetry should adapt the instincts to industrial production in the same way that tribal festivals had adapted them to hunting and primitive agriculture. The twist in his argument was that poetry of this sort could only be written by working people themselves. Since the bourgeois writer is necessarily positioned 'outside' the industrial system, it falls to the 'proletarian poet' (a phrase which betrayed the residual influence of the Proletcult movement) to 'make poetry [out] of what is his native language'.[39] It was a fascinating example of the way that the anthropological element in Marxist criticism can be used to sponsor a democratising vision of artistic activity, even if Lewis's conception of revolutionary poetry had little enough in common with the idea of Socialist Realism.[40]

3. CAUDWELL'S THEORY OF CULTURAL CRISIS

When we turn our attention to Caudwell's theory of cultural crisis,[41] we find a classic example of the autodidact's preference for explaining complex phenomena in terms of a single cause. As we saw in Chapter Two, the Soviet theorists invoked a bewildering variety of factors when trying to account for the 'decadence' of capitalist culture, ranging from the joyless nature of labour in a market system to the modernist preoccupation with the underbelly of modern life. An important aspect of the Soviet argument was the claim that bourgeois literature only descended into outright decadence with the rise of the art-for-art's sake movement, which encouraged writers to turn their backs on the social world and retreat into a private universe of moral and aesthetic experimentation. There is perhaps a sense in which Caudwell's decisive move was simply to extend the critique of art-for-art's sake to the whole of capitalist society. According to Caudwell, who developed his theory in considerable detail in *Studies in a Dying Culture* (1938) and *Further Studies in a Dying Culture* (1948), the root cause of all forms of cultural decline under capitalism is what he famously called the 'bourgeois illusion of freedom'.[42] This is the view that human beings can only flourish when operating independently of wider social influences:

The illusion is that man is naturally free – 'naturally' in this sense, that all the organisations of society are held to limit and cripple his free instincts, and furnish restraints which he must endure and minimise as best he may. From which it follows that man is at his best and noblest when freely working out his own desires.[43]

Although the bourgeois illusion is not quite the same thing as Mill's preference for the 'private sphere' over the public world of institutions, not least because the demand for individual freedom can often acquire institutional expression (Caudwell cited the structure of capitalism itself), it still pivots around the basic contrast between individual judgement (good) and collective purpose (bad). Caudwell's attack on the bourgeois illusion was rooted in a stimulating attempt to outline a Marxist definition of freedom. Apart from pointing out that freedom from social ties is of little use if the individual is too poor to exploit his freedom (a staple Marxist argument which he nevertheless pressed home with great rhetorical flair),[44] Caudwell insisted that human beings can only be described as free if they possess two related powers. The first is the ability to think about the reasons for their actions. If, when responding to an external stimulus, we are able to ask ourselves 'why am I doing this?', we open up the possibility of transcending our habitual responses and identifying new courses of action. However, since we are always responding to external stimuluses in one fashion or another (here we come to Caudwell's second point), we must also seek to maximise our freedom by so ordering our environment that we are largely unaffected by *unwanted* external pressures. There is no such thing as a state of pure freedom, merely a situation in which human beings effectively *choose* the environmental forces which impose restraints (though not absolute restraints) on their freedom of manoeuvre.[45] This is why Caudwell put great store on Engels's famous observation that 'freedom is the recognition of necessity'. Moreover, in a development of the argument which made his reasons for opposing the bourgeois illusion absolutely clear, Caudwell insisted that freedom as he understood it can only be achieved through the medium of collective economic action: 'The essential feature of society is economic production. Man, the individual, cannot do what he wants alone. He is unfree alone. Therefore he attains freedom by co-operation with his fellows.'[46] By making us suspicious of collective action (and by diverting our attention from the issue of why capitalism is unable to adequately transform our physical environment) the bourgeois illusion drains the life out of modern culture by separating human beings from their only source of salvation. It should be clear even from this brief summary that Caudwell's argument can best be seen as a contribution to the venerable debate about the relative merits of 'positive' and 'negative' conceptions of liberty.[47]

Caudwell showed great ingenuity in his attempts to implicate the bourgeois illusion of freedom in the decline of such diverse areas of modern culture as love, psychology, religion, beauty and physics. Most ingenious of all were his efforts to relate the bourgeois illusion to the entire history of modern English literature, both in Chapters IV to VI of *Illusion and Reality* and in the great essay

Romance and Realism.[48] As is well known, Caudwell argued that the bourgeois illusion was first dragged into literature by the conflict between feudalism and emergent capitalism in the sixteenth century. In order to undermine the communitarian values of the feudal age, the writers of the Elizabethan period fashioned characters who embodied an extreme form of individualism – proud, amoral and frenzied heroes such as Doctor Faustus who believed that the transcendence of human limitations can only be achieved through ruthless loyalty to instinct.[49] Writing about Shakespeare,[50] whom he otherwise credited with greater insight into the deficiencies of bourgeois individualism than most of his contemporaries, Caudwell noted that 'His characters know only one law – to be the thing they are; and to be the thing they are is to call into existence, like a magic lantern projection of the soul on the universe, all the phantasmagoria of events and forces that is reality and, revolving around them, is their tragedy or comedy, and claims them or saves them.'[51] Moreover, the representation of extreme individualism did not end with the Elizabethans but has continued in modified form for most of the period since – it is this, more than anything else, which explains the decline of English literature in the capitalist age. Although Caudwell's survey of the history of English literature is extremely well known, not least because it has been singled out for virulent criticism by subsequent Marxist writers, there is a noticeable silence in the academic literature about the moment when Caudwell temporarily abandoned his main thesis and proceeded to argue the precise opposite of what he had been arguing before. In his comments on the century or so between the Restoration and the rise of romanticism (what used to be called the 'Augustan' period), Caudwell accepted that the main purpose of literature became the inculcation of the forms of behaviour most acceptable in an established bourgeois society.[52] Instead of depicting extreme individualists who routinely ignored the standards of the wider society, writers such as Dryden, Pope and Swift specialised in the creation of 'types' – that is, highly stylised characters who exemplified a recognisable form of social behaviour. Each type was evaluated by the standards of the 'bourgeois gentleman', who was implicitly held up to the reader as the acme of what 'reasonable and fashionable men and women should be'.[53] If a character's behaviour conformed to the bourgeois ideal (which very rarely happened) he was treated with sympathy – if not, he was subjected to the most unremitting satire. Augustan literature thus became a sort of behavioural manual in the struggle for capitalist hegemony. Caudwell did not explicitly endorse this tradition, but neither did he relate it to the wider theme of cultural crisis. As such, his account of Augustanism tends to read like a rare example of critical equanimity in the midst of coruscating anguish about the bourgeois illusion of freedom. We perhaps get the feeling that Caudwell has inadvertently cast himself in the unlikely role of the Dr. Johnson of the revolutionary left, rejecting the representation of exceptional people and admiring only work in which 'sublimity is produced by aggregation'.[54] It is an interesting example of the inconsistencies which beset the autodidactic mind when monocausal explanations are suddenly transformed into their opposites.

3.1. An Absence of Radicalism

In seeking to explain the artistic poverty of the age in terms of a single cause, Caudwell clearly aimed to impose a measure of intellectual coherence on the more diffuse doctrine of cultural crisis which had been enunciated by Zhdanov, Radek and other Soviet communists. In this sense his writings on the bourgeois illusion of freedom were entirely orthodox. However, there is also a sense in which his preoccupation with artistic and cultural decadence put him at odds with the Soviet theorists. If it is indeed the case that nearly every modern writer has expressed a deficient understanding of human freedom, it is simply not possible to identify a counter-tradition of 'progressive' poets and novelists who can serve to inspire the new generation of socialist writers. Moreover, since the bourgeois illusion is clearly blessed with a sort of Althusserian ability to impose itself on the writerly mind, it can even be doubted whether a tradition of socialist literature will be able to establish itself in the first place. Caudwell's pessimism about the possibility of literary dissent was especially apparent in his comments on the traditional novel, which he seemed to characterise (at least in *Romance and Realism*) as a form that had been corrupted by the bourgeois illusion at its very origins. According to Caudwell, one of the main assumptions of the bourgeois illusion is that human beings are basically unaffected by their material surroundings. Committed to the view that the individual can slough off all social ties and subsist in a sort of self-determining vacuum, it proposes that '...the bourgeois... [believes himself to be] self-determined and completely cognizant of the laws determining his environment, which laws do not, he thinks, determine *his* being.'[55] The argument of *Romance and Realism* was that the purpose of the novel is to reinforce this belief by creating fictional worlds which the reader can observe but *never feel part of*. Whereas a poem invites the reader to project himself into its distinctive verbal universe, novels give the impression of being 'self-contained' entities to which imaginative entry is simply impossible.[56] Novelists have usually achieved this effect by doing two things: (1) portraying their alternative worlds in substantial detail and linking each element of the narrative in an extended linear sequence, and (2) ensuring that 'every chink is stopped up' by relating events from the perspective of what literary theorists might now call an 'omniscient narrator'.[57] Caudwell also assumed that the line of demarcation between the novel and its reader would invariably be paralleled within the novel itself, specifically by a rigid opposition between the characters and their environment. The characteristics of the people we encounter in novels are never determined by the world in which they live, nor are they significantly affected by their changing circumstances as the narrative unfolds. In his description of *Moll Flanders*, Caudwell noted that 'She [Moll] exists in herself; the world in its fugitive contacts with her is simply environment. She is hard, free, and isolated.'[58] The tension between this sort of argument and Soviet reverence for traditional forms is surely clear. If the novel is indeed a form that owes its very existence to the culture of bourgeois individualism, the likelihood of it being used to express the conviction that social being determines consciousness is limited in the extreme.

Why should Caudwell have referred so obsessively to the bourgeois illusion of freedom, in the process implying that nearly all English writing since the Elizabethan age had been devoid of radical content? Although the main reason was undoubtedly his passion for all-encompassing theories, it might also be case that his dislike of unrestrained individualism tells us something very important about the way that autodidacts relate to other people. As many writers have pointed out, there is often a tendency for the self-taught to feel alienated from 'real life'. This is not so much because their obsessive reading distinguishes them from their less bookish contemporaries (though this is obviously a factor) but rather because of the particular ideology of culture to which they tend to adhere. The majority of autodidacts are instinctive Arnoldians. They naturally tend to suppose that the books to which they devote their lives embody what Arnold famously called 'the best that has been thought and said'. Possessed by the idea that they are floating through life on a cloud of intellectual inspiration, they frequently come to regard their everyday circumstances as sordid and unworthy in comparison. The resulting sense of isolation is vividly described in T.A. Jackson's great memoir *Solo Trumpet* (1953), especially in the remarkable pages evoking the feelings of social paralysis which crippled Jackson during an early period of omnivorous adolescent reading:

The trouble was that all these books – masterpieces though they might be – belonged to the Past, both in their origin and in their mode of expression. Insensibly, preoccupation with these 'classics' treated as a single category – the Best – caused a student to slip into regarding Culture as a fixed Mind-world in which one either ascended with the geniuses to supreme heights or sank with the dullards and the dunces to the uncultured slime. Insensibly in this way, one acquired a complete detachment from – if not a downright contempt for – the 'uncultured' vulgarity and sordidness of everyday life and actuality, with a positive revulsion against the suggestion that this 'vulgar' reality could be, and should be transformed by practical activities which, perforce, 'subdued to the medium they worked in' had to be in some measure, sordid and vulgar likewise.[59]

Although Jackson's point was that Marxism had cured him of these beliefs by encouraging him to relate his books to their social context, it is clearly possible for residual feelings of cultural snobbery to taint the outlook of even the most vehement self-taught Marxist. If we assume that Caudwell suffered from some of these feelings himself (and the whole tenor of his work suggests that he did) his preoccupation with the bourgeois illusion of freedom suddenly becomes more explicable. By condemning the greatest English writers for their ruthless individualism, or so it could be argued, he was simply trying to exorcise his own feelings of guilt by projecting his most anti-social (and anti-Marxist) impulses onto an entire literary tradition. More generally, Caudwell's doubts about the traditional novel were arguably prompted (or at least reinforced) by the difficulties which Marxists had experienced in adapting the novel to their political needs. Although there had been an outpouring of Marxist and *Marxisant* fiction in the years since the October Revolution, much of it had been unsuccessful in evoking realistic characters. Indeed, several Marxist writers had tried to circumvent the novels's individualist bias by abandoning traditional characters altogether. A number of novels written in the USSR in the early 1920s (i.e. before the introduction of Socialist Realism) eschewed individual heroes in favour of a sustained examination of the collective behaviour of the masses. Commenting on *The Iron Flood* by Alexander Serafimovich, a novel of 1924 which follows a band of refugees as they move across the Caucasus during the Civil War, the critic Jurgen Rühle noted that 'There is no hero, only the mass, no psychology, only the power of history, no introduction and no ending, no background and no embellishments. There is only the march, moving on like a force of nature.'[60] Some critics have even suggested that the majority of people depicted in later Soviet novels also lacked individualised characteristics, in spite of the emphasis on positive heroism in orthodox Soviet theory after 1934. In her recent essay 'Socialist Realism *with* Shores' (1997), Katerina Clark argued that many Soviet 'novels' would more accurately be regarded as reversions (conscious or otherwise) to earlier narrative forms, specifically the parable. Just as the protagonists in Christian parables had a 'vertical' relationship with God which guided them through their 'horizontal' relationship with unholy earthly circumstances, so the positive heroes in the Soviet novel had a vertical relationship with the Communist Party that enabled them to revolutionise the social structures to which they were horizontally related. One of the consequences of the revival of parabolic conventions was that protagonists tended to exhibit the same characteristics across a vast range of different books: '...by the mid-1930s, a single, conventionalized system of signs was already evident in virtually all novelistic depictions of positive heroes.'[61] However, if the disappearance of individualised characters in these and other novels (examples could be multiplied) suggests that Caudwell was right in saying that the conventional novel can never transcend its subject/object dualism, it is nevertheless clear that other Marxists see no such limitations in the novel's basic forms. The most distinguished representative of this group is obviously Georg Lukács, whose work can in some ways be seen as a sort of half-way house between Soviet and Western Marxism. While Lukács accepted that a dualistic relationship between the individual and his environment was a central feature of the modernist novel, he famously believed that the great virtue of the 'realist' tradition (exemplified by the work of Balzac and Tolstoy) was precisely that it *laid bare* the social forces that shape human nature. The argument was rooted in a distinctive account of the way that capitalist society reproduces itself. If working people seem largely unwilling to challenge the market system, it is partly because the ongoing process of 'rationalisation' (in the Weberian sense) imbues the individual worker with a sense of increasing disconnection from the system as a whole. By depicting individual characters as a seamless part of the social 'totality' (that is, the network of homogeneous but contradictory relationships which spreads outwards from the economic sphere to encompass the whole of society), the realist novel is able to counter the effects of rationalisation by portraying human nature as an effect of social relationships. Far from being a form which invariably reproduces the perceived gap between subject and object, the novel is potentially one of the most powerful forces of integration.[62] By contrast, Caudwell's theory of the novel comes perilously close to dismissing everyone from Daniel Defoe to Virginia Woolf as a mere cipher of the capitalist class. It is hardly surprising that Caudwell was the only important communist critic of the 1930s who made no contribution to the analysis of the English radical tradition.

CHAPTER SIX

'THE PAST IS OURS':
THE ENGLISH RADICAL TRADITION
AND THE POPULAR FRONT

As we saw in our brief account of *Shelley's Socialism* by Eleanor Marx and Edward Aveling, the desire to identify a radical tradition in English culture[1] has been a part of Marxist criticism in Britain since its earliest days. It is therefore unsurprising that the English communists should have provided a full-scale account of the radical tradition in their work of the 1930s. Although some of this work was a response to the project outlined at the 1934 Writers' Congress, especially the demand that communist intellectuals should trawl through history in search of 'precursors' of Socialist Realism, the most important stimulus was the *political* strategy which the Comintern pursued after the abandonment of the Class Against Class line.[2] Between 1933 and 1939 (and again between 1941 and 1943) the Communist International instructed its member parties to devote their main efforts to resisting the advance of fascism, specifically by joining with social democrats, liberals and even moderate conservatives in the defence of constitutional democracy. One of the main components of the new strategy was the attempt to demonstrate that each country possessed radical traditions which were consonant with the politics of communism. The CPGB's cultural workers were told that they should try to reconstruct the entire history of English radicalism, not only in its political dimension (the long tradition of plebeian revolt) but also in its more cultural aspects (the various attempts by writers and intellectuals to express their disaffection with the *status quo*). This chapter seeks to examine the resulting body of work. Section One identifies the general characteristics which the communists ascribed to the radical tradition. Section Two tries to show how a rather scattered crop of books, essays and articles can be fitted together to provide a coherent account of the development of English radicalism, in spite of the fact that the CPGB's intellectuals were never working with a shared chronological framework. Section Three asks whether the investigation of English radicalism was undertaken along orthodox lines, and examines two theoretical initiatives which grew out of it – one by Edgell Rickword, the other by Jack Lindsay.

1. THE ANATOMY OF ENGLISH RADICALISM

The Communist International began to prioritise its work against fascism in 1933, long after the disastrous consequences of the so-called Third Period had become apparent to everyone except the organisation's most influential figures. When the Executive Committee of the CI met in Moscow in June 1933, shortly after Hitler's accession to power in Germany, it judged that the most effective way of resisting fascism would be for communists to join with social democrats in a 'United Front' to defend civil liberties. There was no longer any question of socialists outside the communist tradition being dismissed as 'social fascists'. Two years later, at the Seventh World Congress of the CI in Moscow, the policy was significantly widened to encompass the idea of a 'Popular Front' against fascism. This was envisaged as an alliance not merely between communists and social democrats but also between liberals, moderate conservatives and other representatives of 'bourgeois' politics who wanted democracy to survive.[3] If we want to understand why the politics of the Popular Front exercised so powerful an influence on cultural Marxism in Britain, we have to look briefly at the famous report which Georgi Dimitrov (the new head of the CI) delivered to the Congress under the title *The Working Class Against Fascism*. Defining fascism as 'the open terrorist dictatorship of the most reactionary, most chauvinistic and most imperialist elements of finance capital',[4] Dimitrov argued that its main purpose was to rescue capitalism from the threat of revolution by abolishing democracy, suppressing the labour movement, sharpening the exploitation of the colonial peoples and reshaping culture along militaristic lines. Since the abolition of bourgeois democracy posed an incalculable threat to the future of the communist movement, it was therefore obvious (or so Dimitrov implied) that the defence of constitutional government and its related liberties was of greater immediate importance than the struggle for socialism. It was this consideration which justified the idea of a Popular Front. Yet there were at least two difficulties which communists would need to overcome if their credibility as opponents of fascism was not to be undermined. The first was that the world communist movement had usually approached the whole idea of bourgeois democracy in a spirit of hostility. Having so often dismissed parliamentary government as the fraudulent shell of an exploitative social system, it was not immediately clear how communists could expect to be taken seriously when they called for its defence. Secondly, communists had done very little to challenge world fascism's highly successful attempt to rewrite history in its own image. According to Dimitrov, one of the main reasons for the success of the fascists was that they had consistently portrayed their approach to politics as the culmination of their respective national traditions. The Italian fascists presented themselves as successors to Garibaldi; their French counterparts identified Joan of Arc as the progenitor of Gallic fascism; while even the American fascists made inroads into public consciousness by identifying themselves with the rebel forces in the War of Independence.[5] By failing to respond to these blatant distortions of history, communists had fatally neglected the element of patriotism in modern politics.

Dimitrov went on to suggest that a single cultural strategy could help to solve both these problems. Communists, he argued, should now give priority to (1) bringing the long history of popular radicalism in their respective countries to the attention of the public, and (2) showing how the militancy of the common people had made a central contribution to the emergence of political democracy:

> Communists who do nothing to enlighten the masses on the past of their people…in a genuinely Marxist spirit, who do nothing to link up the present struggle with the people's revolutionary traditions and past… voluntarily hand over to the fascist falsifiers all that is valuable in the historical past of the nation.[6]

> … being upholders of Soviet democracy, we shall defend every inch of the democratic gains which the working class has wrested in the course of years of stubborn struggle, and shall resolutely fight to extend these gains…How great were the sacrifices of the British working class before it secured the right to strike, a legal status for its trade unions, the right of assembly and freedom of the press, extension of the franchise and other rights! The proletariat of all countries has shed much of its blood to win bourgeois-democratic liberties, and will naturally fight with all its strength to retain them.[7]

It was these passages, more than any others, which established the context in which the British communists attempted to reconstruct the history of the English radical tradition.[8] The attempt was undertaken in a fairly diverse range of books, essays and articles. Edgell Rickword tried to capture the general characteristics of English radicalism in his introductory essay to *A Handbook of Freedom*, the anthology of radical quotations which he edited with Jack Lindsay in 1939 (its title was later changed to *Volunteers for Liberty*).[9] He also contributed another general essay, 'Culture, Progress, and English Tradition', to C. Day Lewis's influential symposium *The Mind in Chains* (1937).[10] The history of plebeian revolt was traced in A.L. Morton's *A People's History of England* (1938) and in Jack Lindsay's pamphlet *England My England* (1939).[11] One of the main themes in the next section is the tension between Morton's scrupulous historical research and Lindsay's more propagandist approach. Three of the most important radical writers (Bunyan, Dickens and Morris) were the subject of book-length studies by Jack Lindsay, T.A. Jackson and Robin Page Arnot respectively.[12] There was a series of essays on these and other writers, including Shakespeare, Spenser, Overton, Swift, Paine and Blake, published in *Left Review* between 1934 and 1938.[13] Lindsay analysed Shakespeare in *A Brief History of Culture* (1939) and John Strachey glanced at More, Winstanley and Morris in *The Theory and Practice of Socialism* (1936).[14] *The English Revolution 1640*, edited by Christopher Hill, appeared at the end of the decade and contained Rickword's important essay on John Milton.[15] Jack Lindsay explored the theoretical significance of the investigation into English radicalism in a series of books and essays.[16] The *Daily Worker* ran a series of brief articles on the history of the radical tradition under the title 'The Past is Ours'.[17] There were also a number of brief references to the radical tradition in a host of other publications.

The logical place to start is Edgell Rickword's account of the general principles underpinning English radicalism in 'On English Freedom'.[18] At the heart of the radical tradition, Rickword argued, was a long history of plebeian revolt which began in the Middle Ages and stretched forward through the English Revolution to encompass such modern movements as Owenism, Chartism and industrial unionism. According to Rickword, the central point to grasp is that the thousands of ordinary people who contributed to this history were ultimately bound together by a shared political outlook, even though the immediate economic demands which prompted them into action were usually quite different. The overriding feature of popular rebellion has been an awareness of exploitation. The peasants of the Middle Ages knew that the manorial system was little more than a form of legalised theft, while the worker under capitalism sees very clearly (in spite of the reifying complexity of the market order) that his employer's profits are actually the fruits of his own unpaid labour.[19] The crucial result is that popular rebellion has always been directed, either explicitly or implicitly, not merely towards marginal economic improvements but towards *the establishment of a classless society based on common ownership*.[20] When the English people rise up against their rulers, Rickword wrote, they are basically asserting 'a common human right which can only find satisfaction in social equality, the demand so to modify the state system that the way will be clear for free and equal collaboration in the productive life of the community.'[21] Although the people have often tried to legitimise their political ambitions by claiming that a communist society has already existed in England, specifically in the period between the departure of the Romans and the arrival of the Normans,[22] the real reason for the durability of the communist impulse is the 'communal nature of labour'[23] under both feudalism and capitalism. Moreover, while it is perfectly true that the English have yet to succeed in establishing a classless society, this does not mean that the history of popular revolt is primarily a record of glorious defeats. Apart from securing a series of economic concessions which have done much to improve the standard of living, its successes in the field of civil liberties have been of epochal significance. Because the common people have always recognised that the state's primary function is to serve the interests of the ruling class, they have had no choice but to balance their struggle for economic justice with a sustained campaign for such crucial democratic rights as freedom of speech, trial by jury and freedom of assembly.[24] In opposition to what Herbert Butterfield had recently called the 'Whig interpretation of history', which explained the establishment of democracy in terms of enlightened government by the commercial elite, Rickword argued that the people's struggle for freedom was the *sole cause* of the comparatively liberal institutions which now existed in England. The political lessons were clear. When the communists called for a Popular Front to defend 'bourgeois democracy' against the threat of fascism, they were not (as their Trotskyist critics claimed) promoting a dangerous diversion from the class struggle so much as honouring the English people's most important political achievement.

Rickword then shifted his attention to the scores of writers, artists and intellectuals who have supported the English people in their struggles against authority. His argument was that the masses have never been stirred into action by ideas introduced to them from outside. The role of intellectuals in the radical movement, though often of immense significance, has always been one of clarification and stimulation rather than outright leadership.[25] Radical intellectuals have been responsible either for giving clear expression to aspirations which the masses might only have expressed inchoately, or else for reviving political energies by imbuing those aspirations with a sort of visionary lustre: '…in the combinations of recalcitrant journeymen, in the staunch bearing of farm labourers in the felon's dock…[we find] the seed of all the formulations of the rights of man and the rhapsodies of the poets on the theme of liberty.'[26] Rickword even came close to suggesting that the relationship between the intellectuals and the masses had been the single most important influence on the nature of modern thought. During periods in which the working people's staunch common sense has attracted the support of the intelligentsia, philosophy and its offshoots have been predominantly optimistic and rationalist. It is only during periods of intellectual elitism that modern thought has been plunged into irrationalist gloom.[27] Writing in the journal *Poetry Nation Review* in 1979,

E.P. Thompson implied that it was precisely this emphasis on the debt which intellectuals owe to ordinary people (so different from Leninist orthodoxy) that made Rickword one of the most trenchant critics of the CPGB's many lapses into authoritarianism in the post-war years.[28]

Rickword's vigorous brand of radical patriotism raised difficult questions about the origins of national character. Anxious to avoid the taint of biological determinism, he was swift to deny that the common people's taste for rebellion was somehow encoded in their genes.[29] If their 'independent turn of mind' has now been raised to the level of an instinct, it is surely because their 'innate' responses have been powerfully conditioned by centuries of class struggle: 'The plain necessity of having to work and fight through long centuries for every advantage has fixed the strain, and has ingrained that deep suspicion of the bosses which Froissart noted as making us a nation very awkward to rule.'[30] Yet it was not entirely possible for Rickword to avoid the sort of English exceptionalism that occasionally marred the work of William Morris. English radicals, he implied, have always been distinguished from their foreign counterparts by a suspicion of abstraction. They have invariably fought for 'some specific form' of freedom and been unconcerned with 'freedom in the abstract'.[31] Aside from suggesting an almost Adornian sensitivity to the way that instrumental reason can be bent to authoritarian purposes, it is possible that Rickword's empiricism had an influence on George Orwell's much more distinguished meditations on Englishness (written about a year later) which also placed a radical construction on the idea that 'the English are not intellectual'.[32] The question of the influence of cultural Marxism on Orwell's work is one which has yet to be adequately explored.[33]

As we shall see in the next section, there were occasional discrepancies between the ideas explored in 'On English Freedom' and those which appeared in more specific accounts of the history of English radicalism. Although many writers tried to substantiate the claim that popular revolt had always been fuelled by communist ambitions, there were others (A.L. Morton was the main example) who took a more realistic perspective on the historical motivations of the English people. Nor was it the case that radical writers and intellectuals were always portrayed as precisely reflecting the wider concerns of the plebeian movement. In order for a writer to be identified as a member of the radical tradition, it was usually enough for his work to contain a critical account of a certain aspect of the capitalist order. Of all the writers whom the communists analysed in the 1930s, it was really only More, Milton and Bunyan who might reasonably be said to have clarified and expanded the concerns of the people. There was also an extremely important feature of communist writing on English radicalism which Rickword failed to even mention. By insisting that popular revolt has been a continuous or near-continuous feature of British life since the end of the fourteenth century, the historians of the Popular Front period were arguably undermining the orthodox Marxist assumption that each mode of production is legitimised by its own political, legal and ideological 'superstructure'. Their response, repeatedly demonstrated in practice though never explicitly stated, was the argument that in each period the dominant ideology contains elements which can be repositioned for radical ends. If such crucial ideologies as Christianity and liberalism have functioned throughout the course of the last 600 years to reinforce support for the existing order, they have also (or so the argument went) furnished many of the assumptions which have underscored popular revolt. When Margot Heinemann suggested that the work of such writers as Rickword, West and Lindsay anticipated many of the concerns of 'Gramscian' Cultural Studies, it might well have been this emphasis on the self-divided nature of ideology which she had in mind.[34]

2. THE SECRET HISTORY OF ENGLISH RADICALISM

Although most of the writers who explored the history of English radicalism shared the assumptions which Rickword outlined in *On English Freedom*, it would be wrong to describe them as an entirely homogeneous group. Most obviously, they never developed the sort of shared chronological framework that would have made their individual studies part of a genuinely collective act of historical investigation. If their individual studies are examined *in toto*, however, it becomes clear that they can be pieced together into a coherent narrative in spite of the existence of minor differences of emphasis. This narrative can be broadly divided into five periods, which can be summarised as follows:

(1) c1380-c1500. The age of peasant revolts against the manorial system, inspired by residual elements of radical egalitarianism in Christian doctrine (Langland).

(2) c1500-c1610. The age of peasant revolts against primitive accumulation and emergent capitalism, inspired by the democratic impulses that fuelled the Reformation (More, Spenser, Shakespeare).

(3) c1610-c1660. The emergence of modern communism and religious dissent in the wake of the English Revolution (Milton, Bunyan, Winstanley, Richard Overton).

(4) c1660-c1760. A period of political quietism in which the spirit of dissent was kept alive by isolated intellectuals (Swift).

(5) c1760-c1900. The birth of the labour movement and the emergence of scientific socialism (Paine, Blake, Dickens, Morris).

The names in brackets refer to the writers and intellectuals who were regarded in the 1930s as the leading radical spokesmen of their respective eras. Other names, such as those of Bacon, Defoe, Wordsworth, Shelley and Hazlitt, would be added to the list by later communist writers. Our task now is to look in detail at how these five periods in the history of English radicalism were portrayed.

2.1. The Peasants' Revolt and the Crisis of Feudalism

The first phase of popular radicalism encompassed the peasant insurrections which swept England in the fourteenth and fifteenth centuries. The most important of these was obviously the Peasants' Revolt of 1381, though the so-called 'Cade Rebellion' of 1450 also received its share of attention. The English communists, while recognising that the late Middle Ages saw the beginning of what was sometimes called the 'transition to capitalism', usually ascribed the tensions of the period to problems arising from a still-dominant feudalism. There was an interesting contrast between the respective approaches of Jack Lindsay in *England My England* and A.L. Morton in *A People's History of England*. According to Lindsay, whose techniques were more those of the pamphleteer than the historian, the Peasants' Revolt was primarily an expression of a longstanding hostility towards the rigidly hierarchical structures of feudal society. Already angered by the wholly unaccountable manner in which the feudal lords had exercised their power, the peasantry was provoked into outright rebellion by the introduction of a penal taxation regime (specifically the Poll Tax of 1380) in the wake of the war with France.[35] Morton, on the other hand, placed more emphasis on the structural changes which had helped to transform the feudal system in its final period of dominance. In the century or so before the Peasants' Revolt, a number of developments had served to loosen the ties which bound the serf to the lord of the manor. These included the introduction of 'commutation' (the replacement of labour services by the payment of a wage), the Hundred Years' War and the extensive cultivation of new land. The crucial feature of the last two decades of the fourteenth century was therefore an attempt by the ruling class to shore up a set of hierarchies which had *already* begun to dissolve.[36] When the government introduced its Poll Tax, it was motivated not only by military considerations (important though these were) but also by the need to undermine the peasantry's new sense of independence by depriving it of most of its wealth. It was this, more than any longstanding sense of social resentment, which ultimately precipitated the mood of plebeian insurgency that drove the likes of John Ball and Wat Tyler.

Yet if Morton insisted that the events of 1381 were stimulated by the demand that the independence of the peasantry should be reinforced and not undermined, he appeared to agree with Lindsay that their ultimate goal was the establishment of a sort of communist Arcadia. 'He demanded the freeing of all enslaved Englishmen', Lindsay wrote in a reference to John Ball, 'but he was too clear-sighted not to see that there could be no peace or happiness settled in the world until classes were altogether abolished'.[37] It was usual to ascribe the peasantry's communist values to a subversion of religious ideology. It was suggested, in the first place, that the poor in the Middle Ages were deeply influenced by a residual element of radical egalitarianism in Christian doctrine.[38] According to this argument, Christianity had been a communist religion at the very moment of its inception. The ambition of its early followers was to create a society in which 'the lowly shall be exalted and the mighty cast into the dust';[39] but since the political realities of late antiquity were incompatible with this sort of uncompromising radicalism, the early Christians were later obliged to moderate their communist ambitions by projecting them into the world hereafter. Equality and universal brotherhood were now presented as a feature of the Kingdom of Heaven, not as values which might reasonably serve as the foundation of a transformed social order. Once this had occurred, it was relatively easy for later generations to transform Christianity into the main ideological buttress for European feudalism. Yet its subversive potential had not been entirely erased. It still contained enough traces of its egalitarian origins to be a potent weapon in the hands of the dispossessed. The communist writers of the 1930s sometimes emphasised the political implications of Christianity's main creation myths, especially that of the Garden of Eden.[40] Because the relationship between Adam and Eve had been an entirely equal one, it was natural for many Christians to assume that God's work on earth could only be achieved if economic and political hierarchies were swept away. This was the assumption that underpinned the famous couplet of John Ball's, quoted by Rickword and Lindsay in *A Handbook of Freedom*, which later provided William Morris with the text of an influential illustration:

Whan Adam dalf and Eve span,
Wo was then the gentleman?[41]

Lindsay and Morton both agreed that the egalitarian element in medieval Christianity found institutional expression in the emergence of the Lollards, led by John Wycliffe. But whereas Lindsay was content to portray Lollardry as a communist doctrine, rooted in the 'new message' that 'only those should eat who worked',[42] Morton saw it as a more ambiguous phenomenon.[43] He argued that the Wycliffe heresy contained two main elements. On the one hand, appalled at the way in which church leaders now ranked among the most important landowners of the age, Wycliffe called for church property to be held in common and not to be treated as a source of surplus value. On the other hand, anticipating the emergence of Protestantism by nearly 150 years, he argued that the distinction between clergy and laity should be loosened and that the more mystifying Christian rituals (especially communion based on the doctrine of transubstantiation) should be abandoned. Morton fully accepted that these ideas had a number of progressive consequences. The emphasis on common ownership of church property was undoubtedly an influence on the wider peasant demand for the abolition of classes, while the attempt to loosen church hierarchies was directly – if not solely – responsible for the first English translation of the Bible. Yet he also insisted that Lollardry had been easily recuperated by the English establishment. As a result of his association with John of Gaunt, the nobleman who effectively ruled England during the childhood of Richard II, Wycliffe had refused to extend his doctrine of common ownership to economic affairs as a whole. And after a lengthy period of state repression, culminating in the abortive Lollard rising at St Giles' Fields in 1414, most of Wycliffe's successors seemed happy to tone down their theological radicalism and espouse a 'bourgeois and democratic' emphasis on 'poverty and thrift'.[44] If the attempt to show that the dominant ideology can often be bent to radical purposes was one of the main intellectual procedures of the Popular Front period, this was a rare example of a communist intellectual, scrupulous in his use of historical evidence, demonstrating that radical ideology is equally susceptible to corruption from above.

It was accepted that the radical movements of the fourteenth and fifteenth centuries had been swiftly suppressed by the state and had not resulted in any short-term changes to the structure of English society. However, it was also implied (in line with the shibboleth that popular rebellion was solely responsible for the existence of 'English liberty') that the Peasants' Revolt had fatally undermined the power of the ruling class and had therefore hastened the transition to capitalism.[45] The peasants were thus portrayed as playing a decisive role in the creation of a society in which a limited conception of democratic rights was allowed to prevail. More interesting was the communist analysis of why the peasants' wider demands had not been realised. In defiance of the view that peasant rebellions tend to be 'vast, shapeless, anonymous, but irresistible movements' (the phrase is Eric Hobsbawm's),[46] both Lindsay and Morton (though especially the former)[47] argued that the political fortunes of the peasantry were inextricably related to the quality of its leadership.[48] When Wat Tyler was able to impose a measure of coherence on the rebels from Essex, Kent, East Anglia and the Home Counties who poured into London in June 1381, there was every possibility that the great Revolt would succeed – things only fell apart when Tyler was executed during his famous meeting with Richard II at Smithfield. 'After that', wrote Lindsay, 'with the leader gone, it was not difficult to bewilder and browbeat the commons and get them dispersed.'[49] Such was the emphasis on leadership that it is difficult to resist the conclusion that the history of peasant insurgency was being rewritten, consciously or otherwise, to conform with the sacrosanct Leninist distinction between 'vanguard' and 'mass'.

The analysis of the cultural aspects of medieval radicalism had scarcely got underway by the 1930s. There was an occasional reference to William Langland (seen as a sort of poetic tribune of the revolutionary peasants)[50] as well as to the 'class conscious' ballads of the fourteenth century;[51] but the only cultural form to be analysed in any depth was religious iconography. The central document in this context was F.D. Klingender's essay 'The Crucifix: A Symbol of Mediaeval Class Struggle', published in Left Review in January 1936.[52] In this piece, which referred primarily to continental art but whose argument was relevant to the whole of Western Christendom, Klingender's aim was to show how the ideologies of the feudal aristocracy, the emergent bourgeoisie and the disaffected peasantry were successively reflected in medieval representations of the Crucifixion. Because the purpose of medieval Catholicism was to legitimise secular hierarchies by portraying humanity as wholly subordinate in its relationship with God, it was not considered appropriate, or so Klingender implied, for the art of the Church to emphasise the suffering of Christ at the moment of his death.[53] If we examine early examples of the crucifix, such as the Imervard Crucifix which was placed in Brunswick Cathedral in the twelfth century, we therefore encounter a Christ figure who radiates divine authority rather than secular anguish. Although his arms are extended in line with the horizontal beam of the cross, he nevertheless appears to be standing on his feet and gazing resolutely outwards. With his 'erect head and wide open eyes', he clearly represents the 'lord whose magic potency must be solicited with ritual action and incantation'.[54] It was only with the start of the long transition to capitalism that a more agonistic image of the Crucifixion began to be used. Since the bourgeoisie needed to legitimise the idea of market competition, they (or at least the religious artists who unconsciously absorbed their outlook) began to conceive of Christ's behaviour in the final hours of his life as the expression of a sort of yearning individualism. The crucifixes which emerged in the thirteenth and fourteenth centuries, typified for Klingender by the one at the Cathedral of Nurnberg, depicted a man whose anguished glimpses of transcendence grew entirely out of his retreat into an inner world. Christ was nailed to the cross, his body was ravaged by suffering and his eyes were sometimes (though not always) cast towards the ground.[55] The lasting impression was of the 'Passion of Christ, the terrible conflict of the lonely human being, during the last twenty-four hours before his death, when he must choose between his life and his cause'.[56]

Klingender recognised that the emotional intensity of the bourgeois crucifix often appealed strongly to the lower orders, but he did not regard it as the main expression of the radical impulse in medieval iconography. He pointed instead towards a number of works of art, exemplified by the crucifix designed by Mathias Grünewald for the altar at St. Anthony's Monastery in Isenheim, which appeared directly to reflect the outlook of the "peasant-plebeian movement"[57] in its revolutionary clashes with the ruling class. In some very compressed remarks on Grünewald's crucifix, Klingender implied that there were at least four ways in which it embodied a revolutionary outlook.[58] The first was that it used anatomical detail to identify God with the interests of the poor – Christ's appearance was clearly that of a peasant. Secondly, it presented the crucifixion of Christ in terms of the peasantry being physically tortured by the ruling class. Christ was flanked on his right by a magisterial figure, clearly of noble origin, who held a Bible in his one hand (presumably symbolising the law) and pointed an accusing finger with the other. Thirdly, it emphasised the indestructibility of the revolutionary impulse. Although the death of Christ represented the temporary defeat of the plebeian movement, there was a figure on one of the panels of the altar piece (confidently identified by Klingender as a 'revolutionary'), who was depicted rising from the grave. Finally, it seemed so devoid of genuine spirituality that it practically invited its audience to redefine the idea of transcendence in purely secular terms:

> The death of Christ…was no longer the sacrifice of the son of God: it was the torture there, and at that moment of the peasant masses, the fiendish terror meted out in those years to the heroic leaders of the peasant revolt… Thus the problem of salvation was stripped of its mystic, transcendental cloak – it was now solely the problem of earthly emancipation from class suppression, its achievement was the task of the suppressed masses themselves.[59]

Klingender's remarks about medieval iconography illustrated the ingenuity with which the British communists could tease out elements of radical sensibility in the art of the past. This ingenuity was to be deployed at greater length in the analysis of subsequent periods.

2.2. The Age of Enclosure

The second period of popular radicalism to which the communists addressed themselves (though it is worth repeating that they were never guided by a shared chronological framework) encompassed the various acts of peasant insurgency that occurred in England between the beginning of the sixteenth century and the start of the English Revolution. The most important were the Pilgrimage of Grace (1536), the Devon and Cornwall Rising (1549), the Norfolk or 'Kett' Rebellion (1549) and the Midlands Rising of 1607. Although these and other rebellions were described as having the same goal as those from the earlier period (that is, the establishment of a communist society administered by the peasants), it was recognised that they were set apart by the very different circumstances in which they occurred. Whereas the medieval rebellions were caused by tensions inherent in the manorial system, the later events were ascribed to dislocations resulting from the transition from feudalism to capitalism. The central claim was that the peasants had been provoked into insurrection by the enclosure of common lands, or what Marxists (in line with the terminology used in Volume One of *Capital*) often called 'primary accumulation'.[60] The purpose of enclosure was said to be twofold: (1) to force the peasantry to sell its labour power to the new capitalist employers, and (2) to increase the amount of land that could be integrated into the new market system. The result was grinding poverty for a significant section of the peasantry and England's first experience of mass unemployment. Morton also pointed to a couple of other factors which had hardened the mood of plebeian discontent. The first was Henry VII's decision to prevent the nobility from keeping 'retainers', on the grounds that they were a potent source of conflict between the various elite groups which aspired to control the state. In an interesting echo of Marx's contempt for the 'lumpenproletariat', Morton argued that the abolition of retainers had swollen the ranks of the unemployed with a group of 'proud, idle, swashbuckling ruffians'[61] (quite unlike their more conscientious peasant counterparts) who tried to remedy their poverty not by seeking work but by resorting to crime. Secondly, the problem of unemployment had substantially worsened after thousands of monastic servants found themselves without an income after the dissolution of the monasteries in the 1530s.[62]

Religion was held to be as important in explaining the communist values of the sixteenth-century peasants as it had been in explaining the similar values of their medieval counterparts; but the emphasis now was less on the egalitarian roots of Christianity than on the rise of Protestantism. Protestantism was usually interpreted by the Marxist writers of the 1930s as an attempt to adapt Christianity to the needs of emergent capitalism.[63] Where medieval Catholicism had promulgated a 'magical' conception of the relationship between man and nature, not least in its doctrine of transubstantiation, the early Protestants adopted a proto-rationalist outlook that was better suited to an age of science. Where Catholicism shored up the hierarchical structures of feudal society by promoting a top/down relationship between clergy and laity, the Protestants tried to parallel the looser relationship between capitalist and worker by speaking in terms of a 'priesthood of all believers'. And where the Catholic idea of personal responsibility was unconcerned to relate Godliness to a capacity for hard work, Protestantism responded to the disciplines of the new market society by developing its famous 'work ethic'. The point which the English communists made was that the new religious ideas were all susceptible to what Perry Anderson would later call 'inflection to the left'. In his great book on Bunyan, to which we shall return in the next section, Jack Lindsay noted that it was common for the early Protestant ideologues to be led by their religious convictions into a hatred for the ruling class. Angered by the pretensions of the Catholic clergy and convinced of the link between diligence and piety, men such as Bishop Latimer, Thomas Becon and Robert Crowley all argued that it could never be acceptable for one group of people to live off the labour of another.[64] Crowley, whom Lindsay quoted, wrote as follows:

> They [i.e. 'the men of law, the gentlemen, the lords'] take our houses over our heads, they buy our grounds out of our hands, they raise our rent, they levy great (yea unreasonable) fines, they enclose our commons. No custom, no law or statute can keep them from oppressing us in such sort that we know not which way to turn to live. Very need therefore constraineth us to stand up against them. In the country we cannot tarry but we must be their slaves and labour till our hearts brast, and then they must have all. And to go to the cities we have no hope, for there we hear that these insatiable beasts have all in their hands.[65]

Insofar as the peasant rebellions of the early-modern period were intended not merely to resist enclosure but to establish a classless society, it was because ideas such as Crowley's had filtered down from the Protestant elite to the common people. Moreover, there were occasions when the peasants actually bested their medieval counterparts by managing to establish an alternative set of political institutions. Lindsay pointed out that the Norfolk rebels had set up a people's court, based at the so-called 'Oak of Reformation' in Mousehold, where landowners were put on trial for enclosing the common lands.[66] Sixty years later, during the Midlands rising, the rebels instituted a system of communal farming after tearing down the fences that had excluded them from the fields.[67] Both these experiments were swiftly suppressed, but they provided evidence (or so Lindsay implied) that English radicalism was rooted in something far more substantial than a purely destructive attitude towards the *status quo*. It is worth emphasising how unorthodox these arguments would have seemed to the majority of British historians in the 1930s. The more conventional understanding of the peasant risings was that the events of 1536 and 1549 (though not necessarily of 1607) were primarily intended not to advance an economic objective but to *halt the Reformation in its tracks*. Far from being the consequence of Protestant scepticism towards existing elites, they actually reflected a streak of extreme religious conservatism on the part of a peasantry which remained overwhelmingly Catholic. The Pilgrimage of Grace was seen as a straightforward act of opposition to the dissolution of the monasteries, while the rebellions of 1549 were related to the efforts of the Protectorate (1547-1553) to introduce a genuine element of Protestant doctrine into a Reformation that had previously been concerned more with organisational matters than with theological fundamentals.[68] The English communists tried to resist this orthodoxy in one of two ways. Either they ignored it altogether (this was Lindsay's approach in *England My England*) or else they resorted to the argument that the peasant risings had been Catholic 'in form' but 'popular' in content.[69] Although the peasants felt obliged to formulate their grievances in the language of the dominant religion, their actions were entirely directed towards radical ends. Morton was able to partially justify this view by pointing out that the Norfolk Rising had been free of Catholic influence and had begun with an act of economic insurgency (an attack on enclosed land at Attleborough on June 20th) rather than a confrontation with the clerical authorities.[70]

Just as unorthodox as the interpretation of the peasant risings was the attempt to assimilate a number of sixteenth-century intellectuals to the radical tradition. The three writers who were singled out in the 1930s were Thomas More (seen as a critic of emergent capitalism and an early exponent of English communism), William Shakespeare (seen as a disillusioned commentator on the alliance between the bourgeoisie and the absolutist state) and Edmund Spenser (seen as a prescient analyst of poetry's incompatibility with market institutions). More's work was examined briefly by Edgell Rickword in 'Culture, Progress, and English Tradition'[71] (1937) and more extensively by John Strachey in *The Theory and Practice of Socialism* (1936), a remarkable introduction to Marxism which was published by the Left Book Club as one of its monthly 'Choices'. Most conventional accounts of More's life and work have been powerfully influenced by the circumstances of his death. Because of his execution in 1535 after refusing to swear an oath of allegiance to Henry VIII, he has usually been regarded either as a stern defender of the Catholic faith (hence his subsequent canonisation) or as an early exponent of religious tolerance. Strachey's tactic was to ignore More's religious side altogether and portray him as a purely political figure. According to Strachey, who was chiefly interested in the ideas contained in *Utopia* (1516), More was primarily important because he identified the dislocations caused by early capitalism and understood how a communist society would be able to eliminate them. There were two aspects of the new bourgeois order which he found especially repellent: enclosure (which linked his concerns to those of the peasant movement)[72] and what Marx would later call 'commodity fetishism'.[73] Enclosure, he implied, was not to be regarded as a necessary element in the transition from one economic system to another, but rather as an act of organised theft whose ultimate consequence would be the breakdown of social order. When the peasantry was deprived of the ability to eke out a living on its own account, it would resort to crime before willingly selling its labour power to one of the new capitalist employers.[74] In Part One of *Utopia*, in which the book's protagonist Raphael Hythloday gives a jaundiced account of the state of contemporary England, More wrote as follows:

> Away they [i.e. the people displaced by enclosure] trudge, I say, out of their known and accustomed houses, finding no place to rest in. All their household stuff, which is very little worth, though it might well abide the sale: yet being suddenly thrust out, they be constrained to sell it for a thing of nought. And when they have wandered abroad till that be spent, what can they then else do but steal, and then justly pardy be hanged, or else go about a begging. And yet then also they be cast in prison as vagabonds.[75]

Strachey also seems to have been impressed by the rhetorical techniques which More developed to satirize the practice of enclosure. Noting that animals now grazed on enclosed land while human beings were allowed to starve, More wrote a famous passage in which he accused the ruling class of callously inverting a set of humane priorities which had proved their worth over centuries: '...they throw down houses; they pluck down towns, and leave nothing standing, but only the church to be made a sheep-house.'[76] Perhaps Strachey admired this form of address because it anticipated the modern rhetorical trick of portraying socialism as nothing more (and certainly nothing less) than the restoration of common sense. Rather less convincing was the claim that More could also be regarded as an early critic of commodity fetishism. According to Strachey, More was deeply troubled by the way that commodities seem to acquire a life of their own when placed for sale on an unplanned market, thereby convincing human beings that economic affairs are largely determined by non-human forces beyond their control. He expressed his discomfort by envisaging a utopian society in which silver and gold, the two main mediums of exchange, were treated with contempt: '...of gold and silver they [i.e. the utopians] make chamber pots, and other vessels that serve for most vile uses – thus by all means possible they procure to have gold and silver among them in reproach and infamy.'[77] Ingenious though it was, this interpretation (in which Utopia's disdain for silver and gold was seen as a direct consequence of its opposition to alienated labour) would not command the support of most other commentators on More's work. A more conventional interpretation would emphasise More's dislike of materialism, specifically the claim that his main reason for opposing capitalism was that it ruthlessly subordinates the cultivation of spiritual values to the acquisition of material wealth. By portraying a society in which it was more usual to defecate on precious metals than use them for ornaments, he was therefore expressing a deeply *ascetic* vision of life. Human beings, he believed, should have everything they need to survive but nothing more.

More's asceticism suggests that his conception of the ideal society was not only quite different from Marx's (it could scarcely have been otherwise in the early-sixteenth century) but also contained elements to which Marxists would be deeply opposed. This perhaps explains why Strachey seemed unwilling to give a detailed account of the structure of Utopian society. He followed Rickword, Lindsay and Morton in describing Utopia as a communist society in which the means of production were held in social ownership, but the less congenial aspects of More's outlook (the emphasis on asceticism, the belief in the regimentation of leisure, the support for imperialism or the dislike of non-believers) were completely disregarded.[78] There was merely a token reference to two of Utopia's more progressive features, one relating to its conduct of international affairs and the other to its treatment of crime. In the first place, Strachey pointed out, Utopia had a definite advantage over its rivals when it went to war. Because its internal affairs were stable and there was no question of popular revolt (not least because the people governed themselves) it could afford to expedite its military engagements by encouraging the citizens of enemy countries to overthrow their respective governments.[79] Secondly, its treatment of criminals was underpinned by an enlightened rejection of the more degrading forms of punishment. The small number of Utopian citizens who broke the law were not sent to prison but forced to do useful work in the community, thereby acquiring (or relearning) an appropriate sense of social responsibility. Writing at a time when Stalin's show trials were about to begin and thousands of Soviet citizens had already been wrongfully executed or sent to labour camps, Strachey insisted that 'We have a development of this system in the Soviet Union to-day, where punishment consists in the retraining of the individual by constructive work, either in an institution or in the outside world, but with a loss of civil rights. How striking it is that More foresaw that in a classless society, based on common ownership, where there is no question of one man's work competing with another's, this solution of the question of punishment (for it is little else) would become possible.'[80] It was a comment worthy of inclusion in Sidney and Beatrice Web's notoriously deluded *Soviet Communism: A New Civilisation?* (1935).[81]

The attempt to portray William Shakespeare as a member of the radical tradition was primarily made by Jack Lindsay, first in an essay in *Left Review* ('William Shakespeare', July 1937) and later in a couple of chapters in his book *A Short History of Culture* (1939).[82] At a time when scholarly work on Shakespeare was dominated by G. Wilson Knight's 'spatial' investigations of the canon's 'burning core of mental or spiritual reality',[83] Lindsay made no attempt to describe Shakespeare either as a partisan critic of early capitalism or as a man of communist sympathies. His more modest claim was that Shakespeare had been a supporter of the capitalist system who later came to loathe its tendency to weaken social cohesion. The radical element in his work was therefore its growing sense of disillusionment with the new market order. The more specific argument was that Shakespeare's work can only be understood against the backdrop of the alliance between the emergent bourgeoisie and the absolutist state which existed in England between the mid-fifteenth and early-seventeenth centuries. For most of this period, Lindsay claimed, the state had generally acted in the interests of the bourgeoisie. It had removed barriers to trade, reformed the established church and given its cautious blessing to the process of enclosure. This was the context in which Shakespeare conceived his early support for capitalism. Anxious that English society would be atomised by the emergence of market institutions, he nevertheless came to believe that the absolutist state could use its authority to create a countervailing sense of social solidarity. However, when the alliance between the Crown and the bourgeoisie began to break down (a process which began in the mid-sixteenth century and reached its crisis point in the Jacobean period) Shakespeare was forced to the conclusion that there was no force on earth that could prevent capitalism from spreading its individualist poisons. At this point, though he could offer no alternative to the existing system, he effectively became a tribune of the radical sensibility.[84]

According to Lindsay, Shakespeare's early optimism about the alliance between Crown and bourgeoisie was reflected in most of the plays of the 1590s. In *Romeo and Juliet* he sketched a portrait of two determined individualists who defied feudal restrictions (represented by the wishes of their respective families) but still managed to achieve a perfect sense of spiritual communion – proof that the new market values were no barrier to social cohesion.[85] In a number of his comedies he satirised the main genres associated with medieval high culture, showing that it was not necessary to recreate the past in order to preserve a sense of national unity. *Love's Labour's Lost* was an attack on the 'courtly love college', *A Midsummer Night's Dream* subverted the courtly masque and *As You Like It* attempted a carnivalesque inversion of the values of pastoral.[86] Shakespeare's purpose in the history plays was to underscore his belief that the maintenance of social cohesion depended entirely on the continued strength of the absolutist state. By surveying the process of state formation over the previous 300 years, he wished to mythologise the moment at which England had been rescued from political division by the emergence of a strong centralised monarchy.[87] If this meant that Magna Carta was written out of history altogether (on the grounds that it represented a destabilising victory for the regions over the centre) it also involved the portrayal of Henry V as a 'fully successful king' who 'achieves national unification and is yet democratic and anti-feudal in his attitude.'[88] Yet even in these early plays, Lindsay went on to argue, there were plenty of signs that Shakespeare was beginning to have doubts about the nature of capitalist society. For example, John of Gaunt's famous evocation of England in *Richard 11* ('this earth, this realm...') was unexpectedly followed by an anguished assault on the predominance of commercial values. England, he said, is:

> ... now leased out, I die pronouncing it,
> like a tenement or pelting farm,
> England, bound in with the triumphant sea,
> whose rocky shore beats back the envious surge
> of watery Neptune, is now bound in with shame,
> with inky blots and rotten parchment bonds.[89]

Lindsay's argument was that passages such as this embodied the dawning recognition that the absolutist state was ultimately quite powerless to mitigate the consequences of capitalist individualism. This became the political assumption that preoccupied Shakespeare in the work of his maturity.[90] In the plays which he wrote in the opening years of the seventeenth century, notably *Julius Caesar, Hamlet, King Lear, Othello* and *Macbeth*, he struggled to understand why neither the bourgeoisie nor the Crown had managed to construct an alliance that might have rescued England from commercial anarchy. His answer, shaped as it was by an unavoidable absence of historical perspective, was that human beings possess a 'blind principle of self-destruction'[91] that invariably corrupts their strivings for wealth and power. This lugubrious doctrine was especially well illustrated in *King Lear*. When Lear invited his three daughters to compete for his estate, he inadvertently encouraged them to set aside their feelings of filial devotion and engage in a brutal struggle for material advantage. Having started the crisis, he then proved by his descent into madness that he had been too corrupted by decades of power to be able to restore order.[92] Although Shakespeare's disillusionment with the alliance between Crown and bourgeoisie would ultimately lead to the 'screaming anarchism' of *Timon of Athens*,[93] there were still occasional signs that he was beginning to identify new sources of political hope. In *Antony and Cleopatra* he wrote admiringly about the same feudal impulses which he had denigrated in his work of the 1590s, holding up the relationship between the lovers as a model of what the human spirit had achieved before the introduction of the cash nexus.[94] More significantly, he also began to reveal a new sympathy for the political aspirations of the masses. In *Coriolanus*, written (as Lindsay noted) just after the Midlands Rising of 1607, Shakespeare endowed the people with a level of political insight and purity of motive that was denied to the other characters:

> Care for us! ...Suffer us to famish and their storehouses crammed with grain. Make edicts for usury, to support usurers. Repeal daily any wholesome act established against the rich, and provide more piercing statutes daily to tie up and restrain the poor. If the wars eat us not up, they will; and that's all the love they bear us.

> The Gods know I speak this in hunger of bread, not in thirst for revenge.[95]

Yet ultimately, Lindsay implied, neither nostalgia for feudalism nor a nascent faith in the masses was enough to rescue Shakespeare from a paralysing political despair. In his final plays he retreated from politics into an aesthetic universe of his own making. *Cymbeline* and *A Winter's Tale* tried to revive the conventions of pastoral, while the *Tempest* was a lengthy meditation on the nature of creativity.[96] 'After that', wrote Lindsay in one of the dramatic observations which peppered his best work, 'there was nothing for him to do unless he was willing to play with hack-work. He had his competence and retired'.[97]

The most unlikely writer to be credited with radical instincts by the English communists was Edmund Spenser, the subject of a subtle essay by Alick West in *Left Review* ('The "Poetry" in Poetry', April 1937). As the author of *The Faerie Queene*, a lengthy allegory on the greatness of Elizabeth I, Spenser is usually regarded as the most inveterately monarchist of English poets. West made no attempt to revise our understanding of Spenser's politics, but instead drew attention to an element of cultural critique in his work that had previously been overlooked. At the heart of many of Spenser's poems, he implied, was a prescient understanding of why capitalist society is 'inimical' to the writing of great poetry. In a passage which probably owed something to the ideas of Christopher Caudwell (but which also recalled the anthropological sections of his own *Crisis and Criticism*) West theorised the opposition between capitalism and poetry in two ways. In the first place, the poetic impulse is compromised under capitalism because poetry is a fundamentally *collective* form which is now called upon to express individualist assumptions. When poetry emerged in primitive society its purpose was to use rhythmic language to bind people together while they worked: its role in an age of markets is to express the poet's sense of his own isolation from others.[98] This tension between collective form and individualist content induces a sense of futility in the poet which serves only to undermine his creativity.[99] His creativity is further undermined (this was West's second point) by the disjuncture between capitalism's indifference to aesthetic values and poetry's obsession with the transformation of sensibility. Of all the forms of literary expression, West implied, it is poetry which works most tirelessly to restore the vitality of our sense impressions. Yet under capitalism, which is 'concerned with the quantity of exchange-value in the commodity, not with the quality of its use-value; and ...operates through the anarchy of free competition',[100] the poet is confronted by a public who have been so deprived of aesthetic stimulation in their work that their capacity to experience pleasure has dwindled almost to nothing. He therefore tries to 'compensate' for the philistine limitations of the age by 'being determinedly poetical in particulars',[101] producing work in which the individual image is smothered beneath language of a self-conscious elegance and density: 'the poem as a whole, for which capitalism has no use, tends to disintegrate into "poetical" phrases.'[102] Spenser, West implied, had an intuitive understanding of these matters which he occasionally dramatised in verse. The argument was illustrated with a detailed analysis of Spenser's poem *Prothalamion*, which contained a typically ornate fantasy about the poet watching a 'Flocke of Nymphes' responding to two swans gliding down the Thames.[103] The two most relevant verses read as follows:

Efstoones the Nymphes, which now had Flowers their fill,
Ran all in haste, to see that silver brood,
As they came floating on the Christal Flood.
Whom when they sawe, they stood amazed still,
Their wondring eyes to fill,
Them seem'd they never saw a sight so fayre,
Of Fowles so lovely, that they sure did deeme
Them heavenly borne, or to be that same payre
Which through the Skie draw Venus silver Teeme,
For sure they did not seeme,
To be begot of any earthly Seede,
But rather Angels or of Angels breede:
Yet were they bred of Somers-heat they say,
In sweetest Season, when each Flower and weede
The earth did fresh aray,
So fresh they seem'd as day,
Even as their Brydale day, which was not long:

Sweete Themmes run softly, till I end my Song.

Then forth they all out of their baskets drew,
Great store of Flowers, the honour of the field,
That to the sense did fragrant odours yeild,
All which upon those goodly Birds they threw,
And all the Waves did strew,
That like old Peneus Waters they did seeme,
When downe along by pleasant Tempes shore
Scattred with Flowres, through Thessaly they streeme,
That they appeare through Lillies plenteous store,
Like a Brydes Chamber flore:
Two of those Nymphes meane while, two Garlands bound,
Of freshest Flowres which in that Mead they found,
The which presenting all in trim Array,
Their snowy Foreheads therewithall they crownd,
Whil'st one did sing this Lay,
Prepar'd against that Day,
Against their Brydale day, which was not long:
Sweete Themmes runne softly, till I end my Song.[104]

Although *Prothalamion* was originally intended to celebrate a wedding, West believed that there are several ways in which it can also be read as a sort of self-reflexive meditation on the limitations of poetry in the capitalist age. The above verses are organised around an implicit comparison between the original function of poetry and the function of poetry in Spenser's time. Captivated by the sight of two swans floating down the Thames, a 'Flock of Nymphes' pay tribute to their beauty in a ritual that is essentially *collective* in nature – they sing, dance, bear flowers and so on. 'The scene', West wrote, 'is a "literary" description of poetry as it was originally sung and acted.'[105] Yet the poet who observes the ritual is completely isolated from the things he records. Unable to join the nymphs in their celebration of the spirit of nature, he exemplifies the inability of the bourgeois artist to experience the sort of group consciousness which lies at the heart of great poetry. The resulting sense that one type of poetic consciousness is now being superseded by another, with disastrous results for poetry, is also reflected at a more formal level, specifically in the tension between the 'I' who speaks in the verses ('A Flocke of *Nymphes* I chaunced to espy') and the 'I' who speaks in the refrain ('Sweet *Themmes* runne softly, till I end my song'). Whereas the former communicates a feeling of isolation, the latter seems to have temporarily recaptured some of the group spirit that has otherwise been sacrificed to market values.[106] But the relationship between the verse and the refrain is not entirely one of contrast. In a passage of what might now be called deconstruction (in Derrida's sense of the term) West argued that Spenser's intention was to show antithetical forms of individual and collective awareness beginning to leak into each other: 'the two tones affect one another...The poem is neither wholly marriage song, nor wholly personal expression. Like the "I", it is indeterminately between the more "individual" and the more "social" Spenser.'[107] Presumably West admired this blurring of categories because it proved that the yearning for social integration can never be entirely suppressed, even in a society which encourages its members to think of themselves as self-determining atoms.[108] At a time when capitalism was still in its infancy, Spenser's genius (and the source of his radicalism) was the ability to diagnose the problems which all bourgeois poets had been forced to endure. In a laconic piece of partisan rhetoric at the end of his essay, West suggested that it was only recently, with the emergence of the communist movement, that the poetic impulse had begun to revive: 'The older poems were not poems of phrases. Nor are the new ones.'[109]

2.3. The English Revolution

If the first two stages in the history of English radicalism were seen as the direct result of economic changes, then the third stage (roughly between 1640 and 1660) was usually described as the unintended consequence of developments in high politics. All the main strands in the plebeian radicalism of the seventeenth century were traced to the influence of the English Revolution. The Revolution was widely interpreted by British Marxists as a 'bourgeois revolution' of the sort which Marx and Engels had analysed in their writings on European history – that is, as a straightforward contest for state power between the emergent bourgeoisie (represented by Parliament) and the feudal aristocracy (represented by the Crown). Its purpose was to free the new capitalist order from arbitrary restrictions imposed by the absolutist state. Yet it was also recognised that many of the revolutionaries were driven by a fervent desire to renew the Protestant impulse. In the period since the Reformation, or so it was argued, the leaders of the established Church had lapsed back into authoritarianism. The aim of groups such as the Puritans, the Presbyterians and the so-called 'anarchists of religion'[110] (Quakers, Congregationalists and so on) was therefore to challenge ecclesiastical power and restructure the relationship between clergy and laity along more egalitarian lines.[111] The idea of bourgeois revolution was explored most fully in Morton's *A People's History of England* (especially Chapters VII, VIII and IX) and Christopher Hill's early essay 'The English Revolution 1640"'(1940).[112] It was only later that British Marxists would propose a much more sophisticated Marxist interpretation of the events of the Cromwellian era, seeing them (in the words of Perry Anderson) as a 'clash between two segments of a landowning class, neither of which were direct crystallizations of opposed economic interests, but rather were partially contingent but predominantly intelligible lenses into which wider, more radically antagonistic social forces came into temporary and distorted focus'.[113]

However, although the communists expended a lot of energy trying to prove that the English Revolution was indeed of bourgeois origins, they also argued that the demand for parliamentary and ecclesiastical reform caused ideological tremors which spread outwards from the elite groups and galvanised the common people. The result was a series of popular movements, some political and some religious, which used the principles of the Revolution as the starting point for a sweeping attack on the privileges of the bourgeoisie, the aristocracy and the clergy. In the 1930s, long before the bewildering variety of radical sects which Hill examined in *The World Turned Upside Down* (1972) were widely known, the only political movements to be singled out for analysis were the Levellers and the Diggers. It was Jack Lindsay who provided the simplest and most dramatic account of these movements in *England My England*. The Levellers, he argued, were the last representatives of rural communism ever to achieve influence in Britain. Strongly plebeian in origin, they struggled to convert Cromwell and his army to a radical programme of constitutional reform (including outright abolition of the monarchy, biennial parliaments and religious freedom)[114] because they thought it would lead to precisely the sort of communist society which the English peasants had been intermittently trying to establish since 1381.[115] By contrast, the Diggers marked the emergence of a distinctively *modern* type of communism. When they established their famous commune on St George's Hill in Surrey in 1649, their aim (or so Lindsay argued) was to create a network of egalitarian communities that would harness scientific knowledge to the task of boosting production.[116] Morton and Hill were both more circumspect than Lindsay. They argued that the Levellers were better understood as a movement of 'small independent men'[117] (tenant farmers and the like) who aimed to challenge the dominance of the bourgeoisie by ensuring that the lower-middle-class had a voice in Parliament. At no time did they embrace communist values or consist primarily of workers and peasants. Convinced that the emerging proletariat was likely to do the political bidding of its employers, they even argued that the parliamentary franchise should be extended to every adult in Britain *with the exception of wage earners*. Insofar as the Levellers deserved their place in the radical pantheon, it was because (1) their hostility to the bourgeoisie inspired a small amount of independent working-class protest in London and elsewhere, and (2) their programme of constitutional reform (embodied in *The Demands of the People*) anticipated that of the Chartists by nearly 200 years.[118] However, there was one point on which Lindsay, Morton and Hill could all agree. Without the influence of the Levellers, they insisted, Cromwell would never have been persuaded at the end of the 1640s to eschew the path of class compromise and institute a genuine republic. The regicide of Charles I was more the product of pressure from below than a reflection of the settled political will of the bourgeois revolutionaries. The Diggers proved to be more contentious. Morton and Hill both argued, *contra* Lindsay, that the experiment on St George's Hill had very little to do with the emergence of modern communism. Although leading Diggers such as Gerrard Winstanley placed a novel emphasis on the need for working people to acquire scientific knowledge (an issue we shall return to in a moment) their vision of the good society was practically identical to that of the earlier peasant communists.[119] A third perspective on the Diggers was provided by John Strachey, who implied in *The Theory and Practice of Socialism* that the extent of their political ambition had sometimes been overstated. Far from seeking to operate across the whole of Britain, their more modest goal was to establish a series of communist colonies on areas of common land which had yet to be enclosed.[120] Strachey's remarks were rooted in the misconception that the original Digger colony had been based on one of the few remaining pieces of common land in Surrey, whereas in fact (as Lindsay and Hill pointed out) it was constructed entirely on waste ground.

The argument was then extended to the issue of *religious* radicalism. Just as the bourgeois exponents of parliamentary rule were inadvertently responsible for stirring the masses into political action, so the Protestant revolutionaries inspired the creation of a network of 'dissenting sects' which served as a major stimulus to working-class revolt over the next 150 years. At first sight, or so it was argued, the aims of 'establishment' groups such as the Puritans and Presbyterians were comparatively modest. The Puritans, inspired by the Calvinist doctrine of predestination and convinced of their status as God's 'elect', merely wanted the right to disregard ecclesiastical rulings on matters such as church ritual, preaching methods and the observance of religious festivals. The Presbyterians wanted to restructure the established Church along the lines of the Scottish kirk. Yet the real significance of both these groups was that they injected an element of democratic idealism into religious debate which revolutionised the organisational forms of popular religion. Composed primarily of working-class and petty-bourgeois congregations, the main Dissenting groups (Quakers, Baptists, Congregationalists etc.) operated on the assumption that the main duty of the clergy was to carry out the wishes of the laity. In doing so they ensured that egalitarian values were to survive unscathed throughout the long period of political stasis between the suppression of the Levellers and Diggers and the emergence of the modern labour movement. Although the writers of the 1930s were largely uninterested in exploring the 'fine tale of the dissenters'[121] (Lindsay's phrase) they nevertheless implied that Dissent was best regarded as a sort of temporary displacement of communist values onto the sphere of religious organisation.[122]

The various strands in seventeenth-century radicalism were reflected by the group of writers to whom the communists devoted individual studies. There was one Leveller (Richard Overton), one Digger (Gerrard Winstanley), one radical Protestant who helped create the intellectual climate in which Dissent could flourish (John Milton) and one *bona fide* Dissenter (John Bunyan). The work of Overton and Winstanley, though not examined in detail, was seen as important because it contained the first real element of freethinking (if not outright atheism) in the history of radical doctrine.[123] Overton, the most important of the Leveller pamphleteers, was the subject of an essay which Montagu Slater contributed to the first issue of *Left Review* under the pseudonym 'Ajax'.[124] Much of the piece was taken up with a brisk account of Overton's arrest by Cromwell's Council of State in 1649, his imprisonment in the Tower of London with John Lilburne and his subsequent acquittal at a legendary treason trial.[125] Yet its implicit point was that Overton had a streak of hedonism in his personality which made him unflaggingly hostile to the bourgeois ideal of self-denial, and which marked him out as an early example of what can perhaps be called the radical clown. During his period in the Tower, for instance, he wrote a passage in which he appeared to urge his fellow Levellers to recognise the political benefits of drinking: 'My Brethren of the Sea Green order [i.e. the Levellers], take a little wine with your water and I'll take a little water with my wine and it will temper us to the best constitution.'[126] He then described alcohol as 'the preserver of being and motion and the original of that habit of laughter".[127] Slater seemed to think that the point of all this boozy exuberance was that it provided Overton with a compelling persona which he could use in his attacks on the existing order. Though always intellectually rigorous, his critique of the dominant ideology was invariably freighted with a seasoned drinker's irreverence and good humour. There was a powerful example of all this in his book *Man Wholly Mortal* (1655), which contained a withering assault on the doctrine of human immortality. It was often argued at the time that the soul could survive death because the responsibility for creating new life was shared between human beings and God, with the latter intervening at the moment of conception to endow the newly created human with a soul. Yet if this were so, Overton argued, then human beings would be capable of producing 'angelic entitie[s]' much superior to themselves, and this is clearly not the case: 'No! Man in his kinde begets corruptable [sic] man, begets nothing but what is corruptable, not half mortal, half immortal, half angel, half man, but compleat [sic] man, totally mortal.'[128] Quite a sophisticated point about the weakness of dualist ideas was thus expressed in the form of a joke. More broadly, Slater implied, the significance of books like *Man Wholly Mortal* was that they symbolised the moment at which the radical tradition began to detach itself from its Christian roots. Aware that the promise of an afterlife has frequently been used as a specific against secular change, Overton was making a conscious effort to ally English radicalism with the tradition of philosophical materialism. From this point on the tension between radical Christianity and militant atheism becomes central to the story of British radicalism.

A similar theme informed John Strachey's brief remarks on the work of Gerrard Winstanley, the most famous member of the Diggers. According to Strachey, Winstanley's great significance was that he developed a predominantly secular conception of the nature of working-class education. In his book *The Law of Freedom*, produced after the collapse of the experiment on St George's Hill, he insisted that the proper role of the clergy was to instruct ordinary people in the first principles of science, economics and politics – there should be no room for irrelevant ideas about God, Heaven or the nature of the afterlife. Although the whole argument was justified in religious terms ('To know the secrets of nature is to know the works of God; and to know the works of God within the Creation, is to know God himself...'),[129] Strachey nevertheless regarded it as sure proof that Winstanley had made the transition from Quakerism to 'magnificently expressed materialism'. As such, his main relevance to the radical tradition was that he anticipated the Marxist conviction that social liberation can only occur once the common people have consciously rejected the lure of religion.[130]

If the English communists saw Overton and Winstanley as pioneers of the link between philosophical materialism and political radicalism, they nevertheless regarded John Milton and John Bunyan as the last great representatives of progressive Christianity. Both, so the argument went, exemplified the mood of democratic idealism which revivified the Protestant vision in the early seventeenth century and led to the emergence of Dissent. An essay on Milton by Edgell Rickword appeared in *The English Revolution 1640* (1940), a book of essays edited by Christopher Hill to mark the 300th anniversary of the outbreak of the Civil War. Rickword virtually ignored Milton's poetry and concentrated instead on his work as a pamphleteer and politician in the twenty years between the establishment of the Long Parliament (1640) and the Restoration (1660). At the heart of the essay was an account of the religious pamphlets which Milton wrote towards the beginning of the period, especially *The Reason of Church Government urged against Prelatry* (1642).[131] According to Rickword, most of these pamphlets were a response to the Bill introduced by Parliament in 1642 to abolish episcopacy. Inspired by the Bill's attempt to restore Protestant values to the established Church, especially its insistence that the principle of divine ordination should now be revoked, Milton set out to explore a model of church organisation that was far too radical for either the Puritans or the Presbyterians (though not the Dissenters) to consider. His basic argument was that congregations should have the right to elect and remove their ministers, on the assumption that religious officials are otherwise inclined to indulge 'their ostentation, their belly-worship, their fostering of superstitious rites, and, basically, their association with the State power' (Rickword's paraphrase).[132] Moreover, he saw very clearly that a relationship of accountability between clergy and laity would only be sustained if certain other reforms were also granted. At various times in the 1640s he called for the disestablishment of the Church of England, an end to priestly interference in the private affairs of the individual (including the relaxation of the divorce laws), complete liberty of action for all Protestant sects and complete freedom of speech. In his *Speech for the Liberty of Unlicensed Printing* (1644), more commonly known as *Areopagitica*, Milton anticipated the Millian argument that freedom of discussion is the essential precondition for discovering the truth.[133]

Between 1649 and 1660, Rickword went on to point out, Milton made a concerted effort to translate his religious convictions into political action. Apart from defending the Commonwealth in a stream of pamphlets, notably *The Tenure of Kings and Magistrates* (1649) and *Eikonoklastes* (1650), he was appointed Secretary for Foreign Tongues in 1649 and thus became central to the new government's relationship with foreign regimes.[134] There were two aspects of Milton's political career that Rickword seemed to find especially significant. In the first place, simply by devoting his time to the business of high politics, Milton proved that political engagement was no barrier to artistic excellence – or, more precisely, he showed how a writer might 'fit himself for a supreme creative effort by many years of intellectual and moral preparation'.[135] Rickword even hinted that the poems of the 1660s and 1670s would never have been written if their author had not spent twenty years 'immersed utterly' in the social struggle. More important still was the epochal contribution to political theory which Milton allegedly made after the regicide of Charles I in 1649. Defending Parliament against the charge of barbarism, Milton argued that no government could be legitimate unless it somehow rested on the consent of the people. In one fell swoop, Rickword appeared to be claiming, he had coined an idea which put the wishes of ordinary people at the heart of political debate, not because of its originality but because of the circumstances in which it was uttered:

It has been said that Milton's thesis is 'in line with the main development of liberal political theory throughout the Middle Ages and Renaissance' and that he 'says nothing that had not been said a hundred times'. But to assert popular sovereignty in general, and in such particular circumstances as the public and ceremonial (for it could not be called legal) decapitation of a king whose legitimacy was indisputable, this is as different as chalk from cheese...But that the lower orders...should not have quietly killed Charles but deliberately challenged popular opinion by the appeal to right and justice, that was what made the ruling classes of Europe realize that something new had entered their circle of calculation.[136]

What was the source of this incendiary emphasis on the will of the people? The other crucial element in Rickword's essay was the claim that Milton's religious and political outlook was partly the result of his fascination with science and scientific method. The most important influence in this respect was Francis Bacon's writings on the philosophy of science, especially *The Advancement of Learning* (1605), which Milton first encountered while still a schoolboy at St Paul's. Milton was especially interested in Bacon's attack on the deductive method and his related account of the role of induction in the accumulation of scientific knowledge. As is well known, Bacon had argued that it is not possible to draw accurate conclusions about the physical universe by applying the laws of formal logic to so-called 'first principles'. The only reliable source of scientific knowledge is the scrupulous observation of abundant data, much of it derived from experimental procedures, with a view to identifying universal laws, processes and 'latent schematicisms'. Milton was also impressed by the note of scientific triumphalism which runs through Bacon's work. Once the inductive method has been applied systematically to the investigation of nature, Bacon predicted, human beings will be able to exercise complete control over their environment. Although Rickword did not make it entirely clear how Bacon's philosophy had affected the political culture of the English Revolution, there were probably several ways in which ideas such as these helped to reinforce the egalitarian cast of Milton's mind. By implying that wisdom could be acquired through something as simple as observation (as opposed to the tortuous processes of formal logic) Bacon seemed to suggest that it would be safe to devolve power from an intellectual elite to the community as a whole. And if it was indeed the case that science could enable human beings to liberate themselves from the elements, the society which resulted would surely be one in which personal autonomy took priority over government control.[137] There were even occasions, Rickword implied, when Milton seemed to be groping towards the cardinal Marxist insight that freedom entails the recognition of necessity.[138] More prosaically, Milton's adherence to Baconian philosophy also led to some early insights into the intransigence of authority. At both school and university (he attended Christ's College, Cambridge between 1625 and 1632) his education was dominated by the assumption that the mark of an educated mind was the ability to use the syllogistic procedures handed down by Aristotle and the medieval Christian philosophers. 'The method', wrote Rickword, 'of testing the qualifications of students then in use was by means of a public debate, in Latin, of course, in which one candidate would defend and another attack a given proposition according to the rules of the prescribed system of logic.'[139] When Milton dismissed all this as 'degenerate learning'[140] and urged his teachers to adopt the Baconian method, he received a scornful response which permanently cured him of the belief that those who wield the greatest power are also possessed of the finest minds. Rickword's argument at this point was probably influenced by the unusual intellectual culture of inter-war communism. At a time when communists liked to claim that their belief in socialism was rooted not merely in a specific understanding of history (i.e. historical materialism) but also in a universal philosophy derived from scientific data (i.e. dialectical materialism), it was doubtless reassuring to point out that John Milton himself had justified his political beliefs with reference to scientific principles.[141]

The writer who most powerfully expressed the Dissenting ethos which Milton had helped to shape was undoubtedly John Bunyan. Jack Lindsay's book *John Bunyan: Maker of Myths* (1937) was by far the most distinguished attempt in the 1930s to analyse the work of an individual member of the radical tradition. Employing ideas drawn from both Marxism and psychoanalysis to relate Bunyan's personal history to the economic, political and religious trends which existed in Britain at the time of the English Revolution, it is the sort of book – typical of Lindsay – that effortlessly holds a range of themes in play at the same time. However, it is most profitably approached as a study of the relationship between Christianity and communism – or, more precisely, as an attempt to balance an optimistic understanding of Christianity's radical potential against a more cautious recognition of the way that supernatural beliefs often blunt the desire for change. On the one hand, Lindsay argued, Bunyan was one of the many thinkers whose communist instincts have been both shaped and reinforced by Christian doctrine.[142] On the other hand, his support for a broadly Calvinist interpretation of the metaphysical foundations of Christianity (specifically the doctrine that the will of God can only be fulfilled in the kingdom of Heaven) ensured that large portions of his work were taken up with a vigorous defence of bourgeois ideology. The argument can only be fully understood if we take a closer look at three elements in Lindsay's book: first, its account of Bunyan's conversion to Christianity; second, its examination of Bunyan's attitude towards the dominant ideology in seventeenth-century Britain; and third, its analysis of the way that Bunyan's suppressed desire for revolution constantly undermined the more fatalistic aspects of his thought.

The account of Bunyan's conversion to Christianity, based on the early sections of *Grace Abounding* (1666), took up most of the first 100 pages of Lindsay's book.[143] Its purpose was to demonstrate the sheer durability of the radical element in Christian doctrine. Bunyan, or so it was argued, rejected Christianity as an adolescent because it appeared to conflict with his egalitarian prejudices, but later returned to it when he realised that communist values were central to the Christian ethic. Lindsay analysed the formation of Bunyan's radical outlook in a way which deftly interweaved the personal and the political. Born in 1628 in a village near Bedford, Bunyan belonged to a family which had endured an appreciable loss of status in the period since the birth of capitalism. Most of his ancestors had been yeoman farmers, yet his immediate relatives (including his father) were reduced to working as 'chapmen and tinkers'. Lindsay argued that Bunyan's hatred of inequality stemmed from the humiliation he must have experienced while living among people who knew only too well that his family had fallen on hard times.[144] It was powerfully reinforced by the behaviour of his own father, who caused a minor scandal in August 1644 by remarrying within two months of his second wife's death. The young Bunyan interpreted this betrayal as a confirmation that authority was nothing but a byword for moral degeneracy.[145] Some months later he began a period of service with Cromwell's New Model Army which inclined his thoughts in a political direction. Inspired by the sense of community which prevailed among his fellow soldiers, exposed (or so Lindsay speculated) to the radical egalitarianism of both the Levellers and the Independents, he at last began to feel that it would be possible to create a society in which all hierarchies had been swept away.[146]

The main consequence of this early rebellion was that Bunyan violently rejected the Christian culture of his elders.[147] The idea of God, he now came to believe, was simply a metaphysical hoax intended to bolster the credibility of temporal authority. Nor was he the sort of man to keep his heretical views to himself. For a number of years he went out of his way to offend believers with scandalous displays of impious behaviour. He became, in Lindsay's vivid phrase, an 'insensate blasphemer and swearer.'[148] And yet, within weeks of being discharged from Cromwell's army in 1647, he was plunged into a period of intense religious anxiety which culminated some years later (in the early 1650s) in his conversion to the brand of Dissenting Christianity that he preached for the rest of his life. In one of his more ingenious attempts to fuse Marxist and Freudian perspectives, Lindsay suggested that Bunyan's yearning for a reconciliation with Christianity was symptomatic of the problems which adolescents tend to encounter in a class-divided society. Adolescence, or so it was argued, is a period in which the advent of physical maturity makes it necessary for the individual to be fully integrated into society. The problem is that class societies are simply too heterogeneous for complete integration to be possible, with the result that the adolescent is oppressed by a sense of being both inside and outside the social group. The consequence is what one writer has called a 'compulsion to think'.[149] Anxious to understand a world that has not fully accepted him, the adolescent embarks on an obsessively cerebral attempt to divine the meaning of existence. Driven back on his undeveloped intellectual resources, wholly indifferent to everything except his own thoughts, he begins to regard himself as the 'centre of the universe'.[150] Crucially, Lindsay argued, this engenders a prolonged state of cosmic paranoia in which everything seems like the product of divine intervention. When Bunyan turned back to Christianity, therefore, he was seeking to contain his religious intuitions in a doctrinal framework that would prevent them threatening his sanity.[151]

Bunyan's behaviour during the period of his conversion was that of a man on the verge of a complete nervous breakdown. Tramping furiously through the village of Elstow, where he now lived with his wife, he endured 'brain-storms of seething heat and intolerable anxiety'[152] in which he wrestled with the malign supernatural forces that appeared to be preying upon him. Lindsay suggested that two episodes in particular were crucial to his eventual reconciliation with Christianity, chiefly (as we have already implied) because they convinced him that the Christian vision was wholly consonant with his egalitarian instincts. The first occurred when one of his imagined 'tempters' tried to incite him to 'sell and part with this most blessed Christ, to exchange him for the things of this life, for anything'.[153] According to Lindsay, the important thing about this demoniacal temptation was that it forced Bunyan to focus on the suspicion of commercial values which lies at the heart of Christian teaching. Appalled that anyone should sacrifice his faith in Christ in order to acquire earthly wealth, he tried to protect himself against mortal sin by invoking the passage in the Bible in which Christ declares that 'the land shall not be sold for ever, for the land is mine'.[154] The second episode occurred when Bunyan became preoccupied with the parable of Esau.[155] His special concern was with the way that Esau had defied his father's wishes through the 'selling of his birthright.'[156] Quoting passages from Lilburne, Crowley, Francis Trigge and Gerrard Winstanley, Lindsay argued that the idea of selling a birthright was widely used by seventeenth-century radicals as a metaphor for the private ownership of the means of production, as when Winstanley complained that:

Before they [i.e. the common people] are suffered to plant the waste land for a livelihood, they must pay rent to their brethren for it. Well, this is the burden the Creation groans under; and the subjects (so-called) have not their Birthright Freedom granted them from their brethren, who hold it from them by club law, but not by righteousness.[157]

When Bunyan came to interpret the parable of Esau, therefore, he saw it not merely as a meditation on the nature of parental authority (though it was certainly that) but more importantly as a representation of God's anger at the institution of private property and the existence of classes. It was in this context that his conversion to Christianity became possible. The young rebel who had dismissed Christianity as a prop of the ruling class was now able to return to it, primarily (or so Lindsay implied) because he had been able to convince himself that his communist convictions were an accurate reflection of God's will. Yet the argument now took a twist which sharply distinguished it from other communist writings on the radical potential of the Christian tradition. Lindsay insisted that Bunyan's interpretation of the parable of Esau was not quite enough to make him a fully-fledged convert – there was still one thing that stood in the way of faith. Having satisfied himself that Christian values were indeed shaped by egalitarian concerns, Bunyan now began to worry that they could *never serve as the basis of earthly behaviour*. At a time when the challenge of the Levellers and the Diggers had just been brutally suppressed, he saw no prospect that English society would ever abandon its exploitative, hierarchical and impious ways. Surely, he began to ask, it is simply not possible to be a Christian while doubting the practicality of the Christian ethic? His anxiety on this score was finally brought to an end when he experienced an auditory hallucination, much less menacing than the ones which had plagued him for years, telling him that 'Thy righteousness is in heaven'.[158] From this point on he came to believe that the purpose of Christianity was to prepare human beings for the life hereafter, where God's values would reign unchallenged. It was simply not possible to promote the observance of Christian values in the here and now, since original sin had reduced human society to a state of irredeemable decadence. The centrepiece of Bunyan's subsequent work was therefore the rigid antithesis between 'Grace' and 'Law'. Grace, in this context, means the ability to recognise God's purpose in the midst of ungodly circumstances, whereas Law signifies the corrupt organisation of earthly society.[159]

Lindsay clearly believed that the contradictions in Bunyan's faith exemplified the big problem with radical interpretations of Christianity. Although an egalitarian reading of the Bible has done a great deal to crystallise opposition to social injustice, there is always a danger that radical Christians will retard political change by becoming fixated on the otherworldly dimension of their creed. One of Lindsay's main concerns was therefore to draw up a balance sheet of what Raymond Williams might have called the 'emergent' and 'hegemonic' aspects of Bunyan's Christianity. On the positive side, it is certainly true that Bunyan has exercised a radicalising influence on successive generations of working people. After joining the Independent Church in Bedford in 1653 and embarking on his life as a preacher, he became a strengthening influence on a dissenting culture which aimed to dissolve the hierarchy between clergy and laity and allow ordinary people to disseminate the Christian message for themselves. Without the force of his contribution, Lindsay implied, English dissent might well have diluted its commitment to democratic values and been reabsorbed into the established Church.[160] Nor did his understanding of Grace serve to lessen his anger at earthly injustice. While he undoubtedly thought of capitalism as the price to be paid for original sin, much of his work (including his sermons) was crammed with denunciations of commerce, inequality and the greed of the ruling class.[161] However, on the negative side, Bunyan's distinction between Grace and Law made him troublingly ambiguous in his attitude towards capitalism. All the dissenting groups of the seventeenth century were preoccupied by the issue of how Christians should behave in a society which they knew to be corrupt. There were several groups, exemplified by the early Quakers, which believed that the prevalence of moral decay implied a positive duty to transgress the standards of the wider society. Yet Bunyan seems to have believed that one of the functions of religion was to specify standards of behaviour that would 'reconcile' the believer with the unavoidable realities of earthly life. It was this, Lindsay suggested, which effectively made him one of the main ideologists of early capitalism. Especially important was his emphasis on the virtues of 'thrift', which corresponded to the economic imperative of subordinating personal consumption to the accumulation of capital. In his allegory *The Life and Death of Mr Badman* (1680), which traced the fortunes of a spendthrift tradesman who 'mouldered away' after a life of excess, he created one of the main sourcebooks of petty-bourgeois morality in the seventeenth and eighteenth centuries.[162] By refusing to believe that the kingdom of Heaven could be established on earth, Bunyan had not merely unbent the springs of resistance – he had gone a long way towards creating the ideas which allowed capitalism to flourish.[163]

Nevertheless, it was a testament to the fundamental optimism of the Popular Front period that Lindsay ultimately allowed his respect for the radical tradition to smother his anxieties about the limitations of Christian communism. If we look at the majority of Bunyan's writings, or so it was implied, we find that the element of religious fatalism is persistently subverted by an irrepressible desire for social revolution. *Pilgrim's Progress*, the book which E.P. Thompson later called 'one of the...foundation texts of the English working-class movement',[164] is ostensibly an illustration of the distinction between Grace and Law. Christian's anguished journey to the Celestial City is an allegorical representation of the ghastliness of earthly existence and the glory of Heaven. Yet the book is full of passages which brush against the grain of its declared theological position.[165] In the first place, Lindsay argued, Christian's progress towards redemption is usually characterised in terms of the trauma of birth.[166] Travelling in darkness, he makes his way through a succession of 'valleys and narrow places'[167] (suggestive of the womb) before he finally emerges into the brilliant sunlight of the Celestial City:

> Apply this analysis to his [i.e. Bunyan's] allegory, and the allegory's meaning is transformed. The world of light is not the land of death. It is the future of fellowship. The tale tells of the passage from privation and obstruction to light and joy and plenty. The heaven-symbol is brought down from beyond-death; it becomes a symbol of what earth could be made by fellowship.[168]

There is also a crucial moment at which Christian's personal quest is suddenly transformed into something more collective.[169] At the end of the book, when he is about to cross the river that will take him to the Celestial City, he is joined by his wife and two small children. The children are instructed to stay on the bank but his wife accompanies him on the swim towards paradise. At this point, Lindsay argued, Bunyan effectively 'confessed his sense that something was wrong about the idea of death as the goal of life',[170] and held out the hope that human beings might still achieve redemption while united in the here and now. Lindsay also detected something highly progressive in the *techniques* which Bunyan employed.[171] He argued that *Pilgrim's Progress* was clearly rooted in the 'pulpit style'[172] that was central to medieval popular culture. In its use of simple language, its personification of moral qualities and its reliance on 'homely metaphor and illustration',[173] it echoed the methods which had been used over centuries to transmit the Christian message to ordinary people. And yet, by achieving a level of expressivity that was simply absent from earlier examples of the tradition, it exemplified the process by which a reviled popular form can be 'canonised'[174] into something of high artistic significance. Moreover, the fact that the pulpit style had been passed down from generation to generation on a largely oral basis (printed texts like *Way to Paradise* were exceptions to the rule) hinted at the sheer durability of plebeian culture.[175] Finally, Bunyan's use of a popular style also enabled him to achieve a balance between 'extreme individual originality and profound mass content'.[176] The conventions which he employed had already appeared in thousands of religious declamations, but this did not prevent him from exploring a novel theological perspective and conveying a lively impression of his own sensibility. There was perhaps a foretaste here of some of Raymond Williams's much later theoretical writings, especially *Marxism and Literature* (1977), which interpreted literature as a 'form of material production' that anchors individual expressivity in a pattern of shared conventions.[177]

2.4. Swiftian Subversions

The third phase in the development of English radicalism encompassed the period between the Restoration (1660) and the Industrial Revolution.[178] It was portrayed by both Lindsay and Morton as something of a political hiatus. Neither the development of primitive forms of trade unionism, nor the continued adherence of the dissenting sects to the ideal of direct democracy, could conceal the fact that popular revolt was at a premium. It was a view of the late-seventeenth and early-eighteenth-Centuries that would prevail among British Marxists until at least the time of E.P. Thompson's revisionist *Whigs and Hunters* (1975). Yet at the height of these bleak years, or so the argument went, there was one writer who kept the best traditions of the dissenting intellectual alive. Jonathan Swift, the subject of brief essays in *Left Review* by Edgell Rickword (March 1935) and Rex Warner (June 1937), might at first have seemed an unlikely recruit to the radical tradition. As a Protestant cleric of solidly aristocratic background who served the Tory government of Lord Oxford as a propagandist, he was regarded by many literary intellectuals as a typical representative of Augustan conservatism. And yet, as Michael Foot has pointed out, Swift has generally been more admired by the British left (from Hazlitt and Cobbett through to Orwell, E.P. Thompson and Foot himself) than by his counterparts on the right.[179] Rickword and Warner, while not denying Swift's Toryism, argued that his sensibility was sufficiently 'various' to encompass a powerful element of scepticism towards the developing capitalist system.[180]

Their main claim was that Swift had been one of the first writers to identify the ways in which capitalism gives rise to war, imperialism and abuses of state power. Not even the most apolitical of critics could have denied that Swift was indeed an opponent of these things. For instance, it was widely known that his pamphlet on *The Conduct of the Allies* (1710) had played a central role in bringing the War of the Spanish Succession to an end, that he had persistently condemned Walpole for manipulating Parliament and that he had been one of the earliest and most vigorous advocates of Irish independence. The novel feature in Rickword and Warner's argument was the claim that Swift possessed a sort of proto-Marxist awareness that war, imperialism and tyranny are ultimately caused by the free play of market forces. Both writers resorted to a certain amount of deviouness when they tried to prove this claim. Since neither could find a quotation which exactly substantiated their case, they both cited the following passage (taken from Part Four of *Gulliver's Travels*) in which Gulliver tried to describe the nature of English economic life to a member of the Houyhnhnms:

> I was at much Pains to explain to him the Use of Money...That the rich Man enjoyed the Fruit of the poor Man's Labour, and the latter were a Thousand to one in Proportion to the former. That the Bulk of our People was forced to live miserably, by labouring every Day for small Wages to make a few live plentifully.[181]

The only thing which this passage demonstrates is that Swift was familiar with the argument that capitalism rests on exploitation – it makes no reference at all to war, imperialism or the destruction of civil liberties. But at a time when the CPGB, following the lead of the Comintern, insisted that the fascist threat to world peace and democracy was ultimately rooted in the general crisis of capitalism, it obviously seemed more important to claim that a great British writer had anticipated the arguments of the 1930s (albeit from a Tory perspective) than to worry too much about his actual beliefs. This makes it all the more ironic that Rickword and Warner should both have revelled so openly in Swift's attacks on the Whig administrations of the eighteenth century, since the modern Liberal Party was one of the organisations which the communists were trying to entice into the Popular Front.

What were the sources of Swift's radicalism? In the first place, Rickword argued, his scepticism towards capitalism was obviously related to his aristocratic background. As a member of a ruling class that was increasingly being sidelined by the bourgeoisie, it was always likely that he would come to regret 'the irresponsibility of man towards man which results when every item of personal worth has been translated into "exchange value"'.[182] More interesting was Warner's claim that Swift's radicalism partly resulted from his classical education. According to Warner, who had graduated in Classics from Oxford and taught the subject at a number of schools, Swift had been greatly influenced by the Stoical assumption that human beings are fundamentally level-headed, group-minded and capable of sorting out their differences in a peaceable manner. It was this which underpinned his hatred of war, his support for the principle of government by consent and his conviction that no nation has the right to dominate another.[183] By thus adding Classical philosophy to Christianity and liberalism as one of the dominant ideologies which the English radicals had managed to bend to their own political ends, Warner was making an audacious break with the more established view (first canvassed by Samuel Johnson in a famously splenetic essay in *Lives of the Poets*) that Swift's conception of human nature was actually a deeply misanthropic one.[184] 'This is not the record of a misanthrope', he said in reference to Swift's involvement in the campaign for Irish independence, 'but of a "defender of liberty".'[185] Although he acknowledged that the Stoical idea of human nature was too static and "rationalistic" to be compatible with the doctrine of historical materialism, Warner also hinted that in some ways it provided a better foundation for radical politics than the sort of moral relativism to which Marxists often subscribe. In addition, towards the end of his essay, Warner strongly implied that Swift's dislike of the establishment was rooted in the feelings of frustration which he (Swift) often experienced while dealing with politicians of inferior intelligence during his period as a Tory propagandist.[186] This was arguably an anticipation of the later claim, first explored by Edward Said in 'Swift as Intellectual' (1984), that Swift was probably the first modern writer to experience the divided loyalties which are characteristic of the intellectual in politics.[187]

Warner commended another aspect of Swift's work on literary grounds. If Swift's belief in humanity's powers of common sense was initially derived from the Roman Stoics, or so Warner argued, it was reinforced by his admiration for the common people. In turn it was his sensitivity to the common people's distaste for theory that made him the greatest propagandist in the radical tradition. If we read one of Swift's pamphlets, notably *The Conduct of the Allies*, we find that he held the attention of the ordinary reader by subordinating the discussion of general principles to a detailed consideration of the effects of politics on everyday life. 'His pamphlet', wrote Warner, 'is a closely reasoned argument from fact, and those points, often comparatively unimportant, which would be most frequently debated by the man in the street, are dealt with most carefully of all.'[188] By furnishing a model of propagandist flair which the modern pamphleteer would do well to emulate, Swift proved that there are lessons to be learned even from a conservative age.

2.5. From Liberalism to Marxism

The final period in the history of English radicalism encompassed the century or so between the Industrial Revolution, when the modern labour movement began to take shape, and the emergence of modern socialism in the last two decades of the nineteenth century. Although Jack Lindsay made a dutiful attempt in *England My England* to show that the common people sustained their communist traditions throughout this period, the relevant section of his pamphlet was too perfunctory to carry much conviction.[189] The more sensible approach was the one adopted by A.L. Morton, who confined himself to providing a broad overview of the period for the benefit of later Marxist writers. The great virtue of Morton's account was that it gave a clear impression of the different stages which modern radicalism had passed through. These can be summarised as follows:

(1) c1760-c1800. Spontaneous protests against the new industrial system. Large sections of the urban proletariat are drawn into political action under the leadership of left-wing liberals (e.g. the 'Wilkesite' movement and the various organisations inspired by the French Revolution).[190]

(2) c1800-c1820. Popular radicalism is driven underground by the repressive legislation which accompanied the French Revolution and the Napoleonic Wars. Occasional acts of industrial sabotage (e.g. the Luddite Rebellion of 1812) and occasional attempts at popular insurrection (e.g. the Peterloo Rising of 1819).[191]

(3) c1820-1835. The legalisation of trade unionism in 1824 leads to the temporary emergence of nationwide industrial unions, some of them (notably the Grand National Consolidated Trade Union) influenced by the socialism of Robert Owen.[192]

(4) c1835-1850. The age of Chartism.[193]

(5) c1850-1880. The decline of working-class militancy and the formation of the 'New Model Unions'.[194]

(6) c1880-1900. The onset of an international slump leads to the renewal of industrial militancy, exemplified by the emergence of 'new Unionism' in the late-1880s. The emergence of modern socialism and the eventual formation of the Labour Party (1900).[195]

As has often been acknowledged, Morton's account of these developments was one of the main influences on the Marxist historians who revolutionised labour history in the period after the war. For example, his analysis of the diverse range of factors which shaped the proletarian response to industrialism was comparable to that of E.P. Thompson, who tried in *The Making of the English Working Class* (1963) to challenge the idea that class consciousness is merely a mechanical response to prevailing economic conditions.[196] And by writing respectfully about the more anarchic elements in the early labour movement (notably the Luddites) he anticipated the pathbreaking efforts of Thompson, E.J. Hobsbawm and George Rudé to rescue the whole process of 'collective bargaining by riot'[197] (Hobsbawm) from the charge of social atavism. On a broader level, it is reasonable to argue that the publication of *A People's*

History of England marked the moment at which Marxism began to displace the liberalism of the Hammonds and the Fabianism of the Webbs as the main intellectual force in the historiography of the British labour movement.[198]

Comparatively few writers from the late-eighteenth and nineteenth centuries were singled out for close examination in the 1930s. Those who were chosen showed that the radical movement had drawn its support from a broad range of political, intellectual and cultural milieux. There was one radical liberal (Thomas Paine), one romantic poet (William Blake), the most influential novelist of the age (Charles Dickens) and the most distinguished member of the first generation of British Marxists (William Morris). An article on Paine by Samuel Mill was published in *Left Review* in May 1937 to mark the 200th anniversary of Paine's birth. It was primarily an exercise in thumbnail biography, charting Paine's career from his early days as an exciseman in Norfolk through to his involvement in the American War of Independence, his authorship of *Rights of Man* (1792) and his exile to the USA during the Pittite 'reign of terror'[199] in the 1790s. But Mill also raised two themes of broader importance. The first was the extent to which modern liberalism (at least in its more radical and egalitarian forms) often transmogrifies under the pressure of circumstances into something more closely resembling socialism. Although Mill recognised that Paine 'was not a Socialist, for the time was not ripe for Socialism',[200] he nevertheless implied that Paine's commitment to the idea of popular democracy made him a natural defender of workers' rights. Among other things he began his political career as a spokesman for striking excisemen in Thetford (this was in 1772), exerted a profound influence on the formation of the London Corresponding Society and made a forceful case in *Rights of Man* for the introduction of state pensions, universal education and unemployment benefit. It was another case of the dominant ideology being repositioned for radical ends, with liberalism now joining Christianity and classical philosophy as one of the unlikely sources from which dissident thinkers had drawn their inspiration. With his second theme, on the other hand, Mill clearly signalled his support for the more pessimistic school of Popular Front thinking about the nature of Christianity. He pointed out that when the British establishment attempted to destroy the Jacobin culture of the 1790s, one of the crucial aspects of its strategy was a calculated appeal to religious sentiment. Its decisive move was to portray the radical challenge to secular hierarchies as a blasphemous assault on God's dominion. Paine's one substantial work on religion (*Age of Reason*, 1794-1796) was an expression of Voltairean 'deism' rather than outright atheism; but it was relentlessly described by Tory propagandists as the effusion of an ungodly degenerate. While Christianity is indeed broad enough to appeal to the communist imagination, Mill seemed to be saying, we should never lose sight of its 'utility in teaching the lower orders their station in life'.[201]

This scepticism towards religion was continued in Randall Swingler's essay on Blake, 'The Imputation of Madness: A Study of William Blake and Literary Tradition', published in *Left Review* in February 1937. Like most other commentators on English romanticism, Swingler recognised that Blake's main theme was the nature of human self-transcendence. All his work illustrated the idea that human beings can advance to a higher stage of evolution by harnessing the visionary capacities of their own minds. And yet, as Hanna Behrend has pointed out, Swingler departed from the majority of Blake scholars by denying that this idea was in any way religious.[202] When Blake tried to identify the mechanism of human evolution, or so the argument went, he was less interested in mystical states of consciousness than in the polymorphous expression of *desire*.[203] If the 'mental deities' which 'reside in the human breast'[204] are ever to be liberated, the individual must open himself up to the feelings of physical rapture which his environment is capable of inspiring – it was these to which Blake was referring in *Songs of Innocence and Experience* when he spoke of 'Love Unconfined'.[205] At the same time, Swingler insisted, Blake was keenly aware that desire must always be harnessed by the power of reason. He believed that the *intellect* precipitates the feelings of physical longing which lie at the heart of the visionary experience, and that it also organises the symptoms of desire and allows them to perform their ultimate role as 'unifier[s] of consciousness'.[206] In other words, or so Swingler implied, the culminating point of the visionary experience is the ability to perceive the physical universe as a coherent whole. This only occurs if the pulsations which traverse the body of the desiring individual are enabled, by means of a conscious intellectual effort, to break through the barriers of the unconscious and liberate what Blake would have called the 'imagination' – that is, mankind's dormant powers of holistic perception. As such, it is quite wrong to regard romanticism as a revolt of the instincts against the intellect. It is better understood as a longing for 'the redemption of human nature by the reuniting of energy with consciousness'.[207]

Swingler went on to argue that much of Blake's work attacked the forces in modern society which obstruct the process of self-realisation, specifically capitalism and religion. Where the former was concerned, Swingler quoted a number of stanzas which portrayed capitalism as a spiritually barren system whose emphasis on self-denial makes it the enemy of all forms of visionary ambition. In one of these stanzas, from the prophetic poem *America*, Blake strongly implied that one of the main problems with capitalism is that it has led to the development of industry:

Let the slave grinding at the mill run out into the field,
Let him look up into the heavens and laugh in the bright air:
Let the inchained soul, shut up in darkness and in sighing,
Whose face has never seen a smile in thirty years,
Rise and look out; his chains are loose, his dungeon doors are open,
And let his wife and children return from the oppressor's scourge...
For Empire is no more, and now the Lion and Wolf shall cease.[208]

By ignoring the opposition between modernity (bad) and nature (good) which lies at the heart of these lines, Swingler was anticipating the tendency among Marxist writers to underplay the element of anti-industrialism in the Romantic sensibility. We will return to this issue when looking at Robin Page Arnot's work on William Morris. By contrast, Swingler's account of Blake's attitude towards religion was much less reticent. Dismissing once again the view that Blake was essentially a mystical thinker, Swingler argued that he (Blake) saw religion as an illusory ideology employed by the 'property owners' to reinforce the puritanical ethic engendered by capitalism.[209] Yet although the rule of 'Urizen', the symbol of religion's 'imposed law' in Blake's prophetic books, is now nearly absolute, there are several ways in which the religious illusion might be challenged. On the one hand, Swingler argued, Blake attached great importance to refuting the idea that human beings possess an innate sense of morality which can be regarded as evidence for the existence of God.[210] Against the whole doctrine of transcendental mental structures, which he presumably encountered in the philosophy of Immanuel Kant, Blake subscribed to a thoroughgoing empiricism which held that the contents of the mind are ultimately derived solely from experience: 'Man has no notion of moral fitness but from Education. Naturally he is only a natural organ subject to sense' (There is No Natural Religion).[211] Blake's other main argument was that the idea of God is basically to be understood as an alienated expression of human potential.[212] When human beings began to create deities, they did so by projecting their own immanent qualities onto a transcendental image which had no basis in fact. It follows that religion will be destroyed when (1) the anthropormorphic origins of the belief in God are exposed, and (2) people are encouraged to focus on the idea of God as an image of their own future evolution. Blake's belief that an immersion in religious imagery (as opposed to religious faith) can serve as the foundation of human evolution was summed up for Swingler in the famous line in All Religions are One: 'Therefore God becomes as we are, that we may be as He is.'[213] Swingler was probably attracted to these ideas because of their similarity to those of Ludwig Feurbach, the 'Young Hegelian' thinker whose work on religion had converted Marx to the doctrines of philosophical materialism. The post-war reader is likely to be reminded of the so-called 'humanist Christians' of the late-twentieth century, represented in Britain by the likes of Don Cupitt,[214] who regard Christianity not as a source of metaphysical truth but as a storehouse of images which can enhance psychological health.

Swingler probably had a number of reasons for putting forward his highly unorthodox interpretation of Blake's work. Most obviously, as he admitted in the early stages of his article, he wanted to make it less easy to ignore the political element in Blake's sensibility. By insisting that the Blakean idea of human evolution was rooted in a secular conception of physical desire (as opposed to an unworldly conception of religious bliss) he was trying to demonstrate that Blake the visionary and Blake the critic of capitalism were both operating in the same realm. Indeed, at one point he came close to implying that the evolutionary scheme in Blake's work was little more than an extravagant metaphor for the Marxist conception of life in communist society. 'This', he wrote after summarising the contents of Blake's prophetic poems, '...is simply the psychology of Marxism'.[215] When Blake envisaged humanity advancing to a new stage of semi-divinity, what he really had in mind (or so Swingler implied) was a non-market society in which the division of labour has been abolished, rationalisation has come to an end and the individual performs a diverse range of economic roles which satisfy both his senses and his intellect.[216] These arguments were undergirded by the claim that Blake's philosophical pronouncements had anticipated the doctrine of dialectical materialism.[217] If his empiricist comments on the origins of knowledge were reminiscent of a materialist belief in the primacy of mind over matter, then (for Swingler) his emphasis on the reconciliation of 'energy and consciousness' suggested a dialectical understanding of the unity and interpenetration of opposites. Blake was thus portrayed as the eighteenth-century prototype of what Jonathan Rée has called the 'proletarian philosophers'.[218]

Speaking of proletarian philosophers, it was entirely appropriate that the work of Charles Dickens should have been analysed by T.A. Jackson, the CPGB's most respected autodidact who traced his love of reading to a youthful obsession with Dickens's novels. Yet the fact remains that no other contribution to the history of English radicalism was anything like as obscure. Jackson examined Dickens's output in a full-length book (*Charles Dickens: The Progress of a Radical*, 1937) and in a brief essay in *Left Review* ('Dickens the Radical', March 1937). If the essay simply reproduced passages from the book in a more or less random manner, the book itself was weighed down by the sheer fertility of Jackson's associative intelligence. Digressive where Lindsay's work on Bunyan had been multi-layered,[219] frequently unconcerned to relate lengthy accounts of individual novels to broader themes, its argument about the nature of Dickens's radicalism is impossible to summarise in its entirety. However, two important themes tend to stand out. In the first place, or so Jackson implied, Dickens is best regarded as a cultural radical who had a particular interest in tracing the effects of capitalist culture on the treatment of children. Secondly, though not exactly a socialist,[220] he clearly believed that the injustices of capitalism could be significantly palliated if power were somehow devolved to working people. The broader point, which Jackson misleadingly identified as the central theme of his book, was that the trajectory of Dickens's populism was directly related to the wider fortunes of English radicalism in the period between 1835 and 1870.[221]

The organising assumption of Jackson's book was that Dickens had a sort of instinctive understanding that the cultural poverty of the Victorian age was rooted in its capitalist base.[222] Since entrepreneurs have no choice but to be parsimonious with their investments (a situation summed up by Mr Gradgrind's injunction to 'buy in the cheapest market and sell in the most expensive'),[223] and since a society's values are invariably based on those of the dominant economic system, it follows that the main characteristic of everyday life under capitalism will be a brutal suppression of emotion. The inevitable consequence of the laws of accumulation is an emphasis on self-denial at the expense of our more generous emotions. Jackson bolstered his case by pointing out that Dickens's attack on capitalism had won the support of John Ruskin, who paid tribute to it in *Unto this Last* (1860).[224] There was also a sense, or so Jackson argued, in which Dickens clearly understood how the capitalist system prevents the majority of people from developing the full range of their capabilities.[225] For example, many of his most celebrated characters were defined almost entirely by a single tic or mannerism. Uriah Heep has become famous for his endless protestations of humility, whereas the only thing which most people remember about Mrs Micawber was her claim that she would 'never leave Mr Micawber'.[226] Noting that many of Dickens's critics had derided this caricatural facility as evidence of a lack of imagination, Jackson argued that it was actually a very powerful means of satirising the destruction of all-round human development at the hands of the modern division of labour. More than anything else, however, the thing which distinguished Dickens from other members of the radical tradition was his preoccupation with the effects of capitalist culture on the development of children. Because he believed that children are naturally exuberant, curious and generous, he recognised that the only way for the dominant culture to adapt them to its needs is to break their spirit at an early age. One of his most significant achievements was his demonstration that the diverse methods of education employed in Victorian Britain were all directed to this single end.[227] In many of his novels he identified what Jackson described as a number of different 'systems' of education – among them the 'Squeers system' (after Wackford Squeers), the 'Pipchin system' (after Mrs Pipchin) and the 'Blimber system' (after Dr Blimber).[228] The central principle of the Squeers system was the belief that the only way to tame a child is to beat it regularly for several years.[229] The 'secret' of the Pipchin system was 'to give them [i.e. children] everything that they didn't like, and nothing that they did.'[230] The Blimber system was ostensibly more 'refined', but its ultimate goal was to stifle spontaneity by encouraging respect for pedantry and inculcating a highly ritualised idea of personal courtesy.[231] Once we have recognised the depths of Dickens's anguish at the modern treatment of children, Jackson implied, many other features of his novels begin to fall into place. Characters such as David Copperfield are clearly intended to advance the idea that children have rights in respect of their elders, with Dickens insisting that the young child has as much of a need for warmth and respect as for food and somewhere to live.[232] And although he rejected fundamentalist Christianity on the grounds that its 'fire-and-brimstone theology'[233] was likely to traumatise the childish imagination, he retained a conviction in personal immortality because 'he could not bear to part with the belief that something other than extinction awaited a bright and dearly-loved child'.[234]

According to Jackson, who was unfairly described by George Orwell as making 'spirited efforts to turn Dickens into a bloodthirsty revolutionary',[235] Dickens responded to the crisis of Victorian culture by calling for power to be taken out of bourgeois hands and devolved to working people. As soon as the workers are assigned a more central role in society, or so Dickens allegedly believed, their natural generosity of mind would pose a major threat to the more self-denying traditions of the ruling class. Working on this assumption, Jackson put forward the startling argument that the various stages in the evolution of Dickens's writings can be precisely correlated with the various stages in the development of Victorian radicalism. The first, between 1836 and 1842, was one of unbounded optimism.[236] At a time when Chartism enjoyed mass support and it seemed likely that the franchise would soon be extended to male wage-earners, Dickens wrote a series of novels (*Pickwick Papers, Oliver Twist, Nicholas Nickleby* etc.) in which class hierarchies were treated as a purely accidental feature of modern society, soon to be replaced by a more fluid set of economic and political relationships. Characters who abused their power were invariably brought to justice, while benevolent employers such as Pickwick and Brownlow were held up as models of democratic virtue. There was also a certain joyous prodigality to the writing, with Dickens creating scores of characters (many of them proletarians) whose existence could not be strictly justified on the grounds of plot alone. However, the retrenchment of English radicalism engendered a noticeable darkening of his perspective. In the years between the collapse of industrial Chartism in 1842 and the failure of the Second Charter in 1848, most of his novels (especially *Dombey and Son*) began to explore the factors which prevent the wealthy from voluntarily surrendering their power.[237] His main theme at this point was the nature of pride, conceived as the natural ally of hierarchy:

> Dickens saw, to his horror, that instead of expanding trade and commerce leading, *via* a growth of Cheerybleism, to a new benevolent-equalitarian harmony, it was leading to the creation of 'Great' commercial houses whose heads wielded a power as great as that of Roman Emperors; and who, in their pride of wealth and power, exacted from their connections and dependants a deference and obedience greater than those for which the Emperor Caligula had had his throat so deservedly cut. That this pride was in itself a selfless pride – since it was pride in the house in which, and to whose glory, the head himself was as subservient as were the humblest of his underlings – made it all the more shocking. As Bernard Shaw was to say, sixty years later, 'Self-sacrifice enables us to sacrifice other people without blushing.' It was their own complete self-effacement before the claims and needs of the House, whose standing and honour was in their keeping, that made these financial-commercial magnates so ruthlessly imperious in exacting an equivalent self-effacement from all beneath their sway.[238]

The final stage of Dickens's career, lasting between 1848 and his death in 1872, saw the growing pessimism of the second period harden into outright despair about the possibility of social change.[239] Looking on as the challenge of Chartism collapsed, he now came to believe that British institutions were specifically designed to prevent ordinary people from exercising power. Some of the best passages in Jackson's book dealt with the legendary portrayal of the legal system in *Bleak House*,[240] seen as representative of Dickens's wider analysis of the mechanisms of class rule. According to Jackson, one of the novel's finest achievements was to show how the dominant institutions are able to establish a sort of admonitory presence in the furthest recesses of everyday life, subjugating the individual with what Foucault might have called the 'panoptical' threat of constant surveillance. This capacity was famously symbolised by the thick fog which hovered around the Chancery buildings and seeped into the souls of all the leading characters.[241] Dickens also had an acute understanding of the way that manifest irrationalities are deliberately built into legal procedure in order to reinforce the power of a professional elite. The case of 'Jarndyce versus Jarndyce' which provided *Bleak House* with its narrative centre (even though its complexities were never fully explained) dragged on endlessly because of (1) an entirely meaningless distinction between Courts of Law and Courts of Equity, and (2) the ability of lawyers to exploit obscure points of law in a manner more consistent with professional self-interest than the public good. 'The one great principle of the English law', Dickens wrote, 'is to make business for itself... Viewed by this light it becomes a coherent scheme, and not the monstrous maze the laity are apt to think it.'[242] By the end of his life (or so Jackson argued) Dickens had become so frustrated with the structure of English institutions that he began to countenance the possibility of armed insurrection. Whereas *Barnaby Rudge*, published in 1841 but written in 1839, seemed to dismiss the Gordon Rioters of 1780 as a bunch of drunkards and madmen, *A Tale of Two Cities* (1859) portrayed the *canaille* of 1789 in a much more favourable light. Only a failure to see beyond the limitations of petty-bourgeois ideology prevented Dickens becoming the greatest revolutionary writer of the age.[243]

If Dickens rejected bourgeois society without ever committing himself to the idea of socialism, William Morris exemplified the moment at which English radicalism was finally transfigured by the influence of Marxism. Yet the starting point for Robin Page Arnot's *William Morris: A Vindication* (1934) was the claim that the communist beliefs which Morris acquired during the last 15 years of his life had deliberately been concealed by the majority of modern commentators.[244] Surveying the books, articles and speeches which marked the 100th anniversary of Morris's birth in 1934, Arnot identified the existence of what he described as two recurring 'myths'. The so-called 'bourgeois myth', typified by a speech given by Stanley Baldwin at the opening of a Morris exhibition at the Victoria and Albert Museum, extolled Morris for his artistic genius but made no reference to his political activities.[245] This was matched on the left by a 'Labour Party and ILP myth', originating in the work of Bruce Glasier, which treated Morris as a 'gentle Socialist' whose politics owed more to the tradition of ethical socialism than to Marx.[246] Although he never really said so, Arnot clearly believed that the main factor underpinning these distortions was Morris's deep nostalgia for the Middle Ages. So long as Morris could be portrayed as an impractical dreamer with a hatred of industry and a love of handicraft, it was easy to either deny, question or merely suppress his support for an ultra-modernist ideology such as Marxism. The main purpose of Arnot's book was therefore to prove that the influence of neo-medievalist ideas on Morris had always been greatly exaggerated.

The goal was pursued in two stages. In one chapter, entitled 'How did Morris come to be a Marxist?', Arnot examined the phase of Morris's career which lasted from his graduation from Oxford in 1856 to his first exposure to Marxism in 1881.[247] As we have seen in the Introduction, Morris's ambition at this time was to combat what he regarded as the decline of high culture. Believing that the root cause of the decline was the inability of the factory system to provide satisfying work for the common people, he established his own furniture company with the aim of promoting 'joy in labour'. The conventional view is that Morris, under the influence of Carlyle and Ruskin, believed that the destruction of pleasurable work had largely been a consequence of the invention of the machine. His company was therefore an attempt to undermine industrial society by restoring handicraft to its rightful place in the labour process. Arnot completely rejected this view. Morris, he claimed, was never an enemy of industrialism but merely an opponent of rationalisation. The modern worker has indeed been 'made into a machine',[248] but this is because the free market tends to fragment production into a series of easily repeatable tasks. It has nothing to do (or so Morris allegedly thought) with anything inherently alienating about the industrial system. It is noticeable that Arnot tried to prove his case not by referring to Morris's work but by quoting the famous passage from Volume One of *Capital* in which Marx described the process of rationalisation as a 'despotism the more hateful for its meanness'.[249] He then went on to consider the nature of Morris's debt to Carlyle and Ruskin. In defiance of the view that Morris had primarily been attracted by their admiration for pre-industrial society, Arnot argued that what he (Morris) had actually absorbed was their 'non-proletarian Socialism'.[250] The idea that there was a socialist element in the work of Carlyle and Ruskin is a deeply controversial one and tends to be derived from two sources, though others are also relevant. In the famous chapter entitled 'The Nature of Gothic' in the second volume of *The Stones of Venice* (1853), working on the assumption that the characteristics of the non-industrial labour process can be deduced from the appearance of medieval cathedrals, Ruskin argued that the element of irregularity in the Gothic façade suggests that the medieval labourer was broadly permitted to follow his own devices.[251] And in *Past and Present* (1843), one of the nineteenth century's most audacious attempts to chart a middle way between left and right, Carlyle spoke of the need to balance the rule of 'heroes' (his favoured solution to the crisis of modern society) with a new system of industrial relations in which workers and employers assumed joint responsibility for running industry.[252] Both texts have been taken to imply a sort of nascent approval on the part of their authors for what would later be called industrial democracy. While Arnot mentioned none of this, he clearly implied that what Morris had inherited from Carlyle and Ruskin was not so much a sentimental attachment to the Middle Ages than a set of egalitarian assumptions about the need for economic reform.

Something similar was argued when Arnot turned his attention to Morris's love for the culture of medieval Iceland.[253] In 1871, still a decade away from his first encounter with Marxism, Morris travelled to Iceland and developed a deep interest in its sagas which eventually resulted in the original poem *Sigurd the Volsung and the Fall of the Niblungs* (1877). Many commentators have suggested that the engagement with the sagas simply deepened Morris's medievalism, not least by forcing him to temper his rather dreamy vision of the Arthurian countryside with imagery drawn from a more inhospitable climate. Arnot tried to challenge this interpretation by proposing what was effectively a theory of Icelandic exceptionalism. For much of the medieval period, he argued, the rigid class structures which existed throughout the rest of Europe were largely absent from Iceland. Because the climate was 'grim, harsh and terrifying',[254] men and women chose to confront the elements in non-hierarchical groups. This was the aspect of medieval Iceland to which Morris had been most attracted. Far from confirming him in a love of feudalism, Morris's immersion in the dark world of the sagas simply reinforced his belief that mankind would do better to dismantle the class system altogether and move forward into a democratic future. 'Iceland of the Sagas', Arnot wrote, 'had nerved Morris for the epic struggle of the classes in Britain.'[255]

The second part of Arnot's argument encompassed the period in which Morris had been an activist on the Marxist left, roughly between 1881 and his death in 1896. After surveying Morris's involvement in the Social Democratic Federation, the Socialist League and the Hammersmith Socialist Society,[256] Arnot confronted the question which has posed the biggest problems for anyone wishing to claim that Morris was a more or less orthodox Marxist during his final years. If Morris was indeed an orthodox Marxist, Arnot asked, then why did his utopian novel *News from Nowhere* (1891) depict a post-revolutionary society that was clearly based on handicraft rather than industry? Was this not a sign that Morris retained his love of the Middle Ages and secretly found the prospect of a non-industrial society more attractive than that of a communist one? Arnot's response was ingenious if not always convincing. If we want to understand why *News from Nowhere* was so crammed with medieval motifs, or so the argument went, we have to refer both to Morris's conception of socialism and to the nature of utopian discourse. To begin with, Morris subscribed to a rather 'unlikely' idea about the social experiments which might possibly be carried out after the establishment of a communist society. Once a new society had been securely built on a foundation of advanced technology, Morris allegedly believed, it was likely that the common people would choose to briefly inaugurate an 'epoch of rest wherein men express their joy in labour largely through handicraft.'[257] The medieval idyll depicted in *News from Nowhere* is not therefore to be seen as a reflection of Morris's idea of socialism, but rather as a sort of historical diversion with which a revolutionary people might seek to refresh themselves before advancing to 'further heights of Communist development'.[258] Arnot's comments on Morris's relationship to the utopian tradition were slightly more plausible. According to Arnot, the great utopian writers of the modern period had often tried to legitimise their vision of the future by invoking a mythical past. The Enlightenment thinkers of the eighteenth century knew perfectly well that there had never been a society which embodied the 'republican virtues' that they wished to recommend, but 'when they wanted symbols of their dreams they evoked the ancient republics of Rome and Sparta, the toga and the Phrygian cap'.[259] By projecting his egalitarian values onto an imaginary rural society which seemed to have more in common with the medieval past than with the communist future, Morris was merely obeying a literary convention too powerful to be ignored. Moreover, he also had a rare understanding of the limitations of the utopian imagination. He knew that if he tried to predict the forms of technology which a communist society might call into being, he would succeed only in describing the 'machines…of a decade, or at most, two decades ahead of 1890'.[260] As such, the dearth of technology in News from Nowhere reflected an understandable desire to sustain the novel's relevance over a number of generations.

3. THE QUESTION OF ORTHODOXY

As we have seen in previous chapters, it was common for the Marxist critics of the 1930s to respond to Soviet influences in highly unorthodox ways. At first sight, however, their writings on the history of English radicalism seem entirely orthodox. It is true that their attempts to translate Dimitrov's exiguous historical precepts into a full-scale narrative showed considerable ingenuity, and that some of the main assumptions of their account (notably the unstable nature of ruling-class ideology) were not derived from Soviet sources. Yet there is very little in the work we have just surveyed which is inconsistent with the critical project outlined at the Seventh Congress of the Communist International in 1935.[261] It could nevertheless be argued that much of this work subtly undermined the CPGB's political identity in ways which had major long-term consequences.[262] When the Popular Front strategy was first introduced, the Party still subscribed to a rigidly Leninist (or Stalinist) approach to politics. It believed that socialism could not be established by peaceful means, that parliament was little more than a 'talking shop' and that socialist institutions in Britain should be closely modelled on their Soviet counterparts. All these positions had been abandoned by the time the Party reconsidered its strategy at the end of the War. From 1950 right through to its dissolution in 1991, the CPGB insisted that socialism could be achieved through the ballot box and that parliamentary democracy should be deepened and not abolished in a socialist society. Moreover, it propagated a vision of socialism that has aptly been described as 'far from revolutionary'.[263] Although the Party continued to pay lip service to the ideal of moving beyond capitalism, it rapidly became clear that its real objective was a mixed economy in which extended public ownership, working-class militancy and demand management would lift the private sector out of its customary inefficiency. This shift from uncompromising Leninism to radical reformism was partly caused by political factors which had nothing to do with the critical projects of the 1930s, notably the Party's brief integration into mainstream British life during the War; but there were several ways in which it was clearly shaped by the new ideas about the nature of English radicalism. The emphasis on civil liberties in the writings of the 1930s is of obvious relevance here. Once the communists had begun to describe the establishment of parliamentary government as one of the great achievements of plebeian revolt, it became virtually impossible to revert to an anti-parliamentary position when fascism was finally defeated. The Party's embrace of reformism might also have been linked to the conception of communism which dominated the historical literature. In order to justify their argument that popular revolt in England had always been motivated by a desire for communism, even in the days before the rise of capitalism, it was necessary for writers such as Lindsay and Morton to equate communism with little more than common ownership of the means of production. In so doing they elided the fact that *modern* communism sees public ownership not merely as a means of securing popular sovereignty (though that is obviously important) but also of transcending 'marketplace anarchy' through the systematic planning of investment and output. This might well have made it easier to defend the Party's new economic policy, which (as we have seen) tended to regard a fair measure of public ownership as an adequate substitute for the abolition of the market.

There was also a hint of unorthodoxy in two theoretical initiatives which had their origins in the investigation of the radical tradition: (1) Edgell Rickword's account of the role of the artist in a socialist society, and (2) Jack Lindsay's seminal attempt to characterise culture as a form of 'productive activity'. Rickword put forward his ideas in the essay 'Culture, Progress, and English Tradition', published in C Day Lewis's symposium *The Mind in Chains* in 1937.[264] In the first part of the essay, which briefly surveyed the history of the radical tradition from the Peasants' Revolt through to Chartism, Rickword concluded that the motivating force of English radicalism has always been the belief that no class has the right to live off the labour of another.[265] He then went on to suggest that one of the most important tasks of socialism is to restore the artist to a position of prominence in the economic process.[266] According to Rickword, the latest phase of capitalism has relegated the majority of cultural workers to a marginal role in society. By dividing each area of productive activity into a series of highly specialised micro-tasks, rationalisation has created a cultural climate in which the inner workings of the mind are regarded as the only legitimate subject matter for a work of art. Artists therefore experience a 'sense of isolation' which invariably engenders 'frustration', 'pettiness' and 'pessimism'.[267] There is also a sense in which the bifurcation of art and society has poisoned the central assumptions of intellectual life. When artists retreat into a world of their own and see no need to test the practicality of their ideas, they tend to surrender to relativism (the belief that 'no statement is more true than another')[268] as well as the irrationalism which usually goes with it. Many of the leading trends in contemporary culture, including surrealism, psychoanalysis and modernism, combine an anguished protest against the poverty of modern life with a stubborn refusal to identify capitalism as the root of the problem.[269]

The point about socialism, Rickword continued, is that it gives a massive boost to production by exploiting the potential of advanced technology, with the result that quantitative considerations ('how do we produce enough?') are replaced by qualitative ones ('how do we ensure that what we produce is beautiful?'). The consequence is a sort of Morrisian idyll in which artists are drawn into economic life in order to embellish the products of human labour.[270] Moreover, there is every possibility that this process will ultimately lead to a complete revolution in the foundations of economic life: 'In the co-operation of artists and scientists...each comes to understand the other's mode of thought; it is a first step towards the realisation of the essential unity of the aims of art and science.'[271] What Rickword appeared to be claiming, in a manner which perhaps recalled Sir Philip Sidney's An Apology for Poetry,[272] was that art and science both give rise to distinct and mutually exclusive forms of knowledge and that the only balanced approach to objective reality is one which combines their respective methods in a higher synthesis. It was an argument that F.R. Leavis would scornfully reject in his famous polemic against C.P. Snow in the so-called "two cultures" debate of the 1950s.

More important than Rickword's proto-Maoist musings was Jack Lindsay's attempt to theorise culture as a form of 'productive activity'.[273] Having made a central contribution to the analysis of the radical tradition, especially in his work on Shakespeare and Bunyan, Lindsay began to argue towards the end of the 1930s that it was not enough to simply identify the elements of progressive thought in the work of individual writers. The broader goal should be to identify the ways in which all forms of cultural activity tend to have progressive consequences. He first addressed the issue in his article 'The Aesthetic Fact' (Dialectics, 1939) and returned to it in a series of books and essays over the next fifty years, including Perspective for Poetry (1944), Marxism and Contemporary Science (1949) and

The Crisis in Marxism (1981).[274] According to Lindsay, Marxism has tended to obscure the progressive aspects of culture (by which he primarily meant the arts) in one of two ways. It has either regarded cultural activity as a *reflection* of the existing economic system (as in the base/superstructure metaphor) or it has seen it as having a purely *extrinsic* capacity for stimulating change, in the sense of raising awareness of systemic transformations which advances in the productive forces have already made possible. Lindsay's counter-thesis was that art can often play a much more fundamental role in society, penetrating to the heart of the economic process and influencing the technological developments which push history forward. It derives this ability from the fact that it characteristically provides an illusory reconciliation of the various contradictions which threaten the coherence of the social system – that is, it takes the tensions between 'inner and outer', 'personal and social' and 'self and audience'[275] (as well as several others) and welds them into an aesthetic continuum. This transformation is primarily effected by a work's form, or what Lindsay insisted on calling 'Form',[276] which he interpreted as an extension of the rhythmic procedures by which the body seeks to orientate itself in a threatening environment. The following passage gives a good impression of the distinctive terminology in which Lindsay often couched his argument, much of it suggestive of the later work of Althusser:[277]

> Art, we can say, is the Structure of human process arrested and objectified at a certain point…the *Pattern* or *Form* is the projection of the structure. *Rhythm* is the movement of the process employed in bringing about this projection, and is revealed in the *Pattern*. The moment of projection reveals further a *Dominance*, the keypoint in the development leading to the work of art, which expresses the particular relation of inner and outer, organism and environment, individual and history…The keypoint, expressing and revealing the Dominance, is *integrative*. It expresses 'the arrangement of organic structure and tension so that *a single characteristic form* is developed'…Development may be defined as *Decrease in Asymmetry* and the Dominance is *the relation of the Form to the Process it facilitates*.[278]

Because of their habit of substituting 'symmetry' for 'asymmetry', or so the argument went, the arts have a remarkable ability to transfigure economic life. Inspired by the spectacle of a social order from which all traces of conflict have been eliminated, the individual is likely to experience a new determination to enhance humanity's control of nature. Either he can intensify the energy which he brings to his everyday tasks, or else (much more importantly) he can turn his mind to the business of improving the instruments of production. While it would be wrong to regard culture as part of the economic 'base', on the grounds that it is neither a productive force nor part of the relations of production, it can nevertheless be regarded as one of the main influences on technology and therefore as a significant indirect influence on the shape of the economic system as a whole.[279] As we have seen, there were many influential theories in the twentieth century which argued that the main role of culture is to reconcile opposites. Lindsay's theory can perhaps be regarded as a Marxist response to I.A. Richards's emphasis on the 'coenaesthetic' function of art (Richards also influenced West and Caudwell) as well as to Claude Lévi-Strauss's pioneering work on the nature of myth. Gorky's remarks about the relationship between myth and economic progress were another possible source of inspiration. However, as Victor Paananen has pointed out, the really important question is not so much who influenced Lindsay as whom Lindsay might himself have influenced. By treating culture as a 'productive activity' with dramatic economic consequences, Lindsay can be regarded (at least in Paananen's opinion) as a precursor of Raymond Williams's attempt to shift the attention of Marxist criticism away from finished artefacts towards the idea of culture as a 'form of material production'. It is for this reason that he has been described, rightly or wrongly, as the 'major British Marxist thinker between Caudwell and Williams'.[280] If his ideas now seems rather unremarkable, it is perhaps because Marxist theory is no longer dominated by the Stalinist version of historical materialism (notoriously summed up in Chapter Four of the *History of the Communist Party of the Soviet Union (Bolsheviks)*),[281] with its dogmatic insistence on the absolute priority of the base over the superstructure.[282]

By way of conclusion, it is worth noting that historical and critical writing on the radical tradition has figured in the post-war history of the Communist Party in a number of interesting ways. For one thing it was central to the process by which communist historians and literary critics were integrated into the mainstream of academic life. When a number of the Party's most distinguished intellectuals first acquired a reputation for academic excellence in the fifties and sixties, thus preparing the way for the academic left's extraordinary influence in British universities in the period since 1968,[283] it was often because of work which took its lead from the research of the 1930s. Eric Hobsbawm, Arnold Kettle, Margot Heinemann, Christopher Hill and E.P. Thompson have all acknowledged their debt to the pioneering efforts of the Popular Front days.[284] Less happily, work on the radical tradition also played its role in the events which led to the dissolution of the Party in 1991.[285] When the 'Eurocommunist' leadership of the Party tried to distance itself from class politics, insisting (though never in so many words) that the working-class had been superseded by the so-called 'new social movements' as the main agency of progressive change, it was considered necessary to challenge the rosy assumptions about proletarian militancy which most communists took for granted. Writers such as Bill Schwarz and Colin Mercer therefore invoked the Nairn/Anderson theses in opposition to what they termed the 'populism' of Thompson and his acolytes, claiming that the populist position was both dangerously complacent and inherently masculinist.[286] Yet even today, when their political fortunes have never been at a lower ebb, British communists retain their interest in the radical tradition. Although none of the so-called 'successor organisations' to the CPGB devotes much time to cultural work, their publications often feature articles on the more famous writers in the radical pantheon – Blake, Shelley and Burns seem especially favoured. Most of this work aims to popularise established ideas rather than break new ground, yet it can still be seen as a dignified if low-key alternative to the presentation of history in mainstream British culture. As Patrick Wright and others have pointed out, one of the main functions of 'heritage culture' is to reinforce the belief that history has somehow come to an end. By presenting the past through the medium of museums, country houses and other spaces which seem remote from everyday life, the heritage industry seeks to persuade us that significant historical change is now impossible, that the British past was characterised by complete unity between the classes and that it was primarily the ruling class which made the greatest contribution to national greatness.[287] However anachronistic their politics might otherwise seem, organisations such as the Communist Party of Britain, the New Communist Party and the Communist Party of Great Britain deserve some credit for challenging this curious blend of postmodern pessimism and conservative triumphalism. With their flow of articles on the periods in British history when the class struggle was at its most intense, most of them published in newspapers and magazines whose low production values make them seem anything but remote, they remind us that history has yet to reach its Hegelian terminus and that popular revolt is still one of the main sources of social progress. More than seventy years after the Seventh World Congress of the Communist International, Dimitrov's legacy is still alive – just.

CONCLUSION

This book has examined the body of literary criticism that was produced between 1928 and 1939 by writers who either belonged to, or were closely associated with, the Communist Party of Great Britain. It has tried to show how the main principles of the new 'revisionist' school of Communist Party historiography can be applied to the CPGB's cultural history. The guiding thread of the book has been an argument about the relationship between the Party theorists and the international communist movement. On the one hand, I have suggested that nearly all the work of the Party theorists had its roots in the influence of the international movement, either in the form of political directives from the Comintern (i.e. the Class Against Class line and the Popular Front line) or in the form of Soviet cultural theory. On the other hand, I have pointed out that the British writers were never reduced simply to parroting the Soviet line. Just as the leaders of the CPGB had to adapt Comintern directives to local conditions, so the Party theorists tried to develop Soviet ideas in distinctive ways, often by drawing on broader English and European traditions of cultural theory. The adaptation of Soviet ideas often had remarkably unorthodox consequences. Whereas some writers (e.g. Ralph Fox) *inadvertently* produced work that was inconsistent with Marxist assumptions, there were others (e.g. Alick West) whose lack of orthodoxy seemed to be the expression of a semi-dissident perspective on the world communist movement. At any rate, the element of unorthodoxy in the work of the Party theorists goes some way towards reinforcing the revisionist argument that British communists were never simply the stooges of Moscow.

By relating Marxist criticism in Britain to developments in the Communist International and to the emergence of Soviet theory, the book intersects with three themes in the history of international communism which historians have only recently begun to address, and which will need to be explored in much greater detail if a balanced assessment of the first wave of socialist revolutions is ever to be achieved. The first is the way that the Soviet Union and its allies often exercised a curiously *positive* influence on economic, political and cultural developments in the capitalist world. As Eric Hobsbawm has pointed out, one of the biggest paradoxes of the twentieth century was that Soviet socialism, which inflicted such misery on most of the people who lived under it, nevertheless played an overwhelmingly progressive role in world affairs.[1] The defeat of fascism, the establishment of the welfare state in Western Europe, the demise of Western imperialism (at least in its colonial form) and the emergence of powerful labour movements throughout the world were all things for which the USSR could take some credit. At the intellectual level, the most important consequence of the October Revolution was that it conferred massive intellectual respectability on what used to be called 'philosophical Marxism', thereby paving the way for the remarkably insightful work on economics, politics, history and culture which has been produced by Marxist intellectuals over the last eighty years. The task facing historians now is to move beyond purely local studies (such as the one in this book) to a more general account of the influence of Soviet Marxism on the development of modern thought.[2] It will also be necessary to ask how communists and other radicals were able to project a radiantly positive image of the USSR at a time when Stalinist depredations were at their height. British historians who wish to answer this question will have to pay close attention to a raft of texts from the 1930s, notably Sidney and Beatrice Webb's *Soviet Communism: A New Civilisation?* (1935), Hewlett Johnson's *The Socialist Sixth of the World* (1939) and Pat Sloan's *Soviet Democracy* (1937), in which men and women of high intelligence and considerable prestige ritually portrayed the USSR as 'the hope of the world'.[3]

A closely related theme is that of the influence of what we might call Comintern Marxism on subsequent trends in Marxist thought, especially those which developed outside the confines of the world communist movement. The tendency of intellectual historians, exemplified in the three volumes of Leszek Kolakowski's *Main Currents of Marxism,* has been to emphasise the *discontinuities* between Western Marxism and what tends to be dismissed as 'Stalinism'. At one level, this is obviously justified – it reminds us that the Marxist tradition is as richly variegated as any of the other major ideologies of the modern period. Yet elements of continuity also need to be explored. As far as British Marxism is concerned, we have already seen how Victor Paananen has begun to draw attention to the similarities (remote though they sometimes are) between the communist criticism of the 1930s and the better regarded work of subsequent decades.[4] Although there is no room here in which to build on his remarks, I would suggest that at least three of the most important post-war developments in Marxist and *Marxisant* criticism all owe some kind of debt to the Party theorists:

The emergence of the New Left and the birth of Cultural Studies. According to the orthodox view, the emergence of the New Left was a consequence of the disillusionment with international communism which set in amongst British intellectuals after the Khrushchev revelations and the Soviet invasion of

Hungary. As such, it is often argued that the early work of Raymond Williams, E.P. Thompson and Richard Hoggart (the three writers who defined the New Left's cultural policy and in so doing invented the discipline of Cultural Studies) was part of a concerted attempt to move beyond the 'deformations' of Soviet Marxism.[5] There is obviously a great deal of truth in this, but what it overlooks are the *parallels* between the communist criticism of the 1930s and the founding texts of Cultural Studies – especially the three books (*Culture and Society, The Long Revolution* and *Communications)* in which Williams laid out his proposals for cultural reform. As is well known, Williams argued that the New Left should strive to create a 'common culture' in Britain that would be rooted in the communitarian values of the working class. This would only be possible once substantial amounts of economic and political power had been devolved to working people (though Williams stopped short of full-blooded socialism), and this would itself be dependent on the skills of 'advanced communication' being extended to the majority. Since the greatest works of English literature embody the ideal of advanced communication in its most sophisticated form, and since many of them give powerful expression to precisely the sort of communitarian values that will underpin the common culture of the future, it follows (or so Williams went on to argue) that the 'great tradition' should be stripped of its elite connotations and integrated into the nation's 'common inheritance'.[6] If arguments such as these can legitimately be read as a sort of quasi-Marxist adaptation of the Leavisite (or Arnoldian) emphasis on the civilising powers of high culture, their consonance with the critical positions of the Popular Front period also seems clear. There is the same belief in the instinctive radicalism of the people, in the peerless ability of the labour movement to extend democracy and in the basic similarities between the values of the great English writers and the values of the working class. Since Williams has admitted that he immersed himself in the writings of the English communists while a student at Cambridge, it is surprising that this aspect of his intellectual formation has been overlooked for so long.[7]

The attack on 'literature'. The most startling aspect of British Marxist criticism over the last thirty years has been the attempt by a number of writers, notably Raymond Williams and Terry Eagleton, to call the very category of 'literature' into question.[8] The idea that 'Literature, in the sense of a set of works of assured and unalterable value, distinguished by certain shared inherent properties, does not exist' (Eagleton)[9] might seem a world away from the canonical certainties of the 1930s, but it was advanced for strategic reasons which the Party theorists would surely have understood. At bottom, Williams and Eagleton both attacked the idea of literature in order to shift attention away from finished texts to *the* *process by which texts are created.*[10] Williams argued (or at least implied) that writing somehow prefigures the experience of unalienated labour in a socialist society, whereas Eagleton wanted to replace English Studies with a new discipline of 'Rhetoric' that would teach students to produce politically persuasive texts of their own.[11] As we have seen, however, the habit of describing literature as a form of 'productive activity' does not originate with Williams and Eagleton but dates back in the English context to the work of Caudwell, West and Lindsay. Since books by all three of these writers were included in the relatively brief bibliography of Williams's *Marxism and Literature* (1977), and since Eagleton has written briefly about both West and Caudwell, it seems reasonable to argue that the thirties writers exercised a direct influence on their successors.

The influence of Gramscian and Althusserian ideas. The biggest influence on Marxist criticism over the last thirty years has been the writings of Antonio Gramsci and Louis Althusser. Both theorists owe their guru status to the *New Left Review*, which has made a sustained effort to bring Western Marxism to the attention of British intellectuals since the 'palace coup' which elevated Perry Anderson to the editorship in 1962. Gramsci's theory of ideology has been used to justify a relatively optimistic approach to literature, with writers such as Raymond Williams, Alan Sinfield and Jonathan Dollimore insisting that all texts contain 'emergent' elements (as well as 'hegemonic' and 'residual' ones) which make them susceptible to oppositional decoding.[12] Althusserian Marxism has generally been used for less sanguine purposes, such as the elaboration of an 'anti-humanist' perspective which categorises literature as one of the 'ideological state apparatuses' which reconcile us to capitalist rule.[13] The Althusser/Gramsci divide has also been evident in Cultural Studies. A large number of writers, ranging from representatives of the so-called 'Birmingham School' (e.g. Stuart Hall, Dick Hebdige and Dorothy Hobson)[14] to the more recent 'cultural populists' (e.g. John Fiske and Paul Willis),[15] have taken the Gramscian view that all popular texts are inherently polysemic – and therefore an important site of 'cultural struggle'. By contrast, the more pessimistic exponents of *Screen* theory, notably Colin MacCabe, Laura Mulvey and Peter Wollen,[16] have analysed popular culture in terms of Althusser's notion of 'interpellation'. There is no question that this body of work represents a major advance on the Marxist criticism of the 1930s, yet even here it could be argued that the reception of Althusserian and Gramscian ideas in Britain was powerfully conditioned by the work of the earlier writers. Take the example of Gramsci's theory of ideology. Nearly everyone agrees that Gramsci's main innovation was to draw attention to the 'contradictory' nature of ideology, specifically the way that the ideas of the ruling group seek to 'frame' the more subversive assumptions drawn from popular culture and folklore, but there is no particular reason why the contradictions of everyday consciousness should be interpreted optimistically – many would argue that they demonstrate the extraordinary ability of the ruling class to 'co-opt' the radical instincts of the people. If the British Marxists of the Seventies and Eighties *did* interpret them optimistically, it was perhaps because they belonged to a radical subculture that was still influenced by their communist predecessors, many of whom (as we have seen at various points in this book) regarded ideologies such as Christianity and liberalism as unstable compounds whose radical elements can easily be disaggregated and put to subversive use. On the other hand, the influence of the communist critics on the reception of Althusser's ideas was probably more negative. One of the things which has distinguished British Althusserianism from its continental and North American counterparts has been a deep suspicion of realism. According to MacCabe and his followers, the 'effect of realism' in the bourgeois novel is created by the 'hierarchical' relationship between the voice of the author and the voice of the characters, which in turn reduces the reader to a position of 'dominant specularity' and guarantees his acquiescence in the dominant ideology.[17] When we think back to the intolerance with which the British communists made the case for realism (and to the venom with which they denounced the modernist writers whom MacCabe so admired), it is clear that the anti-realism of the *Screen* theorists might well have been a response to an orthodoxy that was now regarded as irredeemably philistine.

All of which brings us on to the last theme which needs to be examined – the *internal* culture of the communist movement. Why should so many British communists have turned to the study of literature in a decade as hazardous as the 1930s? Perhaps the main reason was that the world communist movement had one of the most obsessively cerebral cultures in the whole of human history.[18] Committed to an ideology which purported to explain everything between the 'transition from ape to man' (Engels)[19] and the events of the present day, communists were astonishingly polymathic in their ambitions – they insisted that all genuine revolutionaries had a *duty* to immerse themselves in history, science, economics, philosophy and culture. The sense that there was something fundamentally immoral about a lack of intellectual curiosity was well captured in the following observation of Lenin's, which Christopher Caudwell almost used as an epigram for *Studies in a Dying Culture*: 'Communism becomes an empty phrase, a mere façade, and a communist a mere bluffer, if he has not worked over in his consciousness the whole inheritance of human knowledge.'[20] What was especially remarkable was that these exacting standards were imposed not merely on professional intellectuals but on working-class communists as well. The communist parties took thousands of men and women who lacked all but the most rudimentary education and told them that omniscience was a perfectly reasonable goal – or, as Brecht put it in his great poem *Praise of Learning*: 'You must know everything! You must take over the leadership!'[21] Moreover, if the endless pursuit of knowledge was usually justified on strategic grounds, there was also perhaps a feeling that it was one of the few ways in which an impoverished present might anticipate the truly humane culture of the socialist future. Many communists seem to have cleaved almost instinctively to the sort of cultural vision which Gramsci outlined in his *Prison Notebooks*, where the ultimate goal of socialism is seen as the reconciliation of the living elements in all existing systems of thought.[22] In the reading habits of the many 'worker intellectuals' who studied Freud, Bergson or Darwin alongside Marx, Engels and Lenin, we can detect a wish to extract the intellectual pith from 'bourgeois ideology' and assign it to its proper position beneath what Fredric Jameson would later call the 'untranscendable horizon' of Marxism. There even seem to have been communists who had an almost occult or Spinozian faith in the power of knowledge to bring about Promethean changes in human nature. By seeking to recreate the whole of human history in their own minds, they aspired to glimpse 'horizons infinitely remote and incredibly beautiful'[23] that would propel them towards a higher stage of evolution. It was probably no accident that the following lines from Book Three of Keats's *Hyperion* were quoted by Ralph Fox in *The Novel and the People*, even though their meaning was not dwelled upon:

Knowledge enormous makes a God of me.
Names, deeds, grey legends, dire events, rebellions,
Majesties, sovran voices, agonies,
Creations and destroyings, all at once
Pour into the wide hollows of my brain,
And deify me, as if some blithe wine,
Or bright elixir peerless I had drunk,
And so become immortal.[24]

The attempt to document the internal culture of the world communist movement has hardly begun, though in the British context there has been important work by Raphael Samuel, Jonathan Rée, Stuart Macintyre and others.[25] It is nevertheless clear that the true nature of communist history (or that portion of it which began in 1917 and came to an end with the collapse of the USSR in 1991) will never be understood until the 'compliment to man' implicit in communism's hunger for 'intellectual-philosophic sustenance' is more fully recognised (the phrases are George Steiner's).[26] Although thousands of people had their lives ruined by communism, thousands of others were redeemed by it. Once we have condemned them for perpetrating or defending Stalinist barbarism, we must still acknowledge that the constituent parties of the world communist movement were among the greatest *spiritual* institutions of the twentieth century – and perhaps of all time.

APPENDIX:
BIOGRAPHICAL DETAILS

The main text only contains biographical information about (1) those writers who have an entire chapter devoted to their work, and (2) those writers whose work can only be fully understood with some reference to their background. The purpose of this appendix is to provide brief biographical details for the other critics and theorists whom I examine. I have not included information about writers who are only mentioned in passing or the Soviet critics discussed in Chapter Two.[1]

ARNOT, (ROBERT PAGE) [ROBIN] (1890-1986). Historian and critic. Educated at Glasgow University. Secretary of the Fabian Research Department (renamed the Labour Research Department in 1918), 1914-1927. Assistant Director of the Communist International's Eastern Department, 1929. British representative on the Communist International's Executive Committee, 1928-1929/1936-1938. Member of the CPGB's Executive Committee, 1924-1938. Principal of the Marx Memorial Library, 1933-1947. Author of *William Morris: A Vindication* (1934), *A Short History of the Russian Revolution from 1905 to the Present Day* (two volumes, 1937), *Twenty Years 1920-1940: The Policy of the Communist Party of Great Britain from its Foundation, July 31st 1920* (1940), *The Miners: A History of the Miners' Federation of Great Britain* (four volumes, 1949-1979), *A History of the Scottish Miners* (1955), *William Morris: The Man and the Myth* (1964), *South Wales Miners: Glowyr de Cymru* (two volumes, 1967), *The Impact of the Russian Revolution in Britain* (1967) etc.

AUDEN, WYSTAN HUGH [W.H.] (1907-1973). Poet and critic. Educated at Gresham's School and Christ Church, Oxford. Schoolmaster at Larchfield Academy, Dumbartonshire (1930-1932) and Downs School, Herefordshire (1932-1935/1937). Worked as a documentarist for the Film Unit of the General Post Office, 1935. Visited Spain during the Spanish Civil War, briefly working in the censor's office in Valencia in 1937. Heavily influenced by Marxism throughout the 1930s, though never joined the Communist Party. Regular contributor to the Group Theatre. Effectively announced the end of his political phase by emigrating to the USA with Christopher Isherwood in 1939, several months before the outbreak of the Second World War. Lecturer in English at the University of Michigan (1941-1942) and at Swarthmore College, Pennsylvania, 1942-1945. Elected Professor of Poetry at Oxford University, 1955. Author of *Poems* (1928), *Poems* (1930), *The Orators* (1932), *The Dance of Death* (1933), *The Dog Beneath the Skin* (with Christopher Isherwood, 1935), *The Ascent of F6* (with Christopher Isherwood, 1936), *Letters from Iceland* (with Louis MacNeice, 1937), *On the Frontier* (with Christopher Isherwood, 1938), *Journey to a War* (with Christopher Isherwood, 1939), *The Age of Anxiety* (1947), *The Enchafèd Flood* (1950), *Nones* (1951), *The Shield of Achilles* (1955), *Homage to Clio* (1960), *The Dyer's Hand* (1962), *About the House* (1965), *City without Walls* (1969), *A Certain World* (1970), *Epistle to a Godson* (1971), *Thank you, Fog* (1974) etc.

AVELING, EDWARD (BIBBENS) (1849-1898). Writer and political campaigner. Educated at the West of England Dissenters' Proprietary School and University College, London. Lecturer in Comparative Anatomy at the London Hospital, 1876-1881. Fellow of University College, London. Vice President of the National Secular Society, 1880-1884. Editor of *Progress*, 1883-1884. Member of the Executive Council of H.M. Hyndman's Social Democratic Federation, 1884. Founder member of the Socialist League and member of its Executive Council, 1884-1885. Editor of the Socialist League's journal *Commonweal*, 1884-1886. Partner of Jenny Marx, daughter of Karl Marx, from 1884 onwards. Author of *The Student's Darwin* (1881), *The Student's Marx* (1892), *Shelley's Socialism* (with Eleanor Marx Aveling, 1888) etc.

AVELING, ELEANOR (JENNY JULIA) MARX- (1855-1898). Writer, translator and political campaigner. Daughter of Karl and Jenny Marx. Educated at the South Hampstead College for Ladies. Served on the Executive Council of the Social Democratic Federation, 1884. Founder member of the Socialist League, 1884. Member of the Council of the Gas Workers and General Labourers Union. Author of *The Woman Question* (1886), *Shelley's Socialism* (with Edward Aveling, 1888) etc. Translator of Flaubert's *Madame Bovary* (1886) etc.

BERNAL, JOHN DESMOND [J.D.] (1901-1971). Physicist and theorist/ historian of science. Educated at Stonyhurst College, Bedford School and Emmanuel College, Cambridge. Researcher at the Davy-Faraday Laboratory at the Royal Institution, 1922-1927. Lecturer in Structural Crystallography at the University of Cambridge, 1927-1938. Head of X-Ray Crystallography at the Cavendish Laboratories, 1927-1936. Professor of Physics (later Crystallography) at Birkbeck College, London, 1938-1968. Chief Scientific Advisor to Lord Mountbatten during the Second World War. Author of *The World, the Flesh, and the Devil* (1929), *The Social Function of Science* (1939), *Science in History* (four volumes, 1954), *Marx and Science* (1957) etc.

BROWN, ALEC. Novelist, poet, critic, archaeologist and translator. Educated at Cambridge University. Worked briefly for the *Cambridge Magazine*. Became a Lecturer in English at the University of Belgrade, 1920. Contributor to *The Calendar of Modern Letters*. Earned a brief notoriety in the 1930s for his contributions to *Left Review*, some of which enunciated a theory of literature that owed a great deal to the ideas of the Proletkult movement in the USSR. His writings on the class structure of Britain appear to have exercised an unacknowledged influence on George Orwell. Made various attempts to introduce Yugoslavian culture to a British audience in the period after 1940. Author of *The Honest Bounder* (1927), *Daughters of Albion* (1935), *The Fate of the Middle Classes* (1936), *Breakfast in Bed* (1937), *Essays on National Art in Yugoslavia* (editor, 1944), *Yugoslav Life and Landscape* (1954) etc. Translator of D.S. Mirsky's *The Intelligentsia of Great Britain* (1935) etc.

CORNFORTH, MAURICE (1909-1980). Philosopher. Educated at the University College School in London, the University of London, Cambridge University and Trinity College, Oxford. Exercised a deep influence on Stephen Spender while both were pupils at the University College School. Spender later wrote about him in his memoir *World Within World* (1951) and in his contribution to R.H.S. Crossman (ed.), *The God that Failed* (1949). Worked closely with G.E. Moore and Ludwig Wittgenstein while a graduate student at Cambridge. Abandoned the study of philosophy in 1933 to become the Communist Party of Great Britain's District Organiser in the Eastern Counties – a post he held until 1945. Also served on the Party's Executive Committee. Returned to the study of philosopher after the war and rapidly became one of the two most famous communist philosophers in Britain (the other was John Lewis). Aimed in his later years to provide a systematic Marxist account of analytical philosophy. Also wrote an influential attack on the ideas of Karl Popper. Almost singlehandedly responsible for launching the so-called "Caudwell Discussion" in 1950. Author of *Science and Idealism* (1946), *Dialectical Materialism and Science* (1949), *In Defence of Philosophy* (1950), *Dialectical Materialism: An Introduction* (three volumes, 1952-1954), *Rumanian Summer* (with Jack Lindsay, 1953), *Marxism and the Linguistic Philosophy* (1965), *The Open Philosophy and the Open Society* (1968), *Communism and Human Values* (1972), *Rebels and their Causes* (editor, 1977), *Communism and Philosophy* (1980) etc.

ELLIS, AMABEL WILLIAMS- (née **STRACHEY**) (1894-1984). Novelist, critic and writer for children. Educated at home. Literary Editor of *The Spectator*, 1922-1923. Became sympathetic to Soviet communism after visiting the USSR in the late 1920s and early 1930s with her brother John Strachey and her husband Clough Williams-Ellis. Never joined the Communist Party. One of the British delegates at the Soviet Writers' Congress in Moscow, 1934. Co-editor of *Left Review*, 1934-1935. Made a concerted effort while associated with *Left Review* to encourage the work of working-class writers. Author of *The Exquisite Tragedy* (1929), *To Tell the Truth* (1933), *The Big Firm* (1938), *Courageous Lives* (1939), *A History of English Life* (with F.J. Fisher, 1939) etc.

GARMAN, DOUGLAS (1903-1969). Poet and critic. Educated at Caius College, Cambridge. Assistant editor of *The Calendar of Modern Letters*, 1925-1926 (his association with the magazine came to an end when he embarked on a six-month visit to the Soviet Union in November 1926). Worked as an editor for Wishart and Co. in the early 1930s and as a commissioning editor for Lawrence and Wishart in the late 1930s. Joined the Communist Party of Great Britain in 1934 and subsequently served as its National Education Organiser. Frequent contributor to *Left Review* and the *Modern Quarterly*. Distanced himself from the Party in the early 1950s because of his opposition to the strategy outlined in *The British Road to Socialism*, though it is not clear whether he left the organisation – some say he did, others that he followed the example of his friend Alick West and became a sort of permanently disgruntled internal critic. Took up farming in Dorset towards the end of his life and contributed to various editions of the *Shell Guide to England*. Famously named his pigs after his sisters. Author of *The Jaded Hero* (1927).

HILL, (JOHN EDWARD) CHRISTOPHER (1912-2003). Historian. Educated at St Peter's School, York and Balliol College, Oxford. Fellow of All Souls College, Oxford, 1934-1938. Spent a year in the USSR acquainting himself with Soviet writings on English history, 1935-1936. Joined the Communist Party of Great Britain in 1936 and remained a member until 1957. Lecturer in History at University College Cardiff, 1936-1938. Served in British Military Intelligence, 1940-1943. Head of the Foreign Office's Russian desk, 1943-1945. Now believed to have acted as a Soviet mole during his years as a civil servant. Fellow and Tutor in Modern History, Balliol College, 1938-1940, 1945-1958. Lecturer in History at Oxford University, 1958-1965. Master of Balliol College, 1965-1978. Subsequently held a number of visiting professorships in Britain, Australia and the USA. Widely regarded as the pre-eminent post-war historian of the English Revolution. Author of *The English Revolution 1640* (with Edgell Rickword and Margaret James, 1940), *The Soviets and Ourselves: Two Commonwealths* (under the pseudonym K.E. Holme, 1945), *Lenin and The Russian Revolution* (1947), *The Good Old Cause* (edited with Edmund Dell, 1949), *Economic Problems of the Church* (1955), *Puritanism and Revolution* (1958), *Society and Puritanism in Pre-Revolutionary England* (1964), *Intellectual Origins of the English Revolution* (1965), *The Century Of Revolution, 1603-1714* (1961), *Reformation to Industrial*

Revolution (1967), *God's Englishman* (1970), *Antichrist in Seventeenth-Century England* (1971), *The World Turned Upside Down* (1972), *Winstanley: The Law of Freedom and Other Writings* (editor, 1873), *Change and Continuity in Seventeenth-Century England* (1974), *Milton and the English Revolution* (1977), *Some Intellectual Consequences of the English Revolution* (1980), *The World of the Muggletonians* (1983), *The Experience of Defeat* (1984), *A Turbulent, Seditious, and Factious People* (1988), *The English Bible In Seventeenth-Century England* (1993), *Liberty Against the Law* (1996) etc.

JACKSON, THOMAS ALFRED [T.A.] (1879-1955). Historian, journalist and critic. Educated at the Duncombe Road School, Holloway. Employed as a compositor at various times in the 1890s and the first decade of the twentieth century. Founder member of the Socialist Party of Great Britain, 1904. Occasionally employed as a political organiser by the Independent Labour Party and as a Tutor at the North-East Labour College in the period between 1909 and 1920. Founder member of the Communist Party of Great Britain in 1920 and a full-time Party worker between 1921 and 1929. Occasionally served as the editor of the Party journals *Communist* and *Workers' Weekly* in the 1920s. Oversaw the arts pages of the *Sunday Worker* with Ralph Fox, 1925-1929. Thereafter scraped a living as a full-time writer. Author of *Dialectics* (1936), *Charles Dickens: The Progress of a Radical* (1937), *Trials of British Freedom* (1940), *Socialism: What? Why? How?* (1945), *Ireland Her Own* (1947), *Old Friends to Keep* (1950), *Solo Trumpet* (1953) etc.

KLINGENDER, FRANCIS (DONALD) (1907-1955). Art historian. Born in Germany. Emigrated to England in 1925. Educated at the London School of Economics. Employed by the All Russian Co-operative Society (ARCOS) in the 1920s. Joined the Communist Party soon after arriving in Britain but left in the late 1940s. Leading member of the Artists International Association (AIA) from 1933 onwards. Contributor to *Left Review* and to Betty Rea's anthology *5 on Revolutionary Art* (1935). Helped to manage the AIA's Charlotte Street Centre in London, 1941-1944. Lecturer in Sociology at the University College of Hull, 1948-1955. Author of *The Condition of Clerical Labour in Britain* (1935), *The Money Behind the Screen* (with Stuart Legg, 1937), *Marxism and Modern Art* (1942), *Russia – Britain's Ally, 1812-1942* (1942), *Hogarth and English Caricature* (with Milicent Rose, 1943), *Art and the Industrial Revolution* (1947), *Goya in the Democratic Tradition* (1948), *Animals in Art and Thought to the End of the Middle Ages* (1971) etc.

LEWIS, CECIL DAY- (1904-1972). Poet, novelist and critic. Educated at Sherborne School and Wadham College, Oxford. Worked as a schoolmaster at various preparatory and junior schools between 1927 and 1935. Leading member of the Auden Circle in the 1930s. Member of the Communist Party of Great Britain, 1936-1938. Frequent contributor to *Left Review*. Worked as an editor at the Publications Division of the Ministry of Information, 1941-1946. Senior Reader for Chatto and Windus, 1946-1972. Elected Professor of Poetry at Oxford University, 1951. Poet Laureate, 1968-1972. Author of *Beechen Vigil* (1925), *Country Comets* (1928), *Transitional Poem* (1929), *From Feathers to Iron* (1931), *The Magnetic Mountain* (1933), *A Hope for Poetry* (1934), *Revolution in Writing* (1935), *A Time to Dance* (1935), *Noah and the Waters* (1936), *The Mind in Chains: Socialism and the Cultural Revolution* (editor, 1937), *Overtures to Death* (1938), *Word over All* (1943), *Poems, 1943-1947* (1948), *An Italian Visit* (1953), *Pegasus* (1957), *The Gate* (1962), *The Room* (1965), *The Whispering Roots* (1970) etc. Day-Lewis also wrote about twenty detective novels under the pseudonym "Nicholas Blake".

LINDSAY, (JOHN) [JACK] (1900-1990). Novelist, historian, critic and cultural theorist. Educated at Brisbane Grammar School and Queensland University. Co-editor of the Australian anti-modernist journal *Vision*, 1923-1924. After moving to England in 1926, served as co-publisher of the Fanfrolico Press until 1930. Co-editor with P.R. Stephensen of *The London Aphrodite*, 1928-1929. Converted to Marxism in the mid-1930s and joined the Communist Party of Great Britain in 1941. Became the key theorist and practitioner of "mass declamation" during the Popular Front period. Served in the Signal Corps between 1941 and 1943 and as a scriptwriter for the Army Bureau of Current Affairs between 1943 and 1945. Thereafter reverted to full-time writing. Awarded the Order of Znak Pocheta by the Soviet government in 1968 and the Order of Australia in 1981. Author of over 150 books (there is no complete bibliography), including *William Blake* (1927), *Mark Antony* (1936), *Adam of a New World* (1936), *Anatomy of Spirit* (1937), *John Bunyan: Maker of Myths* (1937), *A Short History of Culture* (1938), *England My England* (1939), *Handbook of Freedom* (edited with Edgell Rickword, 1939), *Perspective for Poetry* (1944), *British Achievement in Art and Music* (1945), *Marxism and Contemporary Science* (1949), *Betrayed Spring* (1953), *Rising Tide* (1953), *Moment of Choice* (1955), *After the Thirties* (1956), *Life Rarely Tells* (1958), *Roaring Twenties* (1960), *Fanfrolico and After* (1962), *J.M.W. Turner: his Life and Work* (1966), *Meetings with Poets* (1968), *Origins of Alchemy* (1970), *Origins of Astrology* (1971), *The Normans and their World* (1974), *William Morris* (1975), *William Blake* (1978), *Hogarth: his Art and his World* (1977), *Monster City: Defoe's London* (1978), *The Crisis in Marxism* (1981).

MADGE, CHARLES (HENRY) (1912-1996). Poet, sociologist and co-founder of Mass-Observation. Educated at Winchester College and Magdalene College,

Cambridge. Worked as a journalist on the *Daily Mirror*, 1935-1936. Co-Founded Mass-Observation with Charles Harrisson in 1937. Joined the Communist Party of Great Britain in 1932 but appears to have moved away from Marxism in the 1940s. Contributor to *Left Review* and C. Day Lewis's symposium *The Mind in Chains*. Worked as a researcher at The National Institute for Economic and Social Research (1940-1942) and at Political and Economic Planning (1943). Served as the Director of the Pilot Press in 1944 and as a Social Development Officer in Stevenage between 1947 and 1950. Professor of Sociology at the University of Birmingham, 1950-1970. Author of *The Disappearing Castle* (1937), *Britain* (with Charles Harrisson, 1939), *The Father Found* (1941), *Industry after the War* (1943), *Society in the Mind* (1964), *Art Students Observed* (with Barbara Weinberger, 1973), *Inner-City Poverty in Paris and London* (with Peter Willmott, 1981) etc.

MORTON, ARTHUR LESLIE [A.L.] (1903-1987). Historian and critic. Educated at the King Edward VI Grammar School, Bury St Edmonds, Eastbourne College and Peterhouse, Cambridge. Taught at Steyning Grammar School and at A.S. Neill's progressive school Summerhill in the 1920s. Joined the Communist Party of Great Britain in 1929 and remained a member until the end of his life. Occasional contributor to *Scrutiny* and the *Criterion*. Employed in various capacities by the *Daily Worker*, 1934-1937. Served in the Royal Artillery during the Second World War. Elected to the Urban District Council in Leiston, Suffolk in the late 1940s. Member of the CPGB's East Anglia District Committee until 1974. Active in the Communist Party's Historians' Group from its foundation in 1946. Full-time writer from 1950 onwards. Author of *A People's History of England* (1938), *Language of Men* (1946), *The English Utopia* (1952), *The Everlasting Gospel* (1958), *The Matter of Britain* (1966), *The World of the Ranters* (1970), *Collected Poems* (1977) etc.

MORRIS, WILLIAM (1834-1896). Poet, novelist, critic and designer. Educated at Marlborough College and Exeter College, Oxford. Trained as an architect under G.E. Street, one of the main contributors to the English Gothic revival, 1856-1858. Close associate of the leading Pre-Raphaelites from his days at Oxford onwards. Co-Founder of Morris, Marshall, Faulkner and Co. ("the Firm") in 1861. Founded the Society for the Protection of Ancient Buildings, 1877. Converted to Marxism in the early 1880s and joined H.M. Hyndman's Social Democratic Federation in 1883. Broke with Hyndman and became a founding member of the Socialist League, 1884. Editor of the Socialist League's newspaper *The Commonweal* until 1890. Heavily involved in the dramatic public protests of the late 1880s, including the events on "Bloody Sunday" in 1887. Leading member of the Hammersmith Socialist Society (a breakaway from the

Socialist League), 1890-1896. Founded the Kelmscott Press in 1891. Helped to found the Joint Committee of Socialist Bodies, 1893. Author of *The Defence of Guinevere, and other Poems* (1858), *The Life and Death of Jason* (1867), *The Earthly Paradise* (three volumes, 1868-1870), *A Summary of the Principles of Socialism* (with H.M. Hyndman, 1884), *Chants for Socialists* (1885), *A Dream of John Ball* (1888), *Signs of Change* (1888), *News from Nowhere* (1890) etc.

RICKWORD, (JOHN) EDGELL (1898-1982). Poet and critic. Educated at Colchester Royal Grammar School and Pembroke College, Oxford. Served in France in the Artists' Rifles between 1916 and 1918. Subsequently awarded the Military Cross. Contributor to the *New Statesman*, the *Daily Herald* and the *Times Literary Supplement* in the early 1920s. Chief editor of *The Calendar of Modern Letters*, 1925-1927. Converted to Marxism in the early 1930s and joined the Communist Party of Great Britain in 1934. Editor of *Left Review*, 1936-1937. Editor of *Our Time*, 1944-1947. After the War worked as a bookseller and as the Manager of the Hampstead branch of Collett's bookshop in London. Left the CPGB in 1956 but remained a Marxist. Author of *Behind the Eyes* (1921), *Rimbaud* (1924), *Scrutinies* (editor, two volumes, 1928/1931), *Invocations to Angels* (1928), *Twittingpan* (1931), *Essays and Opinions* (1974), *Literature in Society* (1978) etc.

SLATER, (CHARLES) MONTAGU (1902-1956). Novelist, critic, playwright and librettist. Educated at Millom School and as a non-collegiate student at Oxford University. Worked as a journalist on the *Liverpool Post*, the *Morning Post* and *Reynolds News* in the 1920s and early 1930s. Joined the Communist Party of Great Britain in 1927. Co-editor of *Left Review*, 1934-1935. Served as Head of Scripts in the Ministry of Information's Film Division during the Second World War. Collaborated with Benjamin Britten on a number of plays, documentary films, pageants and operas. Wrote the original libretto for Britten's opera *Peter Grimes* (1946), though it was later revised by Ronald Duncan and Eric Crozier. Author of *Second City* (1931), *Haunting Europe* (1934), *Stay Down Miner* (1936), *Once a Jolly Swagman* (1944), *Peter Grimes and other Poems* (1946), *Englishmen with Swords* (1949), *The Trial of Jomo Kenyatta* (1955) etc.

STRACHEY, (EVELYN) JOHN (ST LOE) (1901-1963). Author and politician. Educated at Eton College and Magdalene College, Oxford. Joined the Independent Labour Party in the early 1920s and collaborated with Sir Oswald Mosley on proto-Keynesian proposals for government reflation of the British economy. Labour MP for Aston, 1929-1931. Became a founder member of Mosley's New Party in 1931, leaving once it became clear that Mosley was increasingly attracted to fascism. Converted to Marxism in 1931 and spent much of the next eight years as Britain's leading populariser of "official" communist doctrine, though he never became a formal member of the Communist Party. Founded the Left Book Club with Victor Gollancz and Harold Laski in 1936. Broke with the Marxist left in 1940 and later became a key thinker on what became known as the "revisionist" wing of the Labour Party. Labour MP for Dundee (later Dundee West), 1945-1963. Under-Secretary of State for Air, 1945-1946. Minister of Food, 1946-1950. Secretary of State for War, 1950-1951. Author of *Revolution by Reason* (1925), *The Coming Struggle for Power* (1932), *The Menace of Fascism* (1933), *Literature and Dialectical Materialism* (1934), *The Nature of Capitalist Crisis* (1935), *The Theory and Practice of Socialism* (1936), *Why You Should Be a Socialist* (1938), *What Are We to Do?* (1938), *A Programme for Progress* (1940), *Contemporary Capitalism* (1956), *The End of Empire* (1959), *On the Prevention of War* (1962), *The Strangled Cry* (1963) etc.

SWINGLER, RANDALL (CARLINE) (1909-1967). Poet, novelist and critic. Educated at Winchester College and New College, Oxford. Worked as a schoolmaster in the late 1920s and early 1930s. Joined the Communist Party of Great Britain in 1934 and made a major contribution to the left's theatrical and musical culture. Editor of *Left Review*, 1937-1938. Founder of Fore Publications in 1938. Literary Editor and staff reporter for the *Daily Worker*, 1939-1941. Co-editor of *Our Time* between 1941 and 1942 and editor in 1949. Served in Italy with the 56th Divisional Signals between 1943 and 1945. Broadcast regularly on the BBC and served as a Tutor in adult education for the University of London in the late 1940s. Left the Communist Party in 1956. Helped to establish the *New Reasoner* in 1957. Author of *Poems* (1932), *Crucifixus: A Drama* (1932), *Reconstruction* (1933), *Difficult Morning* (1933), *No Escape* (1937), *Left Song Book* (edited with Alan Bush, 1938), *To Town* (1939), *We're in the Army Now* (1941), *The Years of Anger* (1946), *The God in the Cave* (1950) etc.

WARNER, (REGINALD ERNEST) [REX] (1905-1986). Novelist and classicist. Educated at St.George's School, Harpenden and Wadham College, Oxford. Began his career as a schoolmaster and held two teaching appointments in Egypt between 1932 and 1934. Leading member of the Auden Circle in the 1930s. Considered himself a Marxist in the 1930s but began to recant after the Nazi-Soviet Pact in 1939. Never joined the Communist Party. Served in Berlin with the Allied Control Commission at the end of the Second World War. Director of the British Institute in Athens, 1945-1947. Held a number of academic posts in the USA in the post-war years, including professorships at Bowdoin College (1962-1963) and the University of Connecticut (1964-1974). Won the Tait Memorial Prize for his book *Imperial Caesar* in 1960. Made an Honorary Fellow of Wadham College, Oxford in 1973. Author of *The Wild Goose Chase* (1937), *The Professor* (1938), *The Aerodrome* (1941) etc.

NOTES

Introduction

1 Most of Auden's critical writings from the 1930s are collected in *The English Auden: Poems, Essays, and Dramatic Writings, 1927-1939*, edited by Edward Mendelson (London: Faber and Faber, 1977). Spender's most important critical statement from the period was *The Destructive Element: A Study of Modern Writers and Beliefs* (London: Jonathan Cape, 1935). Some of Spender's shorter pieces of Marxist criticism were reprinted in *The Thirties and After: Poetry, Politics, People 1933-1975* (London: Fontana/Collins, 1978). C. Day Lewis's only book-length work of Marxist criticism was *A Hope for Poetry* (Oxford: Blackwell, 1934).

2 The book of Empson's which most obviously betrays the influence of Marxism is *Some Versions of Pastoral: A Study of the Pastoral Form in Literature* (London: Chatto, 1935). Knights's most important book, which combines a Leavisite approach to cultural history with Marxist and *Marxisant* insights into the relationship between literature and society, was *Drama and Society in the Age of Jonson* (London: Chatto, 1937). I examine Alick West's response to this work in Chapter Three.

3 The boundaries between the various groups are obviously not watertight. For instance, C Day Lewis, Edward Upward and Stephen Spender, who are usually grouped with the Auden Circle, were all members of the Communist Party in the 1930s – Day Lewis and Upward for several years, Spender for a single month. However, since their critical writings have almost nothing in common with those of the more committed communists, I have only mentioned them in passing. It should also be noted that I have not examined literary *journalism* in this book, primarily for reasons of space.

4 René Wellek, *A History of Modern Criticism 1750-1950, Volume Five: English Criticism 1900-1950* (London: Jonathan Cape, 1986) pp. 142-143. Wellek deals only with the work of Christopher Caudwell.

5 Ron Bellamy, 'The Contribution of Communist Economists' in Socialist History Society, *Getting the Balance Right: An Assessment of the Achievements of the Communist Party of Great Britain* (London: Socialist History Society, n. d.) p. 23.

6 John Gross, *The Rise and Fall of the Man of Letters: English Literary Life since 1800* (Harmondsworth: Penguin Books, 1991) p. 277. If Gross's remarks about West, Lindsay and most of the contributors to *Left Review* were deeply unfair, his judgement on Philip Henderson was perhaps more accurate. At any rate I have chosen not to examine Henderson's work in this book, primarily because Edgell Rickword was right to point out that '...it [i.e. Henderson's approach to literary history] is not specifically Marxist.' See Edgell Rickword, Untitled review of *Literature and a Changing Civilisation* by Philip Henderson, *Left Review*, Vol. 2 No. 1, October 1935, p. 41. Henderson's two most substantial critical statements from the 1930s were *Literature and a Changing Civilisation* (London: John Lane The Bodley Head, 1935) and *The Novel Today: Studies in Contemporary Attitudes* (London: John Lane The Bodley Head, 1936).

7 Victor N. Paananen (ed.), *British Marxist Criticism* (New York: Garland Publishing, 2000) p. 9.

8　　See, *inter alia*, Christopher Hill's remarks about the influence of Edgell Rickword's essay 'Milton: The Revolutionary Intellectual' (1940) on his book *Milton and the English Revolution* (1977): 'Edgell Rickword's essay of 1940 must have sunk deep into my consciousness, but I did not re-read it until I had finished the first draft of my book. I then realized that though I had expanded some factual material and had dealt more fully with Milton's last great poems than Edgell Rickword did, in all essentials I had merely elaborated arguments which he had stated with beautiful brevity and clarity in 1940.' Quoted in Charles Hobday, *Edgell Rickword: A Poet at War* (Manchester: Carcanet, 1989) p. 221.

9　　For Andrew Thorpe, see, *inter alia*, 'Comintern "Control" of the Communist Party of Great Britain', *English Historical Review*, 452, Vol. 112, 1998, pp. 636-662; 'Stalinism and British Politics', *History*, Vol. 83, 1998, pp. 608-627; 'The Communist International and the British Communist Party' in Andrew Thorpe and Tim Rees (eds.), *International Communism and the Communist International, 1919-1943* (Manchester: Manchester University Press, 1993); *The British Communist Party and Moscow, 1920-1943* (Manchester: Manchester University Press, 2000); 'Communist MP: Willie Gallacher and British Communism' in Kevin Morgan, Gidon Cohen and Andrew Flinn (eds.), *Agents of the Revolution: New Biographical Approaches to the History of International Communism in the Age of Lenin and Stalin* (Oxford: Peter Lang, 2005). For Matthew Worley, see, *inter alia*, 'Reflections on Recent Communist Party History', *Historical Materialism*, No. 4, 1999, pp. 241-261; *Class Against Class: The Communist Party in Britain Between the Wars* (London: I.B. Tauris, 2002); For Kevin Morgan, see, *inter alia*, *Against Fascism and War: Ruptures and Continuities in British Communist Politics, 1935-1941* (Manchester University Press, 1989); *Harry Pollitt* (Manchester: Manchester University Press, 1993); 'Harry Pollitt, the British Communist Party and International Communism' in Tauno Saarela and Kimmo Rentola (eds.), *Communism: National and International* (Helsinki: Finnish Historical Society, 1998). For Mike Squires, see, *inter alia*, 'British Communists and the Communist International', *Communist Review*, No. 29, Spring 1999, pp. 25-30. For a Trotskyist critique of the new revisionism, see John McIlroy, 'Rehabilitating Communist History: The Communist International, the Communist Party of Great Britain and Some Historians', *Revolutionary History*, Vol. 8 No. 1, 2001, pp. 195-226. For a fuller list of revisionist (and anti-revisionist) writings, see Dave Cope's *CPGB Bibliography* at www.amielandmelburn.org.uk/cpgb_biblio/searchfrset.htm

10　Quoted in Andrew Murray, *The Communist Party of Great Britain: A Historical Analysis to 1941* (Liverpool: Communist Liaison, 1995) p. 28.

11　See Henry Pelling, *The British Communist Party: A Historical Profile* (London: A & C Black, 1958).

12　See, *inter alia*, James Eaden and David Renton, *The Communist Party of Great Britain since 1920* (Basingstoke: Palgrave, 2002).

13　 See Francis Beckett, *The Enemy Within: The Rise and Fall of the British Communist Party* (London: John Murray, 1995); Keith Laybourn and Dylan Murphy, *Under the Red Flag: A History of Communism in Britain* (Stroud: Sutton, 1999).

14　See, *inter alia*, James Klugmann, *History of the Communist Party of Great Britain, Volume One: Formation and Early Years 1920-1924* (London: Lawrence and Wishart,

1968); Noreen Branson, *History of the Communist Party of Great Britain, Volume Three, 1927-1941* (London: Lawrence and Wishart, 1985); Willie Thompson, *The Good Old Cause: British Communism, 1920-1921* (London: Pluto Press, 1993).

15   See Thorpe, 'Comintern "Control" of the Communist Party of Great Britain, 1920-1943'.

16   See Kevin Morgan, *Harry Pollitt.*

17   For the early history of the CPGB's National Cultural Committee, see, *inter alia,* Andy Croft, 'Writers, the Communist Party and the Battle of Ideas, 1945-1950', *Socialist History,* No. 5, Summer 1994, p. 12f.

18   George Orwell, 'The Lion and the Unicorn: Socialism and the English Genius' in *The Collected Essays, Journalism and Letters of George Orwell, Volume Two: My Country Right or Left 1940-1943* (Harmondsworth: Penguin Books, 1970) p. 95.

19   See Andy Croft, *Red Letter Days: British Fiction in the 1930s* (London: Lawrence and Wishart, 1990) pp. 31-37. The first chapter of Croft's book provides an overview of communist approaches to literature in the 1920s and 1930s. Jackson, Paul and Fox were among the main contributors to the literary pages of the *Sunday Worker* (1925-1929). I hope to examine the *Sunday Worker*'s contribution to the communist understanding of literature on some other occasion.

20   For accounts of *Left Review,* see David Margolies, '*Left Review* and Left Literary Theory' in David Margolies, Margot Heinemann, John Clarke and Carole Snee (eds.), *Culture and Crisis in Britain in the Thirties* (London: Lawrence and Wishart, 1979); Craig Werner, '*Left Review*' in Alvin Sullivan (ed.), *British Literary Magazines: The Modern Age, 1914-1984* (London, Greenwood Press, 1986); Margot Heinemann, '*Left Review, New Writing* and the Broad Alliance against Fascism' in Edward Timms and Peter Collier (eds.), *Visions and Blueprints: Avant-Garde Culture and Politics in early Twentieth-Century Europe* (Manchester: Manchester University Press, 1988); E.P. Thompson, '*Left Review*' in *Persons and Polemics: Historical Essays* (London: Merlin Press, 1994); Glenn Jordan and Chris Weedon, *Cultural Politics: Class, Gender, Race and the Postmodern World* (Oxford: Blackwell, 1995) Chapter Three; David Margolies (ed.), *Writing the Revolution: Cultural Criticism from Left Review* (London: Pluto Press, 1998); Peter Marks, 'Art and Politics in the 1930s: *The European Quarterly* (1934-1935), *Left Review* (1934-1938), and *Poetry and the People* (1938-1940)' in Peter Brooker and Andrew Thacker (eds.), *The Oxford Critical and Cultural History of Modernist Magazines,* Vol. 1 (Oxford: Oxford University Press, 2008). As Margolies points out, *Left Review* replaced the journal *Viewpoint,* two numbers of which appeared in 1934. British communists also published articles on literature in a range of other journals during the 1930s, including *Labour Monthly, Life and Letters Today* and the *Modern Quarterly.*

21   See Noreen Branson, op cit., p. 213.

22   See Julian Symons, *The Thirties: A Dream Revolved,* revised edition (London: Faber and Faber, 1975); Samuel Hynes, *The Auden Generation: Literature and Politics in England in the 1930s* (London: Bodley Head, 1976).

23   Valentine Cunningham, *British Writers of the Thirties* (Oxford: Oxford University Press, 1988) p. 5.

24   Worley, "Reflections on Recent British Communist Party History", p. 256.

25   See John Lucas (ed.), *The 1930s: A Challenge to Orthodoxy* (Sussex: Harvester,

1978); David Margolies, Margot Heinemann, John Clarke and Carole Snee (eds.), *Culture and Crisis in Britain in the Thirties* (London: Lawrence and Wishart, 1979); Geoff Andrews, Nina Fishman and Kevin Morgan (eds.); *Opening the Books: Essays on the Social and Cultural History of the British Communist Party* (London: Pluto Press, 1995); Andy Croft (ed.), *A Weapon in the Struggle: The Cultural History of the Communist Party in Britain* (London: Lawrence and Wishart, 1998).

26   See, *inter alia*, David Smith, *Socialist Propaganda in the Twentieth-Century British Novel* (London: Macmillan, 1978); H. Gustav Klaus 'Socialist Fiction in the 1930s: Some Preliminary Observations' in John Lucas (ed.), *The 1930s: A Challenge to Orthodoxy*; H. Gustav Klaus, *The Literature of Labour: 200 Years of Working Class Literature* (Brighton: Harvester, 1985); H. Gustav Klaus, 'James Barke: A Great-hearted Writer, a Hater of Oppression, a True Scot' in Andy Croft (ed.), *A Weapon in the Struggle*; Ingrid von Rosenberg, 'Militancy, Anger and Resignation: Alternative Moods in the Working-Class Novel of the 1950s and 1960s' in H. Gustav Klaus (ed.), *The Socialist Novel in Britain: Towards the Recovery of a Tradition* (Sussex: Harvester Press, 1982).

27   See, *inter alia*, Colin Chambers, *The Story of Unity Theatre* (London: Lawrence and Wishart, 1989); Colin Chambers, 'Unity Theatre' in David Margolies and Maroula Joannou (eds.), *Heart of the Heartless World: Essays in Cultural Resistance in Memory of Margot Heinemann* (London: Pluto Press, 1995); Jon Clark, 'Agitprop and Unity Theatre: Socialist Theatre in the Thirties' in Jon Clark, Margot Heinemann, David Margolies and Carole Snee (eds.), *Culture and Crisis in Britain in the Thirties*.

28   See, *inter alia*, Bert Hogenkamp, *Deadly Parallels: Film and the Left in Britain, 1929-1939* (London: Lawrence and Wishart, 1986); Bert Hogenkamp, *Film, Television and the Left 1950-1970* (London: Lawrence and Wishart, 2000); Stephen Jones, *The British Labour Movement and Film, 1918-1939* (London: Routledge, 1987).

29   See, *inter alia*, Jonathan Rée, *Proletarian Philosophers: Problems in Socialist Culture in Britain, 1900-1940* (Oxford: Clarendon Press, 1984); Edwin A. Roberts, *The Anglo-Marxists: A Study in Ideology and Culture* (Oxford: Rowman and Littlefield, 1997); Edwin A. Roberts, 'British Intellectuals and the Communist Ideal', *Nature, Society, and Thought*, Vol. 15 No. 2, 2002, pp. 157-181.

30   See Lynda Morris and Robert Radford, *The Story of the Artists International Association 1933-1953* (Oxford: The Museum of Modern Art, 1983); Robert Radford, 'To Disable the Enemy: the Graphic Art of the Three Jameses' in Andy Croft (ed.), *A Weapon in the Struggle*.

31   Raymond Williams, *Culture and Society 1780-1950* (Harmondsworth: Pelican Books, 1979) Part Three, Chapter Five.

32   David Margolies, '*Left Review* and Left Literary Theory' in David Margolies *et al* (eds.), *Culture and Crisis in Britain in the Thirties*; Hanna Behrend, 'An Intellectual Irrelevance? Marxist Literary Criticism in the 1930s' in Croft (ed.), *A Weapon in the Struggle*. Margolies's attitude towards the Soviet influence on English criticism is interestingly ambiguous. Although he has written about the impact of figures such as Bukharin and Dimitrov on the English writers (and although he acknowledges the importance of the political stategies handed down by the CI), his tendency is to portray English Marxist criticism as an independent movement whose debt to Soviet theory was purely incidental.

33 Anand Prakash, *Marxism and Literary Theory* (Delhi: Academic Foundation, 1994).

34 Mention should also be made of Charles Elkins's unpublished PhD thesis *The Development of British Marxist Literary Theory: Toward a Genetic-Functional Approach to Literary Criticism* (Southern Illinois University, 1972), which contains a lengthy chapter on Caudwell and briefer remarks on the work of Philip Henderson, R.D. Charques, Ralph Fox and Alick West. Also worth consulting is the short but perceptive account of British communist criticism in Andrew Milner, *Cultural Theory: An Introduction* (London: UCL Press, 1994) pp. 57-59.

35 E.P. Thompson, *The Making of the English Working Class* (Harmondsworth: Pelican Books, 1972) p. 13.

36 See Paananen, pp. 1-7 *passim*.

37 Prakash, pp. 23-29 *passim*.

38 These echoes are coincidental. Most of my book was completed before *Marxism and Literary Theory* came to my attention.

39 Prakash, op cit., p. 30.

40 James Klugmann, 'The Crisis of the Thirties: A View from the Left' in David Margolies *et al* (eds.), *Crisis and Culture in Britain in the Thirties*.

41 Margot Heinemann, 'The People's Front and the Intellectuals' in Jim Fyrth (ed.), *Britain, Fascism and the Popular Front* (London: Lawrence and Wishart, 1985); Margot Heinemann, '*Left Review, New Writing* and the Broad Alliance against Fascism' in Edward Timms and Peter Collier (eds.), *Visions and Blueprints*.

42 Klugmann, 'The Crisis in the Thirties', p. 25.

43 For Andy Croft, see, *inter alia*, ' "Extremely Crude Propaganda"? The Historical Novels of Jack Lindsay' in Robert Mackie (ed.). *Jack Lindsay: The Thirties and Forties* (London: University of London Australian Studies Centre, 1984); *Red Letter Days: British Fiction in the 1930s* (London: Lawrence and Wishart, 1990); 'Writers, the Communist Party and the Battle of Ideas, 1945-1950', *Socialist History*, No. 5, Summer 1994, pp. 2-25; 'Walthamstow, Little Gidding and Middlesborough: Edward Thompson, Adult Education and Literature', *Socialist History*, No. 8, 1995, pp. 22-48; 'Authors Take Sides: Writers and the Communist Party 1920-1956' in Andrews, Fishman and Morgan (eds.), *Opening the Books*; 'The End of Socialist Realism: Margot Heinemann's *The Adventurers*' in David Margolies and Maroula Joannou (eds.), *Heart of the Heartless World: Essays in Cultural Resistance in Memory of Margot Heinemann* (London: Pluto Press, 1995); 'Culture or Snobology? Writers and the Communist Party' in Socialist History Society, *Getting the Balance Right*; 'Politics and Beauty: the Poetry of Randall Swingler' in Keith Williams and Steven Matthews (eds.), *Rewriting the Thirties: Modernism and After* (London: Longman, 1997); 'The Boys Round the Corner: the Story of Fore Publications' in Croft (ed.), *A Weapon in the Struggle*; 'The Young Men are Moving Together: The Case of Randall Swingler' in John McIlroy, Kevin Morgan and Alan Campbell (eds.), *Party People, Communist Lives: Explorations in Biography* (London: Lawrence and Wishart, 2001); 'The Ralph Fox (Writers') Group' in Antony Shuttleworth (ed.), *And in Our Time: Vision, Revision, and British Writing of the 1930s*, (Lewisburg: Bucknell University Press, 2003); *Comrade Heart: A Life of Randall Swingler*, (Manchester: Manchester University Press, 2003).

44   See, for instance, Croft, 'Authors Take Sides', pp. 94-95.

45   For an early attempt by a British communist to identify the similarities between Soviet and English criticism, see Montagu Slater, 'The Turning Point', *Left Review*, Vol. 2 No. 1, October 1935, pp. 15-23. I examine this article in Chapter Two.

46   See Sir Philip Sidney, 'An Apology for Poetry' in Hazard Adams (ed.), *Critical Theory Since Plato* (New York: Harcourt Brace, 1971).

47   See William Wordsworth, 'Preface to the Second Edition of *Lyrical Ballads*' in Hazard Adams (ed.), op cit.

48   See T.S. Eliot, *Selected Prose of T.S. Eliot*, edited by Frank Kermode (London: Faber and Faber, 1984).

49   For the founding text of the English art-for-art's sake movement, see Walter Pater, 'Preface and Conclusion to *Studies in the History of the Renaissance*' in Hazard Adams (ed.), op cit.

50   See Oscar Wilde, 'The Decay of Lying' in Hazard Adams (ed.), op cit.

51   See, *inter alia*, G.K. Chesterton, *Heretics* (London: John Lane The Bodley Head, 1907) p. 16f.

52   For an introduction to Carpenter's life and work, see Sheila Rowbotham and Jeffrey Weeks, *Socialism and the New Life: The Personal and Sexual Politics of Edward Carpenter and Havelock Ellis* (London: Pluto Press, 1977). For a brief account of the eclectic nature of Carpenter's thinking, see Robert Skidelsky, *Interests and Obsessions: Historical Essays* (London: Macmillan, 1994) p. 14f.

53   For a recent account of the disparate influences on Shaw's work, see Colin Sparks, 'Theatrical Reformism', *International Socialism*, No. 41, Winter 1988, pp. 165-181.

54   See Oscar Wilde, *The Soul of Man and Prison Writings* (Oxford: Oxford University Press, 1990).

55   See, *inter alia*, William Morris, 'The Lesser Arts' in *Selected Writings and Designs*, edited by Asa Briggs (Harmondsworth: Pelican Books, 1968).

56   Ibid., pp. 93-100.

57   See William Morris, 'A Factory As It Might Be' in *Selected Writings of William Morris*, edited by William Gaunt (London: Falcon Press, 1948).

58   See William Morris, 'News From Nowhere' in *Selected Writings and Designs*.

59   See Karl Marx and Frederick Engels, *Selected Works in One Volume* (London: Lawrence and Wishart, 1980) pp. 53-55.

60   Edward Aveling and Eleanor Marx Aveling, *Shelley's Socialism* (London: Journeyman Press, 1979) p. 14.

61   Ibid., pp. 19-22. The Avelings referred not to dialectical materialism but to Shelley's 'evolutionism'.

62   Ibid., pp. 29-33.

63   Ibid., pp. 23-26, 28-33.

64   Ibid., p. 28.

Chapter One

1   Although the Soviet Union began its efforts to intervene directly in the cultural activities of the British communists at about this time, its influence initially proved negligible. A small British delegation attended the Second International Conference of Revolutionary and Proletarian Writers in Kharkov in 1930, where they heard Soviet intellectuals enunciate an approach to literature which owed a great deal to the ideas of the Proletcult movement, but they seem to have felt no obligation to disseminate the Soviet view when they returned home. An attempt to establish a Robert Tressell Club (i.e. a British section of the Association of Revolutionary and Proletarian Writers) was unsuccessful. The only critical issue from the Conference was a couple of inconsequential articles by the novelist Harold Heslop (a member of the British delegation) which bemoaned the absence of a tradition of revolutionary writing in Britain. See H. Gustav Klaus, "Harold Heslop: Miner Novelist" in *The Literature of Labour: 200 Years of Working Class Writing* (Sussex: Harvester Press, 1985) pp. 98-102. Heslop later included a vivid account of his experiences at the Conference in his autobiography. See Harold Heslop, *Out of the Old Earth*, edited by Andy Croft and Graeme Rigby (Newcastle upon Tyne: Bloodaxe Books, 1994), p. 213f.

2   The first revisionist account of the Class Against Class period was probably Alun Howkins, 'Class Against Class: The Political Culture of the Communist Party of Great Britain 1930-1935' in Frank Gloversmith (ed.), *Class, Culture and Social Change: A New View of the 1930s* (Brighton: Harvester Press, 1980). The fullest revisionist account is Matthew Worley, *Class Against Class: the Communist Party in Britain Between the Wars* (London: IB Tauris, 2002). The revisionist case is usefully summarised in Andrew Thorpe, 'Comintern "Control" of the Communist Party of Great Britain, 1920-1943', *English Historical Review*, Vol. 112 No. 452, pp. 636-62. For the more orthodox account of the Class Against Class period, see, *inter alia*, Chapters Two to Eight of Noreen Branson, *History of the Communist Party of Great Britain 1927-1941* (London: Lawrence and Wishart, 1985) and Chapter Two of Willie Thompson, *The Good Old Cause: British Communism 1920-1991* (London: Pluto Press, 1992).

3   Howkins, op cit., p. 243.

4   These were the United Mineworkers of Scotland (UMS) and the United Clothing Workers (UCW), both founded in 1929.

5   For general histories of the cultural work of the CPGB in the Class Against Class period, see Howkins, op. cit. and Worley, *Class Against Class*, Chapter Six.

6   Jack Lindsay, *Fanfrolico and After* (London: Bodley Head, 1962) p. 183. Quoted in Earl G. Ingersoll, 'London Aphrodite, The' in Alvin Sullivan (ed.), *British Literary Magazines: The Modern Age, 1914-1984* (New York: Greenwood Press, 1986), p. 239.

7   Craig Munro seems to suggest that Stephensen's work of this period was not so much a synthesis of Marx and Nietzsche as a move beyond Marxism. Commenting on a heavily Nietzschean essay which Stephensen had written at Oxford just after the collapse of the General Strike in 1926, Munro notes that 'It is significant that Stephensen was reading and absorbing Nietzsche, the evangelist of individualism,

in the wake of the failure of mass consciousness to bring about a proletarian revolution. Stephensen retained communist sympathies for a number of years, but after his Oxford suppression [he had been disciplined by the University authorities for his left-wing activism] and the abortive general strike his rebellious spirit found new creative outlets.' Craig Munro, *Wild Man of Letters: The Story of P.R. Stephensen* (Victoria: Melbourne University Press, 1984) p. 45. For Munro's account of Stephensen's problems with the Oxford authorities, see p. 39f.

8 For a biography of Stephensen, see Craig Munro, *Wild Man of Letters: The Story of P.R. Stephensen*. Munro surveys Stephensen's relationship with Lindsay in his essay 'Two Boys from Queensland: P.R. Stephensen and Jack Lindsay' in Bernard Smith (ed.), *Culture and History: Essays Presented to Jack Lindsay* (Sydney: Hale and Ironmonger, 1984). For brief accounts of *The London Aphrodite*, see Lawrence Coupe, 'Jack Lindsay: From The Aphrodite to Arena' in Robert Mackie (ed.), *Jack Lindsay: The Thirties and Forties* (London: University of London Institute of Commonwealth Studies Australian Studies Centre, 1984) and Earl G. Ingersoll, op. cit.

9 Craig Munro usefully summarises the tenets of Norman Lindsay's philosophy in 'Two Boys from Queensland: P.R. Stephensen and Jack Lindsay', pp. 41f.

10 The biographical material in this paragraph is drawn from Munro, 'Two Boys from Queensland'.

11 See Ingersoll, op cit., p. 237f; Coupe, op cit., p. 49f.

12 Jack Lindsay, 'The Modern Consciousness: An Essay towards an Integration', *The London Aphrodite*, No. 1, August 1928, pp. 4-5.

13 Ibid., p. 5.

14 Ibid., p. 7.

15 Ibid., p. 8f.

16 Lindsay, 'The Modern Consciousness', p. 8.

17 Ibid., pp. 9-24.

18 See Coupe, op cit., p. 46f.

19 Lindsay, 'The Modern Consciousness', p. 9.

20 Ibid., p. 9.

21 Ibid., p. 16. The phrase 'pastoral-sweet rhythm' is Stephensen's. The image of 'gods walking in the harvest' is taken from a poem by Sacheverell Sitwell which Stephensen quoted.

22 Ibid., pp. 17-23.

23 Ibid., p. 17.

24 Ibid., pp. 17-18.

25 P.R. Stephensen, 'Editorial Manifesto', *The London Aphrodite*, No. 1, August 1928, p. 2; 'Notice to Americans', *The London Aphrodite*, No. 3, December 1928, p. 231.

26 P.R. Stephensen, 'Bakunin', *The London Aphrodite*, No. 6, July 1929, pp. 421-432.

27 P.R. Stephensen, 'J. C. Squire (Etc.)', *The London Aphrodite*, No. 2, October 1928, pp. 86-92.

28 P.R. Stephensen, 'Contrapuntals: An Essay in Amiable Criticism', *The London Aphrodite*, No. 3, December 1928, pp. 228-230.

29 P.R. Stephensen, 'The Whirled Around: Reflections upon Methuselah, Ichthyphallos, Wheels and Dionysos', *The London Aphrodite*, No. 5, April 1929,

pp. 338-341.

30   Stephensen, 'The Whirled Around', p. 340.

31   Ibid., p. 338.

32   Ibid., pp. 338-341.

33   Ibid., p. 338.

34   Ibid., p. 339.

35   Ibid., p. 338.

36   Ibid., p. 339.

37   Ibid., p. 339.

38   For brief introductions to Bakunin's life and work, see, *inter alia*, James Joll, 'Bakunin and the Great Schism" in *The Anarchists*, second edition (London: Methuen, 1979) and George Woodcock, 'The Destructive Urge' in *Anarchism: A History of Libertarian Ideas and Movements*, second edition (Harmondsworth: Penguin Books, 1986).

39   Stephensen, 'Bakunin', p. 421.

40   Ibid., p. 427.

41   For the idea of negationism, see Greil Marcus, *Lipstick Traces: A Secret History of the Twentieth Century* (London: Secker and Warburg, 1989).

42   Quoted in Stephensen, 'Bakunin', p. 423. The quotation is from the work of Pierre-Joseph Proudhon.

43   Quoted in ibid., p. 430.

44   Quoted in ibid., p. 423. The quotation is from the work of Alexander Herzen.

45   Ibid., p. 422.

46   Ibid., pp. 423-424.

47   Ibid., p. 427.

48   Ibid., p. 427.

49   Stephensen established the Mandrake Press with Edward Goldston after leaving the Fanfrolico Press, for which he had worked since coming down from Oxford. See Craig Munro, 'Two Boys from Queensland', pp. 63f.

50   Stephensen, 'Bakunin', p. 428.

51   Stephensen, 'The Whirled Around', p. 341.

52   Ibid., p. 341.

53   Ibid., pp. 339-340.

54   Ibid., p. 338.

55   Stephensen, 'Bakunin', p. 428.

56   Ibid., p. 340-341.

57   According to Caudwell, Shaw's obsession with the 'primacy of pure contemplation' was a typical expression of the so-called 'bourgeois illusion of freedom' – that is, the belief (allegedly endemic in capitalist societies and central to the emergence of cultural crisis) that freedom can only be achieved when social restraints are absent. Moreover, it was directly responsible for the two biggest failings of Fabian socialism: (1) the belief that only an intellectual elite can succeed in creating a new society, and (2) the belief that support for socialism can be achieved solely through the dissemination of propaganda. See Christopher Caudwell, 'George Bernard Shaw: A Study of the Bourgeois Superman' in *Studies in a Dying Culture* (London: John Lane The Bodley Head, 1938).

58 Robert Sullivan, *Christopher Caudwell* (London: Croom Helm, 1987) p. 31.

59 For a brief account of Squire's career, see John Gross, *The Rise and Fall of the Man of Letters: English Literary Life since 1800* (London: Penguin Books, 1991) pp. 255-258.

60 Stephensen, 'J.C. Squire (etc.)', p. 86-87.

61 Ibid., p. 87.

62 Ibid., p. 88.

63 Ibid., p. 86.

64 Ibid., p. 92.

65 For a brief recent account of the trial of *The Well of Loneliness*, see Neil Miller, *Out of the Past: Gay and Lesbian History from 1869 to the Present* (London: Vintage, 1995) pp. 183-196.

66 Stephensen, 'J. C. Squire (etc.)', p. 92.

67 Ibid., p. 90.

68 Quoted in Francis Beckett, *Enemy Within: The Rise and Fall of the British Communist Party* (London: John Murray, 1995) p. 45.

69 See J.D. Bernal, *The World, the Flesh and the Devil: An Inquiry into the Future of the Three Enemies of the Rational Soul* (London: Kegan Paul, 1929). For a useful summary of *The World, The Flesh and The Devil*, see Neal Wood, *Communism and British Intellectuals* (London: Gollancz, 1959) pp. 138-144.

70 Among the best introductions to Marx's understanding of the cultural crisis of capitalism is Terry Eagleton, 'The Marxist Sublime' in *The Ideology of the Aesthetic* (Oxford: Blackwell, 1990). For a brief survey of the work of Mehring and Plekhanov, see Peter Demetz, *Marx, Engels, and the Poets* (Chicago: Chicago University Press, 1967) Chapter Seven.

71 For other explorations of the idea of cultural crisis from about the time of the Class Against Class line, see, *inter alia*, John Cornford, 'The Class Front in Modern Art', *The Student Vanguard*, December 1933. Reprinted in Patrick Deane (ed.), *History in our Hands: A Critical Anthology of Writings on Literature, Culture and Politics from the 1930s* (London: Leicester University Press, 1998). R.D. Charques, *Contemporary Literature and Social Revolution* (London: Martin Secker, 1933); Dmitri Mirsky, *The Intelligentsia of Great Britain* (London: Gollancz, 1935).

72 Most academic work on Strachey has focused on his economic writings and his career as a Labour politician. There has been practically nothing on his cultural writings, though Section Three of *The Coming Struggle for Power* is briefly summarised in Edwin A. Roberts, *The Anglo-Marxists: A Study in Ideology and Culture* (Oxford: Rowman and Littlefield, 1997) pp. 78-80.

73 Insofar as Strachey's writings on the theme of cultural crisis had any force, it was largely *cumulative* – that is, a product of the fact that he ranged so widely across the terrain of contemporary culture. This explains why I have included a brief survey of his ideas about religion ansd science in a book which is largely about literary criticism.

74 See John Strachey, *The Coming Struggle for Power*, second edition, (London, Victor Gollancz, 1934) pp. 159.

75 See ibid., p. 159.

76 Ibid., pp. 161-162.

77   For Strachey's relationship with Mosley, see, *inter alia*, Nicholas Mosley, *Rules of the Game/Beyond the Pale: Memoirs of Sir Oswald Mosley and Family* (London: Pimlico, 1998).

78   Contrary to popular belief, this aphorism does not appear in Chesterton's work. Scholars are now inclined to regard it as a corruption of a passage in the work of Emile Cammaerts, whose book *The Laughing Prophet* (1937) was one of the earliest critical studies of Chesterton's ideas. For further information, see the following page at the website of the American Chesterton Society: www.chesterton.org/qmeister2/any-everything.htm.

79   The relevant passages of *The Future of an Illusion* were quoted at length by Strachey in *The Coming Struggle for Power*, pp. 162-164.

80   For other work by Thirties communists which tries to make use of psychoanalytic insights, see, *inter alia*, Christopher Caudwell, 'Freud: A Study in Bourgeois Psychology' in *Studies in a Dying Culture*; Alistair Browne, 'Psychology and Marxism' in C. Day Lewis (ed.), *The Mind in Chains: Socialism and the Cultural Revolution* (London: Frederick Muller, 1937); Jack Lindsay, *John Bunyan: Maker of Myths* (New York: Augustus M Kelley, 1969); Reuben Osborn, *Freud and Marx: A Dialectical Study* (London: Gollancz, 1937). Strachey wrote the 'Introduction' to Osborn's book.

81   For the history of the social relations of science movement, see, *inter alia*, Gary Werskey, *The Visible College: A Collective Biography of British Scientists and Socialists of the 1930s* (London: Free Association Books, 1988); Neal Wood, *Communism and British Intellectuals*, Chapter Five and Edwin A. Roberts, *The Anglo-Marxists*, Chapter Five.

82   Strachey, *The Coming Struggle for Power* pp. 174-176.

83   Ibid., pp. 176-177.

84   Ibid., pp. 177-180.

85   Ibid., p. 181.

86   This paragraph summarises part of the argument of J.D. Bernal, *The Social Function of Science* (London: Routledge, 1939). Bernal's own summary of the argument is contained in his essay 'Science and Civilisation' in C. Day Lewis (ed.), *The Mind in Chains*. For a useful overview of Bernal's ideas, see Edwin Roberts's *The Anglo-Marxists*, pp. 156-178. I am also indebted to Neal Wood's account of Bernal's thought in *Communism and British Intellectuals*.

87   Bernal, 'Science and Civilisation', p. 203.

88   See Wood, *Communism and British Intellectuals*, p. 134f.

89   Strachey, *The Coming Struggle for Power*, p. 186.

90   Ibid., p. 186.

91   Williams explored the distinction between hegemonic, residual and emergent forms of ideology in his essay 'Base and Superstructure in Marxist Literary Theory' in *Problems in Materialism and Culture: Selected Essays* (London, Verso: 1980). The distinction was examined in greater detail in Williams's book *Marxism and Literature* (London: Oxford University Press, 1977). For an introduction to Williams's contribution to Marxist literary theory, see Alan O' Connor, *Raymond Williams: Writing, Culture, Politics* (Oxford: Basil Blackwell, 1989), Chapter Five.

92   See, *inter alia*, Theodor Adorno and Max Horkheimer, *Dialectic of Enlightenment*

(London: Verso, 1995).

93   For a controversial introduction to the new aestheticism, see Dave Beech and John Roberts, 'Spectres of the Aesthetic, *New Left Review*, No. 218, July/August 1996.

94   Strachey, *The Coming Struggle for Power*, p. 206.

95   Ibid., pp. 207-211.

96   Ibid., pp. 211-215.

97   Ibid., pp. 215-216.

98   See Roland Barthes, *Mythologies* (London: Paladin, 1988).

99   See John Strachey, *Literature and Dialectical Materialism* (New York: Covici Friede, 1934) pp. 36-42. Krutch's book was first published in 1929.

100 Strachey, *Literature and Dialectical Materialism*, p. 39.

101 For a recent introduction to Timpanaro's work, see Perry Anderson, 'On Sebastiano Timpanaro', *London Review of Books*, Vol. 23 No. 9, 10 May 2001, pp. 8-12.

102 For an introduction to Marcuse's ideas, see Vincent Geoghegan, *Reason & Eros: The Social Theory of Herbert Marcuse* (London: Pluto Press, 1981).

103 Herbert Marcuse, *The Aesthetic Dimension: Towards a Critique of Marxist Aesthetics* (London: Macmillan, 1978) p. 14.

104 Ibid., p. 68.

105 Strachey, *The Coming Struggle for Power*, p. 358. Quoted in Strachey, *Literature and Dialectical Materialism*, p. 41. Cf. Rodney Barker's observation that 'Even the most optimistic British socialists might have cavilled at the prospect of eternal life which Strachey offered after the revolution.' Rodney Barker, *Political Ideas in Modern Britain* (London: Methuen, 1978) p. 164.

106 Strachey, *Literature and Dialectical Materialism*, p. 28.

107 Ibid., p. 26.

108 Ibid., pp. 23-24.

109 Ibid., pp. 23-24.

110 Ibid., p. 25.

111 Ibid., pp. 26-28.

112 T. S. Eliot, 'Gerontion' in *Collected Poems 1909-1962* (London: Faber and Faber, 1980) p. 39.

113 Montagu Slater, 'The Spirit of the Age in Print' in Edgell Rickword (ed.), *Scrutinies*, Volume 11, (London: Wishart & Company, 1931) p. 270 *passim*

114 Ibid., 264-273.

115 Ibid., pp. 269-273.

116 Ibid., pp. 282-283.

117 The phrase is Roger Fry's, quoted on p. 277 of ibid.

118 Ibid., pp. 273-278.

119 Ibid., p. 279.

120 Ibid., p. 279.

121 For an account of Russian abstraction and its use of geometrical forms, see Boris Groys, *The Total Art of Stalinism: Avant-Garde, Aesthetic Dictatorship, and Beyond* (Princeton: Princeton University Press, 1992) p. 14f.

122 See, *inter alia*, Neal Wood, *Communism and the British Intellectuals*, p. 167f. For some brief remarks about the effects of this anti-intellectualism on the CPGB's approach to culture, see Andy Croft, *Red Letter Days: British Fiction in the 1930s*

(London: Lawrence and Wishart, 1990) p. 37f; Andy Croft, 'Authors Take Sides: Writers and the Communist Party 1920-56' in Geoff Andrews, Nina Fishman and Kevin Morgan (eds.), *Opening the Books: Essays on the Social and Cultural History of the British Communist Party* (London: Pluto Press, 1995) p. 96.

123 Rajani Palme Dutt, *Memorandum on NCLC and Intellectuals*, August 7th 1932. Quoted in John Callaghan, *Rajani Palme Dutt: A Study in British Stalinism* (London: Lawrence and Wishart, 1993), p. 133. The quotation is part of Callaghan's brief discussion of the background to Dutt's response to Mirsky and Dobb. See also Wood, *Communism and the British Intellectuals*, p. 171f.

124 See Croft, 'Writers Take Sides', p. 94.

125 For an overview of the form of cultural conservatism with which the English communists tried to engage, see Iain Wright, 'F.R. Leavis, the *Scrutiny* Movement and the Crisis' in Jon Clark, Margot Heinemann, David Margolies and Carole Snee (eds.), *Culture and Crisis in Britain in the Thirties* (London: Lawrence and Wishart, 1979).

126 See T.E. Hulme, 'Romanticism and Classicism' in David Lodge (ed.), *20th Century Literary Criticism: A Reader* (London: Longman, 1972) pp. 93-104.

127 Ibid., p. 95. Hulme nevertheless pointed out that it is wrong to regard 'the difference between classic and romantic as being merely one between restraint and exuberance.'

128 Hulme did not make this point explicitly but strongly implied it with such phrases as 'man is always man and never a god.'

129 T.S. Eliot, 'Tradition and the Individual Talent' in *Selected Prose of T.S. Eliot*, edited by Frank Kermode (London: Faber and Faber, 1985) p. 38.

130 Ibid., p. 43.

131 This sentence closely matches one from my *Cultural Studies: A Student's Guide to Culture, Politics and Society* (Plymouth: Studymates, 1999) p. 38.

132 F.R. Leavis and Denys Thompson, *Culture and Environment: The Training of Critical Awareness* (London: Chatto and Windus, 1959).

133 See Perry Anderson, 'Components of the National Culture' in *English Questions* (London: Verso, 1992) esp. pp. 96-103.

134 For a brief account of Morton's life, see Maurice Cornforth, 'A.L. Morton – Portrait of a Marxist Historian' in Maurice Cornforth (ed.), *Rebels and Their Causes: Essays in Honour of A..L. Morton* (London: Lawrence and Wishart, 1978).

135 Cf. Iain Wright's comment that 'On their side, the left seemed for a time to be eager for an alliance, understanding the importance of *Scrutiny*'s campaign against the growing power of the advertising industry, the commercialization of the press, the cynically exploitative machinery of the new mass entertainments industry...' Wright, *op cit.*, p. 55. Wright's essay surveys the Marxist attempt to forge an alliance with *Scrutiny* on pp. 54-56.

136 There is another account of the Morton/Leavis debate in Francis Mulhern, *The Moment of 'Scrutiny'* (London: New Left Books, 1979) pp. 63-72.

137 Ibid., p. 66n.

138 See A.L. Morton, 'Poetry and Property in a Communist Society' in *History and the Imagination: Selected Writings of A.L. Morton*, edited by Margot Heinemann and Raphael Samuel (London: Lawrence and Wishart, 1990) pp. 197-202.

139 Ibid., pp. 202-203.

140 Ibid., pp. 203-204.

141 Ibid., p. 204.

142 F.R. Leavis, ' "Under Which King, Bezonian?" ', *Scrutiny*, Vol. 1 No. 3, December 1932, p. 206.

143 Ibid., p. 207.

144 Ibid., p. 208.

145 Ibid., p. 209.

146 Ibid., pp. 210-212.

147 Ibid., p. 212.

148 A.L. Morton, 'Culture and Leisure', *Scrutiny*, Vol. 1 No. 4, March 1933, p. 324.

149 Ibid., p. 325.

150 See Leon Trotsky, *Literature and Revolution* (London: RedWords, 1991), Chapter Six. Francis Mulhern makes a similar point about Morton's attitude to Trotsky in *The Moment of Scrutiny*. See Mulhern, op cit., p. 67n.

151 Morton, 'Culture and Leisure', p. 326.

152 Ibid., pp. 325-326.

153 Raphael Samuel has drawn attention to the influence of Morris on Morton in his essay "A Rebel and His Lineage" in A.L. Morton, *History and the Imagination*, p. 21.

154 Morton, 'Culture and Leisure', p. 324.

155 Ibid., p. 324.

156 Ibid., p. 324.

157 Andy Croft, 'Authors Take Sides', p. 94.

158 Morton, 'Culture and Leisure', p. 326.

159 Mulhern, op cit., p. 67.

160 Morton, 'Culture and Leisure', p. 326. Cf. Mulhern, *The Moment of Scrutiny*, p. 67.

161 Morton, 'Culture and Leisure', p. 326. Quoted in Wright, op cit., p. 55.

162 Morton, 'Culture and Leisure', p. 326.

163 Mulhern, *The Moment of "Scrutiny"*, p. 67.

164 In an attack on an un-named writer who had 'been moulded in the Eliot-Wyndham Lewis complex of ideas' (Edgell Rickword?), the Russian critic D.S. Mirsky argued that a number of literary classicists had been attracted to Marxism because its integrated vision of society corresponded to their desire for order, but that they had largely proved indifferent to Marxism's political objectives. See Dmitri Mirsky, *The Intelligentsia of Great Britain*, pp. 213-214.

165 It is not entirely clear whether Brown can strictly be described as a cultural conservative, though it seems clear from his writings on T.S. Eliot (which I examine here) that he was deeply knowledgeable about Eliot's version of classicism.

166 Croft, 'Authors Take Sides', p. 94.

167 The fullest account of *The Calendar of Modern Letters* can be found in Charles Hobday, *Edgell Rickword: A Poet at War* (Manchester: Carcanet, 1989), Chapter Six. See also Peter Morgan, 'Calendar of Modern Letters, The' in Sullivan (ed.), *British Literary Magazines*; John Gross, op cit., p. 271f.

168 Quoted in John Gross, op cit., p. 271.

169 See Hobday, op cit., p. 92f.

170 The phrases are Garman's, quoted in ibid., pp. 92-93.

171 Alec Brown, 'The Lyric Impulse in the Poetry of T.S. Eliot' in Edgell Rickword (ed), *Scrutinies*, Volume 2, p. 2f.

172 Ibid., p. 21f.

173 Quoted in ibid., p. 30.

174 For a brief survey of Richards's theory of poetry, see René Wellek, *A History of Modern Criticism 1750-1950, Volume Five: English Criticism 1900-1950* (London: Jonathan Cape, 1986), Chapter Seven.

175 Brown, 'The Lyric Impulse in the Poetry of T. S. Eliot', p. 22.

176 Ibid., pp. 22-23.

177 Ibid., p. 25f.

178 Ibid., pp. 25-31. The lines after the colon are from T.S. Eliot, 'Preludes' in *Collected Poems 1909-1962*, p. 23. Quoted in Brown, p. 1.

179 Brown 'The Lyric Impulse in the Poetry of T. S. Eliot', p. 37.

180 Quoted in Frank Kermode, 'Educating the Planet' in *London Review of Books: Anthology One*, introduced by Karl Miller (London: Junction Books, 1981) p. 205.

181 For a useful recent survey of Lewis's ideas (to which my own account is indebted), see John Carey, *The Intellectuals and the Masses: Pride and Prejudice among the Literary Intelligentsia, 1880-1939* (London: Faber and Faber, 1992) Chapter Nine.

182 Ibid., p. 185. The words 'softness' and 'flabbiness' are both quoted by Carey.

183 Ibid., p. 186.

184 Ibid., p. 187.

185 Ibid., p. 187.

186 Edgell Rickword, 'Wyndham Lewis' in Rickword (ed.), *Scrutinies*, Volume 2, p. 151f.

187 Ibid., p. 142.

188 Ibid., pp. 152-153.

189 Ibid., p. 151.

190 Ibid., 156f.

191 Edgell Rickword, untitled review of *Selected Essays* by T.S. Eliot, *Scrutiny*, Vol. 1 No. 4, March 1933, p. 393.

192 Douglas Garman, 'A Professional Enemy', *Scrutiny*, Vol. 1 No. 3, December 1932, p. 280.

193 Ibid., p. 280.

194 Douglas Garman, 'What?..The Devil?', *Left Review*, Vol. 1 No. 1, October 1934, pp. 35-36.

195 Douglas Garman, 'Art and the Negative Impulses', *Scrutiny*, Vol. 2 No. 2, September 1933, p. 193.

196 Ibid., p. 190.

197 Ibid., p. 191.

198 Apart from the essays on Lewis and Celine, Garman also contributed two other pieces to *Scrutiny* in the early 1930s. There was an untitled review of *The Orators* by W.H. Auden (Vol. 1 No. 2, September 1932, pp. 183-184) and a review of Oliver Elton's *The English Muse* entitled 'Sixteen Bobs'-Worth of Culture' (Vol. 2 No. 1, June 1933, pp. 86-87).

Chapter 2

1   For an overview of Soviet cultural criticism between 1917 and 1934, see, *inter alia*, Dave Laing, *The Marxist Theory of Art:An Introductory Survey* (Brighton: Harvester, 1978), Chapter Two. There is now a very large body of work on the development of Soviet culture between the October Revolution and the death of Stalin. Among the most useful sources are the following: Régine Robin, *Socialist Realism: An Impossible Aesthetic* (Stanford: Stanford University Press, 1992); C. Vaughan James, *Soviet Socialist Realism: Origins and Theory* (London: Macmillan, 1973); Boris Groys, *The Total Art of Stalinism: Avant-Garde, Aesthetic Dictatorship, and Beyond* (New Jersey: Princeton University Press, 1992); Matthew Cullerne Bown, *Art Under Stalin* (Oxford: Phaidon, 1991); Thomas Lahusen and Evgeny Dobrenko (eds.), *Socialist Realism Without Shores* (London: Yale University Press, 1997); Brandon Taylor and Matthew Cullerne Bown (eds.). *Art of the Soviets: Painting, Sculpture and Architecture in a One-Party State, 1917-1922* (Manchester: Manchester University Press, 1993); Jurgen Rühle, *Literature and Revolution: A Critical Study of the Writer and Communism in the Twentieth Century* (London: Pall Mall Press, 1969); Igor Golomstock, *Totalitarian Art in the Soviet Union, the Third Reich, Fascist Italy and the People's Republic of China* (London: Harper Collins, 1990).

2   The most important critical statement made by the Futurists was Vladimir Mayakovsky, *How Are Verses Made?* (London: Cape Editions, 1970). Most of the relevant Constructivist documents are contained in Stephen Bann (ed.), *The Tradition of Constructivism* (New York: Da Capo, 1974). A sample of documents produced by the leading exponents of montage cinema (Kuleshov, Pudovkin, Eisenstein, Vertov etc) is contained in Richard Taylor and Ian Christie (eds.), *The Film Factory: Russian and Soviet Documents 1896-1939* (London: Routledge, 1988).

3   See AKhRR, 'Declaration' and 'The Immediate Tasks of AkhRR' in Charles Harrison and Paul Wood (eds.), *Art in Theory 1900-1990: An Anthology of Changing Ideas* (Oxford: Blackwell, 1993).

4   Leon Trotsky, *Literature and Revolution* (London: RedWords, 1991). One of the most useful introductions to Trotsky's cultural writings is Alan Wald, 'Leon Trotsky's Contributions to Marxist Cultural Theory and Literary Criticism' in *Writing from the Left: New Essays on Radical Culture and Politics* (London: Verso, 1994).

5   Robert Hughes, *The Shock Of The New: Art And The Century Of Change* (London: Thames and Hudson, 1991) p. 87.

6   Ibid., p. 87.

7   Quoted in Dave Laing, op cit., *p.* 34.

8   See Boris Groys, op cit., p. 34f.

9   The details in this paragraph are largely derived from Robin, *op cit.*, p. 9 and Golomstock, *op cit.*, p. 86f.

10   The title of this book was later changed to *Soviet Writers' Congress 1934: The Debate on Socialist Realism and Modernism in the Soviet Union*. Its last printing was in

1977.

11   See Cullerne Bown, *Art Under Stalin*, p. 89. Cullerne Bown points out that the name might simply have been endorsed rather than coined by Stalin.

12   A.A. Zhdanov, 'Soviet Literature – The Richest In Ideas. The Most Advanced Literature' in Maxim Gorky, Karl Radek, Nikolai Bukharin, Andrei Zhdanov and others, *Soviet Writers' Congress 1934: The Debate on Socialist Realism and Modernism in the Soviet Union* (London: Lawrence and Wishart, 1977) p. 21.

13   Cf. Cullerne Bown, *Art Under Stalin*, p. 90.

14   For overviews of the related terms *ideinost, klassovost, narodnost* and *partiinost*, see, *inter alia*, C. Vaughan James, op cit., Chapter Four; Cullerne Bown, op cit., p. 91; Toby Clark, *Art and Propaganda in the Twentieth Century: The Political Image in the Age of Mass Culture* (London: Weidenfeld and Nicolson, 1997) p. 87. The terms did not appear in the English translation of the Congress proceedings, but since the concepts to which they referred were invoked throughout the Congress (and since they have been prominent in most British writing on Soviet cultural theory) I have chosen to employ them here.

15   Nikolai Bukharin, 'Poetry, Poetics And The Problems Of Poetry In The USSR' in ibid., pp. 211-223.

16   Ibid., p. 243f.

17   Maxim Gorky, 'Soviet Literature' in ibid., pp. 54-60.

18   Bukharin, op cit., pp. 253-256.

19   Bukharin, op cit., pp. 254-255; Zhdanov, op cit., p. 20.

20   Karl Marx and Friedrich Engels, *The German Ideology: Part One*, edited by C.J. Arthur (London: Lawrence and Wishart, 1982).

21   See, *inter alia*, Dave Laing's discussion of Socialist Realism in Chapter Two of *The Marxist Theory of Art*.

22   Zhdanov, op cit., p. 22.

23   See Laing, op cit., p. 41.

24   Gorky, op cit., pp. 66-68.

25   Ibid., p. 69.

26   Zhdanov, op cit., p. 18.

27   Gorky, op cit., p. 67.

28   There were many occasions when the Soviet theorists tried to legitimise the principle of *partiinost* with an appeal to authority. Their specific claim was that Lenin himself had endorsed the move towards state control of the arts in his article 'Party Organisation and Party Literature' (1905). Written in response to the limited measures of liberalisation that occurred in Russia after the abortive revolution of 1905, Lenin's article was a continuation of the work on democratic centralism which he had begun three years earlier in *What is to be Done?* Its chief concern was to identify the principles on which the revolutionary press should be based in the new conditions of 'semi-legality'. In the first place, or so Lenin argued, the Russian Social-Democratic Labour Party (RSDLP) should ensure that it retained control of the whole process of producing and distributing Party literature, from the initial stage of commissioning work to the final stage of selling it. The Party press should be run on strictly non-commercial lines. And, most importantly of all, the RSDLP should impose an absolute obligation on its writers to reflect its

programme, resolutions, stategy and tactics in all the work they produced for its official publications. Lenin was impatient with the idea that he was advocating a form of censorship. If writers wished to express ideas that were inconsistent with the Party line, they were perfectly free to do so in non-Party publications: '.....we are discussing party literature and its subordination to party control. Everyone is free to write and say whatever he likes, without any restrictions.' He also mocked the ideal of 'absolute freedom' to which many Russian intellectuals seemed to aspire at the time, pointing out that no such freedom was possible in a society whose means of communication were monopolised by the bourgeoisie: 'Are you free in relation to your bourgeois publisher, Mr Writer, in relation to your bourgeois public, which demands that you provide it with pornography in frames and paintings, and prostitution as a supplement to "sacred" scenic art?' Many writers have claimed that Lenin's arguments were only applicable to a revolutionary writer who is operating in a bourgeois-democratic society, and that the Soviet theorists were therefore unjustified in using them to legitimise Soviet arts policy. See V.I. Lenin, 'Party Organisation and Party Literature' in *Selected Works* (Moscow: Progress Publishers, 1977). For a useful discussion of Lenin's article, see Laing, *The Marxist Theory of Art*, p. 22f.

29 Bukharin, op cit., pp. 187-199. For another account of Bukharin's theory of poetry, see, *inter alia*, Laing, *The Marxist Theory of Art*, p. 37f.

30 See Edward Said, *The World, the Text, and the Critic* (London: Vintage, 1991).

31 Bukharin, op cit., p. 192.

32 Ibid., pp. 191-192.

33 Ibid., p. 197.

34 See Kai Hammermeister, *The German Aesthetic Tradition* (Cambridge: Cambridge University Press, 2002) p. 29.

35 Quoted in Bukharin, op cit., p. 197.

36 For Bukharin's discussion of the idea of disinterestedness, see Bukharin, *op cit.*, p. 196f. My comments on Kant, Hegel and Schopenhauer are slightly more extensive than those of Bukharin, who largely contented himself with abuse: 'All this is utter nonsense.'

37 Bukharin, op cit, p. 197.

38 Ibid., p. 197.

39 For another account of Bukharin's remarks about the relationship between form and content, see Laing, *The Marxist Theory of Art*, p. 41f.

40 Ralph Fox, *The Novel and the People* (London: Cobbett Press, 1948) p. 40. Quoted in Terry Eagleton, *Marxism and Literary Criticism* (London: Methuen, 1983) p. 23.

41 Bukharin, op cit, pp. 199-210.

42 See, *inter alia*, Viktor Shklovsky, 'Art as Technique' in David Lodge (ed.), *Modern Criticism and Theory: A Reader* (London: Longman, 1991). Among the most useful introductions to Russian Formalism are Ann Jefferson, 'Russian Formalism' in Ann Jefferson and David Robey (eds.), *Modern Literary Theory: A Comparative Introduction* (London: BT Batsford, 1991); Raman Selden and Peter Widdowson, *A Reader's Guide to Contemporary Literary Theory*, Chapter Two.

43 See Ann Jefferson, op cit., pp. 25-30 and pp. 37-39.

44   Ibid., p. 39.

45   Ibid., p. 39.

46   Ibid., p. 39f.

47   See Leon Trotsky, 'The Formal Method in Literary Scholarship' in *Literature and Revolution.*

48   Bukharin, op cit., p. 205.

49   Ibid., p. 206.

50   Ibid., p. 204.

51   Ibid., pp. 205. Bukharin did not directly link the 'irrationality' of avant-garde poetry with fascism, but the political context in which he was working strongly suggests that it was fascism he had in mind.

52   Gorky, op cit., pp. 45-47.

53   Karl Radek, 'Contemporary World Literature And The Tasks Of Proletarian Art' in Gorky, Radek, Bukharin et al, pp. 79-82.

54   Soviet articles on literature were available in English from 1931 onwards in the monthly journal *International Literature*, published in Moscow. However, it is not clear whether this publication exercised much of an influence on the English communist critics – one gets the impression that it did not.

55   See Karl Marx and Frederick Engels, *Marx and Engels on Literature and Art*, edited by Lee Baxandall and Stefan Morawski (St Louis/Milwaukee: Telos Press, 1973); G.V. Plekhanov, *Art and Social Life* (London: Lawrence and Wishart, 1953); V.I. Lenin, 'Articles on Tolstoy' in David Craig (ed.), *Marxists on Literature: An Anthology* (Harmondsworth: Pelican Books, 1977).

56   For another account of Gorky's remarks about myth, see Laing, *The Marxist Theory of Art*, p. 41f.

57   Gorky, op cit., p. 27.

58   Ibid., p. 28.

59   Ibid., p. 29.

60   Ibid., pp. 28-31.

61   The *Economic and Philosophical Manuscripts* were first published by the Marx-Engels Institute in Moscow in 1932 but would not exert a major influence on Marxist intellectuals for many years.

62   Quoted in Bukharin, op cit., p. 246.

63   The Soviet theorists tended to present these classical Marxist ideas in shorthand rather than examine them in detail. See, for instance, Bukharin, op cit., p. 246.

64   Gorky, op cit., pp. 33-36.

65   Ibid., pp. 36-40.

66   Ibid., p. 37.

67   Gorky, who addressed this theme in detail (see pp. 40-48) did not make explicit reference to the art-for-art's sake movement. It is only his list of names (e.g. Wilde, Huysmans, Des Esseintes) and quotations ('There is no morality, there is only beauty', p. 45) which makes it clear what he had in mind. It should nevertheless be noted that he also referred to a number of writers (e.g. Céline) who would not normally be regarded as aesthetes.

68   Gorky, op cit., p. 44f.

69   Ibid., p. 46.

70   Ibid., p. 45.

71   Ibid., pp. 46-48.

72   Radek, op cit., pp. 74-78.

73   Ibid., pp. 76-78.

74   Ibid., pp. 79-82.

75   Ibid., pp. 86-94. Radek also recognised that a number of writers in the bourgeois democracies were in the process of going over to fascism, citing T.S. Eliot as an example of a British writer who had 'begun to speak in fascist tones'.

76   Ibid., p. 108f.

77   Ibid., p. 153. Radek also devoted a couple of paragraphs to the work of Marcel Proust, which he condemned for its preoccupation with the minutiae of French upper-class life.

78   Ibid., p. 153.

79   Ibid., p. 179.

80   Ibid., p. 154.

81   Ibid., p. 158.

82   Amabel Williams-Ellis, 'Soviet Writers' Congress', *Left Review*, Vol. 1 No. 2, November 1934, pp. 17-28.

83   Ibid., pp. 17-18.

84   Ibid., p. 28.

85   Valentine Cunningham, *British Writers of the Thirties* (Oxford: Oxford University Press, 1990), p. 300.

86   Williams-Ellis, 'Soviet Writers' Congress', p. 23.

87   Ibid., pp. 21-24.

88   Montagu Slater, 'The Turning Point', *Left Review*, Vol. 2 No. 1, October 1935, pp. 15-23. For a less important British account of the Writers' Congress (in the form of a brief review of *Problems of Soviet Literature*), see Charles Madge, 'Writers Under Two Flags', *Left Review*, Vol. 2 No. 5, February 1936, pp. 228-230.

89   Slater, 'The Turning Point', p. 17.

90   Ibid., p. 22.

91   Robert Graves, 'A Letter from Robert Graves', *Left Review*, Vol. 2 No. 3, December 1935, p. 129.

Chapter 3

1   The fullest discussion of West's work can be found in Chapter Six of Anand Prakash, *Marxism and Literary Theory* (Delhi: Academic Foundation, 1994). There is an annotated bibliography of West's work in Victor N. Paananen (ed.), *British Marxist Criticism* (New York: Garland Publishing, 2000). For an unannotated bibliography, with brief introductory remarks, see Alan Munton and Alan Young (compilers), *Seven Writers of the English Left: A Bibliography of Literature and Politics, 1916-1980* (New York: Garland Publishing, 1981). West's work of the 1930s is briefly surveyed in David Margolies, '*Left Review* and Left Literary Culture' in Jon Clark, Margot Heinemann, David Margolies and Carole Snee (eds.), *Culture and Crisis in Britain in the Thirties* (London: Lawrence and Wishart, 1979) and Hanna Behrend, 'An Intellectual Irrelevance? Marxist Literary Criticism

in the 1930s' in Andy Croft (ed.), *A Weapon in the Struggle: The Cultural History of the Communist Party in Britain* (London: Pluto Press, 1998). The posthumous edition of *Crisis and Criticism* which Lawrence and Wishart brought out in 1974 contains a Foreword by Arnold Kettle and an Introduction by Elisabeth West. For an interesting comparison of West and Caudwell, see Christopher Pawling, 'Revisiting the Thirties in the Twenty-First Century: The Radical Aesthetics of West, Caudwell, and Eagleton' in Antony Shuttleworth (ed.), *And in Our Time: Vision, Revision, and British Writing of the 1930s* (Lewisburg: Bucknell University Press, 2003). Also worth consulting are the brief remarks on West in Maynard Solomon (ed.), *Marxism and Art: Essays Classic and Contemporary* (Brighton: Harvester Press, 1979) pp. 492-496; Terry Eagleton, *Marxism and Literary Criticism* (London: Methuen, 1983) p. 56; Terry Eagleton and Drew Milne (eds.), *Marxist Literary Theory: A Reader* (Oxford: Blackwell, 1996) p. 103 and Patrick Deane (ed.), *History in Our Hands: A Critical Anthology of Writings on Literature, Culture and Politics from the 1930s* (London: Leicester University Press) pp. 131-132. This book was completed before the publication of T.G. Ashplant's *Fractured Loyalties: Masculinity, Class and Politics in Britain, 1900-30* (London: Rivers Oram, 2008), which analyses the development of West and other intellectuals of his generation from a psychoanalytical perspective.

2   Alick West, *One Man in his Time: An Autobiography* (London: George Allen and Unwin, 1969).

3   See also Maynard Solomon's slightly different account of the purpose of West's work: 'West proposes that radical movements must come to terms with the complex psychological motivations of their members. He holds out the hope and the possibility that the recognition of such motivations by revolutionary parties, the making conscious of what had been repressed and censored, would prevent the eruption of those irrationalities and disillusionments which periodically decimate the revolution from within its own ranks.' Solomon, op cit., p. 493.

4   West, *One Man in his Time*, p. 192.

5   West's working title for *One Man in his Time* was 'Becoming a Communist'. This accounts for the title of this section. See *One Man in his Time*, p. 192.

6   For brief biographical remarks about West, see, *inter alia*, Solomon, op cit., p. 493f; Munton and Young, op cit., pp. 7-9; Paananen, op cit., p. 9f/pp. 29-30.

7   West, *One Man in his Time*, p. 7.

8   Ibid., pp. 9-19. I have not focused on West's religious background because it seems to me that it features less centrally in *One Man in his Time* than some other writers have assumed. For the alternative view, see, *inter alia*, Elisabeth West, op cit., p. 5; Maynard Solomon, op cit., p. 495.

9   West, *One Man in his Time*, p. 12-13.

10   Ibid., p. 12.

11   Ibid., pp. 24-25.

12   Ibid., pp. 30-31.

13   Ibid., p. 32.

14   Ibid., p. 41.

15   One of West's most obvious reasons for coming to distrust the British establishment was that his brother Arthur had been killed during the War. Arthur West's private

papers were published by Allen and Unwin in 1920. See Arthur Graeme West, *The Diary of a Dead Officer* (London: Allen and Unwin, 1920).

16 West, *One Man in his Time.*, pp. 55-74.

17 Ibid., p. 58.

18 Ibid., pp. 58-59.

19 Ibid., pp. 75-100.

20 For a brief account of Mosley's interpretation of Spengler, see Nicholas Mosley, *Rules of the Game/Beyond the Pale: Memoirs of Sir Oswald Mosley and Family* (London: Pimlico, 1988) pp. 299-305.

21 West, *One Man in his Time*, p. 82.

22 Ibid., pp. 84-85.

23 Ibid., p. 83.

24 Ibid., p. 83.

25 Ibid., p. 83.

26 Ibid., p. 83.

27 Ibid., pp. 87-99.

28 Ibid., p. 93.

29 Ibid., pp. 100-165.

30 Ibid., pp. 147-151.

31 Ibid., p. 30.

32 Ibid., pp. 60-66.

33 See, for instance, his evocation of the onset of economic crisis and the emergence of English fascism in the early 1930s. *One Man in his Time*, p. 138f.

34 Ibid., p. 97.

35 Ibid., pp. 118-119.

36 Ibid., pp. 122-123.

37 Ibid., pp. 124-126.

38 Ibid., p. 157.

39 As is well known, the Bulgarian Communist Georgi Dimitrov, later the head of the Communist International, was charged with burning down the Reichstag and famously acquitted by a Nazi court.

40 West, *One Man in his Time*, p. 101.

41 Quoted in John Callaghan, *Rajani Palme Dutt: A Study in British Stalinism* (London: Lawrence and Wishart, 1993) p. 33.

42 West, *One Man in his Time*, pp. 166-180.

43 See Paananen, op cit., p. 10; *West, One Man in his Time*, pp. 162-163.

44 West, *One Man in his Time*, p. 163.

45 Alick West, *Crisis and Criticism and Literary Essays* (London: Lawrence and Wishart, 1975) pp. 17-19.

46 Ibid., p. 19.

47 Maurice Cornforth criticised Caudwell on precisely these grounds in Maurice Cornforth, 'Caudwell and Marxism', *The Modern Quarterly* (New Series), Vol. 6 No. 1, Winter 1950-51, pp. 16-33.

48 Caudwell outlined his theory of cultural crisis in the Introduction to *Studies in a Dying Culture* (London: John Lane The Bodley Head, 1938).

49 West, *Crisis and Criticism and Literary Essays*, p. 19.

50 See, in particular, T.S. Eliot, 'Tradition and the Individual Talent' in *Selected Prose of T.S. Eliot*, edited by Frank Kermode (London: Faber and Faber, 1985).

51 Although the link between the October Revolution and the shift away from literary individualism was only hinted at in *Crisis and Criticism*, West made the point more explicitly in some of his later writings. See especially Alick West, 'The Abuse of Poetry and the Abuse of Criticism by T.S. Eliot', *The Marxist Quarterly*, Vol. 1 No. 1, January 1954, pp. 22-32.

52 See Douglas Garman, 'What?...The Devil?', *Left Review*, Vol. 1 No. 1, October 1934, pp. 34-36.

53 West, *Crisis and Criticism and Literary Essays*, pp. 43-44.

54 Quoted in ibid., p. 38.

55 Quoted in ibid., p. 38.

56 Ibid., pp. 38-42.

57 Quoted in ibid., p. 40.

58 Ibid., pp. 42-43.

59 Bloom argues that modern poets have been obliged to 'strategically misread' the work of their predecessors in order to acquire enough confidence to write. His most famous formulation of this theory can be found in *The Anxiety of Influence: A Theory of Poetry* (New York: Oxford University Press, 1973). For an introduction to Bloom's work, see Imre Salusinszky, *Criticism in Society* (London: Methuen, 1987) Chapter Three.

60 West, *Crisis and Criticism and Literary Essays*, pp. 42-43.

61 Ibid., p. 43.

62 Ibid., pp. 47-53.

63 Orwell wrote about Richards's experiments in practical criticism in his 'As I Please' column in *Tribune* on 5 May 1944. The column was reprinted in *The Collected Essays, Journalism and Letters of George Orwell, Volume Three: As I Please*, edited by Sonia Orwell and Ian Angus (Harmondsworth: Penguin Books, 1978).

64 West, *Crisis and Criticism and Literary Essays*, pp. 54-65.

65 Ibid., pp. 50-53.

66 Maurice Cowling, 'Raymond Williams in Retrospect' in Hilton Kramer and Roger Kimball (eds.), *Against the Grain: The New Criterion on Art and Intellect at the End of the Twentieth Century* (Chicago: Ivan R Dee, 1995) p. 231.

67 West, *One Man in his Time*, p. 171.

68 Ibid., p. 172.

69 John Carey, *The Intellectuals and the Masses: Pride and Prejudice among the Literary Intelligentsia, 1880-1939* (London: Faber and Faber, 1992) pp. 3-45.

70 Christopher Pawling, *Christopher Caudwell: Towards a Dialectical Theory of Literature* (New York: St Martin's Press, 1989) p. 28.

71 For brief introductions to Richards's work, see, *inter alia*, René Wellek, *A History of Modern Criticism 1750-1950, Volume Five: English Criticism 1900-1950* (London: Jonathan Cape, 1986) Chapter Seven; Frank Kermode, 'Educating the Planet', *London Review of Books: Anthology One*, introduced by Karl Miller (London: Junction Books, 1981).

72 West, *Crisis and Criticism and Literary Essays*, p. 75.

73 Ibid., p. 75. West wrote that 'those feelings of social solidarity which are awakened

in aesthetic experience are still attached to bourgeois society.' I interpret this as a coded reference to fascism, hence my reference to the way in which 'reactionary movements' make use of 'spectacles of intense grandeur'. For another account of West's objections to the inadequacy of communist writing on aesthetics, see Solomon, op cit., pp. 495-496.

74 See Walter Benjamin, 'The Work of Art in the Age of Mechanical Reproduction' in *Illuminations* (London: Jonathan Cape, 1970).

75 Maxim Gorky, 'Soviet Literature' in Maxim Gorky, A.A. Zhdanov et al., *Soviet Writers' Congress 1934: The Debate on Socialist Realism and Modernism in the Soviet Union* (London: Lawrence and Wishart, 1977) pp. 27-32.

76 G.V. Plekhanov, 'Unaddressed Letters' in *Art and Social Life* (London: Lawrence and Wishart, 1953). For a useful introduction to the anthropological element in Plekhanov's thinking, see David N. Margolies, *The Function of Literature: A Study of Christopher Caudwell's Aesthetics* (London: Lawrence and Wishart, 1969).

77 See Margolies, *The Function of Literature*, pp. 28-29.

78 For the anthropological element in Caudwell's work, see, *inter alia*, Francis Mulhern, 'The Marxist Aesthetics of Christopher Caudwell', *New Left Review*, No. 85, May/June 1974, p. 44f. Raymond Williams briefly mentioned the sources for the anthropological element in Caudwell's and West's work in *Culture and Society 1780-1950* (Harmondsworth: Pelican Books, 1979) p. 267.

79 Quoted in West, *Crisis and Criticism and Literary Essays*, p. 76.

80 Victor Paananen draws a similar parallel between West and Williams in Paananen, op cit., p. 11.

81 West, *Crisis and Criticism and Literary Essays*, p. 77.

82 Ibid., pp. 77-78.

83 Ibid., p. 78.

84 Ibid., p. 78.

85 Ibid., p. 76.

86 Ibid., p. 76.

87 Ibid., p. 79.

88 Ibid., p. 79.

89 Cf. Hanna Behrend: 'Like Fox...West did not believe that a work of imaginative literature simply reflected history in the manner in which history actually takes place; in his best criticism he was aware that poetry, fiction and drama present the dynamics of contemporary human development in a polyphonic, contradictory and fragmentary manner...' Behrend, op cit., p. 113. Maynard Solomon makes some similar remarks in Solomon, op cit., pp. 495-496.

90 West, *Crisis and Criticism and Literary Essays*, pp. 85-87.

91 Ibid., p. 86.

92 Ibid., p. 87.

93 Ibid., pp. 87-88.

94 Victor Paananen also makes reference to the relevance of Marx's observation to West's work in Paananen, op cit., p. 11.

95 West, *Crisis and Criticism and Literary Essays*, p. 88.

96 Ibid., pp. 88-89.

97 Ibid., p. 89.

98 Ibid., p. 88.

99 Ibid ., p. 89.

100 For an introduction to Empson's theory of poetic ambiguity, see René Wellek, *History of Modern Criticism 1750-1950, Volume Five*, Chapter Ten.

101 West, *Crisis and Criticism and Literary Essays*, pp. 95-96.

102 Ibid., p. 95.

103 Ibid., pp. 96-97.

104 Ibid., p. 99.

105 Cf. Hanna Behrend, who also situates West in the tradition of Marxist writers who have expresssed scepticism towards the idea of tendentiousness in literature. (Her specific example is 'Marx and Engels's preference for Balzac over Zola'.) Behrend, op cit., p. 113.

106 See, for instance, Phil Watson, 'Whose Legacy?', *Weekly Worker*, No. 336, May 18 2000, p. 7.

107 West, *Crisis and Criticism and Literary Essays*, p. 98.

108 Ibid., p. 97.

109 Ibid., p. 97.

110 Ibid., p. 92.

111 Robert Sullivan, *Christopher Caudwell* (London, Croom Helm: 1987) pp. 87-88.

112 René Wellek, *A History of Modern Criticism 1750-1950, Volume Five*, p. 142.

113 'Linguistic theory is at once very specialized and very controversial, and the question of origins is necessarily to some extent speculative.' Raymond Williams, *Culture and Society 1780-1950*, p. 267.

114 To be fair to West, he briefly signalled his awareness of alternative explanations for the emergence of language on page 78 of *Crisis and Criticism and Literary Essays*.

115 The phrase 'deep structures' is of course one of the key terms in the work of Noam Chomsky.

116 As David Craig has pointed out, commenting on the work of the English classicist George Thomson (often regarded as a disciple of Caudwell's), 'Thomson's theory… that music originated in labour chants has probably to be replaced or very much changed to take account of the theory developed by the German musicologist Hornbostel that the first music was totemistic imitation of animal sounds through wooden masks so made that they altered the human voice as much as possible.' See David Craig, *Marxists on Literature: An Anthology* (Harmondsworth: Pelican Books, 1977). Although Hornbostel's remarks apply primarily to music, they can clearly also be adapted to account for the emergence of language.

117 W.H. Auden, "Writing" in *The English Auden: Poems, Essays, and Dramatic Writings, 1927-1939*, edited by Edward Mendelson (London: Faber and Faber, 1977). Patrick Deane briefly refers to the parallels between West's work and 'Writing' in a footnote in Deane (ed.), op cit., p. 147.

118 See, for instance, Samuel Hynes, *The Auden Generation: Literature and Politics in England in the 1930s* (London: Bodley Head, 1976).

119 Auden, 'Writing', p. 303.

120 Auden did not state explicitly that language had its origins in economic activity, but he strongly implied it when he wrote that oral communication was originally '…a help to doing something with others of his own kind (pulling the boat in).'

121 Auden, 'Writing', p. 303.

122 Ibid., p. 303.

123 There is a useful selection of Bloch's writings in Ernst Bloch, *The Utopian Function of Art and Literature: Selected Essays*, translated by Jack Zipes and Frank Mecklenburg (Massachusetts: MIT Press, 1993). For introductions to Bloch's work, see, *inter alia*, Ruth Levitas, 'Utopian Hope: Ernst Bloch and Reclaiming the Future' in *The Concept of Utopia* (New York: Syracuse University Press, 1990); Jack Zipes, 'Towards a Realization of Anticipatory Illumination' in Bloch, *op cit.*; Vincent Geoghegan, *Ernst Bloch* (Routledge, London, 1996).

124 For an introduction to Marcuse's work, see Vincent Geoghegan, *Reason and Eros: The Social Theory of Herbert Marcuse* (London: Pluto Press, 1981).

125 Quoted in George Steiner, *Real Presences: Is There Anything in What We Say?* (London: Faber and Faber, 1990), p. 228.

126 See, *inter alia*, Raymond Williams, *Culture and Society 1780-1950*, p. 268; Hanna Behrend, op cit., pp. 111-112; David Margolies, '*Left Review* and Left Literary Theory', pp. 75-76. It has sometimes been pointed out that West's position was not so dissimilar from that of Edward Upward, who argued in his essay 'A Marxist Interpretation of Literature' (1937) that only a Marxist could realistically aspire to write a good book in the modern age.

127 For a brief acount of Heslop's life and work, see H. Gustav Klaus, 'Harold Heslop: Miner Novelist' in *The Literature of Labour: 200 Years of Working Class Writing* (Brighton: Harvester, 1985).

128 West, *Crisis and Criticism and Literary Essays*, pp. 104-127.

129 Stanley Edgar Hyman, *The Armed Vision: A Study in the Methods of Modern Literary Criticism* (New York: Alfred A Knopf, 1952) p. 193.

130 For the chapter on Heslop, see Alick West, *Crisis and Criticism* (London: Lawrence and Wishart, 1937).

131 For an attempt by a British writer to relate Soviet orthodoxy to nineteenth-century Russian criticism, see F.D. Klingender, *Marxism and Modern Art: An Approach to Social Realism* (London: Lawrence and Wishart, 1943) p. 17f.

132 West, *Crisis and Criticism and Literary Essays*, pp. 20-21.

133 Ibid., pp. 20-22.

134 Ibid., pp. 23f.

135 Ibid., pp. 23-24.

136 Quoted in ibid., p. 24.

137 Ibid., p. 24.

138 Ibid., p. 24.

139 Ibid., p. 25.

140 Ibid., p. 25.

141 Ibid., pp. 28-29.

142 Quoted in ibid., p. 28.

143 Ibid., pp. 29-30.

144 Samuel Taylor Coleridge, *Biographia Literaria: or Biographical Sketches of My Literary Life and Opinions*, edited by George Watson (London: Dent, 1991) p. 167. Quoted in Harry Blamires, *A History of Literary Criticism* (London: Macmillan, 1991) p. 225.

145 West mentioned it briefly (see pages 26-27 of *Crisis and Criticism and Literary Essays*) but did not refer to Coleridge's comparison between imagination and divine creation.

146 See the bibliography of West's work in Munton and Young, *Seven Writers of the English Left*, pp. 9-14.

147 West, *One Man in his Time*, p. 173.

148 Eric Gill, 'Eric Gill on Art and Propaganda', *Left Review*, Vol. 1 No. 9, June 1935, pp. 341-342.

149 For the history of the AIA, see Lynda Morris and Robert Radford, *The Story of the Artists International Association 1933-1953* (Oxford: The Museum of Modern Art, 1983). See also Julian Symons, *The Thirties: A Dream Revolved*, revised edition (London: Faber and Faber, 1960) Chapter Nine.

150 Eric Gill, op. cit., p. 341.

151 Ibid., p. 341.

152 Ibid., p. 342.

153 Ibid., p. 342.

154 Alick West, 'A Reply to Eric Gill', *Left Review*, Vol. 1 No. 10, July 1935, pp. 410-411.

155 Ibid., p. 410.

156 Ibid., p. 410.

157 Alick West, 'Communism and Christianity', *Left Review*, Vol. 11 No. 4, January 1936, pp. 174-176. *Christianity and the Social Revolution* was edited by John Lewis, Karl Polanyi and Donald K.Kitchen and published by Gollancz in 1935.

158 See Francis Mulhern, *The Moment of 'Scrutiny'* (London: New Left Books, 1979) pp. 70-71.

159 L.C. Knights, *Drama and Society in the Age of Jonson* (London: Chatto, 1937).

160 Alick West, 'Ben Jonson was No Sentimentalist", *Left Review*, Vol. 3 No. 8, September 1937, pp. 468-475.

161 Ibid., p. 468.

162 Ibid., p. 475.

163 Ibid., p. 471f.

164 Ibid., p. 472.

165 Ibid., pp. 473-474.

166 L.C. Knights, 'Mr. Knights Replies to Alick West', *Left Review*, Vol. 3 No. 9, October 1937, pp. 566-567.

167 Ibid., p. 566.

168 Ibid., p. 567.

169 Alick West, 'Wild Goose Chase', *Left Review*, Vol. 3 No. 10, November 1937, pp. 630-631.

170 For another communist assessment of the Auden Group's use of form, see Edgell Rickword, 'Who Is This Noah?', *Left Review*, Vol. 2 No. 7, April 1936, pp. 339-340.

171 West, 'Wild Goose Chase', p. 630.

172 Ibid., p. 630.

173 Ibid., p. 630.

174 Ibid., p. 631.

175 For a brief account of surrealism in Britain, see Symons, *The Thirties: A Dream Revolved*, Chapter Nine.

176 See Alick West, 'Surréalisme in Literature', *Left Review*, Vol. 2 No. 10, July 1936, pp. v-viii; Anthony Blunt, 'Rationalist and Anti-rationalist Art', *Left Review*, Vol. 2 No. 10, July 1936, pp. iv-vi; Anthony Blunt, 'Superrealism in London' in Charles Moore and Christopher Hawtree (eds.), *1936 as Recorded by the Spectator* (London: Michael Joseph, 1986); Anthony Blunt, 'Art Under Capitalism and Socialism' in C. Day Lewis (ed.), *The Mind in Chains: Socialism and the Cultural Revolution* (London: Frederick Muller, 1937); A.L. Lloyd, 'Surrealism and Revolutions', *Left Review*, Vol. 2 No. 16, January 1937, pp. 895-898.

177 See, for instance, André Breton, 'from the *First Surrealist Manifesto*' in Charles Harrison and Paul Wood (eds.), *Art in Theory 1900-1990: An Anthology of Changing Ideas* (Oxford: Blackwell, 1993).

178 Ibid., p. 438.

179 West, 'Surréalisme in Literature', p. vi.

180 Ibid., p. vii.

181 Ibid., p. vii.

182 Ibid., p. viii.

183 See Robert Radford, 'To Disable the Enemy: the Graphic Art of the Three Jameses' in Croft (ed.), *A Weapon in the Struggle*.

184 For an example of this primitive form of Marxist mass-culture theory, see Arthur Calder Marshall, "The Film Industry" in C. Day Lewis (ed.), *The Mind in Chains*.

185 Alick West, 'The Detective Story', *Left Review*, Volume 3 No. 12, January 1938, pp. 707-710; 'The Detective Story – 11', *Left Review*, Vol. 3 No. 13, February 1938, pp. 795-798. For a useful overview of left-wing attitudes towards detective fiction in the Britain of the 1930s, see Chris Hopkins, 'Leftists and Thrillers: The Politics of a Thirties Sub-Genre' in Antony Shuttleworth (ed.), op cit.

186 Raymond Williams, *Culture and Society 1780-1950*, pp. 290-300.

187 Philip Henderson, *Literature and a Changing Civilisation* (London: John Lane The Bodley Head, 1935) p. 105.

188 West, 'The Detective Story' pp. 707-708.

189 Ibid., p. 708.

190 Ibid., pp. 708-709.

191 H.N. Brailsford, *Shelley, Godwin and Their Circle* (London: Oxford University Press, 1949) pp. 143-145.

192 West, 'The Detective Story', p. 710.

193 West, 'The Detective Story – 11', p. 795.

194 Ibid., p. 796.

195 Ibid., p. 796.

196 Ibid., p. 796.

197 Ibid., pp. 797-798.

198 West, *One Man in his Time*, p. 93.

199 Charles Madge, 'Press, Radio, and Social Consciousness' in Day Lewis (ed.), *The Mind in Chains*, p. 160.

200 Ibid., p. 160.

201 Ibid., p. 151.

202 Ibid., p. 150.

203 Ibid., p. 152.

204 For the development of Cultural Studies, see, *inter alia*, Graeme Turner, *British Cultural Sudies: An Introduction* (London: Unwin Hyman, 1990); Dennis Dworkin, *Cultural Marxism in Postwar Britain: History, the New Left, and the Origins of Cultural Studies* (London: Duke University Press, 1997).

205 Dworkin, op cit, p. 172.

206 For Hall, Hebdige and Fiske, see, *inter alia*, Stuart Hall, 'Encoding/Decoding' in Stuart Hall, Dorothy Hobson, Andrew Lowe and Paul Willis (eds.), *Culture, Media, Language* (London: Hutchinson, 1980); John Fiske, *Understanding Popular Culture* (London: Unwin Hyman, 1989); Dick Hebdige, *Subculture: The Meaning of Style* (London: Methuen, 1979).

207 See West, *One Man in his Time*, p. 176; Munton and Young (eds.), op cit., p. 8.

208 Harry Pollitt, *Looking Ahead* (London, The Communist Party, 1947) p. 13.

209 For a partisan account of the development of the CPGB's programme, see Max Adereth, *Line of March: An Historical and Critical Analysis of British Communism and its Revolutionary Strategy* (London: Praxis Press, 1994).

210 For West's approach to the BRS, see *One Man in his Time*, p. 189f. Two other members of the CPGB's cultural intelligentsia, Edward Upward and George Thomson, also opposed the new line and eventually left the Party. Thomson went on to become a leading Maoist. Upward, who died in 2009 aged 105, remained a Marxist until the end of his life and continued to write astonishingly powerful short fiction which combined hallucinatory dreamscapes with witty evocations of the revolutionary left. He provided a fictionalised account of his opposition to the new line in *The Rotten Elements* (London: Quartet, 1979).

211 For the paper which West delivered at the school, see 'The British Road to Socialism' in Jack Lindsay (ed.), *Essays on Socialist Realism and the British Cultural Tradition* (London: Fore Publications, n. d. [1953?]).

212 West, *One Man in his Time*, p. 190. This passage is also quoted in Elisabeth West, 'Introduction' in Alick West, *Crisis and Criticism and Literary Essays*, pp. 7-8; Andy Croft, 'Introduction' in Croft (ed.), *A Weapon in the Struggle*, p. 1; Phil Watson, 'Communist Culture', *Weekly Worker*, No. 305, September 23 1999, p. 3. Watson's article provides an interesting commentary on the idea that the CPGB's approach to culture and the arts was excessively instrumental.

213 Alick West, 'New People', *Communist Review*, November 1947, pp. 330-334.

214 Alick West, 'Marxism and Culture', *The Modern Quarterly* (New Series), Vol. 3 No. 2, Spring 1948, pp. 118-128.

215 For a brief account of the way that the Caudwell Discussion can be related to wider tensions between the CPGB's cultural bureaucrats (e.g. Emile Burns and Maurice Cornforth) and its cultural intelligentsia, see H. Gustav Klaus, 'Changing Attitudes to Caudwell: A Review of Critical Comments on the Author, 1937-87' in David Margolies and Linden Peach (eds.), *Christopher Caudwell: Marxism and Culture* (London: Goldsmiths' College, 1989) pp. 4-10. See also Andy Croft, 'Writers, the Communist Party and the Battle of Ideas, 1945-1950', *Socialist History*, Issue 5, Summer 1994, p. 22.

216 For accounts of the tense relationship between the NCC and the Party's cultural

workers in the early post-war period, see Andy Croft, 'Writers, the Communist Party and the Battle of Ideas, 1945-1950', pp. 2-25; Andy Croft, 'The Boys Round the Corner: the Story of Fore Publications' in Croft (ed.), *A Weapon in the Struggle*.

217 Maurice Cornforth, 'Caudwell and Marxism', *The Modern Quarterly* (New Series), Vol. 6 No. 1, Winter 1950-51, pp. 16-33.

218 Cornforth, 'Caudwell and Marxism', pp. 19-20.

219 Ibid., pp. 20-23.

220 Ibid., pp. 23-28.

221 Ibid., pp. 28-32.

222 Ibid., p. 18f.

223 Alick West, Contribution to 'The Caudwell Discussion', *The Modern Quarterly* (New Series), Vol. 6 No. 3, Summer 1951, p. 266.

224 Ibid., p. 267.

225 Cf. The brief remarks about West's conception of the communitarian nature of aesthetic experience in Solomon, op cit, pp. 493-496.

226 West's second book, *A Good Man Fallen Among Fabians: A Study of George Bernard Shaw*, was published by Lawrence and Wishart in 1950. Although its account of Shaw's work is too intricate to be summarised here, it can also be seen as an implicit expression of West's unhappiness with the state of the communist movement. For one thing, West argued that Shaw remained influenced by Marxism in spite of opting to join the Fabians – the implication was that it is perfectly possible to belong to a political organisation without subscribing to the official outlook. Moreover, West also focused on what he described as Shaw's 'idealist' interest in the Middle Ages, seeing it as an expression of a profound longing for the 'unity' of mankind. In *One Man in his Time*, West admitted that disillusionment with the communist movement had led him to adopt a similar attitude (that is, a quasi-religious yearning for the feelings of 'Godhead' which pervaded the Middle Ages), even though he was highly critical of Shaw's conception of the Middle Ages in his book: 'I was moved by Shaw's conception of a humanity of whose unity all individuals were part. Though I resisted the emotion, I felt myself part of this "Godhead" as I did not feel myself part of the revolutionary movement I opposed to it.' (West, *One Man in his Time*, p. 187).

227 F.R. Leavis, 'Bunyan Through Modern Eyes' in *The Common Pursuit* (Harmondsworth: Penguin Books, 1963).

228 Alick West, *The Mountain in the Sunlight: Studies in Conflict and Unity* (London: Lawrence and Wishart, 1958) p. 10.

229 Ibid., p. 9.

230 In the ten years or so after the publication of *The Mountain in the Sunlight*, a number of communist intellectuals in both Eastern and Western Europe began to express their dissatisfaction with the state of the world movement by endorsing writers whom orthodoxy condemned – Franz Kafka was especially favoured. For West's own endorsement of Kafka, see 'Discussion on Franz Kafka', *Marxism Today*, Vol. 13 No. 7, July 1969, pp. 205-210.

231 Ibid., p. 115.

232 Ibid., p. 114.

233 Ibid., pp. 115-117.

234 Quoted in ibid., p. 117.

235 See the bibliography of West's work in Munton and Young, *Seven Writers of the English Left*, pp. 19-20.

236 In her Introduction to *Crisis and Criticism and Literary Essays*, Elisabeth West pointed out that the essay on Lawrence was intended for a book on modern literature which West was writing at the time of his death. See *Crisis and Criticism and Literary Essays*, p. 10f.

237 West, *Crisis and Criticism and Literary Essays*, p. 261.

238 Ibid., 260f.

239 Ibid., p. 279.

240 Ibid., pp. 281-282.

241 Ibid., p. 282.

242 Ibid., p. 259.

243 A possible exception is Elisabeth West, who summarises the essay in some detail in her Introduction to *Crisis and Criticism and Literary Essays*, p. 11f. See also Hanna Behrend, op cit., pp. 114-115; Paananen, op cit., p. 32.

Chapter 4

1.   The fullest account of Fox's work can be found in Chapter Three of Anand Prakash, *Marxism and Literary Theory* (Delhi: Academic Foundation, 1994). For briefer surveys of *The Novel and the People*, see David Margolies, '*Left Review* and Left Literary Theory' in Jon Clark, Margot Heinemann, David Margolies and Carole Snee (eds.), *Culture and Crisis in Britain in the Thirties* (London: Lawrence and Wishart, 1979) and Hanna Behrend, 'An Intellectual Irrelevance? Marxist Literary Criticism in the 1930s' in Andy Croft (ed.), *A Weapon in the Struggle: The Cultural History of the Communist Party in Britain* (London: Pluto Press, 1998). Several writers have contributed introductions to the various editions of *The Novel and the People*. By far the most useful is Jeremy Hawthorn's preface to the 1979 Lawrence and Wishart edition. Perhaps the most perceptive brief remarks on *The Novel and the People* are those of the American critic Pamela Fox, whose work I was not familiar with when I wrote this chapter. See Pamela Fox, *Class Fictions: Shame and Resistance in the British Working-Class Novel, 1890-1945* (Durham: Duke University Press, 1994) p. 55f.

2   In the essay listed above, David Margolies recognises that Fox was a prescriptive thinker ('He is also too full of prescription...') and quotes his observation that 'the future of the English novel...lies precisely in Marxism.' My claim goes further – that the theoretical material in *The Novel and the People* is organised *around* Fox's prescriptive argument about the novel being the ideal form for the delineation of positive heroes.

3   Ralph Fox, *The Novel and the People* (London: The Cobbett Press, 1948) p. 23. Unless otherwise stated, all references to *The Novel and the People* in this chapter are to the 1948 edition.

4   My biographical sketch of Fox is largely based on the following sources: Ann Brett-

Jones, 'Ralph Fox: A Man in his Time', *Bulletin of the Marx Memorial Library*, No. 137, Spring 2003, pp. 27-41; John Lehmann, C. Day Lewis and T.A. Jackson (eds.), *Ralph Fox: A Writer In Arms* (London: Lawrence and Wishart, 1937); Jeremy Hawthorn, 'Preface' in Ralph Fox, *The Novel and the People* (London: Lawrence and Wishart, 1979) pp. 4-18; Alan Munton and Alan Young (compilers), *Seven Writers of the English Left: A Bibliography of Literature and Politics, 1916-1980* (London: Garland Publishing, 1981) p. 117f.

5   Mulk Raj Anand, 'Preface' in Ralph Fox, *The Novel and the People* (London: Cobbett Press, 1944). Quoted in Hawthorn, op cit., p. 7.

6   See Ann Brett-Jones, op cit., p. 31.

7   Ralph Fox, *The People of the Steppes* (London: Constable, 1925) p. 47.

8   Ann Brett-Jones, op cit., p. 33.

9   Brett-Jones is the only writer on Fox who mentions his employment by the Comintern. Since she is Fox's niece, one assumes that she relied on family sources.

10 For a list of Fox's contributions to the *Sunday Worker*, see Alan Munton and Alan Young, op cit., p. 122f.

11 The description of Fox is by Ann Herbert Richardson, who led the Unigar Strike in Tottenham, London in 1934. Quoted in Hawthorn, op cit., p. 8.

12 See Hawthorn, op cit., p. 9.

13 Hugh Slater, 'How Ralph Fox was Killed' in Lehmann, Day Lewis and Jackson (eds.), op cit., pp. 13-14. Quoted in Munton and Young, op cit., pp. 118-119.

14 Munton and Young, op cit., p. 119.

15 See Fox, *The Novel and the People*, Chapter Four.

16 Karl Marx and Friedrich Engels, *Marx & Engels on Literature And Art*, edited by Lee Baxandall and Stefan Morawski (St Louis/Milwaukee: Telos Press, 1973) pp. 134-136.

17 Fox, *The Novel and the People*, p. 43.

18 Fox himself referred to the use which the early bourgeois economists made of Robinson Crusoe in ibid., p. 45.

19 Ibid., p. 44.

20 Ibid., p. 20.

21 Ibid., p. 103f.

22 Cf. Anand Prakash's observation that 'The empirical outlook inherent in Fox always accepts the dichotomy of the individual and society under which society is seen as constituting a mass of ordinary men and women waiting to be worked upon and mobilised by dynamic individuals.' (*Marxism and Literary Theory*, p. 82).

23 See E.M. Forster, *Aspects of the Novel* (Harmondsworth: Penguin Books, 1988). For a useful introduction to Forster's theory of the novel, see René Wellek, *A History of Modern Criticism: 1750-1950, Volume Five: English Criticism 1900-1950* (London: Jonathan Cape, 1986) Chapter Three.

24 E.M. Forster, *Two Cheers for Democracy* (Harmondsworth: Penguin Books, 1972) p. 76.

25 Forster, *Aspects of the Novel*, p. 56.

26 For another reverent account of Forster's work by a Thirties communist, see A.L.

Morton, 'E.M. Forster and the Classless Society' in *History and the Imagination: Selected Writings of A.L. Morton*, edited by Margot Heinemann and Willie Thompson (London: Lawrence and Wishart, 1990).

27 Margolies, op cit., p. 74.

28 David Margolies comments on Fox's analysis of Cervantes and Rabelais in ibid., p. 74.

29 The classic Marxist account of *Gargantua and Pantagruel* is *Rabelais and His World* by Mikhail Bakhtin. Bakhtin's account of the 'carnivalesque' element in Rabelais' work has recently exerted a profound influence on the work of Marxist and *Marxisant* scholars in Cultural Studies. See, for instance, John Fiske, *Understanding Popular Culture* (London: Unwin Hyman, 1989); John Docker *Postmodernism and Popular Culture: A Cultural History* (Cambridge: Cambridge University Press, 1994).

30 Ralph Fox, *The Novel and the People*, pp. 55-57.

31 Ibid., p. 56.

32 Ibid., pp. 56-57.

33 Ibid., p. 55.

34 Ibid., p. 58f.

35 Ibid., p. 57.

36 Ibid., pp. 57-58.

37 Ibid., pp. 59-62.

38 Ibid., pp. 67-68.

39 Ibid., p. 66.

40 Ibid., pp. 65-66.

41 Ibid., p. 67.

42 Ibid., p. 69.

43 Ibid., p. 69.

44 Ibid., pp. 75-76.

45 Frederick Engels, 'Letter to Margaret Harkness', quoted in Fox, *The Novel and the People*, p. 77.

46 Fox, *The Novel and the People*, pp. 79-81.

47 Ibid., p. 81.

48 Ibid., pp. 78-84.

49 Ibid., p. 37.

50 Ibid., pp. 24-25.

51 Ibid., pp. 87-88.

52 Ibid., pp. 90-91.

53 Ibid., pp. 97-99.

54 Ibid., pp. 93-96.

55 See, for instance, Maxim Gorky, 'Soviet Literature' in Maxim Gorky, Karl Radek, Nikolai Bukharin, Andrey Zhdanov et al, *Soviet Writers' Congress 1934: The Debate on Socialist Realism and Modernism* (London: Lawrence and Wishart, 1977). The Soviet theory of cultural crisis is discussed in Chapter Two of the present book.

56 See Jonathan Rose, *The Intellectual Life of the British Working Classes* (London: Yale University Press, 2001), especially Chapter Four.

57 See, for instance, Jeremy Hawthorn's account of Fox's work as a tutor in his

'Preface' to the 1979 edition of *The Novel and the People.*

58   There is a useful account of Jackson's life and work in Vivien Morton and Stuart Macintyre, *T.A. Jackson: A Centenary Appreciation,* Our History Pamphlet 73 (London: Communist Party of Great Britain History Group, n.d. [1979?]). Jackson is identified as the *ne plus ultra* of the proletarian autodidact in Jonathan Rée, *Proletarian Philosophers: Problems in Socialist Culture in Britain, 1900-1940* (Oxford: Clarendon Press, 1984). Jackson's memoir of the first fifty years of his life is contained in *Solo Trumpet: Some Memories of Socialist Agitation and Propaganda* (London: Lawrence and Wishart, 1953).

59   Quoted in Rose, op cit., p. 130.

60   Quoted in ibid., p. 130.

61   See T.A. Jackson, *Old Friends to Keep: Studies of English Novels and Novelists* (London: Lawrence and Wishart, 1950).

62   See Lehmann, Day Lewis and Jackson (eds.), op cit.

63   Rose, op cit., p. 130.

64   D.H. Lawrence, 'Why the Novel Matters' in David Lodge (ed.), *20ᵗʰ Century Literary Criticism: A Reader* (London: Longman, 1972), pp. 132-135.

65   D.H. Lawrence, 'Introduction to his Paintings' in *'A Propos of Lady Chatterley's Lover' and Other Essays* (Harmondsworth: Penguin Books, 1967), p. 15.

66   Ibid., p. 25.

67   Ibid., p. 26.

68   Fox, *The Novel and the People,* p. 99.

69   Ibid., p. 162.

70   See ibid., Chapter Nine, 'Socialist Realism'.

71   For a brief account of Fox's understanding of the role of the positive hero in the Socialist Realist novel, see Behrend, op cit., p. 111.

72   Fox, *The Novel and the People,* p. 107.

73   Ibid., p. 118.

74   Ibid., p. 108.

75   Ibid., p. 109.

76   Ibid., p. 114.

77   Ibid., pp. 113-118.

78   There is a brief account of Fox's approach to the cultural politics of the Popular Front in Dona Torr, 'Ralph Fox & Our Cultural Heritage', *Left Review,* Vol. 3 No. 1, February 1937, pp. 4-5.

79   David Margolies points to the influence of Dimitrov on Fox in *'Left Review* and Left Literary Theory', p. 73.

80   Georgi Dimitrov, 'Dimitrov To Writers', *Left Review,* Vol. 1 No. 9, June 1935, p. 344.

81   Quoted in Jack Dywien, *Georgi Dimitrov: Fighter Against Fascism* (Nelson: Self-published by Jack Dywien, n.d. [1997]) p. 10.

82   Samuel Hynes, *The Auden Generation: Literature and Politics in England in the 1930s* (London: The Bodley Head, 1976), p. 257.

83   Fox, *The Novel and the People,* p. 127.

84   Ibid., p. 135.

85   See George Orwell, 'Politics and the English Language' in *The Collected Essays,*

Journalism and Letters of George Orwell, Volume Four: In Front of your Nose 1945-1950, edited by Sonia Orwell and Ian Angus (Harmondsworth: Penguin Books, 1984).

86   Fox, *The Novel and the People*, pp. 137-138.

87   Fox's actual point was that more research needed to be done to establish whether the King James Bible was indeed indebted to the language of the lower classes; but he strongly implied that a considerable debt existed.

88   For an account of British hostility to the 'Americanisation' of popular culture, see Dick Hebdige, 'Towards a Cartography of Taste 1935-1962' in Bernard Waites, Tony Bennett and Graham Martin (eds.), *Popular Culture: Past and Present* (London: Croom Helm in association with The Open University Press, 1982). The CPGB led a remarkably successful, if also highly reactionary, campaign against Americanisation in the 1950s. See, for instance, Martin Barker, *A Haunt Of Fears: The Strange History of the British Horror Comics Campaign* (London: Pluto Press, 1984).

89   Fox, *The Novel and the People*, p. 134.

90   For an overview of the debate, see Glenn Jordan and Chris Weedon, *Cultural Politics: Class, Gender, Race and the Postmodern World* (Oxford: Blackwell, 1995) pp. 80-86.

91   Alec Brown, Contribution to 'Controversy: Writers' International', *Left Review*, Vol. 1 No. 3, December 1934, p. 76. Andy Croft has pointed out that Brown's article betrayed the continuing influence on British Marxists of the Soviet Proletcult movement. See Andy Croft, *Red Letter Days: British Fiction in the 1930s* (London: Lawrence and Wishart, 1980), p. 44f.

92   Brown, op cit., p. 77.

93   J.M. Hay, Contribution to 'Controversy: Writers' International', *Left Review*, Vol. 1 No. 6, March 1935, p. 222.

94   Montagu Slater, Contribution to 'Controversy: Writers' International', *Left Review*, Vol. 1 No. 4, January 1935, pp. 125-128; Douglas Garman, Contribution to 'Controversy: Writers' International', *Left Review*, Vol. 1 No. 5, February 1935, pp. 180-182.

95   Hugh MacDiarmid, Contribution to 'Controversy: Writers' International', *Left Review*, Vol. 1 No. 5, February 1935, p. 182.

96   Lewis Grassic Gibbon, Contribution to 'Controversy: Writers' International', *Left Review*, Vol. 1 No. 5, February 1935, pp. 179-180.

97   See *Marx and Engels on Literature and Art*, op cit., pp. 112-113.

98   See Phil Watson, 'Whose Legacy?', *Weekly Worker*, No. 336, May 18 2000, p. 7.

99   Ralph Fox, 'Abyssinian Methods', *Left Review*, Vol. 2 No. 2, November 1935, pp. 81-82; Ralph Fox, 'Gorki', *The Eye: The Martin Lawrence Gazette*, No. 7, June-July-August 1936. Reprinted under the title 'Literature and Politics' in *The Novel and the People*.

100 I am assuming here that Bakhtin was primarily responsible for the bulk of the linguistic theories produced by the so-called 'Bakhtin circle'.

101 For useful introductions to Bakhtin's work, see David Murray, 'Dialogics: Joseph Conrad, *Heart of Darkness*' in Douglas Tallack (ed.), *Literary Theory at Work: Three Texts* (London: B.T. Batsford, 1987) and Robert Stam, 'Mikhail Bakhtin and

Left Cultural Critique' in E. Ann Kaplan (ed.), *Postmodernism and Its Discontents: Theories, Practices* (London: Verso, 1988).

102   See Mikhail Bakhtin, 'Discourse in the Novel' in Julie Rivkin and Michael Ryan (eds.), *Literary Theory: An Anthology* (Oxford: Blackwell, 1998).

103   Ken Worpole, 'The American Connection: The Masculine Style in Popular Fiction' in *Dockers and Detectives: Popular Reading: Popular Writing* (London: Verso, 1983), p. 30.

104   Fox, *The Novel and the People*, pp. 134-135.

105   The most compressed statement of the so-called 'Nairn-Anderson theses' can be found in Perry Anderson, 'Origins of the Present Crisis' in *English Questions* (London: Verso, 1992).

106   See T.S. Eliot, "Little Gidding" in *Collected Poems 1909-1962* (London: Faber and Faber, 1980).

107   For an account of the relationship between British Marxism and cultural conservatism in the 1930s, see Chapter One.

108   See the full bibliography of Fox's work in Alan Munton and Alan Young, op cit.

109   See, for instance, Raymond Williams's remarks on p. 266 of *Culture and Society 1780-1950* (Harmondsworth: Pelican, 1979) about the response of sections of the cultural intelligentsia to the doctrine of base and superstructure.

110   Ralph Fox, 'The Relation of Literature to Dialectical Materialism' in H. Levy, John Macmurray *et al.*, *Aspects of Dialectical Materialism* (London: Watts & Co., 1934), p. 61. This passage was later incorporated into *The Novel and the People*.

111   Fox, 'The Relation of Literature to Dialectical Materialism', p. 62.

112   Ibid., pp. 66-69.

113   Ralph Fox, 'Lawrence The Twentieth Century Hero', *Left Review*, Vol. 1 No. 10, July 1935, pp. 394-396.

114   Stanley Edgar Hyman, *The Armed Vision: A Study in the Methods of Modern Literary Criticism* (New York: Alfred A Knopf, 1952), p. 192.

Chapter 5

1   David N. Margolies, *The Function of Literature: A Study of Christopher Caudwell's Aesthetics* (London: Lawrence and Wishart, 1969); Christopher Pawling, *Christopher Caudwell: Towards a Dialectical Theory of Literature* (New York: St Martin's Press, 1989); Robert Sullivan, *Christopher Caudwell* (London: Croom Helm, 1987). For a useful survey of writing on Caudwell, see H. Gustav Klaus, 'Changing Attitudes to Caudwell: A Review of Critical Comments on the Author, 1937-87' in David Margolies and Linden Peach (eds.), *Christopher Caudwell: Marxism and Culture* (London: Goldsmiths College, 1989).

2   The classic study of communist autodidacticism in Britain is Stuart Macintyre, *A Proletarian Science: Marxism in Britain 1917-1933* (Cambridge: Cambridge University Press, 1980).

3   For brief accounts of Caudwell's life, see, *inter alia*, Sullivan, *Christopher Caudwell*, Chapter Two; Pawling, *Christopher Caudwell: Towards a Dialectical Theory of Literature*, Chapter One; David Margolies and Jean Duparc, 'Introduction' in

Christopher Caudwell, *Scenes and Actions: Unpublished Manuscripts*, edited by David Margolies and Jean Duparc (London: Routledge, 1986); Alan Munton and Alan Young (compilers), *Seven Writers of the English Left: A Bibliography of Literature and Politics, 1916-1980* (London: Garland Publishing, 1981) p. 217f; Valentine Cunningham, 'Sprigg, Christopher St John (1907-1937)' in *Oxford Dictionary of National Biography* (Oxford: Oxford University Press, 2004).

4   See Sullivan, *Christopher Caudwell*, p. 30.

5   Caudwell, *Scenes and Actions*, p. 219. This passage has been quoted by many writers on Caudwell.

6   Sullivan, *Christopher Caudwell*, p. 34f.

7   See, in particular, Jonathan Rose, *The Intellectual Life of the British Working Classes* (London: Yale University Press, 2001),

8   This is the definition of enantiodromia contained in the glossary of Frieda Fordham, *An Introduction to Jung's Psychology* (Harmondsworth, Penguin Books, 1966) p. 146.

9   Since at least one reader has accused me of being 'sniffy' about the phenomenon of autodidacticism, I had better make it clear that I yield to no one in my admiration for the British autodidactic tradition.

10   For Caudwell's theory of poetry, see, *inter alia*, Margolies, *The Function of Literature*, *passim*; David N. Margolies, 'Christopher Caudwell and the Foundations of Marxist Criticism', *Marxism Today*, May 1967, pp. 149-155; David Margolies, '*Left Review* and Left Literary Theory' in Jon Clark, Margot Heinemann, David Margolies and Carole Snee (eds.), *Culture and Crisis in Britain in the Thirties* (London: Lawrence and Wishart, 1979) pp. 77-81; Christopher Pawling, *Christopher Caudwell*, pp. 24-120; Robert Sullivan, *Christopher Caudwell*, Chapter Four; Francis Mulhern, 'The Marxist Aesthetics of Christopher Caudwell', *New Left Review*, No. 85, May/June 1974, pp. 37-58; Maurice Cornforth, 'Caudwell and Marxism', *The Modern Quarterly*, Vol. 6 No. 1, Winter 1950-51, pp. 16-33; René Wellek, *A History of Modern Criticism, Volume Five: English Criticism 1900-1950* (London: Jonathan Cape, 1986) pp. 142-143.

11   Nikolai Bukharin, 'Poetry, Poetics And The Problems Of Poetry In The USSR' in Maxim Gorky *et al.*, *Soviet Writers' Congress: The Debate on Socialist Realism and Modernism* (London: Lawrence and Wishart, 1977) p. 197.

12   Margolies, Pawling and Sullivan all recognise the influence of Bukharin on Caudwell, but, with the possible exception of Margolies (who devotes a chapter to it) they appear to regard it as somewhat incidental. Moreover, they focus on the emphasis which the two thinkers share on the ability of art to convey ideas in sensual or emotional form. My argument here is that Caudwell was also (and perhaps more centrally) influenced by Bukharin's argument about the *quality* of the emotion which art serves to express. See Margolies, *The Function of Literature*, p. 85f; Pawling, *Christopher Caudwell: Towards a Dialectical Theory of Literature*, p. 98f; Sullivan, *Christopher Caudwell*, p. 97.

13   For the influence of behaviourism on Caudwell, see, *inter alia*, Pawling, p. 81f.

14   Christopher Caudwell, *Illusion and Reality: A Study in the Sources of Poetry* (London: Lawrence and Wishart, 1977) pp. 143-144 *passim*.

15   For the influence of Richards on Caudwell, see Mulhern, op cit., pp. 54-55.

16   Caudwell, *Illusion and Reality*, p. 141 *passim*.

17   Ibid. pp. 139-142.

18   Ibid., p. 140.

19   Ibid., pp. 174-177.

20   Ibid., pp. 159-171. For another account of Caudwell's theory of language, see, *inter alia*, Mulhern, op cit., p. 45f.

21   Caudwell, *Illusion and Reality*, p. 160.

22   Cornforth, op cit., pp. 23-28.

23   David Lodge (ed.), *20th Century Literary Criticism: A Reader* (London: Longman, 1972) p. 202.

24   Caudwell, *Illusion and Reality*, p. 227.

25   Ibid., pp. 235-236.

26   Ibid., p. 236.

27   Ibid., pp. 235-242.

28   David Lodge makes a similar point in *20th Century Literary Criticism*, p. 202.

29   See S.V. Pradhan, 'Caudwell's Theory of Poetry: Some Problems of a Marxist Synthesis', *British Journal of Aesthetics*, Summer 1977, pp. 266-274.

30   See Caudwell, *Illusion and Reality*, p. 19f.

31   Ibid., p. 34.

32   Christopher Caudwell, 'Freud: A Study in Bourgeois Psychology' in *Studies in a Dying Culture* (London: John Lane The Bodley Head, 1938) p. 170.

33   Dyer was referring to John Berger, another great Marxist autodidact. See Geoff Dyer, 'Editor's Introduction' in John Berger, *Selected Essays*, edited by Geoff Dyer (London: Bloomsbury, 2001) p. x.

34   Caudwell, *Studies in a Dying Culture*, p. 172. Although Caudwell unsurprisingly described infantile regression as the 'way of defeat', there is reason to suppose that he regarded some form of regression as a *sine qua non* of creative advance. In a letter to his friend Paul Beard (December 21 1934), he wrote that 'Psycho-analytic theories of the unconscious (particularly Baudouin) have greatly influenced my theory of poetry (though not my technique which is empirical) and I explain bouts of "inspiration" by the alternate cycle of regression and progression by which according to Jung, a character individuates itself.' See Caudwell, *Scenes and Actions*, p. 209.

35   See Margolies, '*Left Review* and Left Literary Theory', p. 79; David Margolies (ed.), *Writing the Revolution: Cultural Criticism from Left Review* (London: Pluto Press, 1998) p. 47.

36   C. Day Lewis, 'Revolutionaries and Poetry', *Left Review*, Vol. 1 No. 10, July 1935, p. 399.

37   Ibid., p. 399.

38   Ibid., p. 401.

39   Ibid., p. 402.

40   Caudwell's theory of poetry was brilliantly applied to the development of Ancient Greek literature by George Thomson, perhaps the only disciple whom the communist critics of the 1930s ever had. Although Thomson's most important work was issued from the early 1940s onwards, he began to outline his critical position in the late 1930s. See, in particular, George Thomson, 'The Social Origins

of Greek Tragedy', *The Modern Quarterly*, Vol. 1 No. 3, July 1938, pp. 233-264.

41 For Caudwell's theory of cultural crisis, see, *inter alia*, Margolies, *The Function of Literature*, especially Chapter Four; Margolies, 'Christopher Caudwell and the Foundations of Marxist Criticism', pp. 149-155; Margolies, '*Left Review* and Left Literary Theory', pp. 77-81; Pawling, *Christopher Caudwell*, p. 53f *passim*; Sullivan, *Christopher Caudwell*, Chapter Five; Mulhern, 'The Marxist Aesthetics of Christopher Caudwell', pp. 42f; Cornforth, 'Caudwell and Marxism'; Wellek, *A History of Modern Criticism, Volume Five*, pp. 142-143; Helena Sheehan, *Marxism and the Philosophy of Science: A Critical History* (New Jersey: Humanities Press, 1993) p. 350f; E.P. Thompson, 'Christopher Caudwell' in *Persons and Polemics: Historical Essays* (London: Merlin Press, 1984).

42 Caudwell's most accessible discussion of the bourgeois illusion of freedom is in the 'Foreword' to *Studies in a Dying Culture*.

43 Caudwell, *Studies in a Dying Culture*, pp. xx-xxi.

44 Ibid., p. 195f.

45 Ibid., p. 205f.

46 Ibid., p. 211.

47 David Margolies expands on this point in his chapter on the bourgeois illusion in *The Function of Literature*. See p. 49f.

48 Christopher Caudwell, *Romance and Realism: A Study in English Bourgeois Literature*, edited by Samuel Hynes (New Jersey: Princeton University Press, 1970).

49 Caudwell, *Illusion and Reality*, p. 85f; Caudwell, *Romance and Realism*, p. 40f.

50 For Caudwell's account of Shakespeare, see, *inter alia*, Pawling, p. 59f.

51 Caudwell, *Romance and Realism*, pp. 40-41.

52 Ibid., p. 52f.

53 Ibid., p. 53.

54 Quoted in René Wellek, *A History of Modern Criticism 1750-1950, Volume One: The Later Eighteenth Century* (London: Jonathan Cape, 1970) p. 86.

55 Caudwell, *Romance and Realism*, p. 57.

56 Ibid., pp. 55-56.

57 Ibid., p. 58. Pawling uses the term 'omniscient narrator' in his account of Caudwell's theory of the novel; Sullivan prefers the term "omniscient observer".

58 Ibid., p. 58.

59 T.A. Jackson, *Solo Trumpet: Some Memories of Socialist Agitation and Propaganda* (London: Lawrence and Wishart, 1953) pp. 21-22. Quoted in part in Jonathan Rée, *Proletarian Philosophers: Problems in Socialist Culture in Britain, 1900-1940* (Oxford: Clarendon Press, 1984) p. 11; Pamela Fox, *Class Fictions: Shame and Resistance in the British Working-Class Novel, 1890-1945* (Durham: Duke University Press, 1994) p. 35.

60 Jurgen Rühle, *Literature and Revolution: A Critical Study of the Writer and Communism in the Twentieth Century* (London: Pall Mall Press, 1969) p. 44.

61 Katerina Clark, 'Socialist Realism *with* Shores: The Conventions for the Positive Hero' in Thomas Lahusen and Evgeny Dobrenko (eds.), *Socialist Realism Without Shores* (London: Yale University Press, 1997) p. 31.

62 For the main principles of Lukacs's theory of realism and his related critique

of modernism, see, *inter alia*, *Realism In Our Time: Literature and the Class Struggle* (New York: Harper & Row, 1971); *Writer and Critic and Other Essays* (London: Merlin Press, 1970). There are useful introductions to Lukacs's work in Pauline Johnson, *Marxist Aesthetics: The Foundations within Everyday Life for an Emancipated Consciousness* (London: Routledge and Kegan Paul, 1984) and Stuart Sim, *Georg Lukacs* (London: Prentice Hall/Harvester Wheatsheaf, 1994).

Chapter 6

1   The convention in the 1930s was to refer to the *English* radical tradition. I have followed the convention in this chapter, though it goes without saying that the communists were tracing the history of a movement that was also (at least from the eighteenth century onwards) a *British* phenomenon.

2   For brief accounts of the cultural dimension of the Popular Front policy in Britain, see, *inter alia*, James Klugmann, 'The Crisis in the Thirties: A View from the Left' in Jon Clark, Margot Heinemann, David Margolies and Carole Snee (eds.), *Culture and Crisis in Britain in the Thirties* (London: Lawrence and Wishart, 1979); Margot Heinemann, 'The People's Front and the Intellectuals' in Jim Fyrth (ed.), *Britain, Fascism and the Popular Front* (London: Lawrence and Wishart, 1985); Margot Heinemann, '*Left Review, New Writing* and the Broad Alliance against Fascism' in Edward Timms and Peter Collier (eds.), *Visions and Blueprints:Avant-Garde Culture and Radical Politics in early Twentieth-Century Europe* (Manchester: Manchester University Press, 1988); Mick Wallis, 'Heirs to the Pageant: Mass Spectacle and the Popular Front' in Andy Croft (ed.), *A Weapon in the Struggle: The Cultural History of the Communist Party in Britain* (London: Pluto Press, 1998).

3   It goes without saying that the ecumenical ethos of the Popular Front had definite limits. During the 1930s the CPGB launched a sustained attack on Trotskyism, defended the Moscow Trials and dismissed the Trotskyist and quasi-Trotskyist participants in the Spanish Civil War as fascist fifth columnists. For an especially egregious example of communist anti-Trotskyism, see T.A. Jackson, 'The Moscow Trial', *Left Review*, Vol. 3 No. 2, March 1937, pp. 116-118. The most famous British account of what it felt like to be on the receiving end of communist sectarianism is undoubtedly George Orwell, *Homage to Catalonia* (London: Penguin, 2000). As is well known, Orwell's book was rejected for publication by the Left Book Club.

4   Georgi Dimitrov, *The Working Class Against Fascism* (London: Martin Lawrence, 1935) p. 10.

5   Ibid., p. 69. The relevant passage is quoted in Heinemann, 'The People's Front and the Intellectuals', p. 158.

6   Dimitrov, op cit., p. 70. Quoted in Heinemann, 'The People's Front and the Intellectuals', p. 158.

7   Dimitrov, op cit., pp. 98-99. Quoted in Heinemann, 'The People's Front and the Intellectuals', p. 158.

8   See, *inter alia*, Heinemann, 'The Intellectuals and the People's Front', pp. 157-158.

9   Edgell Rickword, 'On English Freedom' in Jack Lindsay and Edgell Rickword (eds.),

Spokesmen for Liberty: A Record of English Democracy Through Twelve Centuries (London: Lawrence and Wishart, 1941).

10 Edgell Rickword, 'Culture, Progress, and English Tradition' in C. Day Lewis (ed.), *The Mind in Chains: Socialism and the Cultural Revolution* (London: Frederick Muller, 1937).

11 A.L. Morton, *A People's History of England* (London: Lawrence and Wishart, 1984); Jack Lindsay, *England My England: A Pageant of the English People* (London: Fore Publications, n.d. [1939]). The 1930s also saw the publication of a small number of monographs on particular aspects of the *political* history of the English radical tradition. The most important was 'Henry Holorenshaw' [Joseph Needham], *The Levellers and the English Revolution* (London: Victor Gollancz, 1939). However, since this book is primarily concerned with the politics of literature, I have confined myself in this chapter to considering Morton and Lindsay's synoptic accounts of the politics of English radicalism.

12 Jack Lindsay, *John Bunyan: Maker of Myths* (New York: Augustus M Kelley, 1969); T.A. Jackson, *Charles Dickens: The Progress of a Radical* (London: Lawrence and Wishart, 1937); Robin Page Arnot, *William Morris: A Vindication* (London: Martin Lawrence, 1934).

13 The main articles in *Left Review* on the English radical tradition are as follows: Ajax [Montagu Slater], 'Dick Overton, Leveller', *Left Review*, Vol. 1 No. 1, October 1934, pp. 41-44; Edgell Rickword, Untitled review of Jonathan Swift, *Gulliver's Travels and Selected Writings*, *Left Review*, Vol. 1 No. 6, March 1935, pp. 236-237; F.D. Klingender, 'The Crucifix: A Symbol of Mediaeval Class Struggle', *Left Review*, Vol. 2 No. 4, January 1936, pp. 167-173; Randall Swingler, 'The Imputation of Madness: A Study of William Blake and Literary Tradition', *Left Review*, Vol. 3 No. 1, February 1937, pp. 21-28; T.A. Jackson, 'Dickens, the Radical', *Left Review*, Vol. 3 No. 2, March 1937, pp. 88-95; Alick West, 'The "Poetry" in Poetry' (on Edmund Spenser), *Left Review*, Vol. 3 No. 3, April 1937, pp. 164-168; Samuel Mill, 'The Rebellious Needleman: Tom Paine', *Left Review*, Vol. 3 No. 4, May 1937, pp. 202-207; Rex Warner, 'Jonathan Swift', *Left Review*, Vol. 3 No. 5, June 1937, pp. 266-272; Jack Lindsay, 'William Shakespeare', *Left Review*, Vol. 3 No. 6, July 1937, pp. 333-339; Edgell Rickword, 'John Bunyan', *Left Review*, Vol. 3 No. 12, January 1938, pp. 758-759.

14 Jack Lindsay, *A Short History of Culture* (London: Victor Gollancz, 1939) Chapters Fifty-four and Fifty-five; John Strachey, *The Theory and Practice of Socialism* (London: Victor Gollancz, 1936).

15 Christopher Hill (ed.), *The English Revolution 1640* (London: Lawrence and Wishart, 1940). Hill's contribution to this volume was later reprinted as a short book. See Christopher Hill, *The English Revolution 1640: An Essay* (London: Lawrence and Wishart, 1979). Rickword's essay on Milton ('Milton: The Revolutionary Intellectual') was reprinted in Edgell Rickword, *Literature in Society: Essays and Opinions (11) 1931-1978*, edited by Alan Young (Manchester: Carcanet, 1978).

16 The most compressed account of Lindsay's theory of culture can be found in Jack Lindsay, 'Symmetry, Asymmetry, Structure, Dominance' in Victor N. Paananen (ed.), *British Marxist Criticism* (New York: Garland Publishing, 2000).

17 As I indicate in the Introduction, there has not been enough space in this book

to examine the literary journalism of the 1930s. The *Daily Worker* articles on the radical tradition have not therefore been considered in this chapter.

18   For a biography of Rickword, see Charles Hobday, *Edgell Rickword: A Poet at War* (Manchester: Carcanet, 1989).

19   Rickword, 'On English Freedom', p. viif.

20   Ibid., pp. x-xii.

21   Ibid., p. xi.

22   Ibid., p. xii. Rickword's argument here was that English radicals have been continuously influenced since at least 1381 by the doctrine of the 'Norman Yoke', which holds that the English countryside was organised along egalitarian lines for much of the period between the departure of the Romans and the arrival of the Normans. Convinced that the land was owned collectively and farmed by the entire community, or so the argument went, generations of radicals have regarded the class struggle as a means of reversing the baleful decision by a handful of chieftains to collaborate with the invading Normans to establish a feudal society. John Ball, Gerrard Winstanley and John Lilburne were among those who argued that a communist society can be created in Britain because *such a society has already existed.* As extraordinary as it may seem, there were several Thirties communists (Rickword was not one of them) who still affected to take the doctrine of the Norman Yoke seriously, presumably on the grounds that it might still constitute a poweful stimulus to working-class revolt. This approach was exemplified by Jack Lindsay in *England My England*, who wrote that:

A thousand years ago the fight was between the local chieftains and the village group which farmed the land co-operatively. The rulers fought to destroy the rights of the working group, to break up the communal ownership of the soil, and to grab the soil as personal property...As the fight went on, the peasants lost bit by bit their communal rights, their system of shareholding, of yearly dividing up the soil and of sharing out all other things needed by the village community for its work...When the Normans under William conquered England, the dice were heavily weighted against the peasantry, who were now subject aliens as well as a suppressed class... Throughout all the centuries of the later medieval period this struggle went on. It was incomparably the most important fact in the history of those years. So you read nothing about it in the history books at school. It would never do to let the English people know how the land was stolen from them. (Lindsay, *England My England*, pp. 7-8.)

By the time that Lindsay was writing, of course, it was quite unthinkable that the idea of the Norman Yoke could ever be rehabilitated. In a renowned essay which he contributed to a *Festschrift* for Dona Torr in 1953, Christopher Hill (one of Lindsay's friends) pointed out that the working-class movement had abandoned the idea of a pre-Norman Arcadia as long ago as the nineteenth century, not least because the rise of Marxism had exposed it as a historical fiction. As such, the passage quoted above is simply an unusual reminder of the extent to which Marxist intellectuals have occasionally found it necessary to modify or even suppress their own convictions in the interests of populism. It was as if Lindsay, who trained as a classical scholar at Queensland University, was less comfortable with the 'ruthless criticism of everything which exists' (Marx) than with Plato's assumption that one of the main forms of political activity is the dissemination of 'necessary myths'. (For accounts of Hill's essay, see Bill Schwarz, ' "The People" in History: the Communist Party Historians' Group, 1945-56' in Richard Johnson, Gregor McLennan, Bill Schwarz, and David Sutton (eds.), *Making Histories: Studies in History Writing and Politics* (Minneapolis: University of Minneapolis Press, 1982) p. 69f; Harvey Kaye, *The British Marxist Historians: An Introductory Analysis* (Oxford: Polity, 1984). p. 120f.)

23   Rickword, 'On English Freedom', p. xii.

24   Ibid., p. ixf.

25   Ibid., vii-ix.

26   Ibid., p. viii.

27   Ibid., pp. viii-ix.

28   E.P. Thompson, 'Edgell Rickword', *PN Review*, Supplement xxviii, Vol. 6 No. 1, 1979. Reprinted in *Persons and Polemics: Historical Essays* (London: Merlin Press, 1994). For Hanna Behrend's brief comments on Thompson's perspective on Rickword, see 'An Intellectual Irrelevance? Marxist Literary Criticism in the 1930s' in Croft (ed.), *A Weapon in the Struggle*, p. 108. Behrend comments on Rickword's approach to the relationship between intellectuals and the radical movement on p. 117 of the essay.

29   Rickword, 'On English Freedom', p. vii and p. ix.

30   Ibid., p. ix.

31   Ibid., p. ix.

32   George Orwell, 'The Lion and the Unicorn: Socialism and the English Genius' in *The Collected Essays, Journalism and Letters of George Orwell, Volume Two: My Country Right or Left 1940-1943* (Harmondsworth: Penguin Books, 1970) p. 77.

33   I try to assess the influence of British cultural Marxism on Orwell's work in my book *Orwell and Marxism: The Political and Cultural Thinking of George Orwell* (London: I.B. Tauris, 2009).

34   See Heinemann, '*Left Review, New Writing* and the Broad Alliance against Fascism', p. 118. David Margolies also briefly refers to the similarities between Gramscian Marxism and the English communist criticism of the 1930s in David Margolies (ed.), *Writing the Revolution: Cultural Criticism from Left Review* (London: Pluto Press, 1998) p. 11.

35   Lindsay, *England My England*, pp. 9-13.

36   Morton, *A People's History of England*, pp. 120-127.

37   Lindsay, *England My England*, p. 10.

38   My account of the communist analysis of the radical dimension of Christianity is largely derived from Klingender, 'The Crucifix: A Symbol of Mediaeval Class Struggle', pp. 168-169. For a much more extensive discussion of the relationship between communism and Christianity from the 1930s, see John Lewis, Karl Polanyi and Donald K. Kitchen (eds.), *Christianity and the Social Revolution* (London: Gollancz, 1935).

39   Klingender, op cit., p. 168.

40   See, for instance, Lindsay, *England My England*, p. 10.

41   Quoted in Lindsay and Rickword (eds.), *Spokesmen for Liberty*, p. 28.

42   Lindsay, *England My England*, p. 14.

43   Morton, *A People's History of England*, pp. 127-131.

44   Ibid., p. 131.

45   Ibid., pp. 126-127.

46   E.J. Hobsbawm, *The Age of Revolution 1789-1848* (New York: New English Library, 1962) p. 84.

47   Morton merely *implied* that leadership was important but also recognised the inherent weaknesses in all forms of peasant insurrection. See *A People's History of England*, p. 125.

48   See Morton, *A People's History of England*, pp. 125-126; Lindsay, *England My England*, pp. 11-13.

49   Lindsay, *England My England*, p. 12.

50   See, *inter alia*, Morton, *A People's History of England*, p.122 and p. 128; Lindsay and Rickword (eds), *Spokesmen for Liberty*, pp. 20-21 *passim*; Rickword, 'Culture, Progress, and English Tradition', p. 238.

51   See, *inter alia*, Lindsay, *England My England*, p. 14.

52   There is a brief summary of Klingender's essay in Patrick Deane, ' "Building the Just City Now": Exchanges between English Literature, Socialism, and Christianity in the 1930s' in Antony Shuttleworth (ed.), *And in Our Time: Vision, Revision, and British Writing of the 1930s* (Lewisburg: Bucknell University Press, 2003) pp. 32-34. For an intellectual biography of Klingender, see Grant Pooke, *Francis Klingender 1907-1955: A Marxist Art Historian Out of Time* (London: Gill Vista Marx Press, 2008).

53   Klingender, op cit., p. 168.

54   Ibid., p. 168.

55   Ibid., pp. 168-173.

56   Ibid., p. 169.

57   Ibid., p. 173.

58   I have used the reproduction of Grünewald's crucifix on page 172 of 'The Crucifix' to flesh out what I take Klingender to mean in his comments about its revolutionary significance.

59   Ibid., p. 173.

60   See Lindsay, *England My England*, p. 16 *passim*; Morton, *A People's History of England*, p. 166 *passim*.

61   Morton, *A People's History of England*, p. 168.

62   Ibid., pp. 168-169.

63   My account of the communist interpretation of the Reformation is largely derived from Lindsay, *John Bunyan: Maker of Myths*, Chapter Five.

64   Ibid, pp. 43f.

65   Quoted in ibid., p. 44.

66   Lindsay, *England My England*, pp. 17-23.

67   Ibid., pp. 23-28.

68   This reading of the peasant uprisings remained important in post-war attempts to shape popular awareness of English history along conservative lines. See, for instance, Angus Maude and Enoch Powell, *Biography of a Nation: A Short History of Britain* (London: Phoenix House, 1955).

69   Morton, *A People's History of England* p. 172.

70   Ibid. p. 172. Morton recognised that the Pilgrimage of Grace has been an expression of opposition to the dissolution of the monasteries, but he nevertheless implied that ordinary Britons had been hostile to the appropriation of church property but not to the Reformation itself. See page 184 of *A People's History of England*.

71   Edgell Rickword, 'Culture, Progress, and English Tradition', pp. 239-240.

72   Strachey, *The Theory and Practice of Socialism*, p. 272f.

73   Ibid., pp. 277-278.

74   In fact, the quotations from *Utopia* which Strachey reproduced in *The Theory and Practice of Socialism* give the impression that More failed even to recognise that the dispossessed peasantry had an alternative to theft.

75   Quoted in Strachey, *The Theory and Practice of Socialism*, pp. 271-272.

76   Quoted in ibid., p. 272.

77   Quoted in ibid., p. 277.

78   For an account of the aspects of More's *Utopia* which the modern radical is likely to find discomforting, see Pamela Neville-Sington and David Sington, *Paradise Dreamed: How Utopian Thinkers Have Changed the Modern World* (London: Bloomsbury, 1994) p. 29f.

79   Strachey, *The Theory and Practice of Socialism*, p. 278.

80   Ibid., p. 278.

81   As is well known, the Webbs removed the question mark from the title of the second edition of their book.

82   Alick West briefly outlined a radical reading of Shakespeare in a review of A.A. Smirnov's *Shakespeare: A Marxist Interpretation*, a Soviet text which seems to have exercised an (unacknowledged) influence on Lindsay. See Alick West, 'Shakespeare: A Revaluation', *Left Review*, Vol. 2 No. 16, January 1937, pp. 906-909. T.A. Jackson examined Marx's approach to Shakespeare in 'Marx and Shakespeare', *International Literature*, No. 2, 1936, pp. 75-97. This article was later printed in abridged form in *Labour Monthly*, Vol. XLVI No. 4, April 1964.

83   Quoted in Chris Baldick, *Criticism and Literary Theory 1890 to the Present* (London: Longman, 1996) p. 93.

84   Jack Lindsay, 'William Shakespeare', pp. 333-334; Jack Lindsay, *A Short History of Culture*, p. 313-314.

85   Jack Lindsay, 'William Shakespeare', p. 335; Lindsay, *A Short History of Culture*, p. 314.

86   Lindsay, *A Short History of Culture*, pp. 314-316.

87   Lindsay, 'William Shakespeare', pp. 335-337; Lindsay, *A Short History of Culture*, pp. 317-318.

88   Lindsay, *A Short History of Culture*, p. 317.

89   Quoted in Lindsay, 'William Shakespeare', p. 336 and in Lindsay, *A Short History of Culture* p. 318.

90   Lindsay, 'William Shakespeare', pp. 337-339; Lindsay, *A Short History of Culture*, pp. 321-325.

91   Lindsay, *A Short History of Culture*, p. 323.

92   Lindsay, 'William Shakespeare', pp. 337-338; Lindsay, *A Short History of Culture*, p. 323. Lindsay recognised that Cordelia provided a 'counter-force' to the prevailing

mood of rampant individualism and that 'Lear in his madness becomes himself a Fool, uttering the terrible truths which he had spent his power-life in evading.'

93 Lindsay, *A Short History of Culture* p. 324.

94 Lindsay, 'William Shakespeare', p. 337; Lindsay, *A Short History of Culture*, p. 323. Lindsay nevertheless made it clear that Shakespeare rejected the idea that feudalism could ever be re-established, instead regarding the lovers' relationship in *Antony and Cleopatra* as a source of 'prophesies of the future.'

95 Quoted in Lindsay, *A Short History of Culture*, p. 324.

96 Lindsay, 'William Shakespeare', pp. 338-339; Lindsay, *A Short History of Culture*, p. 325.

97 Lindsay, *A Short History of Culture*, p. 325.

98 West did not refer explicitly to the idea that poetry played a directly economic role in primitive societies, but we know from the anthropological sections of *Crisis and Criticism* (see Chapter Three) that this was what he believed.

99 Alick West, The "Poetry" in Poetry', pp. 167-168.

100 Ibid., pp. 167-168.

101 Ibid., p. 168.

102 Ibid., p. 168.

103 Cf. West's own description of the poem: 'A band of nymphs beside the Thames see two swans floating down the river. They gather flowers in honour of the birds. Two of the nymphs sing to them, while the others bear "the undersong". The scene is a "literary" description of poetry as it was originally sung and acted.' West, 'The "Poetry" in Poetry', p. 166.

104 From Edmund Spenser, *Prothalamion* in John Hayward (ed.), *The Penguin Book of English Verse* (Harmondsworth: Penguin Books, 1985) pp. 22-26.

105 West, 'The "Poetry" in Poetry', p. 166. As West pointed out, *Prothalamion* was originally written to celebrate a wedding – another reminder of the collective function which poetry initially fulfilled.

106 Ibid., pp. 165f.

107 Ibid., p. 167.

108 This is assuming that West *did* admire it – a matter which his essay did not make entirely clear. One could also argue that he regarded the 'intederminateness' of Spenser's poem as a depressing symptom of the way in which poetry has been compromised by the emergence of capitalism.

109 Ibid., p. 168.

110 Morton, *A People's History of England*, p. 219.

111 Ibid., p. 192f.

112 For a very detailed, though also debunking, account of the way that the English Revolution has been analysed by British Marxist historians, see Alastair MacLachlan, *The Rise and Fall of Revolutionary England: An Essay on the Fabrication of Seventeenth-Century History* (London: Macmillan, 1996). Interestingly, MacLachlan emphasises the importance of Soviet historiography in shaping the early work of Christopher Hill. See p. 46f.

113 Perry Anderson, *English Questions* (London: Verso, 1992) p. 17.

114 When Lindsay referred to the democratic demands put forward by the Levellers (*England My England*, page 31), he listed 'universal suffrage, annual parliaments,

no conscription'. He was mistaken about the first two demands.

115 Jack Lindsay, *England My England*, pp. 31-33. Lindsay's portrayal of the Levellers' political objectives was slightly obscure. I am assuming that he regarded the Levellers as the last of England's rural communists because (1) he wrote that their main goal was to secure 'the return of the land to the people' (p. 31), and (2) his account of the Diggers stipulated that Gerrard Winstanley's books represented 'the first expression of scientific communism' (p. 34). This would seem to imply that the Levellers did not share this scientific outlook.

116 Ibid., pp. 33-39.

117 Morton, *A People's History of England*, p. 253.

118 Ibid., pp. 253-259; Christopher Hill, *The English Revolution 1640*, p. 48f.

119 Morton, *A People's History of England*, pp. 257-258; Hill, *The English Revolution 1640*, pp. 51-52.

120 Strachey, *The Theory and Practice of Socialism*, pp. 279-283. Strachey also argued that there was a noticeable disjuncture between the practical and ideological aspects of the Diggers' project. While the men who gathered on St George's Hill might only have aspired to prevent the appropriation of England's remaining common lands, Winstanley's writings clearly expressed the desire for complete communism.

121 Lindsay, *England My England*, p. 40.

122 See, *inter alia*, Lindsay, *John Bunyan: Maker of Myths*, pp. 101-106; Morton, *A People's History of England*, p. 219f *passim*.

123 Morton referred to Overton as 'one of the first of English freethinkers' on pp. 256-257 of *A People's History of England*.

124 Slater indirectly admitted to being Ajax in an obituary notice on Charles Donnelly which he contributed to *Left Review* in 1937. See Montagu Slater, 'Charles Donnelly', *Left Review*, Vol. 3 No. 6, July 1937, pp. 318-319.

125 Ajax [Montagu Slater], 'Dick Overton, Leveller', pp. 41-43.

126 Quoted in ibid., p. 43.

127 Quoted in ibid., p. 43.

128 Quoted in ibid., p. 44.

129 Quoted in Strachey, *The Theory and Practice of Socialism*, p. 282.

130 Ibid., pp. 279-283.

131 Edgell Rickword, 'Milton: The Revolutionary Intellectual' in *Literature and Society: Essays and Opinions (11) 1931-1978*, pp. 173-179.

132 Ibid., p. 176.

133 Rickword did not mention John Stuart Mill but revealed his Millian credentials by quoting Milton's belief that he was giving voice to 'the common grievance of all those who had prepared their minds and studies above the vulgar pitch to advance truth in others.'

134 Rickword, 'Milton: The Revolutionary Intellectual', pp. 179-183.

135 Ibid., p. 165.

136 Ibid., p. 179.

137 Ibid., pp. 169-173.

138 Ibid., p. 172.

139 Ibid., pp. 170-171.

140 Quoted in ibid., p. 170. The phrase 'degenerate learning' was Bacon's.

141 For an account of the role of philosophy in British communist culture, see Jonathan Rée, *Proletarian Philosophers: Problems in Socialist Culture in Britain, 1900-1940* (Oxford: Clarendon Press, 1984).

142 It ought to be pointed out that Lindsay never explicitly referred to Bunyan as a communist thinker, instead hinting at his outlook by referring to his yearning for 'unity' and his hatred for the ruling class.

143 Jack Lindsay, *John Bunyan: Maker of Myths*, pp. 1-106.

144 Ibid., pp. 1-6.

145 Ibid., pp. 7-15.

146 Ibid., pp. 16-29.

147 Ibid., p. 12f.

148 Ibid., p. 12.

149 Quoted in ibid., p. 50. Lindsay did not name the contemporary medical author whose words he was quoting.

150 Ibid., pp. 50.

151 Ibid, pp. 47-51.

152 Ibid., p. 56.

153 Quoted in ibid., p. 64.

154 Quoted in ibid., p. 64. For Lindsay's account of this episode, see pp. 64-68.

155 Ibid., pp. 69-95.

156 Quoted in ibid., p. 69.

157 Quoted in ibid., p. 75.

158 Quoted in ibid., p. 84.

159 Ibid., pp. 79-95; p. 107f.

160 For Lindsay's account of Bunyan's contribution to the history of English dissent, see ibid. pp. 96-106 *passim*.

161 Lindsay, *John Bunyan: Maker of Myths*, pp. 113-117.

162 Ibid., pp. 197-211.

163 The metaphor 'unbending the springs of resistance' was famously employed by Richard Hoggart in *The Uses of Literacy*.

164 E.P. Thompson, *The Making of the English Working Class*, (Harmondsworth: Pelican Books, 1972) p. 34. Quoted in Kaye, *The British Marxist Historians*, p. 177.

165 For Lindsay's analysis of *Pilgrim's Progress*, see *John Bunyan: Maker of Myths*, p. 165f.

166 Ibid., p. 189f.

167 Ibid., p. 190.

168 Ibid., p. 192.

169 Ibid., p. 193f.

170 Ibid., p. 193.

171 Ibid., p. 165f.

172 Ibid., p. 166.

173 Ibid., p. 166.

174 The metaphor is that of Viktor Shklovsky, who once argued that great literature is often predicated on 'the canonization of inferior (sub-literary) genres.' Quoted in Ken Worpole, *Dockers and Detectives: Popular Reading: Popular Writing* (London:

Verso, 1983) p. 35.

175 Lindsay, *John Bunyan: Maker of Myths*, p. 166.

176 Ibid., p. 168.

177 See Raymond Williams, *Marxism and Literature* (London: Oxford University Press, 1977). For an introduction to Williams's theory of literary production, see Alan O' Connor, *Raymond Williams: Writing, Culture, Politics* (Oxford: Blackwell, 1989) pp. 109-119.

178 Lindsay, *England My England*, pp. 39-41; Morton, *A People's History of England*, p. 290f.

179 See Michael Foot, 'Round the Next Corner: *the Pursuit of Jonathan Swift*' in *Debts of Honour* (London: Picador, 1981).

180 Rex Warner, 'Jonathan Swift', p. 267f; Edgell Rickword, untitled review of *Swift: Gulliver's Travels and Selected Writings*, p. 236f.

181 Quoted in Warner, 'Jonathan Swift', p. 268 and in Rickword, Untitled review of *Swift: Gulliver's Travels and Selected Writings*, p. 237 (Rickword omitted the passage's first 14 words).

182 Rickword, ibid., p. 237.

183 Warner, 'Jonathan Swift', p. 266f.

184 For an account of Johnson's attempt to describe Swift as a misanthrope, see, *inter alia*, Foot, op cit., p. 185f.

185 Warner, 'Jonathan Swift', p. 270.

186 Ibid., p. 270.

187 See Edward Said, 'Swift as Intellectual' in *The World, the Text and the Critic* (London: Vintage, 1991).

188 Warner, 'Jonathan Swift', p. 269.

189 Lindsay, *England My England*, pp. 41-64.

190 Morton, *A People's History of England*, p. 315f/p. 344f.

191 Ibid., p. 362f/p. 424f.

192 Ibid., p. 423f.

193 Ibid., p. 430f.

194 Ibid., p. 440f.

195 Ibid., p. 447f.

196 For a discussion of Thompson's conception of class consciousness, see, *inter alia*, Bryan D. Palmer, *E.P. Thompson: Objections and Oppositions* (London: Verso, 1994).

197 Eric Hobsbawm, *Uncommon People: Resistance, Rebellion and Jazz* (London: Weidenfeld and Nicholson, 1998) p. 7.

198 For a brief discussion of the early development of labour historiography in Britain, see Kaye, *The British Marxist Historians*, p. 136f.

199 Samuel Mill, 'Tom Paine: The Rebellious Needleman', p. 204.

200 Ibid., p. 206.

201 Ibid., p. 205.

202 Behrend, op cit., p. 119. Behrend surveys Swingler's essay on Blake on pp. 119-120.

203 Randall Swingler, 'The Imputation of Madness: A Study of William Blake and Literary Tradition', p. 22f.

204 Quoted in ibid., p. 24.

205 Quoted in ibid., p. 23.

206 Ibid., p. 24.

207 Ibid., p. 26.

208 Quoted in ibid., p. 25.

209 Ibid., p. 22f.

210 Ibid., p. 23.

211 Quoted in ibid., p. 23.

212 Ibid., p. 23f.

213 Quoted in ibid., p. 23.

214 See, *inter alia*, Don Cupitt, *After God: The Future of Religion* (London: Weidenfeld and Nicolson, 1997).

215 Swingler, 'The Imputation of Madness', p. 27.

216 Ibid., p. 27.

217 Ibid., p. 23.

218 Rée, *Proletarian Philosophers*.

219 Eric Cook inveighed against the digressive nature of Jackson's work in his otherwise highly laudatory review of *Charles Dickens: The Progress of a Radical* in *Left Review*. See Eric Cook, 'Dickens the Radical', *Left Review*, Vol. 3 No. 5, June 1937, pp. 304-306.

220 Jackson argued that Dickens's outlook might have 'deepened into…positive Socialism or Communism' if he had received 'a little outside aid' towards the end of his life. See Jackson, *Charles Dickens: The Progress of a Radical*, p. 11.

221 T.A. Jackson, *Charles Dickens: The Progress of a Radical*, p. 7f.

222 Ibid., p. 33f.

223 Quoted in ibid., p. 33.

224 Ibid., p. 36f.

225 Ibid., p. 250f.

226 Quoted in ibid., p. 250.

227 Ibid., p. 56f.

228 Ibid., p. 58f.

229 Ibid., p. 59f.

230 Quoted in ibid., p. 65.

231 Ibid., p. 68f.

232 Ibid., p. 76f.

233 Ibid., p. 270.

234 Ibid., pp. 271-272.

235 George Orwell, 'Charles Dickens' in *The Collected Essays, Journalism and Letters of George Orwell, Volume Two: An Age Like This 1920-1940*, edited by Sonia Orwell and Ian Angus (Harmondsworth: Penguin Books, 1971) p. 454.

236 Jackson, *Charles Dickens: The Progress of a Radical*, p. 3f and p. 101f.

237 Ibid., p. 7f and p. 111f.

238 Ibid., pp. 112-113.

239 Ibid., p. 7f and p. 129f.

240 Ibid., p. 129f.

241 Ibid. p. 138f.

242 Quoted in ibid., p. 136.

243 Ibid., p. 26f.

244 Robin Page Arnot, *William Morris: A Vindication*, p. 3f. For a recent discussion of Arnot's writings on Morris, see Ruth Levitas, *The Concept of Utopia* (New York: Syracuse University Press, 1990) Chapter Five.

245 Arnot, *William Morris: A Vindication*, p. 4f.

246 Ibid., p. 4f.

247 Ibid., pp. 8-15.

248 Ibid., p. 9.

249 Quoted in ibid., p. 10.

250 Ibid. p. 9.

251 For an introduction to Ruskin's theory of Gothic, see John Unrau, 'Ruskin, the Workman and the Savageness of Gothic' in Robert Hewison (ed.), *New Approaches to Ruskin: Thirteen Essays* (London: Routledge and Kegan Paul, 1981). Arnot made no reference of any kind to 'The Nature of Gothic'. The only text of Ruskin's which he referred to by name was *Unto This Last*, which also addressed the issue of the experience of labour in the industrial system.

252 For an account of the 'socialistic' elements in Carlyle's thought, see Noel O' Sullivan, *Conservatism* (London: J.M. Dent, 1976) pp. 92-99. Arnot briefly referred to Carlyle's *Latter-day Pamphlets* and *Chartism* as well as to *Past and Present*.

253 Arnot, *William Morris: A Vindication*, p. 13f.

254 Ibid., p. 13.

255 Ibid., p. 14.

256 Ibid., pp. 16-21.

257 Ibid., p. 27.

258 Ibid., p. 27.

259 Ibid., p. 28.

260 Ibid., p. 27.

261 Although the central principles of the communist account of English history were derived from Dimitrov, they were applied in ways which clearly owed something to indigenous historiographical influences. As Raphael Samuel has pointed out, the most important of these influences was probably the school of 'people's history' which emerged in the mid-nineteenth cenury. Broadly liberal in orientation and dominated by the likes of Thorold Rogers and J.R. Green, people's history was preoccupied with (1) pointing up the moments in English history when the ruling class had behaved with peculiar callousness towards the lower orders, and (2) identifying the moments when the people had gone some way towards holding the ruling class to account. As such, Rogers and Green both argued that the process of enclosure represented the 'central national tragedy' of recent history, but also insisted that the Middle Ages were a period of egalitarian virtue and that the Reformation had been a largely levelling movement, not simply an expression of bourgeois self-interest. As we have seen, all these arguments survived in modified form in the work of the Thirties Marxists. What is strange is that although the generation of Marxist historians who emerged in the last 20 years of the nineteenth century were also heavily influenced by people's history, there is no evidence that the Thirties communists were even aware of their work. For example, the

bibliography of A.L. Morton's *A People's History of England* contains a number of references to Rogers and Green but none at all to Belfort Bax or Edward Aveling (see Morton, *A People's History of England*, p. 540f). It remains unclear why men as erudite as Morton, Lindsay and Rickword should have known so little about their own ideological forebears. (See Raphael Samuel, 'British Marxist Historians, 1880-1890: Part One', *New Left Review*, No. 120, March-April 1980.)

262 Willie Thompson in particular has emphasised the way that the Popular Front period had profound consequences for the CPGB's post-war political identity. For instance, commenting on the Party's adoption of a parliamentary strategy in the early 1950s, Thompson remarks that 'It seems...reasonable...to suggest that the new line was adopted without any great furore because it fitted in with what had increasingly become the common sense of the party since 1941 if not 1935.' See Willie Thompson, *The Good Old Cause: British Communism 1920-1991* (London: Pluto Press, 1992) pp. 89-90.

263 David McLellan, *Marxism After Marx* (London: Papermac, 1980) p. 308.

264 Cf. Behrend, op cit., p. 117f.

265 Edgell Rickword, 'Culture, Progress, and English Tradition', pp. 237-245.

266 Ibid., p. 245f.

267 Ibid., p. 247.

268 Ibid., p. 250.

269 Ibid., p. 249f.

270 Ibid., p. 251f.

271 Ibid., pp. 255-256.

272 Sidney famously argued that literature involves a distinct mode of cognition which complements that of the natural sciences. See Sir Philip Sidney, 'An Apology for Poetry' in Hazard Adams (ed.), *Critical Theory Since Plato* (New York: Harcourt Brace, 1971).

273 For an overview of Lindsay's attempt to theorise culture as a form of productive activity, see Victor N. Paananen (ed.), *British Marxist Criticism* (New York, Garland Publishing, 2000) p. 51f.

274 Lindsay excerpted some of the most important passages from his theoretical writings in 'Symmetry, Asymmetry, Structure, Dominance', a chapter in *The Crisis in Marxism*. This chapter is reproduced in Victor N. Paananen, op cit.

275 Lindsay, 'Symmetry, Asymmetry, Structure, Dominance' p. 397.

276 Ibid., p. 396.

277 Lindsay himself pointed out the similarities between his own terminology and that of Althusser. See ibid., p. 404.

278 Lindsay, 'Symmetry, Asymmetry, Structure, Dominance', p. 405.

279 Cf. Paananen's account of Lindsay's theory in Paananen, op cit., p. 53.

280 Paananen, op cit., p. 56.

281 See *History of the Communist Party of the Soviet Union (Bolsheviks)*, edited by a commission of the Central Committee of the CPSU (B) (Moscow: Foreign Languages Publishing House, 1939) Chapter Four Section Two. This section also formed the basis of Stalin's influential pamphlet 'Dialectical and Historical Materialism' (1938). See J.V. Stalin, *Problems of Leninism* (Peking: Foreign Languages Press, 1976).

282 Victor Paananen draws attention to the incompatibility between Lindsay's cultural theory and Stalin's account of the base/superstructure distinction in Paananen, op cit., p. 53.

283 For an account of the left's influence in Higher Education since the late 1960s, see Perry Anderson, 'A Culture in Contraflow' in *English Questions*.

284 Cf. Behrend, op cit., p. 108.

285 For a brief account of the dissolution of the CPGB is Nina Fishman, 'The British Road is Resurfaced for New Times: From the British Communist Party to the Democratic Left' in Martin J. Bull and Paul Heywood (eds.), *West European Communist Parties After the Revolutions of 1989* (New York: St Martin's Press, 1994).

286 See Bill Schwarz and Colin Mercer, 'Popular Politics and Marxist Theory in Britain' in George Bridges and Rosalind Brunt (eds), *Silver Linings: Some Strategies for the Eighties* (London: Lawrence and Wishart, 1981).

287 Patrick Wright, *On Living in an Old Country: The National Past in Contemporary Britain* (London: Verso, 1985). Some of the key passages from Wright's book are reproduced in Kenneth Thompson (ed.), *Media and Cultural Regulation* (London: Sage, 1997). The same volume contains an interesting discussion of Wright's ideas in Kenneth Thompson's essay 'Regulation, De-Regulation and Re-Regulation'.

Conclusion

1 For Hobsbawm's account of the history of the USSR, see Eric Hobsbawm, *Age of Extremes: The Short Twentieth Century 1914-1991* (London: Michael Joseph, 1994) and *The New Century* (London: Abacus, 2000). Hobsbawm also explored this theme in a famously candid interview with Michael Ignatieff for BBC television in 1994.

2 The idea that Marxism has exercised a decisive influence on non-Marxist forms of twentieth-century thinking is by no means a new one. For an example of this argument from the 1930s, see Alick West, 'Marxism and Modern Thought', *Left Review*, Vol. 2 No. 1, October 1935, pp. 44-47. More recently, Perry Anderson has argued that classical sociology had its roots in a desire to curtail the influence of Marxism. See Perry Anderson, *English Questions* (London: Verso, 1992) p. 53f.

3 For a brief analysis of the literature of 'authoritarian utopianism', see Vincent Geoghegan, *Utopianism and Marxism* (London: Methuen, 1987) Chapter Five.

4 See Victor N. Paananen (ed.), *British Marxist Criticism* (New York: Garland Publishing, 2000).

5 For accounts of the emergence of the New Left and the birth of Cultural Studies, see, *inter alia*, Graeme Turner, *British Cultural Studies: An Introduction* (London: Unwin Hyman, 1990); Dennis Dworkin, *Cultural Marxism in Postwar Britain: History, the New Left, and the Origins of Cultural Studies* (London: Duke University Press, 1997).

6 See Raymond Williams, *Culture and Society 1780-1950* (Harmondsworth: Pelican Books, 1979), *The Long Revolution* (Harmondsworth: Pelican Books, 1984), *Britain in the Sixties: Communications* (Maryland: Penguin Books, 1962).

7 See Williams's account of his Cambridge years in *Politics and Letters: Interviews*

with *New Left Review* (London: New Left Books, 1979). Stephen Woodhams has begun the task of exploring the effects of Williams's membership of the CPGB on his later work in *History in the Making: Raymond Williams, Edward Thompson and Radical Intellectuals 1936-1956* (London: Merlin, 2001). However, Woodhams does not examine Williams's debt to the work of the communist literary critics.

8   See, *inter alia*, Raymond Williams, *Marxism and Literature* (Oxford: Oxford University Press, 1977); Raymond Williams, *Problems in Materialism and Culture: Selected Essays* (London: Verso, 1980); Terry Eagleton, *Literary Theory: An Introduction* (Oxford: Blackwell, 1989). For an introduction to Williams's attempt to move beyond existing definitions of literature, see Alan O' Connor, *Raymond Williams: Writing, Culture, Politics* (Oxford: Blackwell, 1989).

9   Eagleton, *Literary Theory*, p. 11.

10   Alan O' Connor makes this point in relation to Williams in O' Connor, op cit., p. 111.

11   Eagleton outlines his vision of a new discipline of Rhetoric in 'Conclusion: Political Criticism' in *Literary Theory*.

12   Williams first distinguished between the emergent, hegemonic and residual elements in culture in his essay 'Base and Superstructure in Marxist Cultural Theory', published in *New Left Review*, No. 82 (November/December 1973) and reprinted in *Problems in Materialism and Culture*. Alan Sinfield outlines the main principles of 'cultural materialism', the Gramscian approach to culture of which he is one of the most distinguished exponents, in Chapter One of *Cultural Politics – Queer Reading* (London: Routledge, 1994). The most influential work of cultural materialism is probably Alan Sinfield and Jonathan Dollimore (eds.), *Political Shakespeare* (Manchester: Manchester University Press, 1985).

13   Althusser's classic statement of his theory of ideology is 'Ideology and Ideological State Apparatuses'. For a brief account of the effect of Althusserian ideas on literary studies, see Francis Mulhern, 'Message in a Bottle: Althusser in Literary Studies' in Gregory Elliott (ed.), *Althusser: A Critical Reader* (Oxford: Blackwell, 1994). Although Althusserian criticism has tended to be pessimistic, emphasising the formidable ability of ideology to exercise an iron grip on the minds of subordinate groups, there is also a more upbeat version of Althusserianism which takes its lead from Althusser's (and his follower Pierre Macherey's) point that there is something intrinsic to literary form which serves to reveal the "lacunae" in ideological discourses. The most famous example of this strain of Althusserianism in Britain is Terry Eagleton's *Criticism and Ideology* (London: New Left Books, 1976).

14   For Hall, Hebdige and Hobson, see, *inter alia*, Stuart Hall, 'Encoding/Decoding' in Stuart Hall, Dorothy Hobson, Andrew Lowe and Paul Willis (eds.), *Culture, Media, Language* (London: Hutchinson, 1980); Stuart Hall, *The Hard Road to Renewal: Thatcherism and the Crisis of the Left* (London: Verso, 1988); Dick Hebdige, *Subculture: The Meaning of Style* (London: Methuen, 1979); Dorothy Hobson, *Crossroads: The Drama of a Soap Opera* (London: Methuen, 1982). For a historical account of the development of the Birmingham School, see Dworkin, op cit., p. 125f *passim*.

15   For Fiske and Willis, see, *inter alia*, John Fiske, *Understanding Popular Culture* (London: Unwin Hyman, 1989); Paul Willis, *Common Culture: Symbolic Work at*

Play in the Everyday Cultures of the Young (London: Open University Press, 1990); Paul Willis, *Moving Culture: An Enquiry into the Cultural Activities of Young People* (London: Calouste Gulbenkian Foundation, 1990).

16   For MacCabe, Mulvey and Wollen, see, *inter alia*, Colin MacCabe, 'Realism and the Cinema: Notes on Some Brechtian Theses' in Antony Easthope (ed.), *Contemporary Film Theory* (London: Longman, 1993); Laura Mulvey, 'Visual Pleasure and Narrative Cinema' in Antony Easthope (ed.), op cit.; Peter Wollen, 'Godard and Counter-Cinema: *Vent d'Est*' in *Readings and Writings* (London: Verso, 1982). For a brief introduction to *Screen* theory, see Antony Easthope, *British Post-Structuralism since 1968* (London: Routledge, 1988) Chapter Three.

17   See MacCabe, op cit.

18   For an account of the obsessive intellectualism of the British Party, see Raphael Samuel, 'Class Politics: The Lost World of British Communism, Part Three', *New Left Review*, No. 165, September/October 1987, p. 75f. For a magnificent fictionalised account of the world communist movement's autodidactic culture, see George Steiner, *Proofs and Three Parables* (London: Faber, 1992).

19   See Frederick Engels, 'The Part Played by Labour in the Transition from Ape to Man' in Karl Marx and Frederick Engels, *Selected Works in One Volume* (London: Lawrence and Wishart, 1980).

20   Quoted in Robert Sullivan, *Christopher Caudwell* (London: Croom Helm, 1987) p. 39.

21   Bertolt Brecht, 'Praise of Learning' in Alan Bold (ed.), *The Penguin Book of Socialist Verse* (Harmondsworth: Penguin Books, 1970) p. 236.

22   For a pioneering account of Gramsci's syncretistic vision of socialist culture, see Gwyn A. Williams, 'The Concept of "Egemonia" in the Thought of Antonio Gramsci: Some Notes on Interpretation', *Journal of the History of Ideas*, Vol. XXI No. 4, 1960, pp. 586-599.

23   The phrase is P.D. Ouspensky's. Quoted in Colin Wilson, *The Occult* (London: Grafton, 1989) p. 48.

24   Quoted in Ralph Fox, *The Novel and the People* (London: Cobbett Press, 1948) p. 38. Herbert Read, who also quoted the lines by Keats in a review of *The Novel and the People*, pointed out that '…that is not a description of a socialist-realist. It is a description of the great humanist artist – of Shakespeare, Cervantes, Balzac, Keats himself – who in his art surveys all and transcends all.' See Herbert Read, *A Coat of Many Colours: Occasional Essays* (London: Routledge, 1945), p. 216.

25   For Raphael Samuel, see 'The Lost World of British Communism', *New Left Review*, No. 154, November/December 1985, pp. 3-53; 'Staying Power: The Lost World of British Communism, Part Two', *New Left Review*, No. 156, March/April 1986, pp. 63-113; 'Class Politics: The Lost World of British Communism, Part Three', *New Left Review*, No. 165, September/October 1987, pp. 52-91. For Stuart Macintyre, see *A Proletarian Science: Marxism in Britain 1917-1933* (Cambridge: Cambridge University Press, 1980). For Jonathan Rée, see *Proletarian Philosophers: Problems in Socialist Culture in Britain, 1900-1940* (Oxford: Clarendon Press, 1984). For two more recent works on the CPGB's internal culture – both of them published since the completion of this book – see Kevin Morgan, Gidon Cohen and Andrew Flinn. *Communists and British Society 1920-1991: People of a Special Mould* (London:

Rivers Oram, 2005); Thomas Linehan, *Communism in Britain 1920-1939: From the Cradle to the Grave* (Manchester: Manchester University Press, 2007).

26   George Steiner, Contribution to 'The State of Europe: Christmas Eve 1989', *Granta*, Number 30, Winter 1990, p. 131.

Appendix

1   Much of the biographical information in this appendix is derived from the following sources:

James M. Borg, 'Lindsay, John (1900–1990)' in *Oxford Dictionary of National Biography* (Oxford: Oxford University Press, 2004) [http://www.oxforddnb.com/view/article/54683].

Alec Brown, *The Fate of the Middle Classes* (London: Gollancz, 1936).

Robert Brown, 'Slater, (Charles) Montagu (1902–1956)' in *Oxford Dictionary of National Biography* [http://www.oxforddnb.com/view/article/74935].

Cressida Connolly, *The Rare and the Beautiful: The Lives of the Garmans* (London: 4th Estate, 2004).

C.A. Creffield, 'Aveling, Edward Bibbens (1849–1898)' in *Oxford Dictionary of National Biography* [http://www.oxforddnb.com/view/article/40929].

Andy Croft, 'The Young Men are Moving Together: The Case of Randall Swingler' in John McIlroy, Kevin Morgan and Alan Campbell (eds.), *Party People, Communist Lives: Explorations in Biography* (London: Lawrence and Wishart, 2001).

Andy Croft, *Comrade Heart: A Life of Randall Swingler* (Manchester: Manchester University Press, 2003).

Andy Croft, 'Swingler, Randall Carline (1909–1967)' in *Oxford Dictionary of National Biography* [http://www.oxforddnb.com/view/article/62375].

Maurice Cornforth (ed.), 'A.L. Morton – Portrait of a Marxist Historian' in Maurice Cornforth (ed.), *Rebels and Their Causes: Essays in Honour of A.L. Morton* (London: Lawrence and Wishart, 1978).

A.H. Halsey, 'Madge, Charles Henry (1912–1996)' in *Oxford Dictionary of National Biography* [http://www.oxforddnb.com/view/article/57883].

Charles Hobday, *Edgell Rickword: A Poet at War* (Manchester, Carcanet, 1989).

Claire Harman, 'Rickword, (John) Edgell (1898–1982)' in *Oxford Dictionary of National Biography* [http://www.oxforddnb.com/view/article/40704].

Antony Howe, 'Arnot, Robert Page (1890–1986)' in *Oxford Dictionary of National Biography* [http://www.oxforddnb.com/view/article/40281].

Jonah Jones, *Clough Williams-Ellis: The Architect of Portmeirion* (Bridgend:

Seren, 1996).

Harvey J. Kaye, *The British Marxist Historians: An Introductory Analysis* (Oxford: Polity, 1984).

Martin Kettle, 'Obituary: Christopher Hill', *The Guardian*, 26 February 2003.

Fiona MacCarthy, 'Morris, William (1834–1896)' in *Oxford Dictionary of National Biography* [http://www.oxforddnb.com/view/article/19322].

David McLellan, 'Marx, (Jenny Julia) Eleanor (1855–1898)' in *Oxford Dictionary of National Biography* [http://www.oxforddnb.com/view/article/40945].

Edward Mendelson, 'Auden, Wystan Hugh (1907–1973)' in *Oxford Dictionary of National Biography* [http://www.oxforddnb.com/view/article/30775].

Sean Day-Lewis, 'Lewis, Cecil Day- (1904–1972)' in *Oxford Dictionary of National Biography* [http://www.oxforddnb.com/view/article/31014].

Kevin Morgan, 'Jackson, Thomas Alfred (1879–1955)' in *Oxford Dictionary of National Biography* [http://www.oxforddnb.com/view/article/65941].

Michael Newman, 'Strachey, (Evelyn) John St Loe (1901–1963)' in *Oxford Dictionary of National Biography* [http://www.oxforddnb.com/view/article/36337].

Robert Olby, 'Bernal, (John) Desmond (1901–1971)' in *Oxford Dictionary of National Biography* [http://www.oxforddnb.com/view/article/30813].

Grant Pooke, 'Marxism, Art and Engagement: Francis D. Klingender', *Bulletin of the Marx Memorial Library*, No. 137, Spring 2003, pp. 19-26.

Edwin A. Roberts, *The Anglo-Marxists: A Study in Ideology and Culture* (Oxford: Rowman and Littlefield, 1997).

Hugh Thomas, *John Strachey* (London: Eyre Methuen, 1973).

G.J. Warnock, 'Warner, Reginald Ernest [Rex] (1905–1986)' in *Oxford Dictionary of National Biography* [http://www.oxforddnb.com/view/article/39846].

Index

Also available from Merlin Press

MARGARET LAMBERT & ENID MARX
ENGLISH POPULAR ART
This is a serious study of the variety, origins and durability of popular art in England.
It records the sense of humour of a people – the jug with a toad inside – as well as the
individuality and character of the craftsmen and craftswomen. It illustrates the texture
of popular history.
Contents: Carving, Metal, Painting, Textiles, Pottery, Glass and miscellaneous,
Printing.
xvi+120pp. 109 b/w illus. 978 0 85036 597 9 £14.95

GEORG LUKÁCS
THE MEANING OF CONTEMPORARY REALISM
With a new introduction by Gary Day
An examination of three main trends in modern literature: the literature of the avant-
garde (Kafka, Joyce, Becket, Faulkner); the socialist realists who portray an unreal
Utopia (Sholokov); and the critical realists (Conrad, Mann, Shaw).. "I know nothing
more promising in contemporary literary theory." Raymond Williams, The Listener.
Contents, Preface to the English Edition (1962), Preface to the German Edition
(1957), Introduction, The Ideology of Modernism, Franz Kafka or Thomas Mann?,
Critical Realism and Socialist Realism, Index.
138pp, 978 0 85036 250 3 Pbk £12.95

GEORG LUKÁCS
THE THEORY OF THE NOVEL:
A Historical-Philosophical Essay on the Forms of Great Epic Literature
Translated by Anna Bostock
Lukács is a thinker and critic widely appreciated in cultural and literary studies of the
twentieth century. This book considers the nature and development of the novel and
anticipates its development. It is an essay of prophetic vision, Lukács writes, "anyone
who wants to become more intimately acquainted with the prehistory of the important ideologies of the [nineteen] twenties and thirties ...will be helped by a critical
reading of this book. Library Journal
160pp, 978 0 85036 236 7 Pbk £10.95

E. P. THOMPSON
THE POVERTY OF THEORY
A socialist humanist critique of dogmatic Marxism: and of Althusser in particular.
"There can be no doubt that The Poverty of Theory is an essay that will have lasting
impact. It will resonate throughout discussions of history, Marxist theory and socialist politics." Media: Culture and Society
303pp, 978 0 85036 446 0 Pbk £15.95

www.merlinpress.co.uk